SUFI NON-CONFORMISM

Antinomian Trends
in the Persianate Cultural Traditions

Edited by

Ali-Asghar Seyed-Gohrab

Leiden University Press

This book will be made open access within three years of publication thanks to Path to Open, a program developed in partnership between JSTOR, the American Council of Learned Societies (ACLS), University of Michigan Press, and The University of North Carolina Press to bring about equitable access and impact for the entire scholarly community, including authors, researchers, libraries, and university presses around the world. Learn more at https://about.jstor.org/path-to-open/.

Iranian Studies Series, volume 32

Cover design: Andre Klijsen
Cover illustration: "Dervish Leading a Bear", Folio from the Shah Jahan Album. Painting by Govardhan (active ca. 1596–1645). Calligraphy by Mir 'Ali Haravi (died ca. 1550). Recto: ca. 1630–40; verso: ca. 1530–40. The Met Collection: Purchase, Rogers Fund and The Kevorkian Foundation Gift, 1955.
Lay-out: Crius Group

ISBN 978 90 8728 454 1
e-ISBN 978 94 0060 492 6
https://doi.org/10.24415/9789087284541
NUR 717

Table of Contents

Sufi Non-Conformism

IRANIAN STUDIES SERIES

The *Iranian Studies Series* publishes high-quality scholarship on various aspects of Iranian civilisation, covering both contemporary and classical cultures of the Persian cultural area. The contemporary Persian-speaking area includes Iran, Afghanistan, Tajikistan, and Central Asia, while classical societies using Persian as a literary and cultural language were located in Anatolia, Caucasus, Central Asia and the Indo-Pakistani subcontinent. The objective of the series is to foster studies of the literary, historical, religious and linguistic products in Iranian languages. In addition to research monographs and reference works, the series publishes English-Persian critical text-editions of important texts. The series intends to publish resources and original research and make them accessible to a wide audience.

Acknowledgements

The chapters in this book have been selected from various conferences and workshops hosted at Utrecht University, Department of Philosophy and Religious Studies. The book was edited as part of the ERC Advanced Grant project entitled *Beyond Sharia: The Role of Sufism in Shaping Islam* (www.beyondsharia.nl), funded by the European Research Council (ERC) under the European Union's Horizon 2020 research and innovation programme (Grant agreement No. 101020403). Covering a spectrum of themes, these chapters examine non-conformist aspects of the Islamic world. They explore diverse topics such as gender in Sufism, the concept of *qalandar* ("vagabond"), ʿUmar Khayyām's sceptical philosophy and its European reception, Suhrawardī's doctrine of metempsychosis (*tanāsukh*), an analysis of heresy in the Ottoman Empire, and an examination of antinomianism among the Ahl-i Ḥaqq of Gūrān in Kurdistan. I hope that these chapters will spark inspiration, encouraging scholars to launch new studies on these topics, which have become an integral part of religious discourse in the Islamic world.

I would like to extend my sincere gratitude to the European Research Council (ERC) for their generous financial support, which has enabled us to undertake scholarly activities, reflecting critically on important topics relevant to society and the fields of Persian and Iranian Studies, Islamic Studies, and related disciplines. My heartfelt thanks go out to the dedicated *Beyond Sharia* team – Diede Farhosh-van Loon, Arash Ghajarjazi, Amin Ghodratzadeh, Maarten Holtzapffel, Fatemeh Naghshvarian, Alexandra Nieweg, Zhinia Noorian, and Leila Rahimi Bahmany – for their collegiality and ongoing intellectual engagements. Also, I am grateful to my colleagues at the Department of Philosophy and Religious Studies for creating an inspiring environment, encouraging intellectual flourishment.

Introduction

Islam has a solid intellectual tradition that has debated Islamic doctrines, the nature of the Sharīʿa and its applicability to society, the concepts of belief (*īmān*) and unbelief (*kufr*), thorny questions about the Resurrection and the existence of heaven and hell, and whether one's piety should be based on the fear of God or on passionate love for God. However, over the past fifty years, in scholarly publications and in public debates, discourse on Islamic piety has focused mainly on normative and orthodox Islamic thinking, on correct behaviour according to a precise interpretation of the Sharia. This perspective has been so dominant that some have asked whether more fundamental criticism of Islamic tenets is even possible within Islam. Such views on Islam are simplistic, incorrect, and often politically motivated. From the ninth century onwards, there have been highly influential movements rooted in asceticism that have raised fundamental issues, questioned even the holiest doctrines, and criticised the Sharia. For instance, why did God create Satan if He wanted mankind to be saved? How can practices such as public prayer and fasting be obligatory if true piety is necessarily inward? Should reason be used to gauge Islamic principles and doctrines or should the believer strictly focus on the Quran and the prophetic tradition? Keyvani is right when he writes, in this volume: "Less than two centuries after its establishment, Islam faced numerous forms of opposition from various areas of the lands it had swept through, each with its own historical-cultural background, promoting its specific ideological, religious or political orientations. Over time, the increasing opposition led to factional rivalry, discordance and even physically bloody encounters among people who all professed Islam. The result was the creation of a good number of opposing denominations, and so-called heretical coteries and deviant orders, some minor and short-lived and others relatively powerful and persistent."

These denominations include influential non-conformist movements such as the Karrāmiyya and Malāmatiyya, which go back to tenth century Persia and impressed their influence on Islam in the Persianate world in subsequent centuries. These renunciant movements were partly a reaction to the worldly power and economic gains that Muslim Arabs experienced following the early Islamic conquests of the Persian and Byzantine empires. Melchert suggests using the term 'renunciation' to translate the term *zuhd*, which is often rendered as 'asceticism.' He argues that 'renunciation' more precisely captures the meaning of *zuhd*, indicating "*unconcern*, mainly with the world." The early renunciants revolted against luxurious lifestyles and promoted practices such as fasting, self-flagellation, withdrawal from society, celibacy, and dressing in coarse woollen cloaks. The renunciant movement was a demonstrative rejection of what they considered to be a corrupted society, and a way of protecting their own piety from the danger of hypocrisy, by attracting blame (*malāma*). Convinced that blame had a positive and purifying effect on one's piety, they concealed their religiosity. From the twelfth century onwards, these ideas were perpetuated by several antinomian groups such as the *qalandars*, who spread over the area from India to Anatolia and Egypt.

This book deals with nonconformist aspects of Sufism, and other antinomian movements in the Persianate cultural tradition. It ranges from gender and the role of women in mystical Islam, to doctrinal concepts such as belief and unbelief, the notion of metempsychosis (*tanāsukh*) in the works of the mystic Shihāb al-Dīn Suhrawardī, the question of genuine piety, and the influential role of the Persian sage ʿUmar Khayyām in religious discussions on piety in twelfth century Persia, and his reception history. The book also deals with the religious practices associated with antinomian tenets and how Western scholars connected with such traditions.

The content of the book

This book introduces a critical face of Islam which has been partly overlooked in recent decades. The chapters cross several core subjects in Islamic intellectual tradition such as gender, heresy, piety and impiety in Sufism. In several of these chapters, the authors rely on Persian poetry as a means of critical reflection, theorising themes such as belief and unbelief, and centre and periphery.

A central topic which has been addressed in scholarship from the twentieth century onwards is the place and role of women in Sufism. In recent years, studies on women in Sufism have highlighted women's lack of equality in Sufi literature. Lloyd Ridgeon examines the notion of gender in Sufism from the eleventh to thirteenth century, first in Sufi manuals and hagiographies and then in three case-studies, showing how women feature in the works of three mystics. These are Abū Ḥāmid Ghazālī (d. 1111), Awḥad al-Dīn Kirmānī (d. 1238) and Jalāl al-Dīn Rūmī (d. 1273). Ridgeon's approach is novel as it seeks to understand how these authors discussed women's piety and participation in Sufi activities, and whether their participation would violate the Sharia. As Ridgeon states, the chapter "argues that male Persian Sufis did not trespass "beyond shariah," but they embraced an interpretation of *sharīʿa* that endorsed the complementarity of the sexes, although the idealised version of women offered chances of "spiritual" equality with men."

It can be argued that Islam cannot be fully understood without an appreciation of its "deviant" movements such as the *qalandari*, anarchist or libertine dervishes, whose practices deliberately violated the Sharia to condemn the behaviour of the representatives of the religious establishment in society. The *qalandariyya* is a Sufi antinomian movement, combining the ascetic principles of early Islam with shocking forms of social deviance in protest against urban society, the conventions of mainstream religion, institutionalised Sufism, and the political establishment. The *qalandar*s flouted Islamic rituals such as pilgrimage, prayer and fasting, while praising Christianity, Zoroastrianism, wine-drinking and homo-erotic love. To provoke people, they shaved their beards, eyebrows and heads, had genital piercings and appeared (half-)naked in public. They were deviant not because they were disbelievers, but because they believed that this was the way to attain unity with God. They were condemned as heretics, but at the same time they had an enormous appeal in particular among ordinary people and intellectuals and even for some political actors. Some of the extremist mystic movements attained political power themselves. The legacy of the deviant movements is still affecting Islamic thinking and has shaped Islam as it is lived today.

Three chapters examine the qalandar. Zhinia Noorian's excellent contribution deals with an important verse treatise, entitled *Qalandar-nāma* by Khatīb-i Fārsī ("Persian preacher"). This hagiography introduces the life and philosophy of Jamāl al-Dīn Sāvī (d. about 1232/3), who is considered the founder of the qalandariyya movement. Noorian examines concepts such as "renunciation" (*tajarrud*), "spiritual poverty" (*faqr*) and piety (*pārsā'ī*). Although Sāvī appears as an influential figure in various sources dealing with the qalandariyya, information about him and his mystical philosophy is meagre. The *Qalandar-nāma* was composed long after Sāvī's death. In addition to hagiographical information, the *Qalandar-nāma* imparts information about the *qalandarī* ritual of shaving the facial hair. This tradition is called *chahār żarb* or "four blows," alluding to shaving the skull, eyebrows, beard and the moustache. Qalandari mystics usually removed all their facial hair as a contrast to the beard valued by representatives of the religious establishment as a sign of piety. As Noorian observes, "With the close reading of this hagiographical text and situating it within its historical, religious and political context, this study sheds light on the activities of Sāvī as an Iranian leader in shaping the intellectual-spiritual history of non-conformity in Islamic mysticism."

Keyvani provides a systematic analysis of the concept of qalandar in the poetry of Ḥāfiẓ, the grand lyrical poet of Persia, whose *Dīvān* ("collected poetry"), as Shahab Ahmed says, has been central "to the constitution of a paradigm of identity for Muslims in the world" from the Balkans to the Bengal, being "the most widely-copied, widely-circulated, widely-read, widely-memorized, widely-recited, widely-invoked, and widely-proverbialized book of poetry in Islamic history—a book that came to be regarded as configuring and exemplifying ideals of self-conception and modes and mechanisms of self-expression in the largest part of the Islamic world for half-a-millennium … ."[2] It is remarkable how often Ḥāfiẓ refers to qalandars and various libertine hierarchies in his poetry, to criticise the sham piety of the religious establishment, questioning their religiosity and revealing their hypocrisy. Ḥāfiẓ creates a system of profane and religious ethics, using the contrast between the antinomian conduct of the qalandars and the hypocritical behaviour of religious representatives to define true piety. Keyvani's contribution is indispensable in understanding concepts such as piety and heresy in the Islamic world. It examines how Ḥāfiẓ's poetry introduced a new type of piety, decentring the religiosity of the representatives of the Islamic establishment in society.

A prominent figure to whom various qalandari and nonconformist ideas, and even blasphemous principles, are knitted is the Persian mathematician and astronomer ʿUmar Khayyām. From the twelfth century, various theologically thorny issues were integrated in the quatrains attributed to this sage. Seyed-Gohrab examines the uneasy relationships between Khayyām's provocative statements about the Creator, creation, death and the Hereafter, and the religious beliefs of several Persian scholars. This chapter also elaborates on the scholars' strategies to interpret Khayyāmic themes and motifs such as Bacchanalia to make them acceptable for a Muslim audience. It is fascinating to see that after eight centuries, Khayyām's unorthodox ideas are still used to discuss various aspects of piety and heresy in modern Iranian society.[3]

Seyed-Gohrab's contribution also deals with the theme of qalandari antinomianism. In the concluding part of the chapter, he briefly discusses the authenticity of several quatrains attributed to Khayyām in early sources such as the thirteenth-century collection *Nuzhat al-majālis* by Jamāl Khalīl Shirvānī. One quatrain in this collection mentions the concept of qalandar. Khayyām's earliest poems exhibited hostility toward religious beliefs, questioning the futility of creation, denying the existence of the Hereafter, and emphasising doubt rather than certainty in faith. The attribution of such quatrains to Khayyām reflects a growing antinomian genre in Persian poetry, a trend that emerged as early as the end of the eleventh century.

ʿUmar Khayyām's ideas were regarded by scholars such as Jamāl al-Dīn Yūsuf Qifṭī (1172–1248) as serpents for the Sharia. Quatrains attributed to Khayyām are cited in theological and mystical texts to condemn him. An early example is in an exegesis of the Quran, *Mafātīḥ al-ghayb,* by Fakhr al-Dīn Muḥammad b. ʿUmar Rāzī (d. 1209), who cites one of Khayyām's quatrains to criticise his ideas about the concept of *maʿād* or "the place of the soul's return." Similarly, the mystic theoretician Najm al-Dīn Rāzī, better known as Dāya (1177–1256) cites two of Khayyām's quatrains to condemn him as an atheist and material philosopher.[4] In his *Ilāhī-nāma*, Farīd al-Dīn ʿAṭṭār (d.c. 1221) recounts an anecdote about Khayyām in his grave. Such instances show the impact of Khayyām's ideas and how, by citing such quatrains, scholars of religion discussed key Islamic concepts such as piety, resurrection, the hereafter, and the existence of heaven and hell.

Arash Ghajarjazi's chapter is an excellent example of how Persian religious intellectuals discussed their ideas through quatrains. His chapter deals with a dispute elaborated in two Persian quatrains in a manuscript from 644/1256 that is preserved in the Shahīd ʿAlī Pashā Library in Istanbul. These quatrains deal with the use of reason, as opposed to tradition, to understand doctrinal religious issues. This is an allusion to the animosity between philosophers, who preferred discursive reasoning to explain religious doctrines, and those whose approach to religious principles was theological and based on prophetic tradition. The two approaches are indicated in each poem by a different term: *rāy* or "opinion," and "reason," and *khabar* or "tradition," in both its general sense and as a term for the prophetic traditions, i.e., *ḥadīth*.

Khayyām's legacy extends to Europe and the present day. Amir Theilhaber's chapter studies how Khayyām's quatrains (*rubāʿiyyāt*) were canonised in the German-speaking world through the translation of Friedrich Rosen (1856–1935), *Die Sinnsprüche Omars des Zeltmachers*. Rosen was a diplomat and scholar of Oriental studies, who had an impact on Khayyām studies in Europe. Theilhaber examines Rosen's life and the role Khayyām played in his intellectual and religious life. One of the many interesting topics that Theilhaber examines is how Rosen sees in Khayyām the ideas of a freethinker openly challenging Islamic religious orthodoxy, seeing in the Persian scientist an "Aryan-Indo-Germanic spirit that seeks cognisance, in a cultural war against the dogma of Semitic 'Arabianness.'" Theilhaber demonstrates how such perverse antisemitic ideas were rightly refuted by scholars such as Ignaz Goldziher. The discussion shows how scholars in modern times treated nonconformist mediaeval ideas to explain the rise and popularity of antinomian movements. Aside from such original insights, Theilhaber's chapter elaborates upon Rosen's collaboration with Persian intellectuals such as Taqī Arānī in Berlin.

Colin Imber examines how the notions of faith and unbelief were treated in the Ottoman empire. Here he studies how an Ottoman sultan, as the promulgator of the sharīʿa, had to appoint a religious divine from the hierarchy of the ʿulamā to determine heretic and pious behaviour. In this chapter, we see how apostasy laws shaped the ʿulamā's understanding of heresy and heretics and how they distinguished between the heretic and the pious. External behaviour and words determine whether someone was a heretic; inner beliefs are legally irrelevant. Using historical cases and a range of arguments from original sources, Imber demonstrates how an apostate was judged on the basis of external behaviour. Accusations of apostasy had far-reaching consequences as the penalty was death: the question was whether an apostate should be offered a chance to repent. Imber also shows that there were other definitions, by referring to al-Taftazānī (d. 1390), according to whom a *zindīq* ("heretic") "is someone who is inwardly an unbeliever while outwardly professing belief."[5]

Martin van Bruinessen's invaluable chapter offers original insights into antinomianism in modern times, by analysing perhaps one of the most antinomian community in the Iranian world, the Ahl-i Ḥaqq of Gūrān, and also examining the scholarly works of two of his friends, who are famous scholars of Persian Studies: Peter Lamborn Wilson, aka Hakim Bey (d. 2022), and Vladimir A. Ivanow (d. 1970). While Wilson is known for his interest in Sufism and Sufi poetry, which he also translated, Ivanow is commonly known for his studies on Ismāʿīlism and the Ahl-i Ḥaqq in Kurdistan.[6] Van Bruinessen offers a novel analysis of the "place of Satan and the Peacock Angel in the cosmology and anthropology of the Ahl-i Ḥaqq and the Yezidis." He elaborates on the intricate system of these communities such as "the place in their pantheon of seven angelic beings (*haft tan*) who appear in human incarnations in each cycle of history, and the social and ritual role of holy lineages (*khānadān*) in Ahl-i Ḥaqq communities." Van Bruinessen demonstrates how Zoroastrian ideas have survived "beneath a thin Islamic veneer," among the Kurds in Gūrān, arguing that "there is a much more pervasive influence of early Islam in Ahl-i Ḥaqq religion (as well as Yezidism and Alevism) ... ."

Aside from the communities adhering to Ahl-i Ḥaqq, Yezidism, Ismāʿīlism and various mystical nonconformist groups such as the qalandaris, there are also Islamic mystic philosophers who raised issues which were considered by Islamic orthodoxy to be problematic and even blasphemous. Cornelis van Lit devotes his attention to the reception of the twelfth century Persian philosopher Suhrawardī (d. 587/1191) during the Safavid era (1501–1722). Suhrawardī was popular among various intellectuals ranging from philosophers to theologians, and mystics, who applied his philosophy in their writings and wrote commentaries on his writings. In this chapter, Van Lit discusses the opinions of various scholars, sometimes opposed to one another, to show Suhrawardī's importance in the Persian intellectual tradition. Van Lit concentrates on one unpublished commentary, an eighteenth-century Persian treatise that defends Suhrawardī against accusations of defending "the doctrine of metempsychosis (*tanāsukh*) instead of affirming bodily resurrection (*maʿād-i jismānī*)." Such ideas were discussed from an early period: the fact that such discussions were also conducted with reference to Suhrawardī shows the centrality of the theme for philosophers and theologians.

Certain terms used in this book may be familiar to scholars in the field, while others may require clarification due to their complexity. One such term is "Persianate," which was introduced by Marshall Hodgson in his book *The Venture of Islam: Conscience and History in a World Civilization*. Scholars in Middle Eastern Studies and related disciplines have employed this term in various contexts. It generally refers to the geographic area in which Persian language and culture exerted a significant influence. This influence could manifest itself through the use of Persian as an administrative, religious, or literary language, or as a model for other languages. The term encompasses regions spanning from the Balkans to present-day Turkey, Iran, Afghanistan, the Caucasus, Central Asia, and the Indian subcontinent. Shahab Ahmed introduced the term "Balkans-to-Bengal complex," in which he emphasises the enduring impact of Persian poets such as Ḥāfiẓ and Rūmī across this vast geographic area.[7]

Notes

1 Christopher Melchert, *Before Sufism: Early Islamic Renunciant Piety*, Berlin: De Gruyter, 2020, p. 10.

2 Ahmed, *What Is Islam? The Importance of Being Islamic*, Princeton: Princeton University Press, 2016, pp. 32–33.

3 This chapter was previously published in *Iran-Namag*, Volume 5, Number 3, 2020, pp. 68–93. I am grateful to the editor of the journal Professor Mohamad Tavakoli-Targhi for granting permission to republish this research here. The reason for its republication is that it perfectly fits with several other chapters on Khayyām, complementing them in terms of literary background, critical religious treatment, and Khayyām's reception history in modern times.

4 Muḥammad-Amīn Rīyāḥī in *Encyclopaedia Iranica*, s.v. Dāya, Najm-al-Dīn Abū Bakr ʿAbd-Allāh. www.iranicaonline.org/articles/daya-najm-al-din. For an overview of these mediaeval critics on Khayyām, see Aminrazavi, *Wine of Wisdom*, pp. 40–66.

5 Quoted in Kemālpaşazāde, *al-Risāla fī mā yataʿallaqu bi-lafẓ al-zindīq*, trans. A.Y. Ocak in *Osmanlı Toplumunda zındıklar ve mülhidler*, Istanbul Tarih Vakfı Yurt Yayınlar (1998), 350–351.

6 For secondary literature on these authors see the bibliography of Martin van Bruinessen in this volume. Among the well-known publications of these authors, we can refer to Nasrollah Pourjavady, and Peter Lamborn Wilson, *Kings of Love: The History & Poetry of the Ni'matullahi Sufi Order of Iran*, Tehran: Imperial Iranian Academy of Philosophy, 1978; and W. Ivanow, *The Truth-Worshippers of Kurdistan*. Leiden: Brill for the Ismaili Society, 1953.

7 Shahab Ahmed, *What is Islam?* Also see N. Green, (ed.), *The Persianate World: The Frontiers of a Eurasian Lingua Franca*, California: University Of California Press, 2019; B.G. Fragner, *Die "Persophonie": Regionalitat, Identitat und Sprachkontakt in der Geschichte Asiens*, Berlin: Das Arabische Buch, 1999; and Saïd Amir Arjomand, "Evolution of the Persianate Polity and Its Transmission to India," *Journal of Persianate Studies*, 2 (2009), pp. 115–36.

Whores and Heavenly Beings: Women and Sufism in the Persianate World of the Twelfth to Thirteenth Centuries*

Lloyd Ridgeon
University of Glasgow

Abstract
Much of the recent scholarship on Sufism and gender has focused on the early mediaeval years, prior to the tenth and eleventh centuries (C.E), but little research has been published on the subsequent period in the eleventh to thirteenth centuries in the Persianate world. This chapter seeks to redress this, by firstly assessing the legacy that Sufis of that time inherited, and then by offering three case-studies, each of which represents different genres in Persian in which women feature. The case-studies focus upon three of the major Sufis of the time, namely Abū Ḥāmid al-Ghazālī (d.1111), Awḥad al-Dīn Kirmānī (d.1238) and Jalāl al-Dīn Rūmī (d.1273). The results of the case-studies convey diverse and seemingly conflicting messages, although the difference between them may reflect the dissimilarity and purpose of the respective genre. Moreover, such "conflicting messages" need to be understood in light of the social realities of the times in which there was a strict paradigm of gender complementarity and exclusion for women. This may have resulted in women becoming active in establishing their own forms of Sufi-esque piety and activity, while it should not be discounted that some male Sufis understood that women could achieve very high levels of "mystical" insight (*ma'rifat*). In short, the chapter argues that male Persian Sufis did not trespass "beyond shariah", but they embraced an interpretation of *sharī'a* that endorsed the complementarity of the sexes, although the idealised version of women offered chances of "spiritual" equality with men.

Keywords: Women; Sufism; Ghazālī; Rūmī; Kirmānī; twelfth to thirteenth century Persianate world.

Introduction

Issues pertaining to gender, and in particular to women's rights, have become more prevalent in the late twentieth and twenty-first centuries in Western societies, reflecting the greater awareness of the discrimination and lack of equality that women have suffered in predominantly patriarchal societies. The status of women in pre-modern times, in both Western and non-Western societies, was largely marginalised; the presence of women in mediaeval Persianate society was largely unheard, silenced by male voices; or it was unseen, as writing was overwhelmingly the domain of men. Yet recent scholarship has attempted to provide space for women in Islamicate societies, and re-assess the extent to which women exercised agency, held powerful roles, or were able to have an influential voice in society, whether as rulers,[1] or as authors and poets,[2] or even as patrons of devotional institutions.[3] Research related to Islam in general, and Sufism in particular, typifies this development. Of the more discerning studies, it is worth mentioning the works of Sara Abdel-Latif,[4] Rkia Cornell,[5] Christopher Melchert,[6] Laury Silvers[7] and Arin Salameh-Qudsi[8] who have focused primarily on the ascetic and "early" periods (meaning eighth to eleventh centuries C.E.). The aforementioned authors have been at pains to outline the role of women in Sufism, whilst recognising the anonymity and marginalisation that women were forced to adopt, and the strategies they devised to manage the practice of complementarity.[9]

In contrast, some scholars appear to idealise the Sufi tradition and the position of women within it.[10] For example, Leila Ahmed has argued that "[a]utonomy and a life free of male control – unattainable conditions for women in the dominant society – were thus available to them through Sufism."[11] She also seems to claim in her summary of the life of Rābiʿa al-ʿAdawiyya (d. 801) that women were able to live a Sufi life within convents: "Women dwelling in ribats, and Sufi women in general seemed to have occupied a borderline status between the reputable and disreputable."[12] However, she provides little evidence to legitimise these claims which appear to be anachronistic and an "invention" of women's history in early Sufism. This kind of view is typified by an attachment to the aforementioned Rābiʿa al-ʿAdawiyya who had been adopted as a female Sufi par excellence by the thirteenth century C.E. (as discussed below).

This chapter seeks to build on the efforts of the forementioned scholars, but take a step forward in time, and focus specifically on the twelfth and thirteenth centuries in the Persianate Sufi environment (which therefore excludes a focus on North Africa and Egypt, and it also does not consider the teachings associated with Ibn ʿArabī (d. 1240) and his school of thought).[13] Following a historical introduction in which the position of women within the Sufi tradition is briefly examined, focusing upon different genres (namely the *ṭabaqāt* literature, Sufi manuals and also mentioning how women were portrayed in the "second-class" Sufi associations that gathered under the name of *futuwwat* or *javānmardī*), the chapter provides three case studies that focus on the views related to women of three of the most eminent and distinguished Sufis of the times, namely Abū Ḥāmid al-Ghazālī (d. 1111), Awḥad al-Dīn Kirmānī (d.1238), and Jalāl al-Dīn Rūmī (d. 1273). These case studies also provide examples of three very different kinds of composition: for Ghazālī, the writing is in the form of manuals of advice; the hagiography is assessed in the case study for Kirmānī; and last, the case study for Rūmī primarily utilises his poetry (in this case, his quatrains) but which are complemented by other appropriate writings. There are major differences among the three, and so future research might determine if the genre has an impact on the results. While much has been written on this topic (especially with reference to Ghazālī and Rūmī), this chapter offers a fresh look at material that is often overlooked.

The starting point of this study is the *sharīʿa*, which ties in conveniently with the theme of this volume of "Beyond Shariah". The Sufis of the period had much to say about the *sharīʿa*, typified in the compositions of ʿAzīz Nasafī, a thirteenth century Sufi who wrote solely in Persian. In all of his works, Nasafī structured his arguments based on the worldview of several groups of seekers. At the most elementary and basic were the *ahl-i sharīʿat* (people of the shariah); more sophisticated and intellectual arguments were presented in the form of the views of the *ahl-i ḥikmat* (the people of wisdom, or philosophers); and finally Nasafī presented the worldview of the *ahl-i vaḥdat* (the people of unity),[14] which was clearly his preferred group. Nasafī's methodology allowed him to describe the various mediaeval worldviews which he understood as a hierarchy of law (*sharīʿa*), the Sufi path (*ṭarīqa*) and attainment to God (*ḥaqīqa*). Each stage, however, was a necessary and indispensable building block to the next step. This tripart classification reflected the well-known prophetic dictum: "The *sharīʿa* is my words (*aqwālī*), the *ṭarīqa* is my actions (*aʿmālī*) and the *ḥaqīqa* is my inner states (*aḥwālī*)."[15] Nasafī frequently called the wayfarers to seek perfection through the Perfect Person (*insān-i kāmil*) who "is complete in four things: good words, good actions, good morals and gnosis (*maʿrifat*)."[16] The necessity for Sufis to abide by the *sharīʿa* was unequivocally expressed by Nasafī; it is noteworthy that he emphasised that the need to abide by the lowest level, the *sharīʿa*, was incumbent upon even the Sufi who had advanced to high degrees of insight on the path;

> O dervish! In whatever station you are in, do not trust in your own intelligence and knowledge, and do not consider or name yourself 'Verifier of the Truth'. Neither make a special way (*ṭarīqī*) for yourself, nor establish a religious school (*madhhab*) through your own thought. In other words, you must be an imitator of your prophet in the knowledge and gnosis of any station that you are in, and do not neglect his *sharīʿa* ...[17]
>
> Don't let your caution slip, in other words, don't neglect the *sharīʿa* because anyone who neglects it will certainly be sorrowful since *'renunciation of caution and discretion is poor opinion'*.[18]
>
> Know that the wise people have said that human expediency is to respect the claims of the Verifier of the Truth and not to step outside the bounds of imitation (*ḥadd-i taqlīd*)

> and admit one's own incapacity and ignorance, and know for sure that in reality, one cannot know God as God really is, and in reality, one cannot recognise things as they really are. When this has been understood, the *sharīʿa* has been, and is, respected. The *sharīʿa* includes conforming to commands, abstaining from prohibited things, being abstinent, not neglecting one point in observing the *sharīʿa*, speaking truthfully and behaving correctly.[19] Human liberation and tranquillity in this world and the next is in a mouthful of *ḥalāl* [food] and in association with good people, and the woes and divisiveness of humans in this world and the next is in a mouthful of *ḥarām* [food] and the association of wicked people. [The good person] is one who does not cause difficulties to others and as far as possible brings comfort.[20]

The *sharīʿa,* then, represented the basic and core element for all Sufi activity. Although not as sophisticated and nuanced as other forms of "reality" it was believed that the base building block had to be stable and firm for subsequent endeavours.[21] In short, "normative" Sufis (not the more "unorthodox" types exemplified by the Qalandars) did not seek to go beyond the *sharīʿa,* but attempted to establish their behaviour on firm foundations, thereby giving themselves the opportunity to reach higher levels of meaning.

This acceptance of, and obedience to, the inherited interpretation of *sharīʿa* as it applied to women and how men should relate to them is best exemplified in the writings of Ghazālī, who observed, "… if prostration were possible to any other than God, then women would be commanded to prostrate before men."[22] Yet Ghazālī's comments represent a level of understanding of the social relations between the sexes. The women who observed such a perspective were subsequently idealised as places where it was possible to observe beautiful divine character traits. When Rūmī described women as "rays of God",[23] this idealised version of women did not negate or deny the complementarity paradigm, enshrined by an interpretation of *sharīʿa* that provided strict and different social roles for men and women. In fact, Rūmī utilised the same three-fold classification that Nasafī employed, and in his prose introduction to book five of his *Mathnawī,* he wrote,

> … Religious Law [*sharīʿat*] is like a candle showing the way. Unless you gain possession of the candle, there is no wayfaring [*rāh rafta na-shavad*]; and when you have come on to the way, your wayfaring is the Path [*ṭarīqa*]; and when you have reached the journey's end, that is the Truth [*ḥaqīqa*].[24]

The interrelationship between them all (and the necessity of the *sharī'a*) is highlighted in his comments that:

> the Law [*sharī'at*] may be compared to learning the science of medicine, and the Path [*ṭarīqat*] to regulating one's diet in accordance with (the science of) medicine and taking remedies, and the Truth [*ḥaqīqat*] to gaining health everlasting and becoming independent of them both and becoming independent of them both[25] ... the Law [*sharī'at*] is knowledge, the Path action, the Truth attainment unto God.[26]

Not all scholars accept that the Sufis had this perspective of *sharī'a*. For example, Jawid Mojaddedi discusses Rūmī's "teaching that the Friend of God is unconstrained by the Shariah or any other code of behaviour, because his relationship with God is closer, and therefore at a higher level."[27] However, this kind of view focuses on Sufis who believed they had already mastered the *sharī'a* and *ṭarīqa*, and thus enjoyed intimate relations with God, which the initiate did not enjoy. It is in this sense that the Friend of God becomes "independent" of the *sharī'a* and *ṭarīqa*.

In the three case studies herein that the Sufis investigated, Ghazālī, Kirmānī, and Rūmī all present a vision of women in society, as she is defined by the *sharī'a*, that is, by an understanding of what was considered the "literal" meaning of specific Qur'ānic verses and *ḥadīth*. Ghazālī presents the most "*sharī'a*-faithful" of all three Sufis (perhaps because the genre of writing manuals of advice for Sufis living in society was conducive to this perspective). He offered a vision that conformed to the ideal of complementarity, that is, that females played different roles in society to men, and if they excelled in these roles then their reward would be obtained in the next world. However, the complementarity that was offered for women was very much a patriarchal programme which limited the possibilities open to women in society.

Background

In order to assess the three case studies provided in this chapter, it is instructive to appreciate the inheritance of the mediaeval Sufi tradition in terms of its gender appreciation. This is carried out by reviewing firstly the *ṭabaqāt* literature (a form of writing which provides biographies of previous generations of Sufis) and secondly the manuals of Sufism that were written in this formative period of Sufism up until the eleventh century. The attitudes towards women that come across in the literature were to materialise in society in the form of "second-class" Sufi organisations which were the preserve of males. A third section then assesses the significance of these associations of young men (*javānmardān*).

Ṭabaqāt literature

Ṭabaqāt literature was an early form of biography that depicted the previous "generations" of pious exemplars and leading members of the formative Islamic community (including early ascetics who were duly appropriated as representative of a pious tradition that coalesced into the Sufi movement),[28] and Sufis of the ninth to tenth centuries. These works reveal just as much about the Sufi authors and their intended audience, and their perspectives on gender-related issues, as on the "Sufis" included as biographical entries. One of the first of the *ṭabaqāt* works was written by ʿAbd al-Raḥman Sulamī (d. 1021) whose *Ṭabaqāt al-Ṣūfiyya* ("Generation of Sufis") investigated in some detail one hundred and three male Sufis, most of whom were discussed in entries of several pages in length.[29] Sulamī also wrote another work, much shorter, called *Dhikr al-niswa al-mutaʿabbidat al-Ṣufiyyāt* ("Remembrance of Worshipping Sufi Women") which gave very brief reports of eighty-two females.[30] Although the difference in attention allocated by Sulamī to males and females reflects the relative values accorded to the sexes, it has been argued that equality was accorded to some, as Rkia Cornell observes, females who chose "an independent life as 'career women' of the spirit ... could travel without a chaperone, mix socially with men, teach men in public assemblies, and develop intellectually in ways that were not accessible to their non-Sufi sisters."[31]

Another work in the genre of *ṭabaqāt* was *Hilyat al-awliyā* ("Ornaments of the Friends of God"), written by Abū Nuʿaym al-Iṣfahānī (d. 1038), which described 649 individuals that included a relatively small section on the close female companions of Muḥammad.[32] Perhaps more striking than Abū Nuʿaym's work was that of al-Qushayrī (d. 1074), whose *Risāla* was not strictly a composition in the *ṭabaqāt* genre, although a third of it was devoted to eighty-three leading masters of the path (all of whom were male).[33] Likewise, ʿAbdallāh Anṣārī of Herat (d. 1089) did not include any females in his *Ṭabaqāt al-Ṣūfiyya* ("Generation of Sufis"), a compendium of 274 Sufis.[34] In the same vein, Hujwīrī (d.c. 1063) listed sixty-four male Sufis in his chapter on eminent Sufis in his *Kashf al-Maḥjūb* ("Uncovering the Veiled"). Females were entirely absent in his presentation of illustrious exemplars.[35]

The most positive of all proponents of female piety was Ibn Jawzī (d. 1201) who composed a work entitled *Ṣifāt al-Ṣafwa* ("The Attributes of the Pure"). This treatise describes some two hundred females, which is about one quarter of the total of all individuals. However, it is indicative of the culture that "almost half of the women in Ibn Jawzī have no name, and the stories about them are titled, 'A Devout Woman'".[36]

One of the most significant works of the *ṭabaqāt* genre for the purposes of this chapter is by Farīd al-Dīn ʿAṭṭār (d.c. 1220) whose Persian text *Tadhkirat al-awliyā* ("Remembrance of the Friends of God") was probably composed around the beginning of the thirteenth century and is divided into many "remembrances", each one presenting the life of a Sufi.[37] One of these chapters is devoted to Rābiʿa al-ʿAdawiyya, who is presented as an iconic female Sufi who became (and continues to be) a female paragon who performed miracles, taught that love for God was more important than desire for heavenly reward or fear of hellish chastisement, and instructed eminent males of her time.[38] In his first paragraph of his chapter on Rābiʿa, ʿAṭṭār stated:

> If anyone asks why we placed remembrance of her among the ranks of men, we reply that the Master of the Prophets declares '*God does not regard your forms.*' It is not a matter of form but of right intention. If it is right to derive two-thirds of religion from Ayesha then it is also right to derive benefit from one of his maidservants. When a woman is a man on the path of the Lord most high, she cannot be called woman.[39]

It is possible to understand ʿAṭṭār's last sentence "When a woman is a man on the path of the Lord" in two ways. In the first, his view must be read in conjunction with the *ḥadīth* that he cited '*God does not regard your forms*'. In effect, it is not that a woman must become male, rather, it is at high levels of piety that individuals achieve human perfection.[40] In other words, the word "man" signifies human, rather than a gendered term, an argument advanced by Schimmel.[41] However, this explanation glosses over the significance of the Persian original which uses the word man: (*chūn zan dar rāh-i̤ khudā ... mard bāshad...*).[42] It is to be wondered that ʿAṭṭār chose a specifically gendered term rather than a more neutral word such as *shakhṣ* (person) because he wanted to shame males into achieving higher levels of Sufi piety.

The second understanding reflects a perspective that is typified in an argument offered by Silvers that opinions such as ʿAṭṭār's render women "sexually neuter" and denies their "sexual availability", making them safe. They transcend any notion of sex, and therefore become individuals on the path of God, equal with male Sufis. Moreover, Silvers considers dangerous the "praise" of calling women "men"; this is because "[w]hen men vouch for women's exceptional status by rendering them sexually neuter, depicting them as having transcended their bodies, or by calling them 'men', their praise only confirms that men hold the power to authorize women's value and women on the whole were typically perceived as spiritually and morally weak."[43] Despite Silvers' reservations on ʿAṭṭār's comments, his presentation of Rābiʿa must certainly have challenged some patriarchal ideas. Transcending sexuality and the parameters of what most females in Islamic society could expect in practical day to day living, Rābiʿa was, and is, celebrated as a Sufi whose sole concern was devotion to God, and for many observers, this led her to adopt a celibate lifestyle, thereby positioning herself outside of the restrictions that needed to be enforced for segregation between *maḥram* and *nā-maḥram*.[44] This explains the declaration of Ḥasan al-Baṣrī (depicted as one of the major forefathers of the Sufi tradition) who discoursed with her the whole night and did not notice that he was a man or that she was a woman. It is also worthwhile to point out, as many have done, that Rābiʿa was presented by ʿAṭṭār as the teacher and mentor of Ḥasan al-Baṣrī. It is not important that Ḥasan al-Basrī died when Rābiʿa would have been a girl of fourteen (who at that time probably was not the "rounded" and fully developed pious icon that ʿAṭṭār presented), for historical accuracy is irrelevant to the didactic purpose of the hagiographical work.[45] This contrast between Rābiʿa and Ḥasan al-Basrī occurs not in a single anecdote, but rather in a chain of over ten episodes, during which she instructs other leading "Sufis" including Shaqīq al-Balkhī (d. 810) Ibrāhīm Adham (c. 777) and Mālik-i Dīnār (d. 748).

The idealisation of Rābiʿa in ʿAṭṭār's work of ninety-seven great individuals suggests that her way of celibacy, her refusal to marry, and her rejection of all worldly concerns made up the sole path of female piety. For many women the model of Islamic piety was provided by Muḥammad's wives and daughters, which was that of mother and wife, and as such did not necessarily preclude a Sufi lifestyle.[46] Moreover, her celibacy and denial of any sexual inclination should be contrasted with the way that male Sufis are often presented. For example, the celebrated Junayd of Baghdad (d. 910) is reported to have remarked, "I need sex as much as I need food."[47] Although ʿAṭṭār presented an ideal female Sufi, he did so by producing a "constructed saint," meaning that she was a "composite image of female spirituality whose outline has been shaped through numerous sayings, stories, poems and other popular forms of expression."[48] Importantly, it is a construction of only one kind of female Sufi piety that in practice ignored different types of female religious life.[49] Whilst much Sufi literature simply ignored varieties of female Sufi models, the idealised Rābiʿa became the prominent female Sufi trope to express the desired female qualities. In the thirteenth and fourteenth centuries this was typified by a variety of Sufis: the Persian Sufi Jandī (d. 1301) dedicated a treatise of his to an un-named lady that he refers to as the "Rābiʿa of the age",[50] the Indian Nizām al-Dīn ʿAwliyā (d. 1325) called his mother "the Rābiʿa of the day"[51], and in Anatolia the fourteenth century hagiographer Aflākī reported a prostitute who ran towards Rūmī, lowered her head and fell at his feet, and heard him exclaim, "Rābiʿa! Rābiʿa! Rābiʿa!" Rūmī later explained how the prostitute behaved without hypocrisy or deception and thus deserved to be called by such a praiseworthy name.[52]

The brief survey of these *ṭabaqāt* treatises demonstrates that women were accorded a place within the pious tradition of Islam from an early period, and later were adopted as exemplars by Sufis.[53] Although nowhere near as numerous as reports of male ascetics and "Sufis", the information about these early female "Sufis" is intriguing; Ruth Roded has noted "the recurring image of women flaunting their spiritual superiority over men, rebuking them for lapses in faith and religious duties, and admonishing even men of authority and prominence does not fit the accepted view of women's place in society." Whether this was a realistic depiction of the dynamics at play between female "Sufis" and males needs to be considered, as Roded added a caveat to her observation that "the hyperbole of Sufi discourse can be translated into the notion that even women may achieve a spiritual stage superior to that of men of little faith."[54] Or in other words, the likes of ʿAṭṭār composed the biography on Rābiʿa simply to motivate male Sufis to achieve greater levels of piety: if this can be done by a woman, think what a man can do! Such a perspective resembles how the Egyptian Sufi, Ibn Fārid (d. 1235) reported Rābiʿa's sayings to legitimise certain Sufi teachings, which for some was all the more surprising given her sex: Ibn Fārid added before conveying her instruction, "and she was a woman!"[55]

Manuals

Aside from the *ṭabaqāt* literature there are other works by Sufis prior to the time in question that contain views about women, especially in the treatises of the early and classical authors that discuss the benefits and disadvantages of celibacy and marriage.[56] One of the very earliest manuals is that of Abū Naṣr Sarrāj (d. 988), whose *Kitāb al-Lumaʿ fīʾl-taṣawwuf* ("Book of Light Flashes") does not contain a section devoted to women, but it includes a chapter called the Rules of "Married Men and Those who have Children". Sarrāj does not directly convey his own opinion, instead he speaks through the words of past masters. It is clear that his main concern is not women *per se*, but the distractions that women and children may cause. He opens his chapter with an anecdote about a young man who married, but the couple remained chaste for thirty years. Although the underlying concern of this anecdote was with sexual relations, the subsequent tenor of the chapter suggests that it is the additional worry of having children that was the cause of disquiet. Sarrāj reports from Sufyān al-Thawrī (d. 778) that when a Sufi (*faqīrī*) marries it is like a man who journeys on a ship; when children are born it is as if he has drowned. Sarrāj makes it clear through another anecdote that he is aware that the Prophetic model is to marry and have children; yet he argues that the Prophet was able to provide such guidance to his community through the strength of prophecy and light of messengership, implying that Sufis with children will be prone to making an offence. In fact, it seems that Sarrāj believed that women could be excellent partners for a male Sufi, as he includes a story about Abū Shuʿayb Barāthī who married a worldly woman but who adopted a life of simplicity, and they lived together in poverty and worshipped God in this fashion until they died. Sarrāj also stated from [his] shaykh that Sufis should not marry wealthy women and thereby become slaves to their wishes. A poor Sufi should marry a poor woman and treat her with justice. Nowhere in his chapter on "Married Men And Those Who Have Children" does Sarrāj belittle women, or suggest that they are deficient or non-equal to men.

A contrast to Sarrāj's work is *Qūt al-Qulūb*, ("The Nourishment of Hearts") composed by Abū Ṭālib al-Makkī (d. 996) who has been characterised as a "profound misogynist".[57] He had an extremely negative view of women to the extent that he argued in favour of a celibate life because he disliked women, and regarded the benefits of divorce as greater than the advantages of a couple remaining together. Naturally Makkī could not deny the prophetic model of marriage, however, he argued that women in the Prophet's time were more pious, helpful and supportive, whereas in his own lifetime, the morals of women had deteriorated as their demands had increased.[58] Immenkamp has observed that throughout his text, Makkī referred to women "in the most derogatory and contemptuous terms, claiming, for example, that 'most women are irreligious and unscrupulous ... that their most predominant characteristics are ignorance and caprice' and that 'there is no good in them because they are whimsical and love the world'."[59] Immenkamp concluded her discussion on Makkī by claiming that although he favoured celibacy, and did not conceal his preference, he felt compelled to allow Muslims the freedom to choose a married or celibate life depending upon their own inclinations.[60]

Another influential Sufi who composed a manual for aspiring dervishes, and which also discussed celibacy and marriage was Hujwīrī (d. 1072) whose *Kashf al-Maḥjūb* was one of the earliest Persian Sufi texts. Hujwīrī displayed considerable ambivalence about the advantages of marriage. He offered advantages and disadvantages in his attempt to provide novice Sufis with the requisite theory before making an informed decision. Hujwīrī's largely unstructured chapter mentions three benefits to marriage: it follows the prophetic *sunna*; it provides reverence and security; and there is a possibility of procreation. The disadvantages that Hujwīrī gave were all designed specifically for men. So, for example, the first disadvantage was that marriage was a distraction for the body for the sake of sensual pleasure. Therefore, the Sufi should adopt a celibate lifestyle in the company of likeminded dervishes if he could not control his lust or arrange his marital affairs so that he could devote himself to God. Interestingly, there is no discussion about the sexual demands of women, which some have read into Sufi texts (and will be discussed later). Hujwīrī was writing specifically for men, and so his aim was to ensure that they were able to control their own lusts and desires. The second disadvantage was that marriage was a distraction from the Sufi-lifestyle and God.[61] He seems to be sympathetic towards celibacy and remarked that "Sufism was founded on celibacy: the introduction of marriage brought about a change."[62] Aside from presenting "practical" reasons for adopting a celibate lifestyle, Hujwīrī was careful to mention the scriptural reasons that advocates of celibacy listed: women were behind the "calamity" that overtook Adam, the quarrel between Cain and Abel, the punishment inflicted upon the two angels (Harut and Marut), and in fact such people claim that "down to the present day all mischief, worldly and religious have been caused by women."[63] That he distanced himself from such views by simply listing the opinions of others should not blinker readers to the overall negative portrayal of women that he provided. The fact that, like so many of his contemporaries, he wrote his treatise without referring to female perspectives, suggests that it did not occur to him that women may also have desired to be Sufis, or that women may have sought advice about curbing lust in order to lead a pious life. Hujwīrī's comments were directed towards males to the extent that he was concerned simply with offering advice to male readers: "He should be kind to his wife and should provide her with lawful expenses."[64] Moreover, there are passages which betray a blatant disregard for women and their welfare which is to be provided by men who know what is best for themselves and their wives: "In our times it is impossible for anyone to have a suitable wife, whose wants are not excessive and whose demands are not unreasonable."[65]

Futuwwat (Jawānmardī)

Opposition to female engagement in Sufism appeared within the "second-class" Sufi organisations, that is the *futuwwat*, or *jawānmardī* groups which were developing during the eleventh and twelfth centuries but by the thirteenth century had mushroomed across the Persian and Turkish speaking world. The manuals of these groups stipulated that women could not join. The literal meaning of the term *futuwwat* is indicative of the problem, as it means "manliness", being derived from the Arabic word *fata* (or young man). The origins of these organisations in part lay in groups of brigands who had lofty, ethical views, and as such, the martial aspect and heritage of these groups may have been the motivation for men to join and discourage females from any interest.[66] In effect, the *futuwwat* organisations were societies for men employed in crafts and trades in which there was a large element of ritualised Sufi activity, including gatherings for the performance of *dhikr*, prayer, communal meals and the Sufi devotional singing and dancing (*samā'*). Membership was not necessarily based upon occupation; more important was piety and, significantly, in some of these associations, sex. For example, one mediaeval treatise of *futuwwat* states: "*futuwwat* is not ... for a woman ... there is no *futuwwat* for women because the prophet said, '*They are incomplete in intelligence and in religion.*'"[67] The treatises of Abū Ḥafṣ 'Umar Suhrawardī (d. 1234) on the topic include a number of anecdotes that suggest that he endorsed the complementarity and separation paradigm. In one anecdote Suhrawardī related that some members of the group follow the rules of the *sharīʿa* if a member transgressed their rules in committing a major sin three times; he should be lashed 100 times, and the members should

> ... paint and decorate his hands with henna, just like a woman, anoint his eyebrows and eyelashes with collyrium, and wrap colourful, fine linen around his head [like a hijāb], and give him a certificate which reads, "You did not have the strength for the way of *futuwwat* or of the men of *jawānmardān* ... Now you have fallen to the level of a wicked woman. Your recompense is having colourful hands and the clothing of a woman."[68]

Here is a case of binary distinction, in which the punishment is to degrade the offender in the worst possible fashion. There could have been nothing more shameful than to be cast out of an organisation for males, dressed up as a female. The stigma, disgrace and damage to honour would surely have ensured that transgressions were few in number. It is unclear whether Suhrawardī personally endorsed this view, as he also claimed that according to *futuwwat,* if someone apologised for his sins then he must be forgiven.[69]

Such opposition to female participation in Sufi-like rituals and the establishment of the complementarity and separation paradigm resulted in women creating alternative forms of pious devotion. One option that was open to the wealthier females was that of patronage. Wolper has mentioned this phenomenon with regard to the Mevlevi order in Konya and Anatolia,[70] and Humphries has studied female patronage in Damascus between 1174–1260 and found that twenty-one women underwrote the expenses for religious and charitable institutions, out of a total of 147 individuals (six of these twenty-one women sponsored *khānaqāhs*).[71] A similar trend emerged at the same time in Mamluk Egypt, as one estimate of original donors or superintendents (*nuẓẓār*) of *waqfs* reached 28 per cent.[72]

One last point concerning the *javānmardī/futuwwat* tradition, which in Anatolia was known as *Ahilik*, is that the Ottoman historian ʿĀşikpaşazāde (d. 1484) mentioned just once in his writings a group of female *Ahis* (whom he calls *Baciyan-i Rum*).[73]

First case study: Abū Ḥāmid al-Ghazālī

The figure of Abū Ḥāmid al-Ghazālī, born in Ṭūs in 1058, towers over much of Islamic thought from the time of his death in 1111 C.E. to the modern period. He first achieved prominence on his appointment as head of the Niẓāmiyya *madrasa* in Baghdad, the most famous theological college in the Eastern part of the Islamic world. Indeed, the position has been likened to "being both Archbishop of Canterbury and Regius Professor of Law at Oxford."[74] As an intellectual his range was vast, as he wrote on philosophy, ethics, theology and statecraft, law and political thought.[75] Yet Ghazālī was more than a "dry" academic, as he renounced his professorship, and spent as long as ten years in his "spiritual" quest.

It is perhaps impossible to disentangle Ghazālī the theologian, or ethicist, or Sufi, because the different strands are so interwoven. His *Kīmīyā-yi Saʿādat* ("The Alchemy of Happiness"), a Persian text written towards the end of his life,[76] weaves theological, ethical and Sufi meanings together; indeed some have seen this text as being "replete with many beautifully expressed and valuable insights into the Sufi path."[77] Therefore, his sections in which he dealt with women, according to such an understanding, should include all of the aforementioned elements. However, the long section quoted below, taken from a chapter called "The Courtesies of Marriage" in his *Kīmīyā-yi Saʿādat*,[78] does not render happy reading, depicting the position of women in society, which fully endorses the worst aspects of the complementarity paradigm:

> The rights of men over women are greater [than the rights of women over men] because a woman, in truth, is a man's slave. In the reports it is said that if prostration were possible to any other than God, then women would be commanded to prostrate before men. A man's right over a woman is that she stays in the house and does not leave without permission from him and she does not go out the door or house. She does not mix or chat with neighbours or visit them without need. She says nothing except good things about her husband, and she does not talk about any intimacy that has taken place between them in private. She shares his desire and happiness in all things. She is not treacherous with his property, but seeks his goal in all affairs, and she is kind. When her husband's friend knocks on the door, she answers in such a way that he does not recognise her, and she covers herself from all of her husband's acquaintances so that they do not know her. She is content with her husband in everything, does not seek for anything, and puts his rights over those of [her] relations. She always keeps herself pure so that there may be companionship, physical contact or intimacy [between them]. She does whatever she can by herself. She does not take pride in her own beauty in front of her husband. She is not ungrateful for the goodness that she has witnessed in him, and she does not say, "What did I see in you?" She does not find fault without cause at any time, and she does not get angry. She does not seek to buy and sell, and she does not [ask for a] divorce. The prophet said "I looked into hell, and I saw mostly women. I said, 'Why is it like this?' He replied, 'They curse their husbands much and they are ungrateful with their husbands.'"[79]

Ghazālī also considered the benefits and disadvantages of marriage in his magisterial Arabic work, the voluminous *Iḥyā ʿulūm al-dīn* ("Revivification of the Religious Sciences"). He saw his task as providing useful arguments to help his readers decide on the issue. One group of scholars approved of the institution, but the argumentation indicates that marriage was viewed from the male perspective;[80] a woman was simply expected to assist and promote her husband's life, regardless of her own. The assumption is that by assisting her husbands, a wife would automatically be satisfied.

This group of scholars endorsed the complementarity of the sexes, and they argued for five benefits. The first was to beget children, the second was to guard religion, and the third was to relax the soul. The fourth benefit of marriage allowed the husband "freedom from concern with running the household (and all the chores of cooking, making beds, cleaning dishes and preparing meals)."[81] In the fifth advantage to marriage it is clearly stated that the husband benefited by "enduring their temper, bearing the pain they cause, endeavouring to reform them and guide them on the path of religion."[82] Such comments are hardly conducive to support the idea contained in the Qur'ān that woman are the equals of men.[83] Women are in desperate need of rectification, training and guardianship.

The other group mentioned by Ghazālī commented that "in times like ours it is best to avoid marriage. Marriage used to have its merit in the past, when earning a living was not perilous and women's morals not blameworthy."[84]

The Moroccan feminist scholar Fatima Mernissi (d. 2015) painted a less than positive image of Ghazālī. In her analysis of Ghazālī's writing about women, Mernissi witnessed a correlation between controlled female sexuality and social order.[85] Female sexuality was regulated by both segregation and polygamy which enhanced male domination, and also by regular and sufficient sexual activity that satisfied the female. Thus Ghazālī stated, "It is desirable that [the husband] should have intimate relations with [his wife] once every four nights; that is more just, for the [maximum] number of wives is four which justifies this span. *It is true that intimate relations should be more or less frequent in accordance to her need to remain chaste, for to satisfy her is his duty.*"[86] "According to her needs" was the key phrase for Mernissi because it implied that females would demand more sex due to their inherently active sexual drive. Mernissi understood Ghazālī as positing "the woman as hunter and the man as the hunted, passive victim,"[87] and her investigation also highlighted Ghazālī's discussion of how women had the "power to deceive and defeat men, not by force, but by cunning and intrigue."[88] Although she convincingly showed that males held views that shaped hegemonic perspectives and created cultural deterrents to female activity in the mediaeval public sphere, Mernissi's analysis of Ghazālī's "Proper Conduct in Marriage" glossed over his warnings of the dangers of male passion and lust. One of Ghazālī's conclusions for the benefits to males in marrying was that it offered immunity from Satan, relief from craving, and protection against the perils of lust, a perspective that is also found in earlier Sufi writings.[89] A more balanced conclusion views Ghazālī being equally concerned with the perils of lust and desire among males and females. Moreover, his "negativity" about women should be placed in the context of his views about men in general. He observed, "The common condition of man, however, is foolishness, coarseness, impetuosity, frivolity, bad character, and unfairness combined with the expectation of perfect fairness from others. In this respect, such people will undoubtedly degenerate still further in marriage. For them it is safer to remain single."[90]

The debate over Ghazālī's (un)balanced portrayal of sexuality in the *Ihya 'ulūm al-dīn* deserves more attention.[91] An alternative perspective on Ghazālī's perspective on women has been offered by Omid Safi who argues that his negative statements should be considered in light of the politics surrounding the succession to the Sultanate, and in particular, the role of Tarkān Khātūn, the mother of Sultan's son who was just one of the possible successors to Malik-Shāh (d. 1092). Safi suggests that Ghazālī was in the camp of his patron Niẓām al-Mulk (d. 1092) and preferred the claim of the Sultan's elder son, named Bark-yāruq, who was mothered by another of the Sultan's wives.

While the background to Ghazālī's views on women is obviously complex and defies simple answers, it does appear to be the case that many Muslims came to equate females with sexuality, emotion and irrationality, and males with reason, the intellect and devout piety. Ghazālī himself suggested that the difference between the sexes was based on scriptural foundation and he cited the *ḥadīth* that women "are deficient in intelligence" and confirmed that this particular *ḥadīth* referred to the Qur'ānic verse that the testimony of two women is equal to the witness of just one man.[92] It appears that Ghazālī was concerned with upholding male honour, and one method to achieve this was to control and use women in marriage in order to consolidate or advance within society. His following remarks are instructive in this respect:

> ... the prosperity and peopling of the world depend on women. True prosperity, however, will not be achieved without (sound) planning. It is men's duty, especially after coming of age, to take precautions in matters of choosing wives and giving daughters in marriage, and so avoid falling into disgrace and embarrassment. It is a fact that all the trials, misfortunes and woes which befall men come from women, and that few men get in the end what they long and hope for from them.[93]

Second case study: Awḥad al-Dīn Kirmānī

The second case study focuses upon a Sufi who is perhaps not as well-known in the contemporary West, but in his own lifetime, Awḥad al-Dīn Kirmānī was appointed to one of the highest ranks a Sufi could enjoy: he was the *shaykh al-shuyūkh* of the Mustanṣariyya Sufi complex in Baghdad between 1234 and his death in 1238. This was the leading position to which a Sufi in the capital city might aspire, and it brought with it huge prestige. Prior to Kirmānī the position had been held by the illustrious Shaykh Abū Ḥafṣ ʿUmar Suhrawardī (d. 1234).

This case study differs in the respect that it utilises an untitled hagiography, divided into seventy-two episodes glorifying the virtues of Kirmānī, which was penned in the generation after his death. In this respect it may not reflect Kirmānī's actual words or deeds, but rather it offers an image of what was expected from a leading Sufi shaykh in Anatolia in the late thirteenth century.[94] Although not specifically addressing the issue of gender or female Sufis, the composition may be mined to demonstrate the kinds of perspectives and attitudes that were prevalent among those sympathetic to Kirmānī. Some may object to the use of hagiographies to present historical surveys, as the authors of such works often engage in hyperbole and exaggeration to convey their message; nevertheless, it is likely that many hagiographies contain elements of truth, and indeed they demonstrate the worldview of the author (who lived in the years immediately after Kirmānī's death).

A positive image of women emerges from the very first chapter of the work, which details how Kirmānī was born into a life of privilege, as son of a King. However, as a result of the invading Turkish tribesman, the life of the sixteen-year-old youth was saved by his mother, who told him to flee. Kirmānī escaped, and subsequently made his living in a *madrasa*, but felt something lacking in the disciplines taught there. By good chance he became acquainted with a Sufi called Shaykh Rukn al-Dīn Sujāsī. Kirmānī did not have sufficient resolve for Sufi disciplines when he commenced the path, and so he fled from Sujāsī. However, he was persuaded to return to him by an un-named woman who miraculously knew about his circumstances. Throughout the episode, Kirmānī never saw this woman, who remained in her tent; it was her husband who communicated her words. At first, Kirmānī was offended by the advice of a woman whom he called disparagingly "an impure woman" (*mustaḥāḍa*); however, he was won over by her knowledge, as she miraculously knew of his travails, even though the two had never met previously. He wondered what form of worship and ascetic discipline she observed that enabled her to acquire the light of gnosis. Kirmānī was told that she did not perform ascetic discipline or acts of worship except the obligatory five daily prayers and the fasting of Ramadan. However, during her daily tasks (threading needles, spinning, sewing, making dough, or baking bread, preparing the oven, etc) she performed the *dhikr*.[95] The point that the author of the hagiography desired to convey was that pious attainment was possible for women, even elevated stations beyond which the young Kirmānī had yet to attain. However, all of this was possible within the complementarity paradigm in which women remained at home and performed "women's" work. It is worthy of note that even the old woman's name is not revealed, although readers learn that her husband, an insignificant player in the episode, was called Abū'l Aṣāf, who worked as an oil-maker. The first chapter of the hagiography, then, includes significant roles for women; Kirmānī's mother saved his physical life, and the un-named woman saved his inner life. The situation of both women reveals their relative social insignificance, and yet from the Sufi perspective they could not be of more importance.

The next episode involving women occurs in an anecdote involving Lady Rusūdān, a historical figure, who was the Christian Queen of Georgia between 1223–1245.[96] In this episode, Kirmānī visited Rusūdān in order to rescue a servant boy who had been taken prisoner by the Georgians. Rusūdān fell in love with Kirmānī, but she is not depicted as a woman who is motivated by sexual desire, in fact she is upright and virtuous. She lamented that a book chosen from her library at random by Kirmānī (in order to take an omen) was the *Alfiya wa Shalfiya* (written by Azraqī Hirawī, an eleventh century Persian poet) which was "an illustrated book on sexual matters based on Indian pornographic writings."[97] The Queen was shocked, and questioned why it was that Kirmānī's community and religious school were virtuous, but that he chose this book (even if at random) for an augury. The anecdote details how the Queen struggled to conceal her love for Kirmānī, but ultimately, declared her feelings and an offer of marriage. The anecdote is interesting if only because it would have alerted readers to the reality that females were rulers; although she was a Christian, there were also cases of females becoming rulers in Muslim lands.[98] Even as a woman and a non-Muslim, Rusūdān is still depicted as a courteous and moral individual; although the anecdote does not reveal why Rusūdān was captivated by the Shaykh, the readers would have assumed it was due to his Sufi disposition.[99] Moreover, readers may also have been aware that Rusūdān had a reputation for amorous adventures, and this was exacerbated by associations made by some Muslims of inherent sexual permissiveness among Christian women.[100]

One of the most positive episodes concerning women involves Kirmānī's daughter, Aymāna, which reveals how females in the families of leading Sufis were used to perpetuate lineages and forge strong alliances among those inclined towards the tradition. The author provides the Sufi lineage of Kirmānī through the female line: the daughter of Shaykh Abū'l- Najīb Suhrawardī (d. 1168) was given in marriage to his student, Shaykh Quṭb al-Dīn Abharī (d. 1181). In turn, Abharī's daughter was married to his student, Shaykh Rukn al-Dīn Sujāsī (d. after 1209), and Sujāsī married his own daughter to Kirmānī.[101] (The same anecdote reveals that Kirmānī agreed to the marriage between Aymāna and one ʿImād al-Dīn, the son of the minister of Akhlat in Eastern Anatolia, which breaks the Sufi linkage, but reveals that the daughters of leading Sufis were sought for political patronage).[102] The anecdote also describes that Aymāna's qualities were nurtured by the leading Sufi of the day, Abū Ḥafṣ Umar Suhrawardī. Kirmānī initially handed Aymāna to Suhrawardī as a ward (as the former felt duty bound to obey the wish of the latter, a "superior" Sufi), but he was nevertheless so deeply attached to his daughter that he sent her letters, and eventually requested that Suhrawardī return her to him. When she arrived at Malatiya, Kirmānī "derived much tranquillity, joy and pleasure from conversing with her, and he was amazed at her eloquence, fine words and manner of explanation."[103] The relationship between father and daughter appears to have been warm, and he took Aymāna with him on pilgrimage to Mecca. It appears that Kirmānī was distressed when the marriage between his daughter and ʿImād al-Dīn was not a happy one, as there was quarrelling and exchange of angry words. ʿImād al-Dīn even beat his wife who sought her father's intercession. After the divorce Aymāna stayed with her father and did not remarry. The significance of Aymāna, however, appears after Kirmānī's death, for she moved to Damascus and attracted male and female disciples, and was the *shaykha* of seventeen *khānaqās*.

In a subsequent episode readers learn that Aymāna was not Kirmānī's only daughter. He had another by the name of Fāṭima, whose mother was a female slave (*kanīzak*) that he bought in a market.[104] Kirmānī evidently married her, as one of his leading disciples, Zayn al-Dīn Ṣadaqa, advised him to divorce her after she had proven to be bad-tempered and violent. It would appear that their daughter, Fāṭima, received some form of education, and perhaps Kirmānī wished that she would emulate Aymāna. However, the text simply states that she was unable to memorise anything from the Qurʾān, and as a result she was given "jobs that women do". After one episode during which she distracted Kirmānī from his concentration (*murāqaba*) with her noise, the father finally snapped and said to her "God willing you will be taken prisoner by the infidels". As a hagiographical work that aimed to promote and propagate Kirmānī's status and form of Sufism, it is perhaps inevitable that Fāṭima was indeed taken prisoner by the Mongols after his death. However, the story did not end too miserably as she was eventually released and married a grandee of her brother's followers. The anecdote about the *kanīzak* and Fāṭima is of interest because there is no indication that their bad tempers and moody dispositions reflect an inherent or essential female tendency. It just happened that this was their nature, in the same way that there are many men portrayed in the hagiography who oppose and reject Kirmānī for all number of reasons. The text does not suggest anything related to deficient female intellects, perhaps because it would have been illogical to do so, given the praise that it had already heaped upon Aymāna.[105]

The next anecdote which involves a woman had Kirmānī deeply engrossed in his Sufi exercise of forty-day periods for seclusion. A woman came to plead that Kirmānī intercede for her with the Sultan. Although it is not clear what the woman wished for, the important point is that it reveals that Sufis were influential figures even before powerful dignitaries such as sultans, and that both men and women had access to them.[106]

That there were some Sufis who preferred limited access for women is demonstrated in an important anecdote in which Kirmānī is accused by Shaykh Saʿd al-Dīn Ḥammūya (d. 1252), a leading Sufi from Khorasan, of permitting unrelated women to listen and look upon his teaching or Sufi rituals from a viewing gallery (*mustanẓar*). In reply Kirmānī answered that he knew there were unrelated women in the viewing gallery, for he too had looked up and seen them. Since he too had looked at them, Kirmānī argued that it was impossible to make a complaint. It is assumed that his authority as a leading Sufi legitimised the presence of women, ensuring that nothing illegal would have occurred. However, it does indicate that separation between the sexes was strictly enforced, and as such it may explain why there does not appear to be any "full-time" female Sufi within Kirmānī's circle.[107]

The ritual separation is also evident in another anecdote in which female Sufis (*faqīragān*) in Konya heard that a *samāʿ* was being conducted in a *zāwiya* where Kirmānī had been staying. Without his knowledge the females joined the gathering, and just as the male Sufi disrobed when experiencing a form of unveiling, so too the females removed their head coverings which they then placed into a turban, in agreement with one another. The Shaykh was very angry when he was told of the presence of females at the termination of the *samāʿ*. (The anecdote focuses upon Shaykh Zayn al-Dīn Ṣadaqa (who was a deputy of Kirmānī, who does not seem to have been present). The Shaykh asked his servants,

> Why did you let them enter the house? They are women. Is there a place for them [when there is a] *samāʿ*, dancing and mystical states (*ḥālat*)? They should be engaged in performing acts of obedience, worship and sit in a corner. But they come and listen to the *samāʿ* and dance! They have a different desire when they wish [to participate] in the *samāʿ*. Tell the servant to bring the large pestle that is in the kitchen.

A servant brought the pestle, and the Shaykh told him to place it among the women's head-coverings, to indicate, perhaps, that a woman's task is to perform household chores. He said,

> The punishment of any woman who comes into the circle of men, shakes [her] head to and fro (*sar-andāzī kunad*) [during the *samāʿ*], and does not cover her head, and who also listens to the words of unrelated males is that she must [be like] the female successors of the women of Muṣṭafā (peace be upon him) and the females of his followers (may God be satisfied with them), so that she and others do not fall into iniquity.[108]

A more disconcerting image of females appears in one anecdote that describes a vision (*wāqaʿa*) that was witnessed by one of Kirmānī's disciples. In this vision a woman appeared to the disciple who was sitting in ritual seclusion. She was fat, with one eye, black skin, and tangled hair. She approached the disciple, placed one foot on his knee and another on his shoulder, and then straddled his neck, with both legs hanging down in front of him. The disciple remembered that Kirmānī had said that Satan appeared to those in seclusion, squeezed and whispered to them. The disciple managed to pull the woman off him, and he was able to find a knife and slash open her stomach. When Kirmānī appeared after the disciple had woken up he admitted that he had sent this vision of Satan.[109] Perhaps Kirmānī was thinking of a number of *aḥādīth* which associate women with Satan, such as, "When you see a woman coming towards you it is Satan who is approaching you,"[110] or "When I look into the fire [of hell] most of the people in it are women."[111] Perhaps he was considering that this world, which appears as a beautiful young woman with all of its temptations, was nothing more in reality than an old hag, an image that appears all too frequently in Sufi literature.[112]

The hagiography includes other anecdotes in which women are present, but they play a minor role as the stories unfold. From the summaries of the above anecdotes, it is clear that women were clearly engaged in the Sufi tradition, and encouraged to do so by Kirmānī. However, the culture and paradigm of complementarity and segregation still meant that their aims and ambitions were restricted and that there were limits to what these women could do. As mentioned above, no female Sufis emerge as clearly accepted members of the Kirmānī Sufi circle. Yet there are several episodes that clearly suggest both female "Sufi", and high levels of "mystical", activity. The female Sufis who remove their veils in Konya during the *samā'* is indicative of this, as is the presence of Aymāna in Syria, who took both female and male followers. It is a shame that the text does not elaborate on this further, and so we are left to speculate on the nature of Aymāna's students. Were the female students orphans or widows? Or was there some specific Sufi content or training that Aymāna related? Likewise, it is frustrating that nothing is known of the male-followers.

Female piety leading to deep "mystical" insight (regardless of intense Sufi ritual activity) is also deemed possible by the anecdote of the lady who repeated God's name continually during her household chores. However, the anecdote testifies to the lack of female engagement in formal ritual Sufi practices, and other anecdotes betray an association between females and Satan. Moreover, even the anecdote of the Konyan female Sufis enjoying their *samā'* amongst the male Sufis holds a connotation of the need to control female sexuality. The shaykh reminds the women of the need for chastity and piety by placing a pestle among their headscarves and returns the headscarves in this fashion to them.[113]

Third case study: Jalāl al-Dīn Rūmī

Jalāl al-Dīn Rūmī is perhaps the best known of all Sufis in the West in the contemporary age. Commonly associated with the whirling dervishes and as the author of the *Mathnavī*, a magisterial didactic poem about the Sufi path of approximately 25,000 rhyming couplets,[114] he was reportedly the best-selling poet in the United States in 1997.[115] In his own day too, Rūmī was held in great esteem; hailing from Afghanistan, his family fled the invading Mongols, and were invited to settle in Konya by the Seljuk ruler, Sulṭān ʿAlā' al-Dīn Kay Qubād,[116] and Rūmī himself numbered among his devotees eminent men of rank including the vizier, Muʿīn al-Dīn Parwāneh.[117] Although his depiction of women is by far more positive than Ghazālī's, and complements much of the hagiographical work related to gender in the second case study, still there is an element in Rūmī's writing that does not sit well with modern sensibilities. His presentation of women is one that is highly ambiguous; in this third case-study, the full range of Rūmī's perspectives is presented, commencing with a positive opinion, to one that is ambiguous, and finally to an evaluation that is extremely negative.

Commencing with the positive standpoint, his prose work *Fīhi mā fīhi* advises believers that female beauty (here cast as divine scripture) is transcendent, and if left in peace she will eventually reveal her beauty:

> The Koran is as a bride who does not disclose her face to you, for all that you draw aside the veil. That you should examine it, and yet not attain happiness and unveiling, is due to the fact that the act of drawing aside the veil has itself repulsed and tricked you, so that the bride has shown herself to you as ugly, as if to say, "I am not that beauty." The Koran is able to show itself in whatever form it pleases. But if you do not draw aside the veil and seek only its good pleasure, watering its sown field and attending on it from afar, toiling upon that which pleases it best, it will show its face to you without your drawing aside the veil.[118]

Although his prose works are highly instructive, it is as a poet that Rūmī is primarily known,[119] and many of his verses too offer an extremely positive image of women; the *Mathnawī* provides a perspective of God that lends itself to contemplate a female divine beloved. A familiar trope in Sufi poetry is that of the two lovers, Majnūn and his female partner Laylā.[120] Rūmī often utilised this pair to convey how identities may merge, or unite, with each other. As Majnūn says, "The wise man whose heart is illumined knows there is no difference between Laylā and I."[121] However, Sufis utilised this story to refer to the annihilation of creaturely existence into the divine, e.g. Laylā is a beautiful woman through whom God is manifested.[122] Rūmī developed this story of Laylā and Majnūn, or the merging of identities, in an episode in which some fools criticised Laylā's beauty and compared her unfavourably to the heart-captivating girls in their city. Majnūn responded by stating that people appreciate beauty in different ways, which is another way to describe how God is manifested in a multitude of styles. Rūmī poetically portrays the manifestation of God (through Laylā) which tastes like a fine intoxicating wine for Majnūn, but which is vinegar for the fools.

It is perhaps the genre of poetry that allowed Rūmī to indulge in an antinomian turn of mind. For example, in the *Mathnawī,* he subverts the traditional and negative understanding of women in the *ḥadīth* that mentions how they prevail over wise and intelligent men.[123] Rūmī, however, considers this as beneficial, and remarks sarcastically that ignorant men (with animal natures that are deficient in tenderness, kindness and affection) dominate over women, but concludes that women are in fact rays of God, eternal and creative beings (rather than merely sensual, earthly beloveds).[124] It is in such passages that the revolutionary import of Rūmī's verses should be understood, and which has been neatly expressed by Keshavarz who has observed that Rūmī had an "acute poetic awareness of the emotional and intellectual potency of paradoxes that fuelled his ever-present tendency to subvert."[125] The antinomianism was more than just an appreciation of word-games, for compassion and love in this didactic episode, are the keys to unlock the mystery of God; just as God creates from his compassion and love, so too does the female, both physically and non-physically.

The manifestation of the divine in female forms is also a theme in Rūmī's understudied and weighty compilation of quatrains.[126] These quatrains are complex because the manifestation of the divine appears sometimes as male and at other times as female. One cannot be but suspicious that this was the intention of the poet, refusing to bind the divine into one specific form. In any case, the following lends itself an interpretation that leans towards the identification of the divine being manifested in a female form:

> Your face is the Kaʿba of my heart and the prayer direction of my soul
> I have been burning like a candle for longing, O flame of the soul
> Take off your veil and show your face to the lover
> So that one may tear away with one's own hands the cloak of the soul.[127]

At times, Rūmī's quatrains suggest that a female earthly beloved (*maʿshūqa*) is the place where the divine may be witnessed:

> There is none among the beloveds (*dildārān*) like my beloved (*dilbar*).
> There is no death or end for her, like [there is] for the world.
> If a senseless person objects foolishly, say, "Go ahead and complain!
> There can be no female beloved (*maʿshūqa*) more exquisite than this."[128]

However, such a *maʿshūqa* should not be tied to the household or be devoted to "external" forms of Islamic piety; instead, she must be antinomian and adopt a "Sufi-like" and ecstatic nature:

A maʿshūqa of the household is no use,
She goes behind the veil and does not show her face.
The *maʿshūqa* must have a tavern and musicians,
So that she may come at midnight strumming and singing.[129]

At other times Rūmī wants a non-ecstatic and pious female beloved:

A *maʿshūqa* of the household is no use
Since she flirts and is unfaithful.
The *maʿshūqa* must be at the graveside;
She opens a thousand doors from the gardens of heaven.[130]

However, Rūmī is also hesitant about female beloveds, and it seems that he prefers to witness God through males (*maʿshūq*)[131]:

I have a love that is purer than clear water
And this gambling everything for love is lawful for me
Other people's love changes from state to state
But my love and my *maʿshūq* are imperishable.[132]

Moreover, occasionally the female beloved is belittled, and he favours a male beloved:

Is it right that your hands, your feet and your eyes are two?
But it is wrong that the heart and the *maʿshūq* are two.
The *maʿshūqa* is a pretext (*bahāna*) and the *maʿshūq* is God.
Anyone who imagines "two" is a Jew or a Christian.[133]

Ibrahim Gamard and Rawan Farhadi suggest that it is correct to read the *maʿshūq* as the mystical male beloved and is therefore asexual, and the *maʿshūqa* is a beautiful woman.[134] The issue is confused by portrayals of God that are both masculine and feminine:

Every day you appear anew, O beloved of my soul
And you throw a new yearning into my soul
Give fully, give fully from the cup of life at every dawn

O you are the father and mother of my soul.[135]

The quatrains, then, provide an ambivalent message on gender, and the reader is left in a quandary as to whether this "inconsistency," or oscillation between male and female divine manifestations, is simply the result of Rūmī attempting to fit a specific poetic metre in Persian by either adding an extra sound for the feminine (*maʿshūqa*) as opposed to the shorter sound for the male (*maʿshūq*). According to Schimmel, Rūmī would tire of finding rhymes,[136] and it may be speculated that he occasionally became fatigued by keeping to the metre.[137] Of course the "inconsistency" on gender may also contain a theological message that as yet remains unclear.

Regardless, there is also a dimension of Rūmī's writing in which women are described in a negative fashion. This has been explained by Sachiko Murata in her seminal work, *The Tao of Islam*, where she highlights the use of binary tropes of male and female to convey teachings about the relationship between the spirit and the body. Murata's book is primarily concerned with the idealised nature of human beings and perfection, and its contrast with the baser and lesser dimensions of human achievement. A good example of this is her observation that Rūmī "typically reads all mention of women that suggests negative qualities as referring to the soul that commands to evil."[138] For example, the *Mathnawī* includes verses that compare men with reason and women with the flesh; the former seeks nothing but love for God, whereas the latter is concerned with reputation, food and drink, and social standing.[139] Readers are also invited to compare the woman with the donkey, which is drunk with fodder and is an enemy to be controlled.[140] Perhaps one of the best illustrations of the kind of perspective that belittles women occurs in Rūmī's prose work *Fīhi mā fīhi*:

> Night and day you are at war, seeking to reform the character of women and to cleanse their impurity by yourself. It is better to cleanse yourself in them than to cleanse them in yourself. Reform yourself by means of them. Go to them, and accept whatever they may say, even though in your view their words are absurd ... What is that way [for men that God indicated]? To wed women, so that he might endure the tyranny of women and hear their absurdities, for them to ride roughshod over him, and so for him to refine his character ... By enduring and putting up with the tyranny of woman it is as though you rub off your own impurities on them. Your character becomes good through forbearance; their character becomes bad through domineering and aggression. When you have realised this, make yourself clean. Know that you are a garment; in them you cleanse your own impurities and become clean yourself.
>
> If you cannot succeed with yourself, deliberate with yourself in a rational way as follows. 'Let me pretend that we have never been married. She is a whore. Whenever lust

> overmasters me I resort to her.' Thus rid yourself of manly pride and envy and jealousy, until such time that beyond such deliberation you experience pleasure in struggling and enduring, and in their absurdities discover spiritual joy.[141]

In addition to the kind of argumentation offered by Murata, the discrepancy between the two kinds of perspectives on women may be explained by remembering that all authors live in a context in which in order to convey meaning to their audiences and readers it is necessary to utilise language that is common in their age. Although Rūmī is commonly regarded as an enlightened individual (by today's scholars of Sufism), it should not be forgotten that he was human, suffered the difficulties, anxieties and stresses that beset even the best of individuals. Moreover, it is wise to reflect on the warning offered by Fatimeh Keshavarz who observed that the "Sufi perception and articulation of gender in and around Rūmī's time was shaped with predictable patriarchal notions common to medieval cultures. Despite their comparative willingness to break out of conventional categories, Sufis were not exceptionally liberated in this respect."[142] Even though Rūmī repeatedly made the point that his references need to be read allegorically, it indicates that the Sufi milieu in which he operated was saturated with these fixed categories of male and female and what they represented on a formal level. To use other words, the context of Rūmī's life was one of gender complementarity and segregation, and he utilised such norms which by modern standards are quite surprising and sometimes even vulgar. Such verses, even though they convey stories of uncontrolled sexuality,[143] were meant to be amusing and didactic, and lead to inner, pietistic realities that transcended the problematic forms in which they were wrapped.

The context of Sufism in Rūmī's time is depicted clearly in the hagiography by Aflākī, who relates several episodes involving Rūmī and his wife, Kerā Khātūn. In one of these episodes, Aflākī described how Rūmī flew into a fit of rage on hearing how his wife had left the family home (without his permission) to see some visiting dervishes in Konya. He cursed her and cast coldness into her body, so that even in the hot summer days of Konya she would cover herself in animal furs, and this was a condition from which she was never cured.[144] Even if this story is fictitious, the fact that Aflākī, writing a generation after Rūmī, could attribute such an anecdote to the great poet is suggestive of the kind of culture that existed in Anatolia. Aflākī also included another anecdote which demonstrates the patriarchal culture of Sufism in Anatolia in which he described how Shams al-Dīn (d. 1248) – Rūmī's "spiritual" twin and alter ego – asked him to provide a "good-looking person" (*shāhid*).[145] Rūmī instantly offered him his wife, but Shams refused her.[146] This anecdote may have some basis in fact, for Rūmī himself wrote: "What the shaykh prescribes for you is the same as what the shaykhs of old prescribed, that you leave your wife and children, your wealth and position. Indeed, they used to prescribe for a disciple,

'Leave your wife, that we may take her'; and they put up with that."[147] Even though it serves a didactic purpose, what clearly resonates in this anecdote is that both Rūmī's wife is treated like a chattel, and no concern is expressed for her feeling or possible sense of humiliation. The latent message conforms to the segregationist paradigm in which the domination of the senior male and submission of female is simply taken for granted.

The context in which Rūmī lived may also explain his penchant for offensive gendered terms. This great word-smith in the Persian language seems to have been fond of exclaiming, "Your mother's a whore (*mādar-gharr-ī*)!"[148] This insult appears in one of his quatrains, and indeed, he also employed similar phrases, such as "Your sister's a whore!"[149] According to the aforementioned Aflākī this was uttered by Rūmī whenever he was angry, and he added that it was an expression of abuse employed by those from Khorasan.[150] However, it is pertinent to ask whether the contextual argument is a sufficient clause to escape chastisement, as it surely is and was not an innocent expression.[151] Its impact rests partly upon a perspective that is based upon the tradition that women were to be protected by their husbands, fathers and brothers, and as such, it is an insult to male honour. A woman of marriageable age who did not have such a male guardian was in an undesirable position, and inevitably perhaps, questions would have been raised about her availability. It might be for this reason that insults in Persian were frequently couched in terms of female immorality. Rūmī lived and breathed within the Islamic Persianate cultural context of the mediaeval period which endorsed complementarity and segregation, and in which male honour was frequently understood with reference to control and care over the females in the family. Given such perspectives, it is tempting to speculate that many males were reluctant to provide for females the opportunities for pious development that males enjoyed; instead they remained in *purda*, trapped within the "safety" of their homes. The difficulties that females faced in receiving a similar level of education as males may have been a contributory factor in the absence of treatises and books composed by female Sufis that would probably have addressed issues relating to female piety.

Despite considering the use of such terms in a negative way, some believe the word should be perceived in a different fashion, as Chittick has indicated: "If the witness is the Beloved perceived in a beautiful form, then the whore is the Beloved perceived in ugly form. In other words, whores are images perceived within the heart which at first sight increase the pain and agony of separation."[152] To illustrate his point, Chittick cites the following:

In this lane, I am the whoremonger, I,
– I have pulled off the chador from every beautiful face.
They all put on ugly chadors

So that you will think they are dragons.
But I am fed up with my spirit – I worship dragons!
If you are fed up with your spirit, then hear their calls of welcome![153]

A final observation related to Rūmī and women concerns the highly misogynist views of the aforementioned Shams al-Dīn. Lewis describes Rūmī turning Shams into "a virtual God" and a "picture of apotheosis."[154] The attraction to Shams may explain why Rūmī was keen to clothe God in a masculine form. So, if Rūmī was enlightened about gender issues, how is it possible to explain this relationship, when Shams held opinions that ran counter to every positive perspective of women? The fear among Sufis of a gnostic persuasion that linked females with sexuality is graphically illustrated by Shams who alluded to the feminine gender of the Arabic word for soul (*nafs*): "The soul has the nature of a woman. Or rather, woman herself has the nature of the soul." To clarify his argument, he cited the *ḥadīth 'Consult with them, then oppose them'*."[155] Aflākī also reported that Shams was virulent in his rejection of the possibility of female piety:

> On the day Mawlana Shams al-Dīn [Shams-i Tabrīzī] was describing virtuous women and their chastity. He said: "But despite all this, if a woman were given a place above the Celestial Throne and her sight suddenly alighted on the world and she saw an erect penis on the earth's surface, like a madwoman she would fling herself down and land on top of it. Because in their religion there is nothing higher than this."[156]

Shams' dislike for female sexuality may be related to the possibility that he had sympathies for Qalandars,[157] who became infamous in the Islamic world for shaving away their facial and head hair.[158] It is related that a founder of the Qalandars, Jamāl al-Dīn Sāwī (d. about 1232/3) was trapped in the house of a certain woman who had desired him for some time. In an attempt to escape, Jamāl al-Dīn Sāwī shaved his face and head to appear unattractive, so that she would leave him in peace. The connection between untrammelled sexuality and impiety is obvious, and Sufi literature frequently compared an old, ugly woman who dressed in beautiful clothes and made herself attractive to the world in which we live, which was ephemeral and nothing but a trap.[159] As argued by Mernissi, the associations made of dangerously active female sexuality and the perception of their inferior intellects must have contributed to males promoting and enforcing the segregation of women. Indeed this is precisely the principle that had been advocated by Ghazālī who cited a *ḥadīth* which advises women that their "rightful occupation is staying at home and engaging in female activities such as spinning."[160] Shams-i Tabrīzī, with a clear nod to the same *ḥadīth*, remarked, "It's best that a woman sit behind the spindle in the corner of the house, busy in service of the one who takes care of her."[161]

Shams' dislike of women is also shown in a report which confirms that some female Sufis were acting as Sufi shaykhs, as Aflākī noted that he stated: "If Fatima or A'isha had acted as *shaykhs*, I would have lost my belief in the Messenger."[162] That there were female shaykhs (or more properly *shaykhas*) in Anatolia in the time when Shams was alive is very likely, as Aflākī mentioned that the daughters of Salāḥ al-Dīn Zarkūb (one of Rūmī's principle followers) "were both ladies endowed with miracles and Friendship of God. Most of the ladies of the realms of Rum turned to them and became their disciples."[163] (To this, the case of Aymāna, (see above) should also be included).

Conclusion

It is a difficult task to evaluate the role of women in society and the extent of their involvement in anything that resembles Sufi piety, but historians should not be myopic and distort the material in front of them. "Presentist" research smacks of a concern about the ideals and aspirations of the author rather than an "objective" historical study, as Omaima Abou-Bakr has observed, "modern and contemporary scholars would look into the mirror of the Middle Ages largely in order to reflect back their present-day identities. It is a methodology that admits personal engagement with its subject of study."[164]

The mediaeval period of Islamic history in the Persianate world inherited a legacy that conveys a mixed message for those seeking to determine the involvement of women in Sufism, or how male Sufis considered women. At best, the biographies of women contained in works by Sulamī and Ibn Jawzī testify to active involvement, although the information they provide is often scant and cursory, suggesting that women were not as significant as their male counterparts. Worse are those *ṭabaqāt* works which completely ignore any female Sufi activity. This tendency is fortified by manuals that view with horror anything related to women and marriage because (male) Sufis viewed this as a distraction from God and also due to a perspective that considered women as inherently irreligious and shallow. Even as idealised "female beloveds," wives were expected to conform to the standards of thirteenth century Anatolia, which was patriarchal and largely confined women to a state of *purda* within the home.

Moreover, in conveying the message of the earthly female beloved, Rūmī utilised images and language that were current within the patriarchal society of his age. The awkwardness of some of his verses is also matched by both some of the hagiographic tradition and also the writings of other Sufis in his entourage, such as Shams al-Din. It is surprising that scholars have not focused on Rūmī's gendered message and language, especially as he has become so popular in the West, where research on feminism is also very strong. Given the temptation and distraction that women were for male Sufis (which was made all too abundantly clear in the Sufi manuals by the likes of Qushayrī and Hujwīrī), it is not surprising that such communities were all male, as can be read from the hagiography about Awḥad al-Dīn Kirmānī.

Yet, the mediaeval period from the twelfth to thirteenth centuries offered glimmers of change. While the works of Ghazālī echo the negative legacy that he had inherited from the likes of Makkī and Hujwirī, the poetry of Rūmī indicates a Sufi idealism that transcends notions of gender. There is sufficient evidence in the case studies devoted to Kirmānī and Rūmī to dispel any idea about inherent and essential misogyny. These works suggests that women were engaging in action for themselves, in terms of performing ritual activities and establishing their own organisations, and that some males believed women could achieve extremely elevated levels of piety and insight (*maʿrifat*). Women were probably forced to take such action because the ideal of complementarity persisted, and there were some traditions, such as the *futuwwat* or *javānmardī* associations of the thirteenth century, which, inspired by the Sufi tradition, displayed extreme levels of discrimination against women. The possibility of increasing female pious activity in Persian speaking regions may also offer another reason for the inclusion by ʿAṭṭār (writing in Khorasan just before the age of Rūmī, Shams and Kirmānī in Konya), of his chapter on Rābiʿa in his *Tadhkirāt al-Awliyā*. If the social conditions facing women in Khorasan were the same as those in Konya, was ʿAṭṭār then addressing a female readership/audience, as well as directing his work at males? It is striking, too, that ʿAṭṭār's chapter on Rābiʿa is one of the longest in the book (at sixteen pages in the Persian printed version).

The presence of women is tangible in these three case-studies, yet they are so frustratingly difficult to hear; mostly, the sound that emerges from mediaeval texts is barely an audible whisper, and in the vast majority of cases women are spoken for by men. Scholars should be cautious not to essentialise Sufism. There were different male Sufi attitudes to women, and these were probably influenced by the inherited tradition, individual circumstances and factors related to the local culture.

Notes

* I would like to acknowledge the late Leonard Lewisohn and Laury Silvers who commented on an earlier version of this chapter several years ago and encouraged me to pursue this theme, and to Cyrus Zargar who much more recently read the revised version and offered positive feedback.

1 Fatima Mernissi, *The Forgotten Queens of Islam*, transl. Mary Jo Lakeland (Minneapolis: University of Minnesota Press, 1993). Mernissi's work goes beyond the parameters of this research, as her survey extends to Arab areas such as Yemen.

2 Dick Davis, *The Mirror of My Heart: A Thousand Years of Persian Poetry by Women* (London: Penguin, 2021). Among those included in this book is Mahsatī (c. 1089–1159) who is known to have come from the region of Azerbaijan. Not much is known of her life, and some of the poetry that is attributed to her may have been composed by others.

3 Edith Sara Wolper, *Cities and Saints: Sufism and the Transformation of Urban Space in Medieval Anatolia* (Pennsylvania: Pennsylvania State University Press, 2003), 83. In other work Wolper has cautioned about viewing female patronage as an example of active female participation in society through piety because in the pre-Ottoman period, female names in inscriptions of *khānaqāhs* in, or else mention of women in hagiographies in which they are portrayed as patrons of such institutions, may have functioned to promote dynastic alliances, usually achieved through marriage. Edith Sara Wolper, "Princess Safwat al-Dunya wa al-Din and the Production of Sufi Buildings and Hagiographies in Pre-Ottoman Anatolia," in *Women, Patronage and Self-Representation in Islamic Societies*, ed. D. Fairchild Ruggles (Albany: SUNY Press, 2000), 35–52.

4 Sara Abdel-Latif, "Narrativizing early mystic and Sufi women: mechanisms of gendering in Sufi hagiographies," in *Routledge Handbook on Sufism*, ed. Lloyd Ridgeon (London: Routledge, 2021), 132–145.

5 Rkia Cornell, *Early Sufi Women: Dhikr an-niswa al-muta'abbidāt aṣ-ṣūfiyyāt* (Louiseville KY: Fons Vitae, 1999); Rkia Elaroui Cornell, *Rabi'a from Narrative to Myth: The Many Faces of Islam's Most Famous Woman Saint, Rabi'a al-'Adawiyya* (Oxford: Oneworld, 2018).

6 Christopher Melchert, "Before ṣūfiyyāt: Female Muslim Renunciants in the 8th and 9th Centuries CE," *Journal of Sufi Studies*, 5 (2016), 115–39.

7 Laury Silvers, "Early Pious, Mystic Sufi Women," in *Cambridge Companion to Sufism*, ed. Lloyd Ridgeon (Cambridge: University Press, 2015), 24–52; "God Loves Me": The Theological Content and Context of Early Pious and Sufi Women's Saying on Love, *Journal of Islamic Studies*, 30 (2010), 33–59.

8 Arin Salamah-Qudsi, *Sufism and Early Islamic Piety: Personal and Communal Dynamics* (Cambridge: Cambridge University Press, 2019); "The Economics of Female Piety in Early Sufism," *Religions*, 12(9), (2021), 760. https://www.mdpi.com/2077-1444/12/9/760

9 Scholars have noted how women frequently favoured the study of *ḥadīth*. See Asma Sayeed, *Women and the Transmission of Religious Knowledge in Islam* (Cambridge: University of Cambridge Press, 2013). It is possible that the reason why *ḥadīth* study was popular was with its insistence on a knowledge that did not rely on reason, or which did not necessarily require the judgement of women over men. It might have been thought that Sufism would have permitted women a greater extent of participation. The observation of Jonathan Berkey about women in Mamluk Egypt could also apply to the Islamic world in general between the tenth to fourteenth centuries. "Women were systematically excluded from holding judicial positions that would require them to resolve disputes among men or formal instructional positions that carried a personal, institutional, or metaphorical authority over men." (See Jonathan P. Berkey, "Women and Islamic Education in the

Mamluk Period," in *Women in Middle Eastern History: Shifting Boundaries in Sex and Gender*, eds. Nikki Keddie and Beth Baron (Yale University Press, 1992), 154).

10 A good example is Hülya Küçük, "Female Substitutes and Shaykhs in the History of Sufism: The Case of the Mawlawiyya Sufi Order from its Early Phase to the Eighteenth Century," *Mawlana Rumi Review*, vol. 4, 2013, 106–131.

11 Leila Ahmed, *Women and Gender in Islam* (New Haven: Yale University Press, 1992), 98.

12 Ibid, 115. Ahmad is not known as a scholar of Sufism. Her comments about Rābi'a, and women living in convents requires more clarification; is she referring to the situation in the Islamic world as a whole, or in Egypt (where Ahmad focuses most of her research)? It is not known if there were female convents in Rābi'a's time. In Egypt, most female convents were established in the fourteenth century. Adam Sabra, "Economies of Sufism," in *Handbook of Sufi Studies: Sufi Institutions*, ed. Alexandre Papas (Leiden: Brill, 2021), 33.

13 I have adopted a very loose understanding of the term "Persianate"; it includes all writings in Persian, but also works from areas where Persian culture was strong. So, for example, even areas including Damascus are included within this designation. Ibn 'Arabī is not included, partly because he wrote in Arabic, and partly because of the limitations of space. A separate article would be needed to investigate his ideas and the ideas of his school of thought.

14 See for example, 'Azīz Nasafī, *Kitāb al-Insān al-kāmil*, ed. M. Molé (Tehran/Paris: Institut Franco-Iranien, 1962). In the same work he offers another hierarchy which seems to mirror the *sharī'a, ṭarīqa, ḥaqīqa* classification. In the new hierarchy, the lowest level or the mass of people (*'avāmm*) is represented by "people of imitation" (*ahl-i taqlīd*), the second level includes the "people of reasoning" (*ahl-i istidlāl*) who are the élite, and the third group is the people of unveiling (*ahl-i kashf*) who are the élite of the élite (*Kitāb al-Insān al-kāmil*, 39–44). The same hierarchy appears in his *Maqṣad al-aqṣā*, translated as "The Furthest Goal," in *Persian Metaphysics and Mysticism: Selected Treatises of 'Azīz Nasafī*, trans. Lloyd Ridgeon (Curzon: Richmond, 2002), 85. He seems to offer a similar hierarchy, this time referring to the religious scholars (*'ulamā*), the philosophers (*ahl-i ḥikmat*), and the people of unity (*ahl-i vaḥdat*) (*Maqṣad al-aqṣā, appended to Jāmī's Ashi"at al-lama'āt*, ed. H. Rabbānī (Tehran: Kitābkhāneh-ye 'ilmīyya-yi hāmidī, 1973), translated in full as "The Furthest Goal" in Ridgeon, *Persian Metaphysics and Mysticism*, pp. 110–112). On occasions, Nasafi described the seeking of four groups: in ascending order they were the *ahl-i sharī'at*, the *ahl-i ḥikmat*, the Sufis, and the *ahl-i vaḥdat*. (See "The Furthest Goal," 117).

15 'Azīz Nasafī, *Maqṣad al-aqṣā*, 213. (Ḥājj Mīrzā Ḥusayn Nūrī Ṭabarsī, *Mustadrak al-Wasā'il va mustanbaṭ al-masā'il* (Beirut: n.d. 1408/1988),113.

16 This is similar to the well-known pre-Islamic and Zoroastrian adage of "good thoughts, good words and good deeds."

17 'Azīz Nasafī, *Manāzil al-sā'irīn*, included in *Kitāb al-Insān al-kāmil*, 455.

18 'Azīz Nasafī, *Manāzil al-sā'irīn*, included in *Kitāb al-Insān al-kāmil*, 455–6.

19 'Azīz Nasafī, *Maqṣad al-aqṣā*, 284.

20 'Azīz Nasafī, *Maqṣad al-aqṣā*, 285.

21 Sufis like Nasafī inherited such a perspective on the *sharī'a* from previous generations of Sufis. The following claim by one of the foremost scholars of Sufism is indicative of this: "… the decidedly distanced attitude of the Sufis toward the nascent legal and theological scholars of their time was not the result of a denial or condemnation of God's law (sharī'a). Enthusiastic and total acceptance and implementation of God's commands formed the foundation of the whole Sufi enterprise, and the idea that the divine stipulations could somehow prove to be irrelevant to the endeavour to become true God-servants would have been alien to the Sufis." Ahmet T. Karamustafa, *Sufism: The Formative Period* (Edinburgh: Edinburgh University Press, 2007), 21.

22 Ghazālī, *Kīmīyā-yi sa'ādat*, ed. Ḥusayn Khadiwjam (Tehran, 1983), 323 (my translation).

23 *Mathnawī*, I. 2433–47.

24 Rūmī, *Mathnawī*, Introduction to Book V, trans. R.A. Nicholson (London: Luzac 1934), 1.

25 This does not mean that the *sharī'a* or *ṭarīqa* are irrelevant and may be ignored. On reaching the reality, the wayfarer may express an independence from the previous two realms, but they are still required in order for wayfarers to reach that level.

26 Rūmī, *Mathnawī*, Introduction to Book V, 1.

27 Jawid Mojaddedi, *Beyond Dogma: Rumi's Teachings on Friendship of God and Early Sufi Theories* (Oxford: Oxford University Press), 105.

28 Christopher Melchert, "The Transition from Asceticism to Mysticism at the Middle of the Ninth Century C.E." *Studia Islamica*, 83 (1996), 51–70.

29 *Ṭabaqāt al-Ṣūfiyya*, ed. Nūr al-Dīn Sharība (Cairo: Maktaba al-Khānajī, 1969).

30 Rkia Cornell, *Early Sufi Women*. See for example 162, 176, 184, 232, 238.

31 Ibid, 57.

32 Javid A. Mojaddedi, *The Biographical Tradition in Sufism* (London: Routledge, 2001), 41–48.

33 *Al-Qushayri's Epistle on Sufism*, trans. Alexander Knysh (Reading: Garnet, 2007), 17–74.

34 Anṣārī, *Ṭabaqāt al-Ṣūfiyya*, ed. M. Sarwar-Mawlā'ī (Tehran: Tus, 1386/2007/8).

35 *The Kashf al-Maḥjūb of Al-Hujwiri*, transl. R.A. Nicholson (London: Luzac & Co, 1976), 88–160. All references to this work are taken from Nicholson's English translation.

36 Ruth Roded, *Women in the Biographical Collections* (London: Lynne Rienner Publications, 1994), 93. Also worthy of notice is Ibn Jawzī's criticism of Abū Nu'aym's omission of females in his "Ornaments of the Friends of God." It is of interest that when in Baghdad Ibn Jawzī condemned mixed-sex Sufi meetings, and he remarked, "[Other women] attend Sufi sessions where they allow Shaikhs to put rags on them, and to shake their hands. She becomes his daughter they claim, and do wonders with them." *The Devil's Deceptions* (Birmingham: Dar al-Sunna, 2014), 536.

37 The Persian text first appeared as an edited version in the West in two volumes as *The Tadhkiratul Awliya* (Memoirs of the Saints) *of Faridu'din 'Aṭṭar*, ed. R. A. Nicholson (London: Luzac & Co, 1905–7). A revised Persian edition, *Tadhkirat al-awliyā'*, by M. Isti'lāmī contains 97 individuals: 'Aṭṭār, *Tadhkirat al-awliyā* ed. Isti'lāmī (Tehran: Zuwwar, 1346). An English version of twenty-eight chapters (and which includes Rābi'a) was made by Paul Losensky, *Farid Ad-Din 'Attar's Memorial of God's Friends* (New York: Paulist Press, 2010).

38 *The Tadhkiratul Awliya*, Vol. I. 59–73; *Farid Ad-Din 'Attar's Memorial of God's Friends*, 97–113. For others studies on Rābi'a see a rather dated, though still valuable monograph by Margaret Smith, *Rābi'a the Mystic & Her Fellow-saints in Islām* (Cambridge: University Press, 1928); Heidi A. Ford, "Hierarchical Inversions, Divine Subversions: The Miracles of Râbi'a al-'Adawîya," *Journal of Feminist Studies in Religion*, Vol. 15, No. 2 (Fall, 1999) 5-24; Erin S. Prus, *Divine Presence, Gender, And the Sufi Spiritual Path: An Analysis of Rabi'ah the Mystic's Identity and Poetry*, MA thesis, Xavier University 2009. The most recent addition to the literature is Michelle Quay's PhD thesis submitted to Cambridge University in June 2017, called "'God Does Not Regard Your Forms,': Gender and Literary Representations in the Works of Farīd al-Dīn 'Aṭṭār Nīshāpūrī."

39 Paul Losensky, *Farid Ad-Din 'Attar's Memorial of God's Friends*, 97.

40 See Sachiko Murata, *The Tao of Islam: A Sourcebook on Gender Relationships in Islamic Thought* (Albany: SUNY Press, 1992), 318 who says, "… by calling a woman a 'man' the Sufis meant to show that she had attained to the fullness of the human state in which the soul serves the intellect."

41 See Annemarie Schimmel, *My Soul is a Woman: The Feminine in Islam* (London: Continuum, 2003), 76–77.

42 'Aṭṭār, *Tadhkirat al-awliyā* ed. Isti'lāmī, 72.

43 Silvers, "Early Pious, Mystic Sufi Women," 47.

44 A *maḥram* women is kin with whom one cannot marry, whereas *nā-maḥram* is its opposite.

45 For more on Rābiʿa see Julian Baldick, "The Legend of Rābiʿa of Basra," *Religion*, 19 (1990), 233–47.

46 Silvers has argued convincingly that being a wife and mother did result in challenges to engage in a pious and Sufi-like lifestyle. See her "Early Pious, Mystic Sufi Women," op.cit.

47 A saying often cited by Sufis, e.g. Suhrawardī, *Awārif al-maʿarif* (Beirut: Dār al-Kitāb al-ʿArabī, 1983), 87. *Awārif al-maʿarif;* Ghazālī, *The Proper Conduct*, 24. One wonders what to make of such comments especially as Junayd was known to have been "physically stout and vigorous, [and] some people are said to have doubted the genuineness of his ṣūfī asceticism." See Ali Hassan Abdel-Kader, *The Life, Personality and Writings of al-Junayd* (London: Luzac & Co, 1976), 50.

48 Rkia Cornell, *Rabiʿa from Narrative to Myth*, 33.

49 Maria Dakake, "Guest of the Inmost Heart: Conceptions of the Divine Beloved among Early Sufi Women," *Comparative Islamic Studies*, 3.1 (2007), 72. Dakake argues that segregation for female Sufis resulted in the presentation of their experiences through terms that are "more 'domesticated' than those we find commonly attributed to Sufi men. Rather than conceiving of their souls as lovers journeying in quest of an elusive *rendez-vous* with the Beloved, [women] more frequently imagined their souls as faithful lovers who enjoyed regular or even constant states of intimacy with God," (29). Dakake's work focuses primarily upon the sayings of female "Sufis". It would have been useful to contrast female sayings with those of males from the same time, and this might have produced a more convincing conclusion. It is crucial to point here to the work of Laury Silvers, "'God Loves Me': The Theological Content and Context of Early Pious and Sufi Women's Sayings on Love," *Journal for Islamic Studies*, 30 (2010) 59. Silvers argues that domesticity includes a greater range of experiences such as "doubt and uncertainty [of intimacy with God]" and reflects the various theological arguments that were current in various locations in the formative period of Islamic history, but nevertheless this still reflected "the patriarchal social norm of male guardianship." Sulamī's work on pious believing women included females who were married and those who were mothers. The difficulties encountered by such women should not be overlooked, and they help to explain the reason behind the apparently greater number of pious men that were discussed by the earliest biographers.

50 Muʿayyad al-Dīn Jandī, *Nafhat al-rūḥ wa tuḥfat al futūḥ* (Tehran, 1362/1983–4), 37.

51 Schimmel, My *Soul Is a Woman*, 91.

52 Shams al-Dīn Aflākī, *Manāqib al-ʿārifīn*, transl. John O'Kane, *Feats of the Knowers of God* (Leiden: Brill, 2002), 384.

53 On these early "Sufi " women see Silvers, "Early Pious, Mystic Sufi Women," 24–52; idem, "God Loves Me"; Arezou Azad, "Female Mystics in Medieval Islam: The Quiet Legacy," *Journal of the Economic and Social History of the Orient*, 56 (2013), 53–88. Azad's article focuses upon Umm ʿAlī, a ninth century woman from Balkh who was accorded a high Sufi rank by later generations of Sufis; See also Rkia Cornell's introduction to her *Early Sufi Women* (15–70); Ruth Roded, *Women in the Biographical Collections*, chapter 5, 91–113.

54 Ruth Roded, *Women in the Biographical Collections*, 104.

55 Th Emil Homerin, *From Arab Poet to Muslim Saint: Ibn Fāriḍ, his Verse, and his Shrine* (South Carolina: University Press of South Carolina, 1994), 52.

56 For a very general survey of celibacy in Sufism see Shahzad Bashir, "Islamic Tradition and Celibacy," in *Celibacy and Religious Traditions* ed. Carl Olson (Oxford: University Press, 2007), 133–147.

57 Beatrix Immenkamp, *Marriage and Celibacy in Medieval Islam: A Study of Ghazālī's Kitāb Ādāb al-nikāḥ*, PhD doctorate, University of Cambridge, 1994, 116.

58 Ibid, 116–7.

59 Ibid, 117.

60 Ibid, 132–3.

61 Hujwīrī, *Kashf al-Maḥjūb*, 363.

62 Ibid, 364

63 Ibid, 364.

64 Ibid, 365.

65 Ibid, 364. It is not clear if Hujwīrī was speaking from experience, as his writings do not reveal whether or not he was married. He left a tantalisingly vague reference to his own experience in *Kashf al-Maḥjūb:*
"After God had preserved me for eleven years from the dangers of matrimony, it was my destiny to fall in love with the description of a woman whom I had never seen, and during a whole year my passion so absorbed me that my religion was near being ruined, until at last God in his bounty gave protection to my wretched heart and mercifully delivered me." (*Kashf al-Maḥjūb*, 364).

66 It is of interest that females were sometimes depicted as associating with these brigands and martial groups. See M.A. Mahjub, "Chivalry and Early Persian Sufism," in *Classical Persian Sufism: from its Origins to Rumi*, ed. Leonard Lewisohn (London: KNP, 1993), 562–3. The depiction of women as warriors or soldiers in Arabic literature has been the focus by Remke Kruk, *The Warrior Women of Islam: Female Empowerment in Arabic Popular Literature* (London: IB Tauris, 2014).

67 This misogynist perspective is found in an anonymous *futuwwat* treatise that was probably composed in the early fourteenth century in Persian, most likely from the Anatolian context. (Lloyd Ridgeon, *Jawanmardi: A Sufi Code of Honour* (Edinburgh: University Press, 2011), 131–2). The treatise states:
"There are other people too for whom *futuwwat* is impermissible because they have no beard. This is because the prophet said, '*No futuwwat, no man.*' First, [God] gave *futuwwat* to Adam. When the Truth brought Adam and Eve from the hiding of non-existence to existence there was no beard on his face, and they say that Eve did not respect him, nor was she afraid. Adam complained, 'Oh God! Eve does not respect me.' God Most High granted Adam a beard, and when Eve saw Adam's blessed beard, fear and wonder fell into her heart, and after that, without saying anything, she had such modesty before Adam that they say she never spoke a word to his face, and she never smiled in front of his beard." (Ridgeon, *Jawanmardi*,131–2).

68 Ridgeon, *Jawanmardi*, 64. Further on in the text, Suhrawardī repeats that wearing coloured and decorative clothing is not appropriate for the *jawānmardān*, but it is a habit found in women (82).

69 Ibid.

70 Wolper, *Cities and Saints*, 83.

71 Stephen Humphries, "Women as Patrons of Religious Architecture in Ayyubid Damascus," 35.

72 Carl Perry, "A Paradox of Patronage During the Later Mamluk Period," *Muslim World*, 73 (1983), 199.

73 In the 'Āşikpaşazāde treatise *Tarih-i Al-i Osman*, there is a discussion of four groups: the *Gaziyan-i Rum*, the *Ahiyan-i Rum*, the *Abdalan-i Rum*, and the *Baciyan-i Rum*. The last group were composed entirely of women. (See M. Fuad Kőprűlű, *The Origins of the Ottoman Empire*, trans. Gary Leiser (Albany: SUNY Press, 1992), 98–9. There is no other mention of this kind of organisation in the sources that have come down to the present day, which may explain why Framnz Taeschner believed the manuscript had been incorrectly transcribed. He believed it was more likely that the *Baciyan-i Rum* should be *Haciyan-i Rum* (pilgrims from Rum) or *Bahsiyan-i Rum* (Magicians from Rum). Mika'il Bayram believes that there was indeed a form of Ahilik for women, and interestingly he claims that their leader was one Fātima (the daughter of Awḥad al-Dīn Kirmānī the subject of the second case-study in this chapter). Bayram's argumentation, however, is quite speculative. See his *Fatma Bacı ve Bacıyân-i Rûm* (Konya: Nüve Kültür Merkezi, 2007).

74 Carole Hillenbrand, "al-Ghazālī: In Praise of Sufism," in *Routledge Handbook on Sufism*, ed. Lloyd Ridgeon 63–64.

75 Ibid.

76 Albert Hourani, "A Revised Chronology of Ghazālī's Writings," *Journal of the American Oriental Society*, 104.2 (1984), 300.

77 Ibid, 68.

78 "Ādāb-i Nikāḥ", *Kīmīyā-yi saʿādat*, Vol 1, ed. Ḥusayn Khadiwjam (Tehran, 1983),301–323.

79 Ghazālī, *Kīmīyā-yi saʿādat*, 323 (my translation).

80 The five advantages to marriage are detailed in "The Proper Conduct of Marriage in Islam," 14–33; *Kīmīyā-yi saʿādat*, 302–307.

81 Ghazālī, "The Proper Conduct of Marriage in Islam," 29.

82 Ghazālī, "The Proper Conduct of Marriage in Islam," 30; *Kīmīyā-yi saʿādat*, 306.

83 On this topic see Schimmel, "Women in the Quran and in the Tradition," which is chapter 3 of her *My Soul is a Woman*, 54–68.

84 Ghazālī, "The Proper Conduct of Marriage in Islam," 7. This work is contained in his Arabic *magnum opus*, the *Iḥya 'Ulūm al-Dīn*. The book has been translated twice: Madelain Farah, *Marriage and Sexuality in Islam* (University of Utah Press, 1984); Muhtar Holland, "The Proper Conduct of Marriage in Islam" (*Ādāb al-Nikāḥ*) (Florida: Al-Baz Publishing, 1998). In Persian, the second section of the second book in the second volume of *Kīmīyā-yi saʿādat* is on marriage (301–323).

85 Mernissi, *Beyond the Veil: Male-Female Dynamics in Modern Muslim Society* (Bloomington: Indiana University Press, 1987), 27–45.

86 Cited by Mernissi, *Beyond the Veil*, 39. (My italics).

87 Ibid, 33.

88 Ibid.

89 Ghazālī states, "If a man is restrained by the rein of fear of Allāh, all that happens is that he prevents his organs from responding to lust, thus preserving his modesty and chastity. However, when it comes to guarding the heart against temptation and bad thoughts, this is beyond our freewill; indeed, the lower self never ceases to distract us with sexual concerns." *The Proper Conduct*, 22. Men it would seem, suffer equally from their inherent sexual drive, as women. See also Immenkamp, *Marriage and Celibacy in Medieval Islam*, 103.

90 Ghazālī, *The Proper Conduct*, 36.

91 Omid Safi in *The Politics of Knowledge in Premodern Islam: Negotiating Ideology and Religious Inquiry* (Chapel Hill: The University of North Carolina Press, 2006), 67–71, 117.

92 Ghazālī cites this *ḥadīth* in his *Naṣīḥāt al-Mulūk*, transl. F.R.C. Bagley, *Counsel for Kings* (London: Oxford University Press, 1964, 171): "Once Allah's apostle ... said, 'I have not seen anyone more deficient in intelligence and religion than you [women]. A cautious sensible man could be led astray by some of you.' The women asked, 'O Allah's apostle! What is deficient in our intelligence and religion?' He said, 'Is not the evidence of two women equal to the witness of one man?' They replied in the affirmative. He said, 'This is the deficiency in her intelligence. Isn't it true that a woman can neither pray nor fast during her menses?' The women replied in the affirmative. He said, 'This is the deficiency in her religion'" (*Sahih*, Bukhari: 2.24.541).

93 Ghazālī, *Counsel for Kings*, 172.

94 For the dating of the hagiography and a complete translation, see Lloyd Ridgeon, *Awḥad al-Dīn Kirmānī and the Controversy of the Sufi Gaze* (London: Routledge, 2018). The dating of the hagiography appears on 45. The translation appears on 107–249. On the hagiography see also Lloyd Ridgeon, "A Study of a Medieval Persian Hagiography and Interactions Between Sufis and Christians in Rum and Upper Mesopotamia," in *The Maghreb Review*, 47(3), 2022, 235–359.

95 Anonymous, *Manāqib-i Shaykh Awḥad al-Dīn Ḥāmid ibn-i abī'l-Fakhr-i Kirmānī,* ed. B. Furūzānfar (Tehran: B.T.N.K., 1969), 10–12. For details of a full English translation of this work see note 119.

96 On Rusūdān see David Rayfield, *Edge of Empires: A History of Georgia* (London: Reaktion Books, 2012), 118–131.

97 "Azraqī Heravī", Dj. Khaleghi Motlagh, *Enyclopedia Iranica,* III, Fasc. 3. 272.

98 For female rulers in Islamic communities see Fatima Mernissi, *The Forgotten Queens of Islam.* Perhaps the readers of Kirmānī's hagiography would have been aware that a female, Shajarat al-Durr, ruled Mamluk Egypt from 1250. See Mernissi, *The Forgotten Queens,* 89–99.

99 For this episode see *Manāqib-i Shaykh Awḥad al-Dīn,* 20–23; Ridgeon, *Awḥad al-Dīn Kirmānī,* 117–119.

100 Lloyd Ridgeon, "A Study of a Medieval Persian Hagiography," 248–249.

101 Anonymous, *Manāqib-i Shaykh Awḥad al-Dīn,* 60; Ridgeon, *Awḥad al-Dīn Kirmānī,* 137.

102 Bruno de Nicola, "The Ladies of Rūm", *Journal of Sufi Studies,* 3(2), 2014, 132–56.

103 Anonymous, *Manāqib-i Shaykh Awḥad al-Dīn,* 62; Ridgeon, *Awḥad al-Dīn Kirmānī,* 138.

104 See note 73 for Fāṭima.

105 Anonymous, *Manāqib-i Shaykh Awḥad al-Dīn,* 68–71; Ridgeon, *Awḥad al-Dīn Kirmānī,* 140–143.

106 Anonymous, *Manāqib-i Shaykh Awḥad al-Dīn,* 74–5; Ridgeon, *Awḥad al-Dīn Kirmānī,* 144.

107 Anonymous, *Manāqib-i Shaykh Awḥad al-Dīn,* 103; Ridgeon, *Awḥad al-Dīn Kirmānī,* 155–160.

108 Anonymous, *Manāqib-i Shaykh Awḥad al-Dīn,* 184–5; Ridgeon, *Awḥad al-Dīn Kirmānī,* 204.

109 Anonymous, *Manāqib-i Shaykh Awḥad al-Dīn,* 157–164; Ridgeon, *Awḥad al-Dīn Kirmānī,* 193.

110 Cited in Fatima Mernissi, *Beyond the Veil,* 44 (the reference given by Mernissi is Abu Issa al-Tarmidi, *Sunan al-Tarmidi,* Medina, n.d. vol II, 413).

111 Bukhārī, *Ṣaḥīḥ al-Bukhārī,* "Kitāb al-Nikāḥ," no. 22.

112 See Schimmel, *Mystical Dimensions of Islam,* (Chapel Hill: University of North Carolina Press, 1975), 428. See Rūmī *Dīvān-i Shams* for this world as an old whore (*rūspī*), F. 2303. (All references to the *Dīvān-i Shams* are to *Kulliyāt-i Shasms yā Dīvān-i Kabīr* ("The Collected Shams or the Great Collection"), ed. B. Furūzānfar (Tehran: University of Tehran Press, 1336–46/1957–1967). Henceforth, references to the *Dīvān-i Shams* are given by F. and the number of the ghazal in Furūzānfar's edition.

113 Anonymous, *Manāqib-i Shaykh Awḥad al-Dīn,* 184–5; Ridgeon, *Awḥad al-Dīn Kirmānī,* 204.

114 William C. Chittick, *The Sufi Path of Love* (SUNY Press: Albany, 1981), 5.

115 Franklin D. Lewis, *Rumi, Past and Present, East and West: The Life, Teachings and Poetry of Jalal al-Din Rumi* (Oxford: Oneworld, 2000), 1.

116 Ibrahim Gamard, "Jalāl al-Dīn Rūmī and his place in the history of Sufism," in *Routledge Handbook on Sufism,* ed. Lloyd Ridgeon (London: Routledge, 2021), 104.

117 Chittick, *The Sufi Path of Love,* 2.

118 *Fīhi mā fīhi* has been rendered into English as *Discourses of Rumi,* trans. A.J. Arberry (London: J. Murray 1961), 236–7.

119 As a delicious example of his craft consider the following quatrain:
[Indent each second line of the following quote]
Although sugar is the delight of the soul and heart
It (ū) is one thing and its sugar nature is another.
I said, "Increase my share of sugar from that 'nay'*!"*
It said, "Nay". *For sure that* "nay" *is sugar.*
The Quatrains of Rumi, trans Ibrahim Gamard and Rawan Farhadi (San Rafael: Sufi Dari Books, 2008), #650, 202. (All translations from the quatrains that are cited in this chapter are taken from Gamard and Farhadi's work). Ibrahim Gamard and Rawan Farhadi point out the pun on "*nay*" or "no" and "*nay-shakar*" which means reed-sugar (suggestive of course to the opening lines of the

Mathnawī: "Listen to the Reed". The simple Persian word "*nay*" is also suggestive of the Arabic "*lā*" of the *shahada* – "There is no god but God" which was a great source of inspiration for the Sufis, as it became something of a referent for the idea that God was indeed everywhere, i.e. there is "no" thing in existence apart from God, which renders the negative "nay" extremely sweet for the Sufis.

120 For the ways to understand this trope see edition of collected essays eds. Kamran Talattof & Clinton Jerome, *The Poetry of Nizami Ganjavi: Knowledge, Love and Rhetoric* (New York: Palgrave, 2000).

121 *Mathnawī*, V. 2019.

122 For Rūmī and the human beloved, see A.G. Rawan Farhadi, "The Human Beloved and the Divine Beloved in the Poetry of Mawlana Rumi," *Mawlana Rumi Review*, vol. 1 (2010), 100–107.

123 "I have never seen creatures deficient in reason and religion exert more power and influence over intelligent men than your womenfolk." Cited by Ghazālī, "The Proper Conduct," 23. The *ḥadīth* is recorded by Bukhārī and is regarded as *ṣaḥīḥ* (*Kitāb al-Ḥayḍ*, 6/304).

124 *Mathnawī*, I. 2433–47. A full investigation of how women are portrayed in the *Mathnawī* is beyond the scope of this research. Such a full study would examine all gendered words and phrases, as well as those verses that relate stories about women who appear in the Qur'ān, and which are specific to women.

125 Fatemeh Keshavarz, "Pregnant with God," The Poetic Art of Mothering the Sacred in Rumi's Fihi Ma Fihi," *Comparative Studies of South Asia, Africa and the Middle East*, Vol. XXII, no. 1–2, 2002, 93.

126 A study of how Rūmī portrayed gender in his voluminous collection of sonnets in his *Dīvān-i Shams* would be equally interesting. It has also been translated into English by Jeffrey R. Osborne as the *Divan-i Kabir* in twenty volumes (Independently published: 2017–20). Given the scale of the collection, it is unsurprising that this task has yet to be undertaken.

127 *The Quatrains of Rumi*, #1034, 321. Although a first reading might suggest that the quatrain above is addressed to a female beloved because of the reference to the veil, it is necessary to be aware that Q 42.51 speaks of God communicating from behind a veil, and a well-known *ḥadīth* mentions God's seventy veils of darkness and light. (This is a famous *ḥadīth* which forms the basis for the discussion by Ghazālī about the nature of God in his well-known Sufi work *Mishkat al-Anwār*, transl. W.T.H. Gairdner as *Al-Ghazali's Mishkat al Anwar (The Niche for Lights* (London: Royal Asiatic Society, 1924)). It is the grammatical ambiguity of gender in the third person pronoun in Persian which can mean either he, she or it, that assists the defamiliarisation of Rūmī's poetry and thus the ever-increasing literature to be found in both traditional Islamic regions and in the West. The elasticity of interpretation offers possible the following translation of the last line of the above quatrain: "*So that she may tear away with her own hands the cloak of the soul.*" Ripping away the veil was a metaphor Rūmī used frequently, see *Dīvān-i Shams*, F. 91.

128 *The Quatrains of Rumi*, #133, 43.

129 *The Quatrains of Rumi*, #404, 127. For other verses that lend themselves to such an interpretation see #937, 291.

130 *The Quatrains of Rumi*, #263. That God shines through a female form is also made clear in the *Dīvān-i Shams*, where he compares Mary to Shams-i Dīn: "The eyes and heart of Mary were made bright by those dates: Your tress is a date palm fully laden with dates – shake it loose," F. 1229. (The reference to Mary and the date palm is the Qur'ān 19.25).

131 In addition to the term *ma'shūq*, the male divinity is suggested most obviously when the poet speaks of his beloved having male physical attributes such as a beard. *The Quatrains of Rumi*, #188, 62.

132 *The Quatrains of Rumi*, #1200, 371.

133 *The Quatrains of Rumi*, no. 1202, 372. Other quatrains that use the masculine beloved include #140, 45; no. 465, 145; #898, 279.

134 *The Quatrains of Rumi*, #188, 675.

135 *The Quatrains of Rumi*, #1052, 527. In the *Dīvān-i Shams* it is common to find this kind of description of God (male and female), e.g. "*O Khosrow and O Shīrīn, O* [you whose] *form and image are lovely.*" F. 1228; F. 1863.

136 Annemarie Schimmel, *Mystical Dimensions of Islam*, 319.

137 The *Dīvān-i Shams* includes verses (such as those below) which suggest that the metre became something of a chore:

I have been delivered from these verses and ghazals, oh King and Sultan of Eternity!

Mufta'ilun, mufta'ilun, mufta'ilun *has hounded me to death! …* (F. 38).

The following offers a similar practice of using the poetic metre in the poem:

For God's sake, be silent! Do not break the habit of stillness. When the sweetmeats arrive, cut short the poem.

Mufta'ilun Mufā'ilun Mufta'ilun Mufā'ilun. *Do not open the gate and show off the blossoming rosegarden* (F.46).

(Jeffrey Osborne, *Jalal al-Dín Rumí: Dívan-í Kabír, Vol. XVII, The Seventeenth and Eighteenth Meters*, p. 22). I am grateful to Ibrahim Gamard for pointing me to this reference.

Rūmī does the same in his Arabic ghazals:

People became intoxicated and the regretful fell asleep. So, we drink on our own,

Mufta'ilun, mufta'ilun, mufta'il, fa'lalalan, fa'lalalan, fa'lalalan (F. 2128).

138 Murata, *The Tao of Islam*, 317. The soul commanding to evil is a Qur'ānic term, derived from Q. 12.53.

139 *Mathnawī*, I. 2618–2222.

140 In fact, readers are told to do the opposite of what the donkey desires, which of course is substantiated by referring to the *ḥadīth* when Muḥammad says, "Consult with [women], then oppose their advice. He that does not disobey them will be ruined." *Mathnawī*, I. 2955–7.

141 *Discourses of Rumi*, 1961, 98.

142 Keshavarz, "Pregnant with God," 92.

143 See for example Rūmī's story in book V of the *Mathawī*, called "The story of that maidservant who fucked a lusty lady with a donkey," lines 1333–1405. Nicholson found these verses so sexually explicit and shocking that he rendered them into Latin rather than English. There are also verses in which rampant sexuality is attributed to both men and women. A good example of uncontrolled male sexual appetite is contained in the story of Naṣūḥ in the *Mathnawī*, V. 2227.

144 *Feats of the Knowers of God*, 499–500.

145 There is not necessarily any sexual implication in this anecdote, as a *shāhid* was an individual with a beautiful face, through whom the divine could be witnessed. As such it was a common Sufi practice at the time. However, giving Shams permission to look upon his wife's face, when the common practice was veiling (most likely face-veiling) in front of unrelated males, would have been contrary to social etiquette and perceptions of *sharīʿa* norms. This was recognised by Shams, as Aflākī said that this was a test designed by Shams to assess "the limits of [Rūmī's] forbearance." (*Feats of the Knowers*, 427–8). For a discussion of the *shāhid* see Lloyd Ridgeon, "The Controversy of Shaykh Awḥad al-Dīn Kirmānī and Handsome, Moon-Faced Youths: A Case Study of Shāhid-Bāzī in Medieval Sufism," *Journal of Sufi Studies*, 1 (2012) 3–30, DOI: 10.1163/221059512X617658. In order to glorify Rūmī's masculinity, Aflākī also described an episode in which Rūmī "honored [his wife] with his company and like a fierce rutting lion had sexual intercourse with her seventy times, to the point that she fled from Mawlana's grip." *Feats of the Knowers of God*, 310. The didactic story is meant to demonstrate the power of the "Men of God" who can understand other people's thoughts. Rūmī's wife had begun to doubt his interest and inclination in sexual matters.

146 *Feats of the Knowers of God*, 427.

147 *Fīhi mā fīhi*, translated by A.J. Arberry as *Discourses of Rumi* (London: John Murray, 1961), 107–8.

[148] *The Quatrains of Rumi*, #54, 19.

[149] Such an insult sometimes provokes very strong reactions, even in the contemporary period. One of the most well-known instances occurred during the final match of the Football World Cup in 2006 when an Italian player, Marco Materazzi, audibly uttered the phrase to his French opponent of Algerian descent, considered the best player in the world, Zinedine Zidane. Zidane reacted by head-butting Materazzi, and the former was sent-off. "And Materazzi's exact words to Zidane were ..." *Guardian*, Saturday, August 18, 2007.

[150] Aflākī, *Feats of the Knowers of God*, 106. See also 149, 201, 311 and 352–3.

[151] J. Pitt-Rivers, "Honor", *Encyclopedia of the Social Sciences*, 6 (New York: Macmillan, 1968), 505: See also L. Schneider, "Of Vigilance and Virgins," *Ethnology*, 9, 1971, 1–24; Lila Abu-Lughod, "A Community of Secrets: The Separate World of Bedouin Women," *Signs*, Vol. 10(4), 1985, 637–57; Unni Wikan, "Shame and Honour: A Contestable Pair," *Man*, New Series, Vol. 19(4), 1984, 635–52.

[152] Chittick, *The Sufi Path of Love*, 293.

[153] Chittick, *The Sufi Path of Love*, 293, citing the *Dīvān-i Shams*, F. 2675.

[154] Lewis, *Rumi, Past and Present*, 134,

[155] See *Maqālāt-i Shams*, transl. William Chittick, *Rumi and Me* (Louisville KY: Fons Vitae, 2004), 222, 268.

[156] This report appears in Shams al-Dīn Aflākī, *Manāqib al-'ārifīn, Feats of the Knowers of God*, 441. Although Aflākī is known to have exaggerated and distorted the truth, his words do resonate with Shams' own writings.

[157] See Lloyd Ridgeon, "Shaggy or Shaved", *Iran and the Caucuses*, 14(2), 2010, 233–63.

[158] *The Travels of Ibn Baṭṭūṭa*, transl. H.A.R. Gibb (Delhi: Munshiram Manoharlal Publishers, 1993), p. 38.

[159] This is typified in a quatrain that has been attributed to both Awḥad al-Dīn Kirmānī and Rūmī which states:

If you accept advice, make some effort for two or three days
So that you may 'die before death' *for two or three days*
The world is an old woman. What will it matter if you
Don't associate with an old woman for two or three days.

See *The Quatrains of Rumi*, no. 1798, 562. See also Rūmī's *Dīvān-i Shams*, 3400–01. It should also be noted that not all references to old women are negative as the *ḥadīth* of clinging to the "religion of old women" testifies. See S. Murata and W. Chittick, *The Vision of Islam* (New York: Paragon House, 1994), 55–6

[160] The *ḥadīth* actually provides a gloss in that Muḥammad commented, "Whenever a woman who fulfils God's requirements and is obedient to her husband takes hold of a spinning-wheel and turns it, this is as if she were reciting God's epithets, joining in congregational prayer, and fighting against the infidels." Cited by Ghazālī, *Counsel for Kings*, 162.

[161] Chittick, *Rumi and Me*, 268.

[162] *Rumi and Me*, 268.

[163] Aflākī, p. 698. Schimmel also mentions that Rūmī spoke of one lady who founded a convent in Konya and acted as a *shaykha*. Schimmel, *The Triumphal Sun* (London: Fine Books, 1978), 32.

[164] Omaima Abou-Bakr, "Rings of Memory: 'Writing Muslim Women' and the Question of Authorial Voice," *The Muslim World*, 103 (2013), 322.

Works cited

Abdel-Kader, A.H., *The Life, Personality and Writings of al-Junayd* (London: Luzac & Co, 1976).

Abdel-Latif, S., "Narrativizing early mystic and Sufi women: mechanisms of gendering in Sufi hagiographies," in *Routledge Handbook on Sufism*, ed. Lloyd Ridgeon (London: Routledge, 2021), 132–145.

Abou-Bakr, O., "Rings of Memory: 'Writing Muslim Women' and the Question of Authorial Voice," *The Muslim World*, 103 (2013).

Abu-Lughod, L., "A Community of Secrets: The Separate World of Bedouin Women," *Signs*, Vol. 10(4), 1985, 637–57.

Aflākī, Shams al-Dīn, *Manāqib al-ʿārifīn*, transl. John O'Kane, *Feats of the Knowers of God* (Leiden: Brill, 2002).

Ahmed, L., *Women and Gender in Islam* (New Haven: Yale University Press, 1992).

Al-Qushayri's Epistle on Sufism, trans. Alexander Knysh (Reading: Garnet, 2007), 17–74.

Anonymous, *Manāqib-i Shaykh Awḥad al-Dīn Ḥāmid ibn-i abī'l-Fakhr-i Kirmānī*, ed. B. Furūzānfar (Tehran: B.T.N.K., 1969).

Anṣārī, ʿAbd Allāh, *Ṭabaqāt al-Ṣūfiyya*, ed. M. Sarwar-Mawlāʾī (Tehran: Tus, 1386/2007/8).

ʿAṭṭār, Farīd al-Dīn, *Tadhkirat al-awliyā* ed. Istiʿlāmī (Tehran: Zuwwar, 1346).

ʿAṭṭār, Farīd al-Dīn, *The Tadhkiratul Awliya* (Memoirs of the Saints) *of Faridu'din ʿAṭṭar*, ed. R. A. Nicholson (London: Luzac & Co, 1905–7).

Azad, A., "Female Mystics in Medieval Islam: The Quiet Legacy," *Journal of the Economic and Social History of the Orient*, 56 (2013), 53–88.

Baldick, J., "The Legend of Rābiʿa of Basra," *Religion*, 19 (1990), 233–47.

Bashir, S., "Islamic tradition and celibacy," in *Celibacy and Religious Traditions* ed. Carl Olson (Oxford: University Press, 2007), 133–147.

Bayram, M., *Fatma Bacı ve Bacıyân-i Rûm* (Konya: Nüve Kültür Merkezi, 2007).

Berkey, J.P., "Women and Islamic education in the Mamluk Period," in *Women in Middle Eastern History: Shifting Boundaries in Sex and Gender*, eds. Nikki Keddie and Beth Baron (Yale University Press, 1992).

Chittick, W.C., *The Sufi Path of Love* (SUNY Press: Albany, 1981).

Cornell, R., *Early Sufi Women: Dhikr an-niswa al-mutaʿabbidāt aṣ-ṣūfiyyāt* (Louiseville KY: Fons Vitae, 1999)

Cornell, Rkia Elaroui, *Rabi'a from Narrative to Myth: The Many Faces of Islam's Most Famous Woman Saint, Rabi'a al-ʿAdawiyya* (Oxford: Oneworld, 2018).

Dakake, M., "Guest of the Inmost Heart: Conceptions of the Divine Beloved among Early Sufi Women," *Comparative Islamic Studies*, 3.1 (2007), 72.

Davis, D., The Mirror of My Heart: A Thousand Years of Persian Poetry by Women (London: Penguin, 2021).

Farah, M., *Marriage and Sexuality in Islam* (University of Utah Press, 1984).

Ford, H.A., "Hierarchical Inversions, Divine Subversions: The Miracles of Râbiʿa al-ʿAdawîya," *Journal of Feminist Studies in Religion*, Vol. 15, No. 2 (Fall, 1999) 5–24.

Gamard, I., "Jalāl al-Dīn Rūmī and his place in the history of Sufism," in *Routledge Handbook on Sufism*, ed. Lloyd Ridgeon (London: Routledge, 2021).

Ghazālī, Abū Ḥāmid Muḥammad, *Kīmīyā-yi saʿādat*, ed. Ḥusayn Khadiwjam (Tehran, 1983).

Ghazālī, Abū Ḥāmid Muḥammad, *Mishkat al-Anwār*, transl. W.T.H. Gairdner as *Al-Ghazali's Mishkat al Anwar (The Niche for Lights* (London: Royal Asiatic Society, 1924).

Ghazālī, Abū Ḥāmid Muḥammad, *Naṣīḥāt al-Mulūk*, transl. F.R.C. Bagley, *Counsel for Kings* (London: Oxford University Press, 1964)

Hillenbrand, C., "al-Ghazālī: In praise of Sufism," in *Routledge Handbook on Sufism*, ed. Lloyd Ridgeon 63–64.

Holland, M., "The Proper Conduct of Marriage in Islam" (*Ādāb al-Nikāḥ*) (Florida: Al-Baz Publishing, 1998).

Homerin, T.E., *From Arab Poet to Muslim Saint: Ibn Fāriḍ, his Verse, and his Shrine* (South Carolina: University Press of South Carolina, 1994).

Hourani, A., "A Revised Chronology of Ghazālī's Writings," *Journal of the American Oriental Society*, 104.2 (1984).

Humphries, S., "Women as Patrons of Religious Architecture in Ayyubid Damascus," *Muqarnas*, 1994, Vol. 11, pp. 35–54.

Ibn Battuta, *The Travels of Ibn Baṭṭūṭa*, transl. H.A.R. Gibb (Delhi: Munshiram Manoharlal Publishers, 1993).

Ibn Jawzī, *The Devil's Deceptions* (Birmingham: Dar al-Sunna, 2014).

Immenkamp, B., *Marriage and Celibacy in Medieval Islam: A Study of Ghazālī's Kitāb Ādāb al-nikāḥ*, PhD doctorate, University of Cambridge, 1994, 116.

Karamustafa, A.T., *Sufism: The Formative Period* (Edinburgh: Edinburgh University Press, 2007).

Keshavarz, F., "'Pregnant with God,' The Poetic Art of Mothering the Sacred in Rumi's Fihi Ma Fihi," *Comparative Studies of South Asia, Africa and the Middle East*, Vol. XXII, no. 1–2, 2002.

Khaleghi Motlagh, Dj., *Enyclopedia Iranica*, s.v. Azraqī Heravī.

Kőprülü, M.F., *The Origins of the Ottoman Empire*, trans. Gary Leiser (Albany: SUNY Press, 1992).

Kruk, R., *The Warrior Women of Islam: Female Empowerment in Arabic Popular Literature* (London: IB Tauris, 2014).

Küçük, H., "Female Substitutes and Shaykhs in the History of Sufism: The Case of the Mawlawiyya Sufi Order from its Early Phase to the Eighteenth Century," *Mawlana Rumi Review*, vol. 4, 2013, 106–131.

Lewis, F.D., *Rumi, Past and Present, East and West: The Life, Teachings and Poetry of Jalal al-Din Rumi* (Oxford: Oneworld, 2000).

Losensky, P., *Farid Ad-Din ʿAttar's Memorial of God's Friends* (New York: Paulist Press, 2010).

Mahjub, M.A., "Chivalry and early Persian Sufism," in *Classical Persian Sufism: from its Origins to Rumi*, ed. Leonard Lewisohn (London: KNP, 1993).

Melchert, C., "Before ṣūfiyyāt: Female Muslim Renunciants in the 8th and 9th Centuries CE," *Journal of Sufi Studies*, 5 (2016), 115–39.

Melchert, C., "The Transition from Asceticism to Mysticism at the Middle of the Ninth Century C.E." *Studia Islamica*, 83 (1996), 51–70.

Mernissi, F., *The Forgotten Queens of Islam*, transl. Mary Jo Lakeland (Minneapolis: University of Minnesota Press, 1993)

Mernissi, F., *Beyond the Veil: Male-Female Dynamics in Modern Muslim Society* (Bloomington: Indiana University Press, 1987).

Mojaddedi, J., *Beyond Dogma: Rumi's Teachings on Friendship of God and Early Sufi Theories* (Oxford: Oxford University Press).

Mojaddedi, J.A., *The Biographical Tradition in Sufism* (London: Routledge, 2001).

Muʿayyad al-Dīn Jandī, *Nafhat al-rūḥ wa tuḥfat al futūḥ* (Tehran, 1362/1983–4), 37.

Murata S. and W. Chittick, *The Vision of Islam* (New York: Paragon House, 1994).

Murata, S., *The Tao of Islam: A Sourcebook on Gender Relationships in Islamic Thought* (Albany: SUNY Press, 1992).

Nasafī, ʿAzīz, *Kitāb al-Insān al-kāmil*, ed. M. Molé (Tehran/Paris: Institut Franco-Iranien, 1962).

Nicola, B. de., "The Ladies of Rūm", *Journal of Sufi Studies*, 3(2), 2014, 132–56.

Nūrī Ṭabarsī, Ḥājj Mīrzā Ḥusayn, *Mustadrak al-Wasā'il va mustanbaṭ al-masā'il* (Beirut: n.d. 1408/1988).

Osborne, J., *Jalal al-Dín Rumí: Dívan-í Kabír, Vol. XVII, The Seventeenth and Eighteenth Meters.*

Perry, C., "A Paradox of Patronage During the Later Mamluk Period," *Muslim World*, 73 (1983).

Pitt-Rivers, J., "Honor", *Encyclopedia of the Social Sciences*, 6 (New York: Macmillan, 1968).

Prus, E.S., Divine presence, gender, and the Sufi spiritual path: An analysis of Rabiʿah the mystic's identity and poetry, MA thesis, Xavier University 2009.

Quay, M., 'God does not regard your forms,': Gender and Literary Representations in the Works of Farīd al-Dīn ʿAṭṭār Nīshāpūrī. PhD thesis submitted to Cambridge University, June 2017.

Rawan Farhadi, A.G., "The Human Beloved and the Divine Beloved in the Poetry of Mawlana Rumi," *Mawlana Rumi Review*, vol. 1 (2010), 100–107.

Rayfield, D., *Edge of Empires: A History of Georgia* (London: Reaktion Books, 2012).

Ridgeon, L., "A Study of a Medieval Persian Hagiography and Interactions Between Sufis and Christians in Rum and Upper Mesopotamia," *The Maghreb Review*, 47(3), 2022, 235–359.

Ridgeon, L., "Shaggy or Shaved," *Iran and the Caucuses*, 14(2), 2010, 233–63.

Ridgeon, L., "The Controversy of Shaykh Awḥad al-Dīn Kirmānī and Handsome, Moon-Faced Youths: A Case Study of Shāhid-Bāzī in Medieval Sufism," *Journal of Sufi Studies*, 1 (2012) 3–30.

Ridgeon, L., *Awḥad al-Dīn Kirmānī and the Controversy of the Sufi Gaze* (London: Routledge, 2018).

Ridgeon, L., *Persian Metaphysics and Mysticism: Selected Treatises of ʿAzīz Nasafī*, trans. Lloyd Ridgeon (Curzon: Richmond, 2002).

Ridgeon, L., *Jawanmardi: A Sufi Code of Honour* (Edinburgh: University Press, 2011).

Roded, R., *Women in the Biographical Collections* (London: Lynne Rienner Publications, 1994).

Rumi, Jalāl al-Dīn, *Fīhi mā fīhi*, translated by A.J. Arberry as *Discourses of Rumi* (London: John Murray, 1961).

Rūmī, Jalāl al-Dīn, *Dīvān-i Shams* are to *Kulliyāt-i Shasms yā Dīvān-i Kabīr* ("The Collected Shams or the Great Collection"), ed. B. Furūzānfar (Tehran: University of Tehran Press, 1336–46/1957–1967).

Rumi, Jalāl al-Dīn, *Fīhi mā fīhi* has been rendered into English as *Discourses of Rumi*, trans. A.J. Arberry (London: J. Murray 1961).

Rumi, Jalāl al-Dīn, *Maqālāt-i Shams*, transl. William Chittick, *Rumi and Me* (Louisville KY: Fons Vitae, 2004).

Rūmī, Jalāl al-Dīn, *Mathnawī*, Introduction to Book V, trans. R.A. Nicholson (London: Luzac 1934).

Rumi, Jalāl al-Dīn, *The Quatrains of Rumi*, trans Ibrahim Gamard and Rawan Farhadi (San Rafael: Sufi Dari Books, 2008).

Sabra, A., "Economies of Sufism," in *Handbook of Sufi Studies: Sufi Institutions*, ed. Alexandre Papas (Leiden: Brill, 2021).

Safi, O., *The Politics of Knowledge in Premodern Islam: Negotiating Ideology and Religious Inquiry* (Chapel Hill: The University of North Carolina Press, 2006).

Salamah-Qudsi, A., "The Economics of Female Piety in Early Sufism," *Religions*, 12(9), (2021), 760. https://www.mdpi.com/2077-1444/12/9/760

Salamah-Qudsi, A., *Sufism and Early Islamic Piety: Personal and Communal Dynamics* (Cambridge: Cambridge University Press, 2019).

Sayeed, A., *Women and the Transmission of Religious Knowledge in Islam* (Cambridge: University of Cambridge Press, 2013).

Schimmel, A., My *Soul is a Woman: The Feminine in Islam* (London: Continuum, 2003).

Schimmel, A., *Mystical Dimensions of Islam*, (Chapel Hill: University of North Carolina Press, 1975).

Schimmel, A., *The Triumphal Sun* (London: Fine Books, 1978).

Schneider, L., "Of Vigilance and Virgins," *Ethnology*, 9, 1971, 1–24.

Silvers, L., "Early pious, mystic Sufi women," in *Cambridge Companion to Sufism*, ed. Lloyd Ridgeon (Cambridge: University Press, 2015), 24–52;
Silvers, L., "God Loves Me": The Theological Content and Context of Early Pious and Sufi Women's Sayings on Love, *Journal of Islamic Studies*, 30 (2010), 33–59.
Smith, M., *Rābiʿa the Mystic & Her Fellow-saints in Islām* (Cambridge: University Press, 1928).
Suhrawardī, *Awārif al-maʿarif* (Beirut: Dār al-Kitāb al-ʿArabī, 1983).
Sulamī, ʿAbd al-Raḥman, *Ṭabaqāt al-Ṣūfiyya*, ed. Nūr al-Dīn Sharība (Cairo: Maktaba al-Khānajī, 1969).
Talattof, K., & J. Clinton, *The Poetry of Nizami Ganjavi: Knowledge, Love and Rhetoric* (New York: Palgrave, 2000).
The Kashf al-Maḥjūb of Al-Hujwiri, transl. R.A. Nicholson (London: Luzac & Co, 1976)
Wikan, U., "Shame and Honour: A Contestable Pair," *Man*, New Series, Vol. 19(4), 1984, 635–52.
Wolper, E.S., "Princess Safwat al-Dunya wa al-Din and the production of Sufi buildings and hagiographies in pre-Ottoman Anatolia," in *Women, Patronage and Self-Representation in Islamic Societies*, ed. D. Fairchild Ruggles (Albany: SUNY Press, 2000), 35–52.
Wolper, E.S., *Cities and Saints: Sufism and the Transformation of Urban Space in Medieval Anatolia* (Pennsylvania: Pennsylvania State University Press, 2003).

Jamāl al-Dīn Sāvī's Codification of Qalandarī Rites and Rituals

Zhinia Noorian
Utrecht University

Abstract
The *Qalandariyya* has remained a significant social-spiritual pious movement with a profound impact on the Islamic cultural zone from the Balkans to Bengal. In different primary and secondary sources, Jamāl al-Dīn Sāvī (d. about 1232/3) is considered as the founder of this influential movement founded upon an extreme form of renunciation (*tajarrud*), namely, *faqr* (lit. poverty). Nevertheless, little to nothing is known about his life, or the conceptualisation of the *qalandarī* spirituality, rites and rituals by this Iranian spiritual leader. In this chapter, I focus on the only extant *Qalandar-nāma* on Sāvī and his spiritual career written by an anonymous author, and a devout *qalandarī* disciple, who introduced himself as Khatīb-i Fārsī ("Persian preacher"). Although written years after Sāvī's death, this hagiography is highly significant in the field of Sufi studies. This text is the only known manuscript that provides details about the non-conformist *qalandarī* ritual of shaving the head, eyebrows, the beard and the moustache (*chahār żarb*), which later became known as the hallmark of the *qalandarī* path. Through the analysis of *Qalandar-nāma* by the Persian preacher, this chapter provides details about the formation of the *Qalandariyya* movement and its distinctions from the other non-conformist, impactful spiritual movement within Islamic mysticism known as the *Malāmatiyya*. This in-depth examination sheds light on Sāvī's *qalandarī* manner in developing a significant, non-conformist piety within Islamic mysticism. With the close reading of this hagiographical text and situating it within its historical, religious and political context, this study sheds light on the activities of Sāvī as an Iranian leader in shaping the intellectual-spiritual history of non-conformity in Islamic mysticism.

Keywords: *Qalandariyya*; Jamāl al-Dīn Sāvī; non-conformity in Islam; Khatīb-i Fārsī; *Qalandar-nāma*; renunciation (*tajarrud*); poverty (*faqr*); Sufi piety.

The formation of the *Qalandariyya* movement is associated with the Sufi master, Jamāl al-Dīn Sāvī (d. about 1232/3). Drawing from the principles of the *Malāmatiyya*, the *qalandars* tried to preserve their piety inwardly while provoking extreme blame or contempt from the respectable Muslim society.[1] We have little information about Sāvī as the founder of this movement and his role in systematising what already existed as a tendency described in Persian literature and Sufi treatises. In this chapter, I will closely examine the only available hagiography of Sāvī, the *Qalandar-nāma*, written in Persian by an anonymous author, who introduces himself as Khaṭīb-i Fārsī ("Persian preacher"). With this investigation, I aim to shed light on Sāvī's spiritual journey, ending in his becoming a *qalandar*. The original contribution of this study to the field is to provide information about the spiritual career of Sāvī as a *qalandar* guide, and his role in shaping what became known as the *Qalandariyya* movement after the thirteenth century. The questions I ask are as follows: How did Sāvī systematise the *qalandarī* rites, rituals and doctrines into the *Qalandariyya* movement? What characteristics did he introduce as the key elements of this tradition? What type of piety did Sāvī, as a *qalandar*, promote with his behaviour? Were the *qalandar*s pious Muslims?

The *Qalandariyya* was an eclectic non-conformist movement, hypothetically shaped by a diversity of antinomian strands of thought, such as *Khurram-dīniyya* (*Mazdakism*), *Karrāmiyya*, and *Malāmatiyya*, among others. According to Madelung, the *Khurram-dīniyya* was one of the revolutionary movements that emerged in the eighth and ninth centuries. It is an overt amalgamation of Persian and Islamic religious motives and beliefs. In Muslim heresiographies, it is generally recognised as the teachings of Mazdak who started a social and religious revolution during the reign of the Sassanian monarch, Kavād (r. 488–531).[2] The other movement with an important role in shaping the *Qalandariyya* is *Karrāmiyya*, founded by Muḥammad ibn Karrām (d. 869). As Madelung stated, it was "the most important ascetic movement in Iran" from the ninth to the twelfth centuries. This movement, at times stigmatised as heretic, "represented an activist and ostensive asceticism".[3] The last movement, probably heavily inspiring the *Qalandariyya* in its particular context of time and place, was the pious movement of *Malāmatiyya*. In Shafīʿī-Kadkanī's words, "*Qalandariyya* and *Malāmatiyya* were the sides of a coin", therefore, inseparable.[4]

To situate the case of Sāvī as a *qalandar* saint in its historical context, I start with a brief history of Sufism. Since the *Malāmatiyya* has a special place in shaping the *Qalandariyya*, I shall also give a brief account about the *Malāmatiyya*. Then, I trace a chronological outline of the *qalandarī* movement and the character of the *qalandar*, according to previous research. I shall proceed with Khaṭīb-i Fārsī's representation of the *qalandarī* piety, as projected through the image of Sāvī as the perfect saint. My focus will be on the couplets where Sāvī defines the *qalandarī* piety and its components. I also investigate Sāvī's use of what he refers to as prophetic *ḥadīths* (one of the fundamental elements of sharīʿa law) in his codification, to provide an example of his point of departure from the Islamic norms.

The *Qalandariyya* movement: an overview in Sufi history

Researchers have approached the study of Sufism in various ways, but I would like to open my discussion with a definition of Sufism that recalls the image of Sāvī, as portrayed in Khaṭīb Fārsī's hagiography. With a summarising comment, the major Sufi master Bāyazīd Basṭāmī (d. 848 or 875) defined Sufism as "shutting the door of comfort and sitting with one's arms around the knees of self-denial".[5] According to Melchert, Sufism can be defined as "Islamic mysticism", with the qualifications that Islamic mysticism is not limited to Sufism.[6] Knysh suggests that Sufism is "the ascetic-mystical stream in Islam". Emerging from the onset of Islam, Sufism developed into a variety of doctrinal, devotional, institutional and artistic forms.[7] In their histories, tenth- and eleventh-century Sufi authors implied that Sufism emerged from an earlier renunciatory movement.[8] They tended to ignore the disreputable and marginal figures, who were also called "Sufis" before the ninth century, but were not associated with mysticism.[9] According to the spiritual lineage worked out in the early eleventh century, Sufism goes back to the prophet's companions. The immediate forbears of the Sufis were identified by various biographers (ʿAbd al-Raḥmān Sulamī (d. 1021), and Abū Nuʿaym (d. 1038) being the most important ones) as eighth- and ninth-century renunciants who were known as *zuhhād* (pl. "ascetic"), *nussāk* (pl. "pious"), or *ʿubbād* (pl. "servants of God"). These people underwent austerities and devoted themselves to reciting the Qurʾān, praying and thinking steadily of God. Although a few of these early renunciants wore outfits of wool (Arabic: "*ṣūf*"), the term "Sufi" only appeared in the late eighth century, so few of these renunciants were called "Sufis" during their lifetimes.[10] In his new research, however, Melchert contends that contrary to the believers' views, Sufism did not manifest itself in the lifetime of the prophet, nor during the conquest period, or immediately after that. Instead, Melchert suggests that classical Sufism was developed under the spiritual leadership of Junayd (d. 910), the Baghdadi master, although mystical piety had already emerged in the literary tradition in the mid-ninth century.[11]

Muslim renunciatory piety, which was attributed mainly to the early companions and followers of the prophet, typically involved obsessive fear and sadness, to the extent of wishing to avoid the Resurrection. In the mid-ninth century, however, a mystical trend associated with persons known as Sufis emerged in Iraq. Later in the ninth century, the term *ṣūfiya* was used in referring to this tradition. These Sufis spoke about a reciprocal love relationship with God, and they told of being addressed by Him through the things of the world. Naturally, the Sufi trend aroused opposition from pious Sunnī scholars, who instituted an inquisition toward Sufis in 264/877–8 in Baghdad, to protect the idea of divine transcendence.[12] This incident, which led to the execution of two prominent Sufis (Ḥallāj and Ibn ʿAṭāʾ in 309/922), was the most spectacular manifestation of hostility between the Sufis and the more old-fashioned ascetics. After this inquisition, Junayd presented a less controversial form of mystical piety by advocating an inward mysticism that would not interfere with following *ḥadīth*, jurisprudence or making a living, among other things.[13] Despite facing hostility and measures such as executions, arrests or exiles, classical Sufism had taken shape by the end of the century in Baghdad, from where it started to spread and merge with other pious movements over the two centuries to come.[14] One of the major pious movements, which merged with Sufism, and had a major role in spreading it out of Baghdad, was the undemonstrative *Malāmatiyya* of Nīshāpūr.[15] To clarify the important role of *Malāmatiyya* in shaping the antinomian movement of *Qalandariyya*, a more detailed explanation of *Malāmatiyya* is significant.

The *Malāmatiyya*

Although the *Malāmatiyya* started in Nīshāpūr, it gained particular importance in Central Asia, and considerable success from Turkey to the Balkans, as well as regions of the Arab Middle East.[16] Founded by Ḥamdūn al-Qaṣṣār (d. 884), *Malāmatiyya* was "an extremely introverted reaction to extroverted and ascetic forms of spirituality (*zuhd*)", and it later took other forms such as the *Qalandariyya*.[17] These Ṣūfīs adhered to the practice of *malāma* (blame), which was pivotal to the *malāmatī* doctrine, and which promoted the mystic's total indifference to other people's positive or negative judgements.[18] The scarce information available about the *Malāmatiyya* is based on the only source specifically dealing with this movement, the *Risālat al-Malāmatiyya* (*Malāmatiyya Epistle*), by Abū ʿAbd al-Raḥmān al-Sulamī.

Sulamī was from one of the most eminent families of Nīshāpūr, and a disciple and grandson of Abū ʿAmr Ismāʿīl ibn Nujayd. This is significant because Sulamī's grandfather was actually a distinguished disciple of Abū ʿUthmān al-Ḥīrī, a prominent *malāmatī* shaykh at the end of the ninth century. It is also significant to mention that Sulamī's *Risālat* was never intended to be a historical text about *Malāmatiyya*. His purpose was to situate this movement in the mystical tradition of Islam (probably to counterbalance the Baghdadi centre), to promote this Nīshāpūrī school as the purest mystical tradition, and to vindicate it from accusations of antinomianism and nonconformity.[19] It is also worth mentioning that Sulamī was severely criticised by scholars, particularly those of the Hanbalite school. He was censured for his fabrication of prophetic *ḥadīths* and for his method of exegesis, although later writers such as Qushayrī (d. 1072), Hujvīrī (d. 1072), Ghazālī (d. 1111), Shihāb al-Dīn ʿUmar Suhravardī (d. 1234), Ibn al-ʿArabī (d. 1240) and others have quoted his works extensively.[20]

Early *malāmatī* activities took shape in Nīshāpūr while it was the capital of Khurāsān and the governmental centre under the Tahirid Dynasty (820–873). After the Buids captured Baghdad in 945, Nīshāpūr became, and remained, the centre of Sunnite Islam until at least the mid-eleventh century. From the ninth century, Nīshāpūr and its people were severely affected by factional and sectarian struggles known as "wild sectarian struggles", or *al-ʿaṣabiyyāt al-waḥsha*. The two major schools of religious law (the *madhāhib*) that clashed most intensely were the Ḥanafites and Shāfiʿites, as the Mālikites, Ẓāhirites and Ḥanbalites were merely small minorities in Nīshāpūr. Sectarian clashes were also noticeable among other groups such as the *Shiʿites* and the *Karrāmiyya*, as well as the "vigilantes" (*mutaṭaw-wiʿa*) and the extremists, such as the Khawārij.[21] These sectarian hostilities were not limited to Nīshāpūr. Throughout the tenth century they extended to communities across Khurāsān, which was an important crossroads connecting Baghdad, the Persian Gulf, India, Central Asia and China.

It was in this milieu that the *malāmatī* masters promoted a system of sincere self-scrutiny, which was interwoven into an esteemed social code of chivalry and altruism. *Malāmatiyya* advocated the realisation of psychological purity as a spiritual experience. Through *ikhlāṣ* (sincerity), and by freeing one's actions and perceptions from the contamination of the lower self (*nafs*), the adherents aimed to reach a stage in which their spiritual and psychological attainments become completely introverted.[22] Tracing the origins of their tradition to the prophet, who was extolled by the Qurʾān as impervious to blame (5:54), the *malāmatīs* considered all hopes of heavenly rewards, or even private thoughts of success in religious deeds, as a spiritual failure.[23] Schimmel postulated that the deeds of *malāmatīs* were probably shaped by two other verses from the Qurʾān. The first says, "and they do not fear the blame of a blaming person" (5:59), and the second concerns the *nafs lawwāma* ("the blaming soul") "that warned them at every step in religious life" (75:2).[24] The following lines from Sulamī's *Risāla*, attributed to Abū Ḥafṣ al-Ḥaddād (d. about 260), and many similar sayings encountered in the relevant literature, succinctly expresses this key *malāmatī* aspiration:[25]

> They [the *Malāmatīs*] show off what is blameworthy and conceal what is praiseworthy. Thus people blame them for their outward [conduct] while they blame themselves for their inward [state] ...[26]

In the *Malāmatiyya* school, the call to abandon all outward and inward claims of spiritual distinction or superiority meant abidance by the Islamic *sharīʿa*.[27] In other words, these mystics "saw their piety as a deepening or expansion of legalistic observance".[28] One fundamental *malāmatī* question, therefore, was "how far can one proceed on a spiritual path of uncompromising introverted purification, which entails elimination of any external traces of vanity (*ʿujb*), presumptuous pretension (*iddiʿāʾ*) and delusion (*ghurūr*), to the point of incurring constant blame, without undermining the ethical and practical precepts of extroverted religion?"[29]

By the twelfth century, Sufism was recognised as a part of religious life and religious knowledge "Iʿlm". This form of piety gradually "came to dominate religious life" among both Sunni and Shiites.[30] By the end of the twelfth century, the Sufi tradition was well institutionalised. As part of their intuitive journey to know God, Sufi saints founded *ṭarīqas* (lodges, lit. "pathways") and attracted pupils (*murīds*, "those willing to enter the path" or *sāliks*, "wayfarers").[31] It was in this period that the most important developments in Sufism took place. Two major literary figures of the thirteenth century, Ibn ʿArabī and Rūmī, played a crucial role in this spiritual revival.[32] Despite orthodox condemnation, the institutionalised *ṭarīqas* attracted chronically anxious people by promising them salvation. Yet, these Sufi masters had to compete with other sects such as the *Qalandariyya* that had no established doctrine "beyond the urgent quest for a transcendent state of consciousness".[33]

The *Qalandariyya* as a tendency

As mentioned before, the *Malāmatiyya* probably inspired the *Qalandariyya* movement. Yazici, however, argued that the *qalandarī* adherents gave a different interpretation to the *malāmatī* doctrines. Although the *malāmatīs* adhered to God's commands without boasting or ostentation, the *qalandarīs* tried to destroy all tradition, and conceal their deeds from the public.[34] According to Karamustafa, the *malāmatīs* almost certainly conformed to social and legal norms, since the hallmark of their piety was blending into society.[35] Yet, De Bruijn's opinion about these two groups differs slightly from that of Yazici and Karamustafa. According to De Bruijn, the essence of the *malāmatī* principle was that the mystic must strive to reach a state of mental detachment from any form of positive or negative judgement about his deeds. To attain this state, *malāmatīs* could go as far as seeking to provoke harsh criticism by engaging in blameworthy behaviour. However, as De Bruijn argued, the pitfall of such an excessive attitude was that the antinomian behaviour could be practised for the sake of mere self-indulgence. The great mystic Suhravardī was deeply concerned with this issue. That is why, in his *ʿAwārif al-maʿārif*, Suhravardī drew a clear line between "the acceptable and unacceptable forms of *malāma*". He sought to restrict *malāmatī* behaviour to efforts towards pursuing "the principle of *katm al-ʿibādāt* (the dissimulation of acts of obedience)". De Bruijn contended that Suhravardī's argument indicated that antinomian behaviour was the primary manifestation of the *Qalandariyya* in that era. For De Bruijn, the *Qalandariyya* was an excessive consequence of the sophisticated *malāmatī* attitude adopted by those whom Suhravardī accused of pursuing the "destruction of conventions" (*takhrīb al-ʿādāt*). De Bruijn asserted that despite such severe disapproval in the

Sufi tradition, the adherents of this extreme form of antinomianism emerged under the name of *qalandars*.[36]

In its early stage, the *Qalandariyya* was no more than a corpus of basic principles. It is highly probable that the *Qalandariyya* was influenced by Indian, non-Muslim wandering ascetics who practised poverty, sought uprightness (*ṣidq*), sanctity and purification during the ninth century, in Mesopotamia and adjoining regions. Probably these holy men, travelling in pairs, impressed Muslim ascetics, who sought to imitate them by looking for and finding authority in the Qur'ān and the *ḥadīth*.[37] Opinions differ over where the *Qalandariyya* first appeared. Karamustafa contended that the movement originated in Syria and Egypt, mainly under the leadership of Iranian masters, most notably Jamāl al-Dīn Sāvī, and then it rapidly spread to Asia Minor and India.[38] Yazici however, argues that *Qalandariyya* took shape in Khurāsān, Turkistān and other parts of the Eastern Islamic world, and then was introduced to the Western Islamdom.[39]

From a tendency to a movement: the activities of Jamāl al-Dīn Sāvī

According to Yazici, *Qalandariyya* arose as a movement when the *qalandarī* trend entered a new phase during the early thirteenth century, after Jamāl al-Dīn Sāvī (d. c. 1232/3) added to and systematised the existing corpus. Sāvī's role was so instrumental in transforming the *Qalandariyya* that it was basically a new movement, and Sāvī was then considered its founder.[40] This opinion harmonises with Karamustafa's argument that apart from literary evidence, we know very little about the *qalandar* as a social type prior to the thirteenth century.[41] The origin of shaving the head and bodily hair by *qalandarī* adherents, known as the ritual of *chahār żarb* (lit. "four blows") is unknown, but there is historical evidence that similar rituals were seen in other spiritual creeds.[42] However, we know that *qalandar*s shaved their heads and facial hair, wore hair-cloth garments and practised any illicit actions that were legally permissible.[43] Trimingham's list of the *qalandarī* characteristics is slightly different, as he claims the *qalandar*s did not shave their moustaches.[44] Trimingham also mentions a kind of behaviour adopted from the ascetic followers of Quṭb al-dīn Ḥaydar. Referring to Ibn Baṭṭūṭa's observation, Trimingham asserts that the *Ḥaydarī* group, centred in Khurāsān south of Mashhad, wore iron rings in their necks, hands and ears. They even wore rings in their male members, to deprive themselves of sexual intercourse. The *Ḥaydariyya* reached Iran, Anatolia, Syria and India, where it was finally absorbed into the *Qalandariyya*.[45] Thereafter, *Qalandariyya*-style non-normative behaviour had a significant impact on the whole Muslim world. Although the movement was provocative, it attracted a notable following, and it influenced a number of literary works.

Sāvī was also regarded as the founder of *Jawlaqiyya*, a branch of the *Qalandariyya* movement. The term *Jawlaqiyya* was based on a reference to the master's distinctive garment, the *jawlaq* (taken from the Persian *jawlaq* (lit. "sack-cloth"). In the first half of the thirteenth century, the movement spread into Anatolia. *Jawlaqī* convents were principally located in Anatolia and Egypt, but the movement also reached the Maghrib and India.[46] In India, the *Jawlaqī* adherents wore nothing but a blanket as their clothing, and they wrapped their loins in pieces of blanket or cotton sheet. They lived a carefree life, and utterly ignored all sorts of religious or social norms. Like the *Qalandar*s, the *Jawlaqī*s always created trouble upon visiting a *khanaqāh* or a *jamā'at khāna*. They did not conform to any established social convention or tradition, and unlike other mystics, they believed in intimidation and violence.[47] During the early fourteenth century in Anatolia, the *Qalandar*s were also referred to as *Abdālān-i Rūm* or *Shamsīyān*, and they remained active during the Ottoman period until the eighteenth century.[48] The word *abdāl* has been used, mainly in the Bektashi tradition, as "a sort of sobriquet for mystics such as Kaygusuz Abdāl and Pīr Sulṭān Abdāl". References to the *abdāl*, however, have appeared in Sufi texts as early as Sanā'ī's poetry, usually in discussing ascetics. Later, the word meant "a saint who after his death would be "substituted" for (*badal*) by another person".[49]

Sources on the *Qalandariyya*

The sources on the *Qalandariyya* are scarce and permeated with contradictions. Shafī'ī-Kadkanī mentions that much of what we know about the *Qalandariyya* is accusations marked by invective. He believes that the *Qalandar*s were known for different behaviour in the unknown period of their existence. They would break social norms, bring havoc to communities, and perform mendicancy in some eras. While in other periods, they were esteemed for their doctrine and intellectual worldviews.[50]

The information available about the early phase of the *Qalandariyya* comes from one source, namely the *Qalandar-nāma* by 'Abd Allāh Anṣārī (d. 1089). This book explained that the *qalandarī* system of thought advocated inner contentment, the avoidance of pretension, neglect of learning, and contempt for the ephemeral world.[51] However, both De Bruijn and Karamustafa referred to at least one other Sufi treatise, Suhravardī's *'Awārif al-ma'ārif*, in which we can find some additional information about the *Qalandariyya*.[52] In this treatise, Suhravardī enumerated the characteristics of *qalandar*s, while making a distinction between them and the adherents of the *Malamatiyya*.[53] Suhravardī wrote his treatise upon the formation of the Sufi *silsilas* ("orders"):

> The term *Qalandariyya* is applied to people so possessed by the intoxication of 'tranquillity of heart' that they respect no custom or usage and reject the regular observances of society and mutual relationship. Traversing the arenas of 'tranquillity of heart' they concern themselves little with ritual prayer and fasting except such as are obligatory (*farā'iż*). Neither do they concern themselves with those earthly pleasures which are allowed by the indulgence of divine law .... The difference between the *qalandarī* and the *malāmatī* is that the *malāmatī* strives to conceal his mode of life whilst the *qalandarī* seeks to destroy accepted custom.[54]

Some evidence in Persian literature indicates the existence of the *qalandarī* religious attitude before it developed into a full-fledged movement after the thirteenth century.[55] The *qalandar*, as a motif in Persian poetry, existed in the lyric genre and some other genres. However, it was only in the late eleventh and early twelfth century that *qalandar* appeared as a central character in a cluster of images in the *Qalandariyyāt* by Majdūd ibn Ādam Sanā'ī (d. 1131). The key motifs in the *qalandarī* cluster of images revolved around wine-drinking, gambling, sexual promiscuity, playing games of chess or backgammon and adherence to non-Islamic faiths (Christian and Zoroastrian in particular). These images were situated in the *kharābāt* (lit. "ruins", referring in reality to "taverns" or "brothels").[56] In the *qalandarī* terminology, the values normally attached to these words were nearly always reversed. Most of these key terms originally had strongly negative connotations, but they acquired highly positive meanings after being adopted as *qalandarī* terminology.[57]

The most recent study on the figure of the dervish (an umbrella term he uses for spiritual figures such as *qalandar*s and *abdāl*s among others) by Papas deserves a mention here. He does not approach these figures from the perspective of religious studies, but he gives different examples of the living presence of this spiritual figure in the vast expanse of Central Asia. Using the term "dervish" and "*qalandar*" interchangeably, Papas does not make a distinction between these two spiritual figures. He sees his book as "a fragmented historical journey" exploring "a desire for transgression and a return to the wild side of life" in Muslim societies.[58] In five chapters, he investigates cases in different regions of Central Asia and gives an overview of the rites and rituals performed by the *qalandar* dervishes, some of which still function as spiritual practices. He uses criteria such as these *qalandar* dervishes' religious tolerance and acceptance of believers and unbelievers alike, living in grottoes, using particular vernaculars, mendicancy, and having an itinerant life style among the reasons to categorise them as marginal figures.[59] Papas does not clarify what he considers as central when he argues marginality. However, his line of argument implies that he considers the institutionalised Sufi orders and the discursive Islamic tradition as orthodoxy versus *dervishhood* as heterodoxy.

Such a binary, as Ahmed argues, privileges the orthodox forms as the "powerful statements of Islam", versus the heterodox as the "less powerful forms".[60] The figures Papas introduces as *qalandar* dervishes may have a marginal position in Islamic societies. Such a marginal position, however, is meaningful when these figures are compared to dervish figures such as the Persian poet, Ḥāfiẓ (d. 1390), who according to Ahmed, was a "pervasive poetical, conceptual and lexical presence in the discourse of educated Muslims" across the Balkans-to-Bengal complex from the fifteenth to the late nineteenth century.[61] What is also unrecognised in Papas' argument is the conceptualisation of Islam as Ahmed does it, "a capacious manner that is attentive to and inclusive of the widest possible range and loci of self-statement of *being Muslim*".[62] Nevertheless, Papas' case studies are worthwhile for this chapter because they show the unbroken continuity of the diverse expressions that branched out of the centuries-old spiritual trend of *Qalandariyya*.

This overview of the limited sources available on the *Qalandariyya* movement indicates the importance of the *Qalandar-nāma* by Khaṭīb-i Fārsī. This hagiographical account is the only book available that focuses on Jamāl al-Dīn Sāvī and his spiritual career. The writer is an anonymous Persian preacher who wrote his account decades after Sāvī's death, probably with more than one intermediary. We also know that he was a devoted disciple, so probably, his account of Sāvī's life and spiritual career is tinted with bias. Nevertheless, and regardless of its historical accuracy, the investigation of this book can contribute to our knowledge of Sāvī's role in systematising the *Qalandariyya* as a movement.

Qalandar-nāma by Khatīb-i Fārsī: an introduction

Qalandar-nāma-yi Khatīb-i Fārsī or *Sīrat-i Jamāl al-Dīn Sāvī* is a book that mainly concerns the spiritual career of Jamāl al-Dīn Sāvī. It also discusses his interaction with three other well-known masters whom he initiates into the *qalandarī* path, namely, Jalāl al-Dīn Dargazīnī, Muḥammad Balkhī and Abū Bakr Ṣafāhānī. The book does not have a distinct title and its content describes the virtues and manners (*sīrat*) of Jamāl al-Dīn Sāvī. Apparently, Ḥamīd Zarrīnkūb, its editor, has chosen the title based on this content.[63] The other edition of this book, published by Tahsin Yazici in Ankara, is titled *Manāqib-i Jamāl al-Dīn Sāvī*.[64] *Manāqib*, as a genre, has specific characteristics.[65] It is a biographical account centred on not only an individual's "traits of character" and "acts and deeds", but also on their moral qualities. From the tenth century onwards, *manāqib* was used to refer to "laudatory biographies of the *īmāms*" who founded major legal schools, and elaborated on the *Sharīʿa*. Over time, it assumes a more pronounced hagiographical nature. It is used to narrate the manners, actions and qualities of revered saints or Ṣūfīs or any human being, considered a prodigy in the public mind.[66]

Zarrīnkūb used a manuscript version of the *Qalandar-nāma* that was available in the Suleymāniya library in Turkey.[67] This book was written in the *mathnavī* poetic form ("rhyming couplets"), and it consisted of 1,770 couplets, composed by an anonymous author who called himself 'Khaṭīb-i Fārsī' ("Persian preacher") at several points within the text.[68] Later, I shall continue this introduction of *Qalandar-nāma* and discuss Khaṭīb-i Fārsī's own explanation of his reason for authoring the book. However, since the structure of *Qalandar-nāma* is more important for my investigation, I shall now proceed with a close examination of the book's sections, according to Khaṭīb-i Fārsī's organisation.

Khaṭīb-i Fārsī begins the *Qalandar-nāma* with a section entitled *Yā mufattiḥ al-abvāb* ("O the Opener of the Doors"), which refers to one of God's attributes. Following tradition, the author dedicates this section to the praise of God and the Prophet Muḥammad, who chose "poverty" (*faqr*) although he was given command over the sky, the sun and both worlds. In his *Sharḥ-i iṣṭilāḥāt-i taṣavuf*, an encyclopaedic book, explaining terminology in Sufism, Sayyid-Ṣādiq Gowharīn, explains that for the Sufi seekers, the term *faqr* means "annihilation in God".[69] A reference in the Qur'ān may further clarify the connotations of *faqr* as a mystical term. In referring to the *Sura* Muḥammad, verse 38, Bonner postulates that *faqr* probably refers to mankind's neediness, in contrast to God's self-sufficiency. It may also refer to the human being's need for God, according to a verse in the *sura* Fāṭir.[70] The concept of poverty is central to the study of *Qalandar-nāma* and of Sāvī's role in shaping *Qalandariyya* as a movement, and I will return to this concept later in the chapter. However, for now it is important to mention that the first reference to *faqr* appears early in the *Qalandar-nāma*, and that Khaṭīb-i Fārsī connects this concept to the prophet. The other pivotal concept in this text, which I will interpret later, is that of being isolated (*mujarrad*). According to Shafīʿī-Kadkanī, *qalandars* would wish lasting *tajrīd* for each other.[71] In his study on Bābā Ḥājī ʿAbd al-Raḥīm's *Qalandar-nāma*, Afshari contends that "*tajrīd* is the most important *qalandarī* principle".[72]

۱۷. اگرچه هر دو عالم زان او بود
سپهر و مهر در فرمان او بود

نکرد او التفاتی بر دو عالم
که خاک پای او بد هر دو عالم

ز هر چیزی که در عالم ببخشید
مجرد گشت و ملک فقر بگزید[73]

17. Although both the worlds belonged to him
The sky and the sun were under his command

He did not pay attention to both the worlds
for, both the worlds were the dust under his feet

From all he gave away in the world,
he became a renunciant and chose the kingdom of poverty[74]

The book's next section is entitled "On the Reason for Versification of the Book". In this section's 62 couplets, Khaṭīb-i Fārsī explains why he wrote *Qalandar-nāma*.[75] He begins with a story of his quest for knowledge in schools (*madrasas*), where he learned about several secrets of the world and met perfect guides (*pīrān-i kāmil*). However, as many of his questions remained unanswered, he begged his guides to show him a way of searching for "Archetypal Ideas" (*maʿānī*). When they told him that he would find his answer through travelling, he left Shiraz, his hometown, and went to different Islamic cities. During his trip to Damascus to seek perfect masters, he went on pilgrimage to various places where the companions (*aṣḥāb*) of the prophet were buried. After his pilgrimage to the holy shrine of Bilāl Ibn Rabāḥ (d. 640), the Prophet Muḥammad's *muʾaẕẕin*, he met a group of peculiar *dervishes*.[76]

In describing such people, Khaṭīb-i Fārsī uses terms such as perfect guides (*pīrān-i kāmil*), *dervish*es and mystics (*ʿārifān*).[77] However, his encounter with a shaykh called Muḥammad from Bukhārā and his disciples is the first occasion where he refers to a group of *dervish*es as *qalandar*s. Khaṭīb-i Fārsī's description of this group and their saint is noteworthy for its references to the principle of poverty. In couplet 55, we read that this group of mystics are willing not only to gamble their heads, but also their world and religion to pursue the path of love. This couplet implies that the *qalandar*s are ready for absolute detachment from everything. The next couplet states that the world is a palm-full of dust before the *dervish*es' aspiration (*himmat*), which re-emphasises their readiness for giving up every form of worldly possession.[78] However, when describing their master, Khaṭīb-i Fārsī uses the term *faqīr* (lit. "a mendicant" (n.) or "poor" (adj.)). Gowharīn explains *fuqarā* (pl. of *faqīr*) as the people who, for the sake of seeking the Truth, have abstained from gaining any worldly possessions.[79] The application of *faqīr*, a derivative of the key term *faqr*, indicates that this guide is a perfect *dervish*, a mendicant, a drunk and an eloquent mystic:[80]

۵۵. گروهی عارفان دیدم سرانداز
به کوی عاشقی دنیا و دین باز

قلندرصورتانی چند چالاک
جهان در پیش همتشان کف خاک

یکی درویش کامل پیر ایشان
فقیری عارفی مست سخندان[81]

55. I saw a group of mystics, (ready to) offer their heads,
gambling the world and religion on the path of love

The *Qalandar*-faced so vigilant
that the world was a palm-full of dust before their aspiration

A perfect mystic was their saint
A man of poverty, a drunk, eloquent mystic.

As a result of this encounter, Khaṭīb-i Fārsī is entrusted with the versification of the *Qalandar-nāma*. He becomes a devout disciple of Shaykh Muḥammad, and benefits from his presence. After some time, Shaykh Muḥammad gives him a pamphlet describing the spiritual states of Jamāl al-Dīn Sāvī, and asks him to versify it. The principle of poverty also plays a role in this entrustment. Couplet 64, where *faqr* is explicitly mentioned, implies that being immersed in poverty is the condition for being entrusted to write about Sāvī:

ازو دریوزه می کردم دمادم
همی گشتم زانفاسش مکرم

٦۴. مرا فرمود پیر راه روزی
که گر داری ز درد فقر سوزی

فرو خوان سیرت پیر زمانه
جمال الدین ساوی آن یگانه[82]

I begged of him breath by breath
while I became from revered through his breaths

64. One day the master of the path told me,
If you have a fire from the pain of poverty

Call to read the manners of the saint of Time
Jamāl al-Dīn Sāvī, the unique one

This introductory section also bears some information about the date of Khaṭīb-i Fārsī's encounter with the *qalandar*s, and when Sāvī founded his path. At the beginning of the *Qalandar-nāma*, Khaṭīb-i Fārsī states that Sāvī established the *qalandarī* path 382 years after *Ḥijra* (961 CE). This claim does not correspond to the date given in other sources, or in other parts of the book:

زهجرت سیصد و هشتاد و دو بود
که سید سکه ای بنیاد فرمود[83]

It was 382 (years) after *Ḥijra*
that the Sayyid founded his path

Still later in the book, the author states that he was appointed to versify the account of Sāvī 748 years after the *Ḥijra* (1327 CE):

زهجرت بود هفتصد و چهل و هشت
که این اقبال و دولت یار من گشت[84]

It was 748 (years) after *Ḥijra*
that this ascending fortune and prosperity became my companion.

In the closing lines of this section, Khaṭīb-i Fārsī emphasises the principle of poverty again. This time he refers to it as a distinguishing characteristic for *dervishes* who have some understanding of its importance. He hopes that his readers will grasp the power of the book's Archetypal Ideas, and that they will make his soul joyful with *a takbīr*[85].

The next part of the *Qalandar-nāma* is essential to this investigation of the role that Jamāl al-Dīn Sāvī played in systematising the *Qalandariyya* movement.

Poverty: a prerequisite for becoming a *qalandar*

To better understand how the *Qalandariyya* grew into a movement, it is essential to trace how the concept of a "journey of poverty" is developed in the *Qalandar-nāma*. In a forty-one-couplet section entitled "On the Qualities of the Virtue of Poverty", Khaṭīb-i Fārsī theorised the concept of poverty in the context of the post-Sāvī *Qalandariyya* community. As the title reveals, *faqr* is a virtue with qualities that deserve to be explained. Khaṭīb-i Fārsī was entrusted to versify Sāvī's hagiography because he was a devout and trusted disciple of Shaykh Muḥammad Balkhī, who was one of the three saints in Sāvī's immediate circle of companions. Therefore, his treatment of "poverty" can probably be taken as a reliable representation regarding the central role of this principle after the *Qalandariyya* had become a systematised movement. A close reading of Khaṭīb-i Fārsī's attitude towards poverty, and his account of Sāvī's life, can shed light on this saint's process of codifying the *Qalandariyya*, and the role of poverty in the process. To follow the structure of the book, I begin with the close reading of Khaṭīb-i Fārsī's argument about poverty.

"On the Qualities of the Virtue of Poverty" presents an intricate design of coherent parts, each with their own subsections. For the sake of clarity, I use capital letters for the names of the main "parts", and small letters for the names of the subsections. Part A comprises couplets 85–105, part B comprises couplets 106–122 and part C comprises couplets 123–127. Part A has four subsections. In subsection a) (couplets 85–88), the poet introduces himself, hints at his reason for versifying the text, and refers to the high spiritual rank of people who embrace poverty. These couplets serve as the introduction to both part A and to the whole section. Subsection b) elaborates on the superior rank of the prophet (couplets 89–95), and then subsection c) links the Prophet's superior rank to his choice of poverty (couplets 96–100). Finally, subsection d) (couplets 101–105) summarises the importance of poverty, the Prophet's devotion to it, and its connection to the book's Archetypal Ideas. Khaṭīb-i Fārsī quotes a prophetic *ḥadīth* to separate this part from the rest of his argument. Part B presents a theorisation of poverty through explaining the characteristics and deeds of people who seek poverty as a spiritual practice. Finally, part C gives an overall conclusion (couplets 123–127). With this structural outline of Khaṭīb-i Fārsī's arguments, I shall proceed with its translation and interpretation:

Part A

Subsection a

در صفت فضیلت فقر

On the Qualities of the Virtue of Poverty

۸۵. الا ای بلبل گلزار اسرار
کلید از بند گنج نطق بردار

اگر خواهی که از فقرت رسد بوی
سخن چندان که بتوانی در آن گوی

حدیث از فقر [و] درویشی کن آغاز
سخنهای فقیرانه بپرداز

خوشا و خرمّا وقت فقیران
که سلطانند بر شاهان و میران[86]

85. O the nightingale of the rose garden of secrets,[87]
lift the key off the chain on the treasure of speech

If you want to get into the tradition of poverty,[88]
speak about it however much you can.

Start stories of poverty and dervishhood
adorn speeches about manners of the poor

May the Time of the poor be pleasant and cheerful
for they are the sultans (ruling) over kings and rulers.

Khaṭīb-i Fārsī's language in theorising the concept of poverty is mystical. In the first three couplets he uses the famous metaphor of the nightingale and the rose garden from Persian poetry to address himself as the poet. As Schimmel explains, the nightingale has long symbolised the longing soul in Persian literature.[89] She draws on the words of Rūzbihān Baqlī (d. 1209), one of the great Iranian mystics, to show that in mystical language the nightingale represents "the soul longing for eternal beauty". The nightingale tirelessly praises the rose, suffers the stings of its thorns without complaint, and tells the story of its longing.[90] In addition to this mystical layer of meaning, the metaphor of the nightingale probably has a connection with depictions of the Prophet Muḥammad given by Sufis. Schimmel argues that the Sufi love of roses probably reflects Muḥammad's love for the red rose, which is commonly described in Sufi stories. In one such story, the prophet reportedly showed his love for roses by putting one on his eyes, and saying that "The red rose is part of God's glory". Schimmel indicates that such accounts might have led a number of poets to call Muḥammad "the nightingale of the Eternal Garden," because it was Muḥammad who disclosed the mysteries of the Everlasting Rose to the faithful.[91] Therefore, we see an implied similarity between Muḥammad and Khaṭīb-i Fārsī. The poet praises himself by mentioning that he also is aware of the secrets of the rose garden.[92] Yet in the next two couplets, he elevates the rank of *faqr* by implying that although he may be "the nightingale of the garden of secrets" he is still longing for its scent. In the next couplet, he praises the poor, describing them as the rulers of the kings of the world. These couplets establish the idea that these people have the highest rank imaginable in this world.

Subsection b

خدای ذوالجلال پاک جبار
جهان و هر چه در وی کرد اظهار

۹۰. همه از بهر ذات مصطفی کرد
پس او را بر دو عالم پادشا کرد

ز آب و آتش [و] از باد [و] از خاک
سپهر و انجم و ارواح و افلاک

هر آن چیزی که در کون و مکان است
طفیل خاتم پیغمبران است

دو کون از بهر آن مهمان او بود
که ما زاغ البصر در شأن او بود

اگرچه لطفهای حق تعالی
بدو بخشیده بد دنیا و عقبی

۹۵. بدان سلطانی و شاهی ننازید
رها کرد او جهان و فقر بگزید

قال النّبی علیه السلام: انا سیّدُ ولدِ آدمَ ولافَخرَ[93]

The prophet said, 'I am the pride of the children of Adam but I do not take pride (in it)'.

God, the Glorious, the Pure, the Almighty
manifested the world and all there is in it

90. He did all of that for the sake of Muṣṭafā's soul[94]
Then He assigned Muṣṭafā the kingdom of the two worlds

From water and fire and wind and dust
the sky and stars and spirits and spheres

Whatever that there is in existence and the world
is the uninvited guest (or parasite) of the seal of the prophets[95]

The two worlds are his guests, for
'his eye swerved not' was said of his rank[96]

Although God's benevolence
had entrusted to him the world and the hereafter

95. He did not take pride in that authority and kingdom
He gave up the world and chose poverty.

In this section, Khaṭīb-i Fārsī describes and justifies the superior rank of poverty among spiritual practices. To make his argument more powerful, he deploys the two central elements of the Qur'ān and the Prophet's *ḥadīth*s in the following five couplets (89–93). First he elaborates on the status of Muḥammad, stating that he is the reason for God's creation (89–90), and asserts that all the created beings in the universe are Muḥammad's guests. This is Khaṭīb-i Fārsī's allusion to an inauthentic *ḥadīth* that says, "Allah Most High says I swear it by My Power and My Glory! Were it not for you [O Muḥammad], I would not have created the world".[97] Then, by using the phrase «ما زاغ البصر», he alludes to a Qur'ānic verse, 53:15, which states that Muḥammad's eyes were not distracted when he saw Gabriel. Then, in couplets 94–95, Khaṭīb-i Fārsī connects Muḥammad with poverty, by stating that he chose poverty over all that God gave him in this world.

Subsection c

اگرچه کرده یزدانم مکرم
بزرگم کرد بر اولاد آدم

اگرچه روز محشر پیش دیوان
شفیع امتان باشم [به] یزدان

اگرچه انبیا چندان که باشند
مرا هم تابع و هم خواجه تاشند

به قدر همتم کون و مکان نیست
وزینها مرمرا فخر جهان نیست

۱۰۰. نمی نازم به سلطانیّ [و] صدری
فقیری جسته ام الفَقرُ فَخری[98]

Although God has held me revered,
[and] has put me [in rank] above the children of Adam

Although on the day of resurrection before the court
I will be the people's intercessor

[and] however [high] the prophets may be,
They are my subjects and fellow-servants

What is in existence and in the world does not match me in rank
And through these I do not take pride in the world

100. I do not take pride in kingdom and supremacy
I have sought poverty; poverty is my pride.

The argument enters its most crucial phase in couplets 96–100, as Khaṭīb-i Fārsī continues presenting Muḥammad as the speaker. Therefore, it is as if Muḥammad himself is endorsing Khaṭīb-i Fārsī's claims regarding the Prophet's rank. He asserts his status as being the intercessor (or intermediary) for all people on the day of resurrection, and claims his superiority over all of the other prophets. Probably, the author is reiterating claims that already existed in the tradition. By emphasising Muḥammad's rank over all other prophets, and by including him in the circle of *faqīrān*, Khaṭīb-i Fārsī recalls the image of the prophet in the Sufi tradition. According to Lindholm, Muḥammad is considered in the Sufi tradition to have been sent by God as both the final Prophet, and as a perfect man "to maintain the order of the universe". In esoteric language, the prophet was the cosmic pivot (*quṭb*) bringing the world to perfection.[99] Yet the most important couplet in Khaṭīb-i Fārsī's elaboration on the virtue of poverty is couplet 100, in which he alludes to an allegedly prophetic *ḥadīth*. So in addition to having the prophet himself say that he has chosen poverty, Khaṭīb-i Fārsī reports that he also said, "Poverty is my pride". The *sīra* (the Prophet's biography) contains intermittent references to poverty and the poor.[100] However, it is significant that the *ḥadīth* reported by Khaṭīb-i Fārsī is evaluated as a fabrication.[101] It is also noteworthy that although accumulating wealth is described as useless in numerous *sura*s in the Qurʾān (e.g., 15:84; 69:28; 92:11; 111:1–2, etc.), or a temptation that leads humanity away from God, wealth is generally regarded as permissible, and even desirable under certain conditions. What the tradition reproaches is hoarding, arrogance and avarice, because such behaviour indicates a desire for independence from God.[102]

It is also important to mention that, as Schimmel contends, the Sufis transmitted stories surrounding the prophet through their interpretation of *ḥadīth* and the

Qur'ān, which shaped their ideas about him. The Sufis used Muḥammad's poverty as their model for mystical poverty. According to Schimmel, this was the Prophet's way to educate his *shayṭān*, (base faculties), which prefigured the Sufis' ceaseless struggles with their *nafs* (lower selves).[103] It is also worth mentioning that a specific form of poverty was a highlighted aspect of piety promoted by Ibn Karrām, the founder of the *Karrāmiyya*. Believing that work interfered with complete trust in God's provision (*tawakkul*), Ibn Karrām prohibited work for profit. This doctrine flourished in the tenth and eleventh centuries in Nishapur. It was promoted by Ibn Karrām's followers who advocated renunciation (*zuhd*), self-mortification (*taqashshuf*), mendicancy, prohibition of work for profit and complete trust in God.[104] Through my discussion, however, I shall demonstrate how poverty was transformed into a sophisticated *qalandarī* concept through Sāvī's linking it to self-imposed death as the ultimate form of detachment from the material world. I shall also argue that, based on the reports of Sāvī's reception as described in the *Qalandar-nāma*, the teaching of holy poverty evoked criticism from the Muslim society. Sāvī's linkage between the prophet and the virtues of poverty probably did not contribute to popularisation of the *Qalandariyya*.

Subsection d

ببین تا فخر و آزادی چه کارست
که او را بر دوعالم اختیار است

کسی کو رنگ [و] بوی فقر دارد
بدو شاه جهانبان[105] فخر دارد

اگر از فقر بودی هیچ بهتر
بکردی اختیار آنرا پیمبر

دو عالم را بنگرفت اعتباری
فقیری جست از هر کار و باری

۱۰۵. محقق شد از آن عالم که معنی است
به از فقرو تجرّد دولتی نیست[106]

Behold what affair pride and liberation are
for he has authority over both worlds

The one who has the majesty of poverty[107]
The world-guardian king envies him

If there was anything better than poverty,
The prophet would choose that

He did not take the two worlds as a warning[108]
He sought poverty from every affair and burden

105. It is ascertained from the (other) world that is Archetypal Idea,
There is no fortune better than poverty and detachment.

Praise for poverty is the heart of Khaṭīb-i Fārsī's conclusion for section A. His repeated reference to this keyword supports his argument in terms of both its content and structure. In the remaining couplets he goes back to his main argument concerning the merits of poverty by emphasising that despite his superior rank, Muḥammad chose poverty. He concludes his argument with a declaration that nothing is better than poverty. This statement is presented not as Khaṭīb-i Fārsī's personal opinion, but as the result of "ascertaining" truths from the world of Archetypal Ideas. In this way, he aims to secure the place of poverty as credible, and leave no room for any doubts.

Part B

۱۰۶. فقیران کمزنان کایناتند
که صاحب[109] همّت و عالی صفاتند

فقیران اهل اسرار کمالند
که ایشان خاصگان ذوالجلالند

فقیرانند کاندر ملک سبحان
بدیشان قایمست افلاک [و] ارکان

فقیرانند کاندر روز محشر
بدیشان مفتخر باشد پیمبر[110]

106. The poor are the professional gamblers in the world of created beings
who are esteemed for aspiration and the highest virtues

The poor are the people of secrets of perfection
For, they are the intimates of God, the Glorious

It is for the poor who in the kingdom of the most Holy

Spheres and pillars are upright[111]

It is the poor in whom on the Judgement Day
The prophet takes pride.

Khaṭīb-i Fārsī starts his theorisation of poverty as the highest virtue by presenting a well-organised catalogue of the characteristics of *faqīrān*. With 21 couplets, this is the longest part in the book. The first four couplets in section B almost serve as an introduction to the catalogue. As his recurrent references to the terminology of gambling indicate, the most prominent quality of *faqīrān* is being like a professional gambler. Khaṭīb-i Fārsī introduces *faqīrān* as professional gamblers in the first hemistich, but he adds a paradoxical twist to this description. In the second hemistich of the same couplet, he states that *faqīrān* are the people most esteemed for aspiration and the highest virtues. This description prepares the reader for an introduction of a specific type of gambler. Next the author proceeds to praise the *faqīrān*'s rank in relation to God, to the created world, and finally in relation to the Prophet Muḥammad, while also referring to their ranks on the Judgement Day. In addition to creating a coherent structure, Khaṭīb-i Fārsī strengthens his case of promoting poverty as a superior characteristic of Sufis by asserting their rank before God and his Prophet.

۱۱۰. فقیرانند کاندر هر دو گیهان
ندارند التفاتی جز به جانان

فقیرانند صاحب دولتانی
که دربازند[112] هر ساعت جهانی

فقیرانند کاندر پرده راز
غزل خوانند خوش بی حرف [و] آواز

فقیرانند کز دلشان خبرهاست
ز جانان سوی جانانشان نظرهاست[113]

فقیرانند عشاق سرانداز
بیک بازی دو عالم را برانداز

۱۱۵. فقیرانند در دنیا سبکبار[114]
گرانبارند دیگر خلق ناچار

فقیرانند کز خلق دو عالم
سر مویی ندارد جانشان غم

فقیرانند اهل ذوق [و] عرفان
که ایشان راست عشق [و] شوق سبحان

فقیرانند اصحاب طریقت
فقیرانند ارباب حقیقت

فقیران راست معراج و مقامات
که بر سر هستشان تاج کرامات

۱۲۰. فقیران راست بر آفاق شاهی
که ایشانند عشاق الهی

فقیران راست ذوق [و] شوق صحبت
فقیران ساختند آداب صحبت

فقیران از دو گیتی بی نیازند
که صاحب دولتان پاکبازند[115]

110. It is the poor in both the worlds
Pay attention to nothing but the beloved

The poor are esteemed for fortune
who gamble a world in every hour

It is the poor who in the veil (or melody) of secrets
Sing *ghazal*s cheerfully without letters and songs

It is the poor who are aware of the heart
Towards whose soul there are gazes from the beloved

The poor are the lovers ready to throw their heads
In one game [of polo] uprooting two worlds[116]

115. The poor are light-burdened in the world
[while] The other people [are] helpless

It is the poor who among the people in both worlds
whose souls do not have sorrow, as much as the tip of a hair

The poor are the people of spiritual savour and mysticism
who have the love and passionate longing for the most Holy

The poor are the companions of the path
The poor are the masters of the truth

As for the poor, they have Muḥammad's rank and night of ascent to heaven,
for they have the crown of miracles on their heads

120. As for the poor, they have the kingdom of horizons
for, they are the Godly lovers

As for the poor, they have spiritual savour and passionate longing of intimacy
The poor created the manners of intimacy

The poor are needless of the two worlds
For they are the all-gambling, esteemed for fortune.

In couplets 100–122, the tone of praise vanishes, and the catalogue of poverty's characteristics is presented. Through these couplets, we see who the *faqīrān* are and how they have gained their rank. Their first characteristic is their unwavering attention to the Beloved, above all that there is in both this world and the hereafter. Couplet 111 is Khaṭīb-i Fārsī's bridge to the first couplet, which reiterates his statement about the *faqīrāns*' dexterity in gambling. In addition to representing the *faqīrān* as notorious gamblers, the couplet implies that the people of poverty have access to an endless fortune. Despite giving away a world every hour, they are esteemed for their fortune, which implies that their fortune is otherworldly in essence. Couplet 114 is another reference to gambling; this time these professional gamblers are ready to gamble their heads and lose both worlds. This implies that these Sufis expect a reward neither in this world nor in the hereafter. The next couplet conveys a similar meaning: the poor are *sabuk-bār*, light-burdened and ready to start a journey, which is a metaphor for their detachment from the material engagements of this world. Referring to the prophet in couplets 119 and 120, Khaṭīb-i Fārsī once more elevates the rank of the poor as high as that of Muḥammad. The author then closes the catalogue with another reference to the poor's detachment from both worlds, and a final reference to their being gamblers.

Part C

خداوندا به استغنای ذاتت
به لطف عام و آثار صفاتت

که ما را با فقیران آشنا کن
دل ما معدن صدق و صفا کن

۱۲۵. ز خاک درگهت بویی به ما بخش
گناه ما به موی مصطفی بخش

بیا تا دست ازین عالم بشوییم
قلندروار تکبیری بگوییم[117]

O God, for the sake of the needlessness that is your essence,
for the sake of your universal benevolence and the effects of your attributes

Acquaint us with the poor
Turn our hearts into the mine of truth and purity

125. From the dust of your court, entrust us with [some] scent
Forgive our sin for the sake of Muṣṭafā's hair

Let's wash this world off our hands
Utter a *takbīr* like a *qalandar.*

Part C of the section on the virtues of poverty is Khaṭīb-i Fārsī's conclusion, in which he begs God to bestow upon him (and his readers) acquaintance with the poor. He also makes a final reference to the prophet as the intercessor to redeem humans from their errors. The very last couplet is an invitation for the readers to join him in detachment from this world, and to shout a *takbīr* like a *qalandar*. This significant couplet is repeated as the closing line of all sections in the book, and it implies longing on the part of Khaṭīb-i Fārsī, and of all those seeking *maʿnī* ("meanings," "Archetypal Ideas"), to adopt *qalandarī* manners. In this section, glorifying poverty and its adherents takes on a much deeper significance. It can be interpreted as saying that even those who have adopted poverty, including the Prophet, have not attained the rank of a *qalandar*.

The spiritual career of Jamāl al-Dīn Sāvī

Sāvī is regarded as the founder of the *Qalandariyya* by all the sources on the movement. However, as mentioned before, the term *qalandar* had already appeared in Sufi treatises and Persian poetry. Also, we have little information about the transformation of *Qalandariyya* into a movement, or about Sāvī's role in the process. According to Karamustafa, Sāvī's spiritual life can be divided into three stages. In the early stage of his career he was a very well-respected young Sufi master, delivering sermons on the Qur'ān and on *ḥadīth* (the reported sayings of Muḥammad), and expressing mainstream views on *taṣawwuf*. In the second stage, Sāvī sought to practise what he had preached, and started roaming with forty of his disciples. In the last stage of life, he became a *qalandar*, who had freed himself from the two worlds through *muwt-i irādī* (self-imposed death). At this stage, Sāvī appeared as the embodiment of the *ḥadīth* "die before you die": he went about naked and hairless, he sat on graves facing the direction of Mecca, was motionless and silent, without any sleep, and fed on nothing but wild weeds.[118]

This account presents a picture of how a *qalandar* looks, yet the close reading of the *Qalandar-nāma*, the only hagiography of Sāvī, can reveal how this influential character systematised the movement. The *Qalandar-nāma* is structured into stories revolving around Sāvī and his interactions with his masters, disciples or the Muslim community. I shall go through the whole book, and focus on the main accounts in which the codification of *Qalandariyya* happens.

Khaṭīb-i Fārsī introduces Sāvī early in the *Qalandar-nāma*, describing him through the eyes of the great mystic Bāyazīd Basṭāmī. This introduction begins as Bāyazīd Basṭāmī is sending Shaykh ʿUthmān-i Rūmī to Sāvī. ʿUs̱mān-i Rūmī is a seeker who has gone through forty stages of the spiritual journey under Bāyazīd Basṭāmī's guidance, and is now ready to complete it under Sāvī's guidance. It is important to examine Basṭāmī's description of the stages that ʿUthmān-i Rūmī has gone through, because it shows Sāvī's rank when he is introduced later:

پس از بسیار سالش پیر بسطام
به خلوت گفت روزی کای نکونام

بسی اندر طریقت سعی کردی
دراین ره خون دل بسیار خوردی

خداوندت بسی نور [و] صفا داد
در تحقیق بر روی تو بگشاد

۱۶۵. چل و یک منزلست اندر طریقت
که بروی بگذرد اهل حقیقت

قدم در ره نهادی تا به مردی
چهل منزل از آنها قطع کردی

ترا باقیست یک منزل در این راه
که از توحید گردد جانت آگاه

اگرچه با تو ما را اتفاق است
حوالتگاه تو ملک عراق است

یکی از دوستان ما در آنجاست
تمامی کارت از وی می شود راست[119]

After many years, the saint of Basṭām
one day said in intimacy, O you well-reputed (one)

You tried so much on the path of *ṭarīqa*
On this path you drank much blood of the heart

God bestowed upon you much light and purity
He opened to you the gate of ascertaining the truth

165. There are forty-one stages in *ṭarīqa*
through which pass the people of Truth

When you set foot on the path in a manly manner
you have cut through forty of them

As for you, there remains one stage
until your soul becomes aware of *towḥīd*[120]

Although we are in communion with you,
your next resting place is the territory of Iraq

One of our friends is there
your work will become completely upright by him.

When ʿUthmān-i Rūmī asks about the signs by which he can find Sāvī, Basṭāmī describes Sāvī as follows:

۱۸۰. یکی مردیست اندر ساوه امروز
مبارک روی [و] صاحب فر و پیروز

که اندر علم و اند زهد و تقوی
میان عاشقان مانند او نی

پسر دارد یکی صاحبقرانی[121]
ز منظوران ربانی جوانی[122]

زهر علمی که در ملک جهان است
سراسر پیش ذهن او عیانست

ز شرعیات و معقولات یکسر
خبر دارد زهی نور منور

۱۸۵. ز اولاد محمد و آل پاکست
وجودش بس شریف و خاکناک است
...

۱۹۱. چو تاج فقر بر فرقش نهادند
کلید گنج توحیدش بدادند
...

۱۹۳. کنونش با فقیران اتفاق است
چنان دانم که در ملک عراق است[123]

180. There is a man today in Sava,
auspicious-faced and esteemed for glory and favoured by fortune

Who, in knowledge and asceticism and piety
there is no one like him among lovers

The boy has such fortune and invincibility
in divine approval, (he is such) a youth

From every knowledge in the kingdom of the world
(it is) all visible before his mind

From affairs of *sharīʿa* and reasoning (or philosophy) in total,
he is aware; what a face! the illuminated (or the elucidated light)[124]

185. He is from the children of Muḥammad and the pure progeny
His existence is so noble and down to earth
...

191. When they crowned him with poverty,
they gave him the key to *towḥīd*
...

193. Now he is in company of the poor
As [far as] I know, he is in the kingdom of Iraq.

As these lines show, Sāvī was already an esteemed, knowledgeable preacher, and an ascetic who was practising *faqr*, probably before he settled in Iraq and became a *qalandar*.[125] The significance of this point is that it shows how the station of being a *qalandar* is acknowledged as higher than all other stages for those on the spiritual path. Later, Khaṭīb-i Fārsī gives examples of incidents by which his reader can observe and attest that Basṭāmī's description of Sāvī is true. He takes the readers through sessions starting with questions, where Sāvī demonstrates his knowledge of *sharīʿa*, mysticism and reasoning through his persuasive answers. One of these sessions concerns the virtue of *faqr* and the other concerns travelling, both of which Sāvī claims are recommended by the Prophet.

The first place where traces of the codification of the *Qalandariyya* can be found is the story of Sāvī's meeting with Jalāl al-Dīn Dargazīnī. To practise what he preaches, Sāvī decides to set foot on the path, and is accompanied by ʿUthmān-i Rūmī.[126] Now, Khaṭīb-i Fārsī has prepared the readers for the final station on Sāvī's spiritual journey.

When they reach Iraq, Sāvī meets Jalāl al-Dīn Dargazīnī, a naked ascetic near the Shrine of Zaynab in Damascus. Dargazīnī has eaten nothing but vegetables (*giyāh*) for thirty years, and has spoken to others only if necessary. Sāvī is moved by his encounter with this ascetic to improve his soul through *maʿnī*. Dargazīnī's reply to Sāvī is key here: he asks Sāvī to detach himself from everything all at once, as a result of which Sāvī will see or perceive the countenance of the Soul, or the Beloved. This is what Sāvī was longing for, and was sent to Dargazīnī by Bāyazīd Basṭāmī to experience, as the forty-first and final station on the spiritual path:

٥٧٦. بگفت ای پیر در حالم نظر کن
بمعنی جان ما را بهره‌ور کن

جوابش داد پیر صاحب اسرار
که گر خواهی که یابی ذوق دیدار

برون رو یکدم از چاه عوایق
ببر یکبارگی بند علایق

که آنگه طلعت جان را ببینی
محقق روی جانان را ببینی[127]

576. He said, O saint, cast a glance at my state
Benefit our soul through the Archetypal Idea

The saint esteemed for secrets replied to him
If you want to find the spiritual savour of vision

Go out of the well of obstacles for [as long as] a breath
Cut the bonds of attachments

For, at that moment you will see the countenance of the soul
It is ascertained that you will see the countenance of the beloved

In the following couplets Dargazīnī becomes silent again, and the transformation of Sāvī begins through experiencing a strange state (*ḥālat-i ʿajīb*) in his soul and heart:

۵۸۰. بگفت این چند لفظ و دم فروبست
جمال الدین بشد یکباره از دست

بمعنی شورشی در جانش افتاد
خروشی در دل سوزانش افتاد

عجایب حالتی او را شد املا
نماندش طاقت صبر و مدار[ا][128]

580. He said these words and became silent
Jamāl al-Dīn was lost all at once

In essence, some insurrection befell his soul
Some state of commotion befell his burning heart

Some strange state filled him up
As for him, there remained no tolerance of patience or forbearance

He becomes restless and impatient, and prays for divine intervention, while he states that the only thing he longs for is God himself. For him, his union with God means liberation from both religion (or the material world) and the hereafter. Couplets 585 and 586 are noteworthy because of the distinctions that he makes between different parts of his being. Referring to the agreement of his tongue and heart as a witness for his truthful aspirations articulated verbally, he longs for the joy of his soul (*ravā*) through the light of acquaintance with God. This implies that the medium through which he would perceive God is his soul. He is longing for total union, so that there will remain no distance, even as thin as a (filament of hair):

دعا کرد آنزمان گفتارالهی[129]
تویی داننده حالم کماهی

تو می‌دانی که من هر دم ز دنیا
ترا می خواهم از دنیا و عقبی

۵۸۵. اگر هستم درین گفتار صادق
زبان و دل بهم دارم موافق

روانم کن به نور معرفت شاد
مرا از دینی و عقبی کن آزاد[130]

چنان گردان به نور حق مزین
که از دنیا نماند هیچ با من

غبار ظلمتم از پیش بردار
حجاب راه من یک موی مگذار[131]

At that moment, he prayed and said,
'You are aware of my state as it is'.

You know that [at] every breath from the world, I
want you from the world and the hereafter

585. If I am truthful in this speech,
[If] I have [my] tongue and heart in agreement

Make my soul cheerful through the light of acquaintance (or knowledge)
Liberate me from this world and the hereafter

Embellish [me] through the light of Truth in such a way that
There remains nothing from the world with me

Lift the dust of error (or darkness) from before me
Do not allow a [filament of] hair to be the veil of my path

Khaṭīb-i Fārsī's shift to the third person narrator to recount the rest of the story, and his presentation of Sāvī's movement to isolation, boost the central motif of this saint's initiation to perfection. In the first couplet, the narrator describes the mysterious space in which Sāvī's spiritual transformation to complete detachment from the material world is about to happen:

بگفت اینها [و] سر در خود فرو برد
پس از یک ساعتی چو[ن] سربرآورد

۵۹۰. نبوده بر همه اعضاش یک موی
نه اندر سر نه اندر ریش و ابرو

چو مجنونی از آن مشهد برون جست
ز مستی شیشه سالوس بشکست

سراسر حرفها از دل برآورد
نثار جمعی از نظارگان کرد

به صحرا شد حشایش پاره‌ای چند
زاطراف و کنار جوی برکند

از آنها کرد خود را سترپوشی
دلش هر دم فزون می زد خروشی[132]

He said these and carried his head down.
when he raised his head after an hour,

590. There was no [filament of] hair on his [body] members
neither on [his] head, nor his beard or eyebrows

He jumped out of that holy sepulchre like a madman
[and] broke the glass of hypocrisy through drunkenness

He uttered all the words
[and] offered them to an assembly of spectators

He went to the desert [and] plucked some dry grass
from sides of the stream

From them, he made a loin-cover for himself
[while] his heart cried in lamentation more and more at every breath

Sāvī sinks into a deep meditative state, and when he comes out of that state he has become hairless. The representation of this incident implies that (if his prayers have been answered) there is a connection between his hairlessness and reaching the final station on the spiritual path: total detachment from everything, and union with God. This is interesting because Sāvī is already represented as practising poverty, which may seem like a similar concept, but Dargazīnī makes a distinction between the two concepts. The rest of the piece explains Sāvī's new level of detachment, and differentiates it from poverty as presented up to this point. This is worth meticulous attention, because up to this point in the text, poverty has been praised particularly as a prophetic practice. From now on, "poverty" is replaced with another concept or practice, i.e., total detachment from everything, through a particular and previously inexplicable (at least up to this point in the text) state of consciousness.

The characteristics woven into Sāvī's image from this moment on can be taken as defining what being a *qalandar* means. The first, most obvious and probably the most important characteristic is hairlessness. Then Sāvī is described with the word *majnūn*, which is ambiguous, as it can be interpreted as an allusion to Niẓāmī's *Laylī and Majnūn*.[133] In this epic romance, Qeys ibn Mulawwaḥ al-ʿĀmirī, who fell madly in love with Laylī, became known as *Majnūn*. However, he transcended his love for her, and as Seyed-Gohrab postulates, became a *qalandarī* mystic.[134] This term can also be taken as indicating its literal meaning: "mad". Then comes drunkenness. However, we were told earlier that Sāvī was a devout preacher and that during their journey, he was the *Imām* (the leader of the congregational *ṣalāt* prayers) of his companions in the mosque for the morning prayers.[135] After fulfilling this religious duty, Sāvī would visit the holy shrines alone, as was the tradition of ascetic elder guides.[136] We cannot be certain about the nature of Sāvī's drunkenness mentioned here. However, as there is no talk of (grape) wine, his drunkenness refers to the intoxicating effect of his spiritual experience in the grave. Moreover, Khaṭīb-i Fārsī associates drunkenness with breaking the glass of hypocrisy. Khaṭīb-i Fārsī's old image of Sāvī was as a respected Sufi master, preaching to large crowds of people. Khaṭīb-i Fārsī's metaphoric language implies that Sāvī became drunk after being initiated into the rank of a *qalandar*, and that his previous socio-religious status was one of hypocrisy. The last characteristic, completing the new image of Sāvī, paints him as naked, with a loin cover made of dried plants.

۵۹۵. بیامد در حضور پیر و بنشست
بیکبار از حکایت دم فرو بست

کم و بیش آنچه بودش جمله درباخت
بکلی صورت ظاهر برانداخت

زبهر خود مرتب کرد یکی گور
نشست اندر میانش همچنان عور

جلال درگزینی آن ولایت
چو از سید بدید آن حد [و] غایت

یقین گشتش که پیر از کاملانست
بمعنی در مقام واصلانست

٦۰۰. دگرگون گشت وی را جمله احوال
ز جای خویشتن برجست فی‌الحال

چو بود اندر مقام عشق صادق
شد او هم با جمال الدین موافق

بیامد پیش سید پیر معنی
سری بنهاد او بی کبر [و] دعوی[137]

595. He came and sat in the presence of the guide
[and] all at once, closed down his breath (or became silent) from recounting [the story]

He gave away all that he possessed
He threw down[138] the manifested form in total

He arranged a grave for himself
He sat amidst it, still [and] naked

When Jalāl Dargazīnī, that *vilāyat*[139]
saw that limit and destination from the *Sayyid*

He became certain that the guide is [one] of the perfect [men]
[That he is] in essence in the station of those in union

600. His states all became altered
he sprang from his place at once

He came in the presence of the *Sayyid*, the guide of Archetypal Idea
[and] put down his [head] without any arrogance and claim

As he was truthful in the station of love,
he became harmonious with Jamāl al-Dīn.

The next set of characteristics are defined in the light of Sāvī's interaction with Dargazīnī, the Elder guide whose presence initiated Sāvī's transformation. Sāvī returns to this guide and becomes silent, which is another characteristic of his nature as a guide. Then, we hear that Sāvī gives up his "manifested form". This is explained by what he does next: he prepares a grave and sits in it. Through Dargazīnī's eyes, Khaṭīb-i Fārsī implies that this is the final stage of Sāvī's spiritual journey. Now Dargazīnī, who by way of spiritual guidance has initiated the strange state in Sāvī, recognises him as a "perfect" man – among those who have attained union. Dargazīnī comes and sits before him as a disciple. This is the second time that Khaṭīb-i Fārsī elevates the status of Sāvī as a disciple, by placing his rank above that of the master. Already, Basṭāmī, the renowned Sufi master, had introduced Sāvī, his disciple, as the perfect man, who could guide Shaykh ʿUṣmān to the forty-first stage of his spiritual journey.[140] The last couplet reminds us that Dargazīnī and Sāvī are both disciples of the school of love, and that it is only through truthfulness on this path that the wayfarer can aspire to the final destination.

The importance of dissecting these events becomes clear when we juxtapose them with the rituals of the mainstream, institutionalised Sufism that existed before Sāvī. As Schimmel explains, the path that leads the mystics toward God in the Islamic tradition is defined as *sharīʿa*, *ṭarīqa* and *ḥaqīqa*. Schimmel uses the analogy of a highway for *sharīʿa*, out of which a narrower path, *ṭarīqa*, branches out. *Sharīʿa* is the God-given law, which every Muslim must obey faithfully, but *ṭarīqa* is more difficult to follow. It is by wandering through stations (*maqām*) on the path of *ṭarīqa* that the *sālik* ("wayfarer") can arrive at the perfect *tauḥīd*, or "the existential confession that God is One".[141] Sāvī is a Sufi master who has already stepped on the path of *sharīʿa*, and has gone through all the stations (*maqām*) on the path of *ṭarīqa*. What Khaṭīb-i Fārsī's account implies is that Sāvī attains *ḥaqīqa* when he becomes a *qalandar*.

فرومالید سید دست به اعضاش
فروپاشید از تن جمله موهاش

نه موی و ریش و سبلت تا به ابرو
نماند اندر تن مست ملک خو

۶۰۵. چو شد در صورت و معنی قلندر
نشست آنگا[ه] رودررو برابر

بکلی از جهان معذور گشتند
به فکر و ذکر حق معمور گشتند

فرو بستند از گفتارها دم
نگفتی این حدیث و آن دگر هم

بهنگام نماز آن هر دو ابرار
بکردندی اداء فرض جبار

فرو رفتند آن هر دو بحیرت
شدندی غرقه دریای فکرت[142]

The *Sayyid* touched upon his [body's] members
all his hair crumbled down from his body

Neither on his head, nor his beard and moustache [up] to [the, or his] eyebrows,
there remind on the body of the drunken one with manners of angels

605. When he became a *qalandar* in form and essence
then he sat face to face before [him]

They became dismissed from the world in total
[and] became abundant in the thought and *ẕikr* of Truth

They closed down their breath from speeches
[and] neither one said any stories

> At the time of prayers, both those pious [men]
> performed the obligations of the *Jabbār*
>
> They both sank into amazement
> (and) drowned in the ocean of contemplation.

The new relationship between Sāvī and Dargazīnī depicts the first stages of the ritualisation of becoming a *qalandar*, with Sāvī as the master. After going through the previous stages and being truthful, the final step is to become hairless. Sāvī touches Dargazīnī's body, which also becomes hairless. This act is reminiscent of a ritual that in Sufi tradition is called *baraka* (i.e., blessing, spiritual power). Schimmel explains that when an adept is accepted by a master, he or she needs to complete three years of service, after which he may deserve the *khirqa* (lit. "a patched garment"). This patched frock, which distinguishes the adept as an aspirant of Sufism, has a symbolic significance. The aspirant receives some of the *baraka* from his master.[143] In the *qalandarī* tradition being established by Sāvī, however, the frock is nudity and hairlessness; the master's *baraka* is acquired through his touch on the disciple's body. Dargazīnī, like Sāvī, is described as drunk (couplet 604).

After this ritual, Dargazīnī becomes a *qalandar* both inwardly and outwardly, and he sits in front of Sāvī. In the remaining couplets, we read that they both become totally detached from the world. They become silent and find abundance through meditation and *ẕikr* ("recollection"). They both say their prayers at the right time as fulfilling God's obligation, and then go back to their state of amazement and meditation.

The next place where we find hints of Sāvī's codification of *Qalandariyya* is the story of Shaykh ʿUthmān's encounter with Sāvī, after he becomes a *qalandar*:

> ٦۴۵. چو دید آن نقش او را شیخ عثمان
> تعجب کرد او و ماند حیران
>
> بپرسید از جمال الدین که ای شاه
> تا چه افتادت زناگاه؟
>
> طریق زینت خود دور کردی
> ز مردم خویش را مهجور کردی
>
> جمال الدین جوابش داد در حال
> که] ای پیر سخندان کهن سال]
> ...

۶۵۰. که [هر] کو رنگ معنی می‌پذیرد
چو اهل عشق پیش از مرگ میرد

هر آنکس را که باشد شوق دیدار
بباید مرد پیش از مرگ ناچار[144]

645. When Shaykh ʿUthmān saw that image of him
he was astonished and remanded amazed

He asked Jamāl al-Dīn, 'O king,
what happened to you all at once?'

'You removed the manner of adorning yourself
You have alienated yourself from people'

Jamāl al-Dīn answered him right away,
'O, the elderly eloquent guide'
…

650. 'those who accept the colour of Archetypal Idea,
will die before death, like the people of love'

'As for those who have passionate longing for the vision
they have no way except to die before dying'.

Shaykh ʿUthmān, amazed at seeing Sāvī in his new condition, asks him about the reason for removing his hair (which he refers to as "adornment") and for his self-isolation. Sāvī's answer leads us to the key characteristic of being a *qalandar*: death before death, for which Sāvī introduces a prerequisite: *rang-i maʿnī paẕīruftan* ("to accept the colour of Archetypal Idea"). Then he implies that *qalandar*s like himself, are people of love, who in longing for the countenance of God, have no choice but to die before they die. This is the most important line among these couplets, because it alludes to a (reportedly) prophetic *ḥadīth*, which Khaṭīb-i Fārsī includes after it:

قال النّبی علیه السلام: موتوا قبل ان تموتوا

'The prophet, peace be upon him, said, "Die before you die!"'

What is noteworthy here is the recurrence of Sāvī's use of what we now know as an inauthentic (or unestablished) *ḥadīth*. "Die before you die!" is a central teaching in the *qalandarī* movement, but as we shall see later, this is considered a Sufi saying, and not a prophetic *ḥadīth*. The term is generally interpreted as follows:

> The meaning is die voluntarily before you are forced to die. Voluntary death stands for abandoning lusts, idle amusements, and all the sins and errors that pertain to them.[145]

Schimmel elaborated on the mystical concept of death as "the annihilation of the individual qualities, the lifting of the veil that separates the primordial beloved from the lover created in time". According to her, the Sufi tradition "die before ye die" provides for "the possibility of pondering the implications of the slaying of the lower qualities and the ensuing spiritual resurrection in this life".[146] In the following lines, Sāvī directly refers to himself as a man who has died and has entrusted himself to the graveyard:

من آن مردم که پیش از مرگ مردم
وجود خود به گورستان سپردم

از این پس من ندارم اختیاری
که از مرده نیاید هیچ کاری

الف را نقطه هرگز نیست در کار
از این معنی شدم عریان الفوار

٦٥٥. الف را زان گزیدم اندرین باب
که بتوان یافت اینجا فتح الباب

الف را خوب دیدم اندرین راه
که هست اندر حروفش نام الله
...

دگر گفتی که ارباب شریعت
همی گویند ما را اهل بدعت

من از خلق جهان آن روز مردم
که وضعی بس عجب بنیاد کردم

٦٩٠. جنون است این ولیکن بس عیانست
که این معنی جنون عاشقانست

درست این دم که من دیوانه مردم
که این طور عجب انشا بکردم

برای آن ز خلقم هیچ غم نیست
که] بر دیوانه و عاشق قلم نیست]

تو ای عثمان کرم کن روز پیشم
رها کن با جنون [و] مرگ خویشم

چه می خواهی ازین برگشته احوال؟
چه می جویی ازین شوریده افعال؟

۶۹۵. من اینها [را] و آنها را ندانم
برو زین پس [مده] تصدیع جانم

گرم پروای گفت و گوی بودی
ورم سودای جست و جوی بودی

نمی گشتم زدنیا این چنین عور
نمی کردم چو مرده پای در گور
...

۷۰۰. بیا تا دست از این عالم بشوییم
قلندروار تکبیری بگوییم[147]

I am the man who died before he died
I entrusted my existence to the graveyard

From now on, I do not have any volition
For, no work can be done by a dead [person]

There is never a dot involved in the work of an *alif*
I became naked from this Archetypal Idea like an *alif*

655. I chose *alif* in this affair
for, here one can find victory

I saw *alif* appropriate on this path
for, in its letters, there exists the name of *Allah*
...

And he said that the masters of *sharīʿa*
call us the people of *bidʿa*

I died from the people of the world the day
that I established a very strange state

690. This is madness, but it is surely visible
that this essence is the *junūn* ("possession," "love-madness")

It is true at this moment that I am a madman
that I created this strange manner

I do not feel any sorrow [caused] by people
because there is no verdict on madmen and lovers

O you ʿUthmān! be kind today before me
leave me with my madness and death

What do you want from this unfortunate [one]?
What are you seeking from this [man with] delirious deeds?

695. I do not know these and those
Go, do not vex my soul more than this!

If I feared to start a conversation
if I had the desire for searching

I would not have become naked from the world like this
I would not step into a grave like this

700. Let's wash this world off our hands
Utter a *takbīr* like a *qalandar*

Sāvī's argument is filled with *qalandarī* elements. Comparing himself to the letter *alif* in nudity, Sāvī refers to his detachment from the world. Sāvī's comparison is in line with the mystical connotations of the letter *alif*. As Schimmel informs us, inspired by the detached letters that start 29 *sūra*s in the Qurʾān, the Sufis interpret *alif* as *Allāh*, who connected everything, but remained isolated from his creation. "To know the *alif* meant, for the Sufis, to know the divine unity and unicity". In Sufi symbolism, the letter *alif* represents "the spiritually free, the true mystics who have reached union with God".[148] By using this Sufi symbol, Sāvī re-emphasises his complete detachment from the created world. Then he responds to the masters of *sharīʿa* who have accused him of *bidʿa* ("reprehensible innovation") by referring to his "death", implying complete indifference. The next characteristic Sāvī refers to is his *junūn* (lit. "insanity", or "being possessed") as in love madness, which renders him indifferent to others' judgements. Sāvī's words in these couplets recall the doctrine of *Malāmatiyya* out of which *Qalandariyya* was born. Later, when Sāvī asks Shaykh ʿUthmān to leave him in peace, he reiterates that he has detached himself from the world. He does not care about the others' judgements. Otherwise he would not have become nude, sitting like a dead corpse in a grave. The repetition of the motif of death and nudity shows the importance of these key elements in Sāvī codification of the *qalandarī* doctrine.

The next stage of Sāvī's formation of the movement is shown as he meets his next (future) disciple, Muḥammad Balkhī. This event also happens in Damascus. When Sāvī asks Shaykh ʿUthmān to leave him in peace, he predicts that a master whose soul is familiar with the secret of *Ideas* (*sirr-i maʿnī*) will come to the mosque the next day. He asks Shaykh ʿUthmān to send that master to Sāvī.

۷٦۵. که اهلا مرحبا ای سالک راه
بیا گرزانکه داری عزم درگاه
...
تو را سوزیست اندر دل شب و روز
که می نالد از آن زاری به صد سوز

نشان حضرت از مشتاقی توست
دوای [آن] تجرد باشد ای دوست

۷۷۰. مجرد شو به اسرار الهی
عیانش بین بچشم دل کماهی

چو بلخی آن کرامت دید از پیر
ز حیرت گفت اندر حال تکبیر

روان پاک او شد غرقه نور
فکند از خویش رخت زرق را دور

بیامد پیش پیر آن مرد ابدال
فرو مالید بر او دست در حال

فروپاشید آن دم موی از او
چو ایشان شد چه در شکل و چه در رو

۷۷۵. روان شد اندر آن دم سوی صحرا
گیاهی چند جمع آورد آنجا

از آنها سترپوش خویشتن ساخت
دلش یکبارگی از خویش پرداخت

دو عالم کرد در یکدم فراموش
چو آن پاکان نشست آن پیر خاموش

جمال الدین نخوردی و نخفتی
بچندین روزها لفظی نگفتی

میان مردم از نزدیک و از دور
حدیث آن جماعت گشت مشهور

۷۸۰. همی گفتند هر کس در روایت
به دیگر شهرها رفت آن حکایت[149]

765. that welcome O, you wayfarer of the path
come, for you have the intention of [reaching] the court
...

In your heart, you have a burning [desire] day and night
from that lamentation [your heart] weeps for a hundred burnings

the sign of the Presence is visible from your eagerness
the cure for it is renunciation, my friend

770. Become a renunciant through divine secrets
see Him visible through the eyes of the heart as He is

When Balkhī saw that blessing (*karāmat*) from the guide
out of amazement, he uttered a *takbīr* at the moment (immediately)

his pure soul became drunk in light
[He] threw away from himself the garment of hypocrisy

the *abdāl* man came to the guide[150]
[He] touched upon him at the moment

all his hair crumbled down (or disintegrated from his body)
He became like them whether in form or face

775. he ran to the desert at that moment
he collected some plants there

From them, he made a loin-cover for himself
his hair, all at once, became polished from himself

he forgot both the worlds at one breath (at once)
That guide sat silent like the pure

Jamāl al-Dīn did not eat, nor did he sleep
For a few days, he did not utter a word

Among people from far away and nearby
the story of those people became well-known

780. Everyone told [it] in a story
and that story went to other cities.

In terms of Sāvī's initiation of Muḥammad Balkhī into *Qalandariyya*, a similar set of events happens. When the two masters meet, Muḥammad Balkhī is struck by Sāvī's clairvoyant powers in seeing through his state of consciousness, to perceive his burning desire to continue the spiritual journey. Sāvī blesses Balkhī, which means that he receives the master's *karāma* ("blessing") and then utters a *takbīr*, after which his pure soul drowns in light. This sequence results in Balkhī discarding the garment of hypocrisy. Now he is ready to be touched by Sāvī, to lose his hair and become a *qalandar*. After the ritual is performed, Balkhī is nude like Sāvī, with merely a loin cover made of dry grass. The most significant difference between this initiation process and the previously described process is the use of the term *tajarrud* ("renunciation").[151] The substitution of the previous vague references to states of consciousness with the term *tajarrud* shows a development in conceptualising Sāvī's spiritual journey. Sāvī introduces "renunciation" as the cure for Muḥammad Balkhī's burning desire to reach the court of the Presence. To renounce everything would mean to see Him through the eyes of the heart.

The third and last disciple hears about Sāvī and the *qalandar*s when the story of these strange-looking mystics is spread to other cities.

۷۹۰. که در ملک دمشق امروز جاییست
ز بهر عاشقان خلوت سراییست

گروهی از فقیران پریشان
که حیرت می کند انسان از انسان

در آن موضع سراسر جمع گشته
زبانها در کشیده شمع گشته

عجب رسم غریب آورده پیدا
که در عالم نمی ورزد کس آن را

به نام بدعت ایشان جمله فاشند
که ریش و سبلت و ابرو تراشند
...
۷۹٦. نمی پوشند از رخت جهان هیچ
نمی گویند هم با مردمان هیچ

مجال خلق یکساعت ندارند
بجز خاموشی و طاعت ندارند[152]

790. that in the territory of Damascus, today there is a place.
It is a quiet house for the lovers

a group of confounded poor
[in a shape and form] that human beings are amazed by human beings

have gathered all over in that place
[whose] withdrawn tongues have become candles

what a strange tradition they have created
that no one follows in the world

They are all known with the name of *bid'a*
for, they shave the beard, moustache and eyebrows
...

896. They neither wear any of [these] worldly garments
nor do they speak with the people

they do not have time for the people for an hour
They do not have any [obligations] except silence and worship.

Abū Bakr Ṣafāhānī hears these words about Sāvī and his disciples, eagerly sets foot on the path, and journeys to Damascus to see them:

۸۰۵. سری بنهاد اندر خدمت پیر
سلامی کرد و حالی گفت تکبیر

جمال الدین چو اندر وی نظر کرد
همانگه آن نظر در وی اثر کرد

بدو گفت ای جوانمرد همایون
ترا مقدم مبارک باد و میمون
...

۸۱۱. هلا گر عشق ما داری تمنا
ریاضت کش شوی اهلا و سهلا

چو پیر از حال او اینها خبر داد
برآمد از نهاد مرد فریاد
...

۸۱۸. مرا اول بیان کن خوش به فرهنگ
که خاصیت چه دید[ی] اندرین رنگ

چرا آن صورت اول ببردی
سرو ابرو [و] ریشت را ستردی؟

۸۲۰. ز سر صورت خویشم خبر کن
پس آنگه جامه ما را بدر کن[153]

805. He put his head in the service of the guide
he said hello, and at this moment [immediately] uttered a *takbīr*

when Jamāl al-Dīn gazed upon him
at that moment, that gaze made an impression on him

he told him, O blessed *javānmard*[154]
may your arriving be blessed and auspicious
...

811. Draw near if you desire our love
become an ascetic, welcome!

When the guide informed him of these
a cry raised from the man's heart
...

818. First explain to me pleasantly in a cultured manner
what quality did you see in this colour?

Why did you remove the first form?
Why did you shave your head, eyebrows and beard?

820. Inform me of the secret of my own form
and then remove our garment.

This conversation with Ṣafāhānī differs from the previous encounters between Sāvī and his future disciples. Sāvī invites Ṣafāhānī to the path by asking him to practise *riyāżat* ("asceticism"), which is another key term in the codification of *Qalandariyya*. The key Sufi elements, such as relinquishing oneself to the master (showing complete trust), uttering *takbīr* and *naẓar* ("gaze"), are present. However, before Ṣafāhānī is ready to let Sāvī discard his previous garment, he has questions about Sāvī's change of appearance, namely shaving his head and facial hair.

جوابش داد پیر صاحب اسرار
که هست این سکه مردان عیار

من اول روز سر در گور کردم
بدیدم روضه [ای] آغاز کردم

بگفتم این چه جای بوالعجیب است
ریاضی بس لبیب [و] بس غریب است

ندیدم بیش از یک کشک ماقوت
در آنجا باغها و میوه ها قوت

۸۲۵. محمد با علی شبیر و شبّر
دگر بد فاطمه زهرای انور

دگر زینب بد و دیگر سکینه
که بد معصوم [و] پاک از بغض و کینه

دگر جبریل با جمله ملایک
زیارت آمده اعلی الارائک

چو دیدم جمله را کردم سلامی
تو گویی یافتم من جمله کامی

پس آنگه حضرت سید بخواندم
ستادم دست را بر هم بماندم
۸۳۰. [به] گفتا ای جمال الدین چه مقصود
بگفتم یک نظر کن مر مرا زود

قلندرصورتی بشنیده ام من
بفرما مر مرا شاها در این فن

فروماليد دست بر فرق و بر رو
نماند اندر سر[و] پایم یکی مو

پس آنگه گفت رو شاکر همی باش
به خلوتگاه رو ذاکر همی باش[155]

The guide esteemed for secrets answered him
that this is the path of *ʿayyār* men

[When] I put my head the first day,
I saw a garden; I entered

I said, what is this marvellous place?
It is a very vibrant and strange meadow!

[Although] I did not see (or have) anything but a [piece] of *kashk*[156]
there were orchards, and fruits as food

825. Muḥammad with ʿAlī, Ḥasan and Ḥusayn
The others were Fāṭima, and the most luminous Zahrā

[And] there was Zaynab and Sakīna,
who was innocent and pure from hatred and malice

[And] there was Gabriel and all [the other] angels
[who] came to visit the people of the Paradise

When I saw them all, I said hello
It was as if I found (or was given) my desire

And then the presence of the *Sayyid* called me [to himself]
I stood with [one of] my hands on top of the other

830. He said, O Jamāl al-Dīn, what do you desire?
I said, 'Cast a gaze at me swiftly!'

I have heard about a *qalandar*-appearance
Initiate me in this manner O king![157]

He touched upon the crown of [my] head, and face
There remained no strand of hair in my [body from] head to toe

Then he said, 'Go and be grateful,
Go to a place of solitude and praise God'.

Sāvī's conversation with Ṣafāhānī in detail is significant in more than one way. First, in these couplets Sāvī reveals to Ṣafāhānī how he becomes a *qalandar*. He recounts that when he went into the grave the first time, he saw a paradise-like place with the Prophet, ʿAlī, Fāṭima, Ḥasan and Ḥusayn. In the Islamic tradition, this pentad is referred to as the *Ahl al-Kisāʾ* or *āl al-ʿabāʾ* ("the people of the cloak").[158] Adding Zaynab (Ḥusayn's sister) and Sakīna (Ḥusayn's daughter) to the original pentad, Sāvī reports that he sees Gabriel and all the other angels, who have come for a pilgrimage to the people of paradise.[159] The prophet then bestows on Sāvī what he desires, which is the prophet's gaze (*naẓar*) and the transformation of becoming a *qalandar*. The prophet touches Sāvī on the crown of his head and his face, and he loses all hair on his body. The prophet then advises him to go into solitude, to praise God and practice remembrance.

The other significance of these couplets is that they demonstrate how Sāvī connects the spiritual rites and rituals of the path that he is promoting to the prophet of Islam. Schimmel reports that according to Sufi tradition, the *silsila* is a spiritual lineage through past generations that connects the Sufi masters to the

Prophet.[160] Although we know of Sāvī as a *Sayyid* ("descendent of the Prophet"), his words in this anecdote highlight the importance of prophetic association in the formation of Sufi *silsilas* ("orders," "chains"). As Lindholm contends, the *ṭarīqas* (pl. lit. "paths") traced their origins back to the Prophet, to validate their authenticity and maintain the charismatic relationship of the founding master and his disciples, which served as a reiteration of the prophet's bond with his enlightened *umma*.[161] However, the fact that the *ḥadīth* used by Sāvī are invariably evaluated as inauthentic or fabricated opens the door to a number of questions that are worth mentioning, even though delving deeply into them would require another study. One wonders if Sāvī knew that the *ḥadīth* he cited were invalid, and in any case why he used them the way he did. Was it, as Lindholm and Schimmel contended, a matter of using prophetic associations as a means of validating the establishment of the *Qalandariyya* movement? Or can we regard Sāvī's prophetic associations as attempts to demystify the Prophet of Islam, and to establish *Qalandariyya* as a divergent medium of spiritual expression? Bearing in mind that the final station of Sāvī's spiritual path was union with God, the image painted of Sāvī's experience in the grave recalls the ascension of the Prophet.

According to *mi'rāj-nāmas*, the books about Muḥammad's night journey (*isra'*) and his ascension into the skies (*mi'rāj*), the prophet was accompanied by Gabriel, met other prophets, communicated with God, and visited Heaven and Hell.[162] In Sāvī's journey, he met, not the previous prophets, but Muḥammad and the members of his household – Gabriel, the other angels and those dwelling in the paradise. The prophet directly spoke to Sāvī, asked him what he desired, and granted it to him. Unlike Muḥammad's experience of communicating with God, Sāvī's arrival at his spiritual destination was facilitated by Muḥammad's touch, resulting in his hairlessness and becoming a *qalandar*. The most significant difference between these two experiences is that Sāvī's vision happens in a grave on Earth and not in the skies, which sounds like a subversion of Muḥammad's sanctified experience. Moreover, Sāvī's narrative makes his encounter with the prophet and the angels (including the archangel Gabriel) suggest that these holy figures are accessible on Earth. After recounting how he became a *qalandar*, Sāvī reveals another Archetypal Idea to Ṣafāhānī, so that Ṣafāhānī joins Sāvī in his *qalandarī* practices like a brother.[163] Then Sāvī reiterates the well-known prophetic *ḥadīth* as what God said on Muḥammad's ascension night:

دگر گویم یکی معنی انور
که دریابی شوی با ما برادر

۸۳۵. چنین گفتست خلاق جهاندار
شب معراج با سید در اخبار

قوله تعالی: «إنّ الله لا ينظر إلی صورکم، ولا إلی أموالکم، ولکن ينظر إلی قلوبکم
وأعمالکم»[164]

'The words of the most High are: "Truly, God looks neither upon your appearances, nor on your possessions, but He looks at your hearts and deeds."'

And I will tell (you) a luminous Archetypal Idea
so that you perceive it and become a brother of ours

835. This is what the creator and ruler of the world has said
On the ascension night with the *Sayyid* as is in the *ḥadīth*

Later, Sāvī goes back to the central motifs of poverty and self-imposed death as central elements in his narrative of *qalandar*hood. Upon hearing about the two types of death, Ṣafāhānī asks for more explanation, and Sāvī elaborates on these types. From couplet 849, where Sāvī focuses on self-imposed death, we read another set of codified *qalandarī* elements:

تو این معنی شنیدستی که پیران
همی گویند دایم با فقیران

که هر کو رنگ معنی می پذیرد
چو اهل عشق پیش از مرگ می رد

۸۴۰. حکیمانی که هستند اهل معنی
چنین گفتند با ارباب تقوی

که مرگ این جهانی بر دو قسمت[165]
که هر یک را به دیگرگونه اسمست

یک موت طبیعی نام دارد[166]
که آن یکسر خواص و عام دارد

دگر مرگیست آن اندر جهادی
همی خوانند خود موت ارادی
...

۸۴۹. ولیکن آن بود موت ارادی
که پیش از مرگ شخصی در مبادی

۸۵۰. بگوید ترک خورد و شهوت [و] خواب
براندازد بکلی مال و اسباب

هم از خشم و هم از کبر و هم از ناز
هم از بخل و هم از مکر و هم از آز

به یک ره شمع همت برفروزد
سراسر هستی خود را بسوزد

کم و بیش آنچه دارد برفشاند
بجز یاد خدا چیزی نماند

نماند در دلش نقش مناهی
شود تسلیم تقدیر الهی

۸۵۵. نماند در سر و پایش بجز دوست
بدیشان گر تواند مرد نیکوست[167]

Have you heard the Idea that the guides
keep telling the poor?

Whoever acquires the colour of Archetypal Ideas
like the people of love, dies before death?

840. The sages, who are the people of Archetypal Ideas,
said this to the masters of piety

That death in this world is of two types,
that each has a different name

One is called the natural death
which all have, whether the intimates or the commoners

The other is a death with a *jihād* within
which they call the self-imposed death

849. But it is the self-imposed death
[in which] the person in the beginning, before he dies

850. Repels food, lust and sleep
[and] totally throws down [all] possessions and means

[He will also throw down] rage, and arrogance and self-sufficiency [from the Beloved]
[and also] avarice and deception and greed

[He] lights the candle of aspiration on one path
[and] will burn the entirety of his existence

[He] discards all he has, little or much
[until] there remains nothing but recollection of God

There remains no stain of [any] vices
[Until he] totally surrenders to the divine portion (or destiny)

855. [Until] there remains nothing but the Friend in his entire existence [from head to toe]
To these, if one can die, it is pleasant

Sāvī elaborates on self-imposed death as detachment from all material needs and attachments. The seekers must prevent themselves from lust, eating, sleeping, any possessions, or any of the vices such as anger, avarice, arrogance and deception. They must aspire to remain on the path, and burn all their existence to the point that nothing remains in their hearts but the recollection of God. Then their hearts become pure, they surrender to God's will, and this is when all their existence becomes the Beloved.

کنون ما از خود و عالم بمردیم
جهان را با جهان خواهان سپردیم

کسی کو نقش ما خواهد بیکبار
بباید مردن از دنیاش ناچار

۸٦۰. چو هست این سکه ما صورت مرگ
نباشد هر کسی را طاقت مرگ

هلا گر قوت این راه داری
بیا با ما بساز از روی یاری

وگرنه رخت بخت خویش بردار
مده تصدیع [و] ما را مرده انگار

بگفت اینها جمال الدین [و] آنگاه
دم اندر بست [و] شد این قصه کوتاه

ابوبکر صفاهانی همان دم
مجرد شد زجزو [و] کل عالم

۸٦۵. بیامد پیش سید از دل و جان
نشست و دم ببست در یاد سبحان

برو مالید دست آن مرد ابدال
فرو پاشید مو از رو همان حال

تراشید از ارادات ریش [و] ابرو
چو ایشان شد چه در شکل و چه در خو

چو ایشان هم گیاهی چند برچید
و ازآنها سترپوش خود بیافید
...

۸۷۰. چو با هم آن جماعت یار گشتند
چو یاران محمد چار گشتند
...
۸۷۵. به قبله کرده رو آن چار درویش
سخن با کس نمی گفتند کم و بیش

به یک ره دست از عالم کشیده
ز غیر حق طمع کلی بریده
...
۸۲۸. ولی زیشان سر مویی خبر نیست
ازین رو این حکایت را اثر نیست[168]

Now, we died from ourselves and the world
[we] entrusted the world to those desiring the world

The one who desires our character at once
must inevitably die from the world

860. Since this path of ours is the face of death
Not everyone has the strength for death

Draw near if you have the strength for this path
Come and be our companion by way of friendship

Otherwise take the garment of your fate
Do not vex [us, and] consider us dead

Jamāl al-Dīn said these [words, and] then
He closed in his breath and this story was cut short

Abū Bakr Ṣafāhānī at that very breath
became a renunciant of the entire world

865. He came before the *Sayyid* from [his] heart and soul
[He] sat and closed his breath (or became silent in recollection of the most High)

The *abdāl* man touched upon him [with his hand]
[His] hair crumbled down from his face at that moment

He shaved [his] beard and eyebrows out of devotion
He became like them in both form and manner

Like them, he plucked a bunch of grass
and out of it, he wove his loincloth

870. When that community became friends with each other
Like Muḥammad's companions, they became four
...
875. Those four dervishes faced the *qibla*
They would not speak with anyone less or more

All at once, they withdrew their hands from the world (or detached themselves from the world)
They gave up hope in everything but the Truth

878. But there is no news of them, as little as the tip of a hair
That is why this story is not handed [down] by tradition.

This is the last time in the *Qalandar-nama* that we read about Sāvī initiating someone into his path. As with his other disciples, the realisation of the initiation is indicated by Sāvī's touch, the disciple's subsequent loss of hair, and the disciple's nudity, referring back to the hallmark of the *Qalandariyya*. Khatīb-i Fārsī ends this section on the encounter of Ṣafāhānī and Sāvī with a conclusion about the four masters sitting in silence facing the *qibla*. He reiterates that they were detached from the world and from anyone but God. This image recalls not only *faqr*, but also *tawakkul* (complete trust in God's provision), which are two pivotal themes in the *Karrāmiyya* doctrine.[169] Khatīb-i Fārsī's last sentence in this section, concerning the lack of news about these four masters, gives a clue about the reception of the *Qalandariyya*, and they probably indicate why the author is writing this account.

After going through a *chilla*, (a period of forty days) living merely on water and herbs (*giyāh*), Ṣafāhānī feels weak. Fearing death, he asks Balkhī to get Sāvī's permission to go out and beg (*parsa*) for food.[170] Balkhī refuses to go to Sāvī, as he considers such a request contrary to the principles of *adab* ("respect, politeness"):

۹۳۴. جوابش داد پیر بلخی آن دم
که من ترک ادب هرگز نکردم

ترا گر خود تمناییست کاری
نخواهد کرد کس منع تو باری

برو زان سان که خودخواهی همی ساز
نمی دارد تو را زین کار کس باز[171]

934. Balkhī replied to him at the moment,
'that I never abandoned respect and politeness

If you desire to do something,
no one forbids you [from doing it]

Go, carry [it] out the way you want
No one prevents you from doing this work

Ṣafāhānī travels to Damascus, goes to the Sultan's court and asks to see him. The king's servants describe Ṣafāhānī as a man who is extremely poor and unpleasant (*faqī-u nā-murād*). The Sultan deems seeing such a complexion as "not blessed" (... *nīst ... mubārak*), and the ruler has no awareness of the light ("*āgāhī az nūr*") that Ṣafāhānī bears. Rejected by the king and beaten by his servants, Ṣafāhānī returns to the graveyard.

خبر دادند سلطان را بناچار
که آن دیوانه باز آمد دگربار

۹۷۵. دگر بار آمده ست امروز بر در
نمی خواهد کسی غیر از تو دیگر

ملک در خشم شد گفتا برانید
شما بر در ستاده مردگانید؟

ندانستید کان صورت که اوراست
خرابیّش از آن صد گونه پیداست[172]

زجل شکلست این ویوانه خوار
ندارد پیش ما خود آنچنان کار

اگر بودی در او آثار طاعت
نکردی آشکارا رسم بدعت

۹۸۰. ولی در وی چو از سنّت اثر نیست
یقین شد کز خدایش هم خبر نیست

چنین کس را بدین درگه چه کارست
که صاحب بدعت و مجنون [و] خوارست

چو مردم حکم ساطان را شنیدند
از آن پس در دمشق او را ندیدند[173]

برون کردند از شهرش به خواری
نمی کرد او حدیث [از] بردباری

فتادندش هزاران کودک از پس
همی زد سنگ و مشت [و] چوب هر کس

۹۸۵. همی راندند [و] از پس می دویدند
سوی باب الصغیر اندر رسیدند

دکان کوزه گر بد بر سر راه
در آنجا کوزه ها مقدار پنجاه

ابوبکر از میان یک کوزه برداشت
سوی دروازه آمد نعره برداشت

به پیش درگه دروازه بردش
بزد بر آستان [و] کرد خردش

گشاد انگه زبان چون تیغ الماس
به بانگ و ناله می گفت ایّهاالناس

۹۹۰. مرا فرمود سلطان تا برانند
سراپایم به خون اندر نشانند

منم مردی چنین عریان و درویش
کنون کردند سر تا پای من ریش

چو سلطان را زاهل [دل] خبر نیست
فقیران را ولایت مختصر نیست

نماند اندر وجود ما مدارا
بکشتیم ار غضب شاه شما را

برای آنکه تا از اهل ابصار
فقیران را نرنجانند دگربار

۹۹۵. بگفت اینها و همچون باد بگذشت
ز چشم خلق در ساعت نهان گشت[174]

They helplessly informed the king one more time
that the madman came one more time

975. He has come to the court today one more time
he does not want to see anyone except you

The king entered in a rage and said, ‘Drive [him] away!’
You, standing at the gate, are you dead?

Did you not know the face belonging to him
his corruption shows from [the face] a hundred ways.

This lowly madman has the form of death
He does not have anything to do before us

If there existed signs of worship in him
he would not manifest a tradition of *bid'a*

980. But because there is no sign of *sunna* in him
It becomes certain that he does not have any news from God

What does such a person have to do in this court,
Who is known for *bid'a* and is mad (*majnūn*) and lowly?

When the people heard the verdict of the Sultan,
they did not see him [Ṣafāhānī] in Damascus anymore

They threw him out of the city in a humiliating manner
[although] he would not complain due to humility

Thousands of children followed him
while hitting him with rocks and fists and wooden [sticks]

985. They continued driving him away while running after him
[until] they reached the *Bāb al-ṣaqīr*

There was a potter's shop on the way
In which there were fifty earthen bottles

Abū Bakr took one from among them
Coming to the gate, he raised a cry

He took it to the gate of the court
[He] hit it on the threshold and crushed it

Then he opened his diamond-sharp tongue
and said, shouting and weeping, 'O people!

990. The Sultan commanded to drive me away
to immerse my head to toe in blood!

I am a man so naked and poor
They wounded me, head to toe

As the sultan is not aware of the people of [heart]
the poor do not have [even] small guardianship

There remained no humility in our existence
We killed your king out of anger

So that the people of perception through eyes
do not molest the poor one more time'.

995. He said these [words] and passed like wind
He became invisible to the eyes of the people instantly.

The next day, Ṣafāhānī returns to see the Sultan, and is rejected one more time as a madman. The Sultan's verdict clearly establishes that Ṣafāhānī is a man of *bid'a*, and his appearance reveals that he is not just an unbeliever, but an atheist. The Sultan's verdict about Ṣafāhānī, particularly regarding his belief, influences the mindset of his subjects in Damascus. This is significant because it demonstrates the religious authority that the sultan of Damascus, as ruler of a major political centre in the mediaeval Islamic world, had over his citizens. In response to their ruler's actions, the people humiliate and injure Ṣafāhānī, driving him out of the city. He loses his patience, curses the Sultan to death and disappears. Khatīb-i Fārsī's account of the people's opinions about Ṣafāhānī echoes the Sultan's verdict. Ṣafāhānī returns to the graveyard, and the death of the Sultan is publicly announced the next day. At this, the people start believing in the *qalandar*s as perfect men who are in union with God.[175]

This event, which Khatīb-i Fārsī refers to as Ṣafāhānī's *karāmāt* ("blessings"), and the resulting change of people's views, is significant. It demonstrates the religious and political challenges that non-conformist movements such as the *Qalandariyya* posed at the Islamic establishment.

Next, Khatīb-i Fārsī relates that after the story of Ṣafāhānī and the Sultan circulates around the city, a lot of people gather around the *qalandar*s. Sāvī decides to leave and find solitude. When Balkhī hears this, he begs Sāvī to take him along.[176] Before leaving, Sāvī explicitly defines the *Qalandariyya* to Balkhī, who insistently demands to accompany the teacher. This is where Sāvī actually installs Balkhī as the leader, and refers to adherents of the doctrine as *qalandar*s. This is significant, because it implies that Sāvī was actually more than a solitary hermit, detached from the idea of *Qalandariyya* as an influential movement. Sāvī's instructions are described as follows:

۱۲۰۰. مرا بگذار تا با یاد سبحان
بمانم چند روزی فرد و عریان

چو من شکلی برآوردم الف وار
الف را نقطه هرگز نیست در کار

تو همچون نقطه خواهی گشت یارم
الف وارم من این طاقت ندارم

ولیکن بر تو واجب نیست این کار
که همچون من شوی عریان الف وار

گرت باید رضای خاطر من
برو نزدیک آن یاران کم زن

۱۲۰۵. ترا من پیشوا کردم بر ایشان
مباش از غلغل ایشان پریشان

وگر خواهی که دانی معنی آن
شنو تا گویمت روشن به برهان

کسی کو شد به رنگ ما منور
لقب باشد چنان کس را قلندر

قلندر آن بود کز هر دو عالم
سر] موئی نباشد در دلش غم]

زر و سیم و هوی و شهوت و آز
نکونامی و جاه [و] نعمت و ناز

۱۲۱۰. براندازد به عشق ما بیکبار
نماند در دلش جز یاد جبّار[177]

1200. Let me, with the remembrance of the Pure,
remain a few days solitary and naked

Since I have branched out an *alif*-like form
there is never a dot in the work of an *alif*

You will become my companion like a dot
I am like an *alif*, I cannot bear this

But this work is not obligated on you
to become naked like I [am]

If the contentment of my mind suits you
Go to those humble companions[178]

I assigned you as their leader
Do not become disturbed from their rageful mutterings

And if you want to know the essence of it,
listen so that I tell you clearly with proof

Qalandar is the one who from two worlds
has no grief in his heart [even] as much as the tip of a hair

Gold and silver and lust and greed,
good repute [and] position and convenience and pride

[He] drops for our love all at once
there remains in his heart nothing but the remembrance of the Almighty.

These lines are immediately followed by Sāvī's reiteration of what he has referred to as the characteristics of an adherent:

بگویم با تو یک معنی دیگر
قلندر پنج حرفست ای برادر

یکی قاف و یکی لام و یکی نون
یکی دال و یکی رای همایون

از اینها هر یکی [را] معنیی هست
که آنها بر قلندر عین فرضست

که هر یک را بشرط خود بداند
ز لوح معرفت نقشش بخواند[179]

I will tell you another Idea
'*Qalandar*' is five letters, O brother,

A *qāf* and a *lām* and a *uūn*
a *dāl* and an auspicious *rā*

As for every one of these, there is an Idea
which is an essence of obligation

1215. that he reads each [letter] under its own condition
[that] he reads the imprint of each from the tablet of knowledge (or knowing).

This reiteration in the form of letters forming the word *qalandar* is a detailed, systematised codification of the doctrine, given in a cryptic manner. Apart from the significance of this manner of codification, it implies that those bearing the epithet of *qalandar* must also embody these characteristics. As each letter represents an element of the essence of the doctrine, it is clear that being a *qalandar* is not merely having the title. It requires internalising what the title essentially means: *qināʿat* ("contentment"), *luṭf* ("benevolence"), *nidāmat* ("penitence"), *diyānat* ("religiosity"), and *riyāżat* ("asceticism"). Each letter of the word bears one of the pillars of the creed that the adherents must abide by to be *qalandars*.[180]

Conclusion

The *Qalandariyya*, as an eclectic, non-conformist movement, probably took shape under the leadership of the Iranian Sufi master, Jamāl al-Dīn Sāvī (d. about 1232/3). This spiritual movement had a considerable following in the vast expanse of Islamic societies from the Balkans to Bengal. Recent research by Papas shows the living presence of the *qalandar* in different regions of Central Asia. According to De Bruijn's original research, we know that from the eleventh century, the figure of the *qalandar* appears in *Qalandariyyāt* by Sanāʾī although it existed in different genres of classical Persian poetry in earlier centuries. The figure of the *qalandar* also appears in Sufi treatises. Nevertheless, little is known about the *Qalandariyya* and its doctrine as a non-conformist movement. This chapter focuses on a *Qalandar-nāma*, the only hagiographical account available on Sāvī and his spiritual career. It is written decades after Sāvī's death by a devout disciple, Khaṭīb-i Fārsī (lit. "Persian preacher"), who is actually assigned to compose the hagiographical account. Despite the chronological gap, and the probable bias of the writer because of his spiritual adherence, this account is unique in terms of being solely dedicated to Sāvī.

Sāvī is known as the founder of the most outstanding *qlandarī* ritual, *chahār żarb* (lit. "four blows"). This ritual, which refers to shaving the head, eyebrows, the beard and the moustache, becomes the hallmark of the *qalandarī* path. According to the *Qalandar-nāma*, this ritual begins with Sāvī becoming hairless when reaching union with God as the final station on the spiritual path. Sāvī initiates his four intimate disciples into the path by touching them, as a result of which they also become hairless. According to the text, Sāvī's hairlessness and nudity go hand in hand and symbolise the ultimate renunciation (*tajarrud*) and detachment from all worldly values and possessions. In his interactions with his disciples, as a *qalandarī* master, Sāvī used his own example to systematise the *qalandarī* doctrine. He invited his followers to adopt complete and spiritual self-sufficiency, or poverty (*faqr*), by detaching themselves from eating, sleeping, speaking, fulfilling any worldly desire or passion, and possessing objects or belonging to a place. In his systematisation of the *Qalandariyya*, Sāvī referred to inauthentic or unauthorised "prophetic" *ḥadīth*s. References to such *ḥadīth*s are part of the Sufi tradition, but they also reveal an important fact about the question of piety in the Sufi tradition. What deserves special attention in Sāvī's spiritual leadership is his proximity to the divine in Islam. This is clearly seen in the anecdote in which Sāvī meets Gabriel, Muḥammad and his descendants. This anecdote can be seen as almost an earthly replica of Muḥammad's ascension night. Muḥammad needed his steed, *Burāq*, to ascend the spheres. Sāvī sits in a graveyard, sinks into a meditative state and experiences a similar journey and is elevated to the station of union with God.

Notes

1 This chapter was written at Utrecht University as part of the ERC Advanced Grant project entitled *Beyond Sharia: The Role of Sufism in Shaping Islam* (www.beyondsharia.nl), funded by the European Research Council (ERC) under the European Union's Horizon 2020 research and innovation programme (Grant agreement No. 101020403). Johannes T. P. de Bruijn, 'The *Qalandariyyāt* in Persian Mystical Poetry, from Sanā'ī Onwards,' in *The Legacy of Mediæval Persian Sufism*, ed. Leonard Lewisohn, (London and New York: Khaniqahi Nimatullahi Publications, 1992), 76. See also Ahmet T. Karamustafa, *God's Unruly Friends: Dervish Groups in the Islamic Later Middle Period 1200–1550* (Salt Lake City: University of Utah Press, 1194), 36. Jean-Jacques Thibon, in *The Encyclopaedia of Islam Three* s.v. Malāmatiyya.

2 Wilferd Madelung, *Religious Trends in Early Islamic Iran*, Columbia Lectures on Iranian Studies 4 (Albany, N.Y.: Bibliotheca Persica, 1988), 1.

3 Wilferd Madelung, *Religious Trends in Early Islamic Iran*, 39, 44.

4 Muḥammad-Riżā Shafīʿī-Kadkanī, *Qalandariyya dar tārīkh: digardīsīhā-yi yik īdi'uluzhī*, 3rd repr., (Tehran: Intishārāt-i sukhan), 2008, 32–33.

5 John Renard, *Friends of God: Islamic Images of Piety, Commitment, and Servanthood.* 1st ed. (Berkeley: University of California Press, 2008), 81.

6 Christopher Melchert, *Before Sufism: Early Islamic Renunciant Piety* (Berlin, Boston: De Gruyter, 2020), 178–179.

7 Alexander Knysh *Sufism: A New History of Islamic Mysticism* (Princeton: Princeton University Press, 2017), 1.

8 Christopher Melchert, *Before Sufism*, 185.

9 Ibid., 177. Other scholars have argued that the Sufi tradition was not limited to mystics, but was a tradition aiming to emulate the prophet in matters such as ritual activities and ethics. It was only from the ninth century that we can trace mystical content in the tradition. For the complete discussion, see Lloyd Ridgeon, 'Mysticism in Medieval Sufism', in *The Cambridge Companion to Sufism*, ed., Lloyd Ridgeon (Cambridge: Cambridge University Press, 2014), 125–149.
For the year of al-Junayd's death as 910, I have used *The Encyclopaedia of Islam Three.*

10 Christopher Melchert, 'Origins and Early Sufism,' in *The Cambridge Companion to Sufism*, edited by Lloyd Ridgeon, (Cambridge: Cambridge University Press, 2014), 11.

11 Christopher Melchert, *Before Sufism*, 1, 177, 179. Other scholars have argued that the Sufi tradition was not limited to mystics, but was a tradition aiming to emulate the prophet in matters such as ritual activities and ethics. It was only from the ninth century that we can trace mystical content in the tradition. For the complete discussion, see Lloyd Ridgeon, 'Mysticism in Medieval Sufism', in *The Cambridge Companion to Sufism*, ed., Lloyd Ridgeon (Cambridge: Cambridge University Press, 2014), 125–149. For the year of al-Junayd's death as 910, I have used *The Encyclopaedia of Islam Three.*

12 Christopher Melchert, 'Origins and Early Sufism', 11, 3–6.

13 Ibid., 16. See also Christopher Melchert, *Before Sufism*, 189.

14 Christopher Melchert, 'Origins and Early Sufism', 3.

15 Melchert further argues that through travelling to Baghdad and back, the Nīshāpūrī adherents of this movement – along with the followers of the more populist Karāmiyya movement – reinforced the teachings of Abū Bakr al-Wāsitī (d. after 320/932), the figure who introduced Sufism from Baghdad. By the turn of the eleventh century, these two movements had merged into Sufism. One indicator is perhaps the continuation of the *khānaqāh*, formerly a Karāmi institution, as a Sufi institution. See Christopher Melchert, 'Origins and Early Sufism', 19.

16 John Renard, *Friends of* God, 153.

17 Sara Sviri, 'Ḥakīm Tirmidhī and the *Malāmatī* Movement in Early Sufism', in *The Heritage of Sufism: Classical Persian Sufism from its Origins to Rūmī (700–1300)*, ed., Leonard Lewisohn (Oxford, Oneworld Publications, 1999), 596, 584.

18 Johannes T. P. de Bruijn, 'The *Qalandariyyāt* in Persian Mystical Poetry', 75–79.

19 Sara Sviri, 'Ḥakīm Tirmidhī and the *Malāmatī* Movement in Early Sufism', 588.

20 Hussaini, S. Sh. Kh., in *Encyclopœdia Iranica*, s.v. Abū ʿAbd-Al-Raḥmān Solamī.

21 Sara Sviri, 'Ḥakīm Tirmidhī and the *Malāmatī* Movement in Early Sufism', 592.

22 Ibid., 584, 595.

23 John Renard, *Friends of God*, 152–153.

24 Annemarie Schimmel, *Mystical Dimensions of Islam* (Chapel Hill: The University of North Carolina Press, 1975), 86.

25 Sara Sviri, 'Ḥakīm Tirmidhī and the *Malāmatī* Movement in Early Sufism', 595.

26 Ibid., 600; see also 600, n 45.

27 Ibid., 584.

28 Ahmet T. Karamustafa, 'Antinomian Sufis: Between Sublimation and Subversion: Divergent Attitudes Towards Social Norms and the Sharīʿa in Early Sufism (850–1200),' in *The Cambridge Companion to Sufism*, ed. Lloyd Ridgeon (USA: Cambridge University Press, 2015), 102.

29 Sara Sviri, 'Ḥakīm Tirmidhī and the *Malāmatī* Movement in Early Sufism', 592.

30 Marshall G. S. Hodgson, *The Venture of Islam: Conscience and History in a World Civilization.* Vol II (Chicago and London: Chicago University Press, 1974), 203.

31 Charles Lindholm, 'Prophets and Pirs: Charismatic Islam in the Middle East and South Asia'. in *Embodying Charisma: Modernity, Locality and the Performance of Emotion in Sufi Cults*, eds., Pnina Werbner and Helene Basu Werbner (London: Routledge, 1998), 213.

32 Leonard Lewisohn, *Beyond Faith and Infidelity: The Sufi Poetry and Teachings of Mahmud Shabistari* (Richmond, Surrey: Curzon Press, 1995), 104–105.

33 Charles Lindholm, 'Prophets and Pirs', 220.

34 Tahsin Yazici, in *Encyclopaedia of Islam*, Second Edition, s.v. Ḳalandariyya.

35 Ahmet T. Karamustafa, 'Antinomian Sufis', 102. See also Karamustafa, *God's Unruly Friends*, 36.

36 Johannes T. P. de Bruijn, 'The *Qalandariyyāt* in Persian Mystical Poetry', 75–76.

37 Tahsin Yazici, in *Encyclopaedia of Islam*, Second Edition, s.v. Ḳalandariyya. It is worth mentioning that Khatīb-i Fārsī refers to Indian ascetics when he describes the ways of the *qalandars*:

۲۰۹. به هندوستان نظر کن هندوان را
که چون بگذاشتند ایشان جهان را

Behold the *hindūs* in India,
the way they gave up the world.

See Khatīb-i Fārsī, *Qalandar-nāma-yi Khatīb Fārsī* or *Sīrat-i Jamāl al-Dīn Sāvajī*, ed. Ḥamīd Zarrīnkūb (Tehran: Intishārāt-i Ṭūs, 1983), 41.

38 Karamustafa, Ahmet T., *God's Unruly Friends*, 3–4.

39 Tahsin Yazici, in *Encyclopaedia of Islam*, Second Edition, s.v. Ḳalandariyya.

40 Ibid.

41 Ahmet T. Karamustafa, 'Antinomian Sufis', 114.

42 According to Muṭahhar bin Ṭāhir-i Maqdasī, among the people of India there was a sect that considered Muslims as impure. If one of them converted to Islam, they killed that person, but first they purified him by shaving all his head and bodily hair. See Muṭahhar bin Ṭāhir-i Maqdasī, *Āfarīnish-u tārīkh* (Vols. 4–6) translated and with an introduction by Muḥammad-Riżā Shafīʿī-Kadkanī (Tehran: Āgah, 1995), 563–564.

43 Tahsin Yazici, in *Encyclopaedia of Islam*, Second Edition, s.v. Ḳalandariyya.

44 J. Spencer, Trimingham, *The Sufi Orders in Islam* (Oxford: The Clarendon Press, 1971), 268.

45 J. Spencer, Trimingham, *The Sufi Orders in Islam*, 39.

46 Tahsin Yazici, in *Encyclopaedia of Islam*, Second Edition. s.v. Ḳalandariyya.

47 Khaliq Ahmad Nizami, *Religion and Politics in India During the Thirteenth Century* (New Delhi: Oxford University Press, 2002), 311.

48 Tahsin Yazici, in *Encyclopaedia of Islam*, Second Edition, s.v. Ḳalandariyya.

49 Annemarie Schimmel, *Mystical Dimensions of Islam*, 202.

50 Muḥammad-Riżā Shafīʿī-Kadkanī, *Qalandariyya dar tārīkh*, 17. See also, Bābā Ḥājī ʿAbd al-Raḥīm, *Qalandar-nāma-'ī ba nām-i ādāb al-ṭarīq*, ed., Meharn Afshari (Tehran: Chishma, 2016), 17–18.

51 Tahsin Yazici, in *Encyclopaedia of Islam*, Second Edition, s.v. Ḳalandariyya. See also ʿAbd Allāh-i Anṣārī, *Risāla-yi Qalandar-nāma*, ed., Vaḥīd Dastgirdī (Tehran: Kitābfurūshi-yi Furūghī, 1970).

52 Johannes T. P. de Bruijn, 'The *Qalandariyyāt* in Persian Mystical Poetry, 76; Karamustafa, Ahmet T., *God's Unruly Friends*, 34.

53 Shihāb al-Dīn ʿUmar Suhravardī, *ʿAwārif al-maʿārif*, trans. Abū Manṣūr ʿAbd al-Muʾmin Iṣfahānī, ed. Qāsim Anṣārī (Tehran: Intishārāt-i ʿlmī farhangi, 1985), 30–31.

54 J. Spencer, Trimingham, *The Sufi Orders in Islam*, 39, 267.

55 See Johannes T. P. de Bruijn, 'The *Qalandariyyāt* in Persian Mystical Poetry', 75–86; Ahmet T. Karamustafa, 'Antinomian Sufis', 110; Ahmet T. Karamustafa, *God's Unruly Friends*, 32–34.

56 Ahmet T. Karamustafa, 'Antinomian Sufis', 110.

57 Johannes T. P. de Bruijn, 'The *Qalandariyyāt* in Persian Mystical Poetry', 86.

58 Alexandre Papas, *Thus Spake the Dervish: Sufism, Language, and the Religious Margins in Central Asia, 1400–1900* (Leiden and Boston: Brill, 2019), 206.

59 Alexandre Papas, *Thus Spake the Dervish.*

60 Shahab Ahmed, *What is Islam: the Importance of Being Islamic* (Princeton and Oxford: Princeton University Press, 2016), 274.

61 Shahab Ahmed, *What is Islam*, 32.

62 Ibid., 538.

63 Khatīb-i Fārsī, *Qalandar-nāma*, 7.

64 Haṭīb Fārisī, *Manāqib-i Jamāl al-Dīn Sāvī*, ed. Tahsin Yazici (Ankara, Turk Tarih Kurumu Basımevi: 1972).

65 My purpose here is to give a brief introduction of Manāqib as a genre. For an overview of the complicated semantic development of the term, which goes beyond the scope of this chapter, see Charles Pellat, in *Encyclopaedia of Islam*, Second Edition, s.v. Manāqib.

66 Charles Pellat, in *Encyclopaedia of Islam*, Second Edition, s.v. Manāqib.

67 Khatīb-i Fārsī, *Qalandar-nāma*, 7–8. For the sake of clarity and uniformity, I refer to the book as *Qalandar-nāma* throughout this study.

68 The editor of the book, Ḥamīd Zarrīnkūb has referred to this point in his introduction to the book. See Khatīb-i Fārsī, *Qalandar-nāma-yi Khatīb Fārsī* or *Sīrat-i Jamāl al-Dīn Sāvajī*, ed. Ḥamīd Zarrīnkūb (Tehran: Intishārāt-i Ṭūs, 1983), 7. For two examples of the writer's reference to himself as Khaṭīb-i Fārsī, see pages 36 & 59 of *Qalandar-nāma*.

69 Sayyid-Ṣādiq Gowharīn, *Sharḥ-i iṣṭilāḥāt-i taṣavvuf* (Tehran: Zavvār, 1382/ 2003–2004), vol. 7–8, s.v. فقر.

70 Michael Bonner in *Encyclopaedia of the Qur'ān Online*, s.v. Poverty and the Poor.

71 Muḥammad-Riżā Shafīʿī-Kadkanī, *Qalandariyya dar tārīkh*, 371.

72 See Afshari's discussion on the *qalandarī* characteristics in Bābā Ḥājī ʿAbd al-Raḥīm, *Qalandar-nāma-ʾī ba nām-i ādāb al-ṭarīq*, 71. I will elaborate on this concept in the context of Khatīb Fārsī's *Qalandar-nāma* on page 39.

73 Khatīb-i Fārsī, *Qalandar-nāma*, 34.

74 The word *mujarrad* in Persian means naked; unmarried; solitary, alone; bodiless, incorporeal; immaterial. Steingass, *A Comprehensive Persian-English Dictionary*, s.v. مجرد. The infinitive form of the word, *tajarrud* ('renunciation'), is also used in the *Qalandar-nāma*. For the sake of uniformity, I translate *mujarrad* as 'renunciant'.

75 Ibid., 34–36.

76 Later when Khatīb-i Fārsī describes Sāvī's conversion to asceticism, he explains that Sāvī did a pilgrimage to the holy shrine of Zaynab, too. See Khatīb-i Fārsī, *Qalandar-nāma*, 56; ʿArafat, W., in *Encyclopaedia of Islam*, Second Edition, s.v. Bilāl b. Rabāḥ.

77 The term *pīr* (pl. *pīrān*) literally means old as an adjective. In texts on mysticism, it can be translated as saint. It also means a founder or chief of any religious body or sect. Steingass, *A Comprehensive Persian-English Dictionary*, s.v. پير.

78 The word *himmat* has a wide range of connotations. A number of its literal equivalents are desire, aspiration, and ambition. In the Sufi discourse, *himmat* is the unwavering attention of the seeker, summoning all his/her spiritual competence to attain perfection. See Sayyid-Ṣādiq Gowharīn, *Sharḥ-i iṣṭilāḥāt-i taṣavvuf*, vol. 9–10, s.v. همت.

79 Sayyid-Ṣādiq Gowharīn, *Sharḥ-i iṣṭilāḥāt-i taṣavvuf*, vol. 7–8, s.v. فقر.

80 The term *faqīr* is an adjective which can have two literal equivalents in English: poor (adj.) or a mendicant (n.). As the English equivalents do not convey the deeper meaning of *faqīr* in this context, I substitute it with 'man of poverty'.

81 Khatīb-i Fārsī, *Qalandar-nāma*, 35.

82 Khatīb-i Fārsī, *Qalandar*-nāma, 35.

83 Ibid., 36.

84 Ibid.

85 *Takbīr* literally means to utter the words *Allah-u akbar*, praise. Steingass, *The Student's English-Arabic Dictionary*, s.v. تکبیر. This is a key term in the *qalandarī* tradition in Khaṭīb-i Fārsī's book, to which I will return later in this chapter.

86 Khatīb-i Fārsī, *Qalandar*-nāma, 36.

87 The word *gulzār* in this couplet is ambiguous, because it means both a blooming garden of roses and a flourishing, well-populated town. It is also the name of a note in music. Since the author is referring to himself with the metaphor of a nightingale, the third meaning of the word, namely of a note in music, may also be taken into consideration. Steingass, *A Comprehensive Persian-English Dictionary*, s.v. گلزار.

88 My choice of using 'tradition' as an equivalent for *bū-y* needs some clarification. The word *bū-y* refers to whatever that can be perceived with the sense of smell. The metaphoric meaning of the word is *nishān* or *athar*. One of the idiomatic expressions in which this metaphoric meaning appears is *bū-y chīzī ba kas-ī risīdan*. Anvari, *Farhang-i buzurg-i sukhan*, s.v. بو. *Nishān* means a sign, signal, mark, character, and *athar* means a footprint, sign, mark; result, consequence; tradition. Steingass, *A Comprehensive Persian-English Dictionary*, s.v. نشان and اثر. Therefore the word *būy* can be ambiguous. Since the author is describing poverty as a spiritual state, and a *qalandarī* tradition, I choose to take the metaphoric meaning of 'tradition' for *būy* in my translation.

89 Annemarie Schimmel, *Mystical Dimensions of Islam*, 299.

90 Ibid., 296, 307.

91 Ibid., 222.

92 The poets taking pride in their poetic credentials is known as *fakhr* ('self-praise') in classical Persian poetry. It is interesting to see that Khatīb-i Fārsī, a devout disciple of a *Qalandar* saint, praises himself for knowing and disclosing mystical secrets. For more on *fakhr*, see E. Wagner, and Bichr Farès, in *Encyclopaedia of Islam*, Second Edition, s.v. Mufākhara.

93 Khatīb-i Fārsī, *Qalandar-nāma*, 36–37.

94 The word *ẕāt* means soul, essence, substance; body, person, self; generation, breed, tribe, caste. Steingass, *A Comprehensive Persian-English Dictionary*, s.v. ذات.

95 The word *ṭufail* is the name of a poet of Kūfah who used to go uninvited to wedding-feasts (also called *ṭufailu'l-a'rās* (*'arā'is*); hence any uninvited guest; one who accompanies a guest without being invited. Steingass, *A Comprehensive Persian-English Dictionary*, s.v. طفیل.

96 The *Qur'ān* 53: 17. The translation is by Arthur J. Arberry, *The Koran Interpreted: A Translation* (Oxford: Oxford University Press, 1983).

97 Mullā 'Alī Al-Qārī, *Encyclopedia of Hadith Forgeries: Al-Asrār Al-Marfu'a Fil-Akhbār Al-Mawżū'a Sayings Misattributed to the Prophet Muḥammad*, translated and with an introduction by Gibril Fouad Haddad (Rochdale UK: Beacon Books, 2013), 147.

I will come back to the role of using inauthentic *ḥadīth* in shaping the *Qalandariyya* movement by Sāvī later in this study when I discuss his rendering of *faqr*.

98 Khatīb-i Fārsī, *Qalandar-nāma*, 37.

99 Charles Lindholm, 'Prophets and Pirs', 214–215.

100 Michael Bonner in *Encyclopaedia of the Qur'ān Online*, s.v. Poverty and the Poor.

101 Mullā ʿAlī Al-Qārī, *Encyclopedia of Hadith Forgeries: Al-Asrār Al-Marfuʿa Fil-Akhbār Al-Mawżūʿa Sayings Misattributed to the Prophet Muḥammad*, translated and with an introduction by Gibril Fouad Haddad (Rochdale UK: Beacon Books, 2013), 422. As mentioned in the footnote above, I elaborate on the role of using inauthentic *ḥadīth* in shaping the *Qalandariyya* movement by Sāvī later in this study when I discuss his rendering of *faqr*.

102 Michael Bonner in *Encyclopaedia of the Qur'ān Online*, s.v. Wealth.

103 Annemarie Schimmel, *Mystical Dimensions of Islam*, 222.

104 Margaret Malamud, 'The Politics of Heresy in Medieval Khurasan: The Karramiyya in Nishapur,' *Iranian Studies* 27, 1/4 (1994): 42–43.

105 As a suffix, one of the meanings of *bān* is a prince, lord, chief or governor. When it is affixed to a noun, it signifies a keeper or a guardian, as in *bāghbān* (a gardener). Steingass, *A Comprehensive Persian-English Dictionary*, s.v. بان.

106 Khatīb-i Fārsī, *Qalandar-nāma*, 37.

107 The expression *rang-u būy* means majesty, power; aptitude, capacity. Steingass, *A Comprehensive Persian-English Dictionary*, s.v. رنگ.

108 The expression *iʿtibār giriftan* means to take an example or warning. Steingass, *A Comprehensive Persian-English Dictionary*, s.v. اعتبار.

109 The word *ṣāḥib* means 'esteemed' or 'enjoying reputation'. Steingass, *A Comprehensive Persian-English Dictionary*, s.v. صاحب.

110 Khatīb-i Fārsī, *Qalandar-nāma*, 37.

111 The word *rukn* has a wide range of connotations. It can mean the firmer side of anything, the side on which it is supported; a pillar, prop, support; the foot of a verse; a foundation, a cornerstone; the black stone at Mecca. Steingass, *A Comprehensive Persian-English Dictionary*, s.v. رکن

112 *Dar-bāḵẖtan* means to play; to buy and sell; to give away; to lend. Steingass, *A Comprehensive Persian-English Dictionary*, s.v. درباختن.

113 Khatīb-i Fārsī, *Qalandar-nāma*, 37.

114 The word *sabuk-bār* means, of a light weight, ready to rise and travel; lightly loaded, unencumbered; jocund, blithe, free from care. Steingass, *A Comprehensive Persian-English Dictionary*, s.v.سبکبار.

115 Khatīb-i Fārsī, *Qalandar-nāma*, 37–38.

116 The imagery of throwing heads in this couplet can imply the game of polo. For more on the imagery of polo in Persian classical literature and its mystical interpretations, see Ali-Asghar Seyed-Gohrab, '"My Heart is the Ball, Your Lock the Polo-Stick": Development of the Ball and Polo-stick Metaphors in Classical Persian Poetry', in *The Necklace of the Pleiades*, eds. Franklin Lewis and Sunil Sharma (Leiden: Leiden University Press, 2010).

117 Khatīb-i Fārsī, *Qalandar-nāma*, 38.

118 Karamustafa, Ahmet T., *God's Unruly Friends*, 40–41.

119 Khatīb-i Fārsī, *Qalandar-nāma*, 39–40.

120 *Towḥīd* means making one; declaring (God) to be one; a belief in the unity of God; unitarianism, antitrinitarianism; the fifth degree of perfection in Sufi life, where the divine essence is contemplated as void of any attribute conceived by thought. Steingass, *A Comprehensive Persian-English Dictionary*, s.v. توحید.

Within the Sufi paradigm, *Towḥīd* means purification and detachment of the heart from anything except the Truth. Sayyid-Ṣādiq Gowharīn, *Sharḥ-i iṣṭilāḥāt-i taṣavvuf*, vol. 9–10, s.v. توحيد.

121 The word *ṣāḥib-qirān* means lord of the happy conjunction; a fortunate and invincible hero. It is also a title given to a monarch who has ruled forty years; Muḥammad; Jesus. Steingass, *A Comprehensive Persian-English Dictionary*, s.v. صاحب قران.

122 The word *manẓūr* can mean looked at, seen, visible; admired; chosen, approved of, admitted, accepted; sanctioned, granted; agreeable, acceptable; designed, intended; aim, object in view (m.c.); advantage (m.c.). In the combination *manẓūri k̲h̲udā*, it means approved of God. Steingass, *A Comprehensive Persian-English Dictionary*, s.v. منظور.

123 Khatīb-i Fārsī, *Qalandar-nāma*, 40–41.

124 The word *zihe, zahe* means How good! excellent! Well done! Steingass, *A Comprehensive Persian-English Dictionary*, s.v. زهی.

125 The chronological sequence of events in Bāyazīd Basṭāmī's account is different from the logical order one might expect. I suggest that this is probably not merely Khatīb-i Fārsī's errors in reporting the events as Karamustafa postulated and that it might have a value in terms of Sufi tradition of compiling hagiographies. See Karamustafa, *God's Unruly Friends*, 116, notes 2 and 3.

126 Khatīb-i Fārsī, *Qalandar-nāma*, 55–56.

127 Ibid., 57.

128 Khatīb-i Fārsī, *Qalandar-nāma*, 57.

129 This couplet is different in Yazici's edition:

دعا کرد آنزمان گفتا الهی
تویی داننده حالم کماهی

See Haṭīb Fārisī, *Manāqib-i Jamāl al-Dīn Sāvī*, 31. In my translation, I have used Yazici's edition, because semantically and grammatically it is correct.

130 This couplet is different in Yazici's edition:

روانم کن به نور معرفت شاد
مرا از دینی و عقبی کن آزاد

See Haṭīb Fārisī, *Manāqib-i Jamāl al-Dīn Sāvī*, 32. I have used Yazici's edition because of the congruence of images: the combination of this world and the other world.

131 Khatīb-i Fārsī, *Qalandar-nāma*, 57.

132 Ibid, 57–58.

133 Niẓāmī Ganjawī, *Laylī u Majnūn*, ed. W. Dastgirdī, (Tehran: Armaghān, 1313/1934, second edition, ʿIlmī, 1363/1984).

134 See Ali Asghar Seyed-Gohrab, *Laylī And Majnūn: Love, Madness and Mystic Longing in Niẓāmī's Epic Romance* (Leiden: Brill, 2003), 337–339.

135 Stijn Aerts, in *The Encyclopaedia of Islam Three* s.v. Imām (technical term).

136 Khatīb-i Fārsī, *Qalandar-nāma*, 56.

جمال الدین ساوی هر سحرگاه
امامت کردی ایشان را و آنگاه
به رسم و عادت پیران زاهد
بتنها آمدی بیرون ز مسجد

Every dawn, Jamāl al-Dīn Sāvī
was their *Imām* and then
as (was the) tradition and habit of ascetic Elderly guides
he went out of the mosque alone.

137 Khatīb-i Fārsī, *Qalandar-nāma*, 58.

138 The compound verb *bar-andākhtan* means to throw out or down, s.v. برانداختن.

139 Literally, the word *valāyat* means helping, assisting or governing. It can be pronounced as *valāyat* or *vilāyat*. It can also connote being master of; authority; guardianship or sanctity; holiness; and mystical union with God affected by self-denial. Steingass, *A Comprehensive Persian-English Dictionary*, s.v., ولایة. According to Gowharīn, in *valāyat* is a state in which there remains in a person nothing but "the friend" (i.e., God). Sayyid-Ṣādiq Gowharīn, *Sharḥ-i iṣṭilāḥāt-i taṣavvuf*, vol. 9–10, s.v. ولایت.

140 Already, Basṭāmī, the renowned Sufi master, introduced Sāvī, his disciple, as the perfect man who could guide Shaykh ʿUṣmān to the forty-first stage of his spiritual journey. See Khatīb-i Fārsī, *Qalandar-nāma*, 40–41.

141 Annemarie Schimmel, *Mystical Dimensions of Islam*, 98–99.

142 Khatīb-i Fārsī, *Qalandar-nāma*, 58.

143 Annemarie Schimmel, *Mystical Dimensions of Islam*, 101–102.

144 Khatīb-i Fārsī, *Qalandar-nāma*, 60.

145 Mullā ʿAlī Al-Qārī, *Encyclopedia of Hadith Forgeries*, 307.

146 Annemarie Schimmel, *Mystical Dimensions of Islam*, 135.

147 Khatīb-i Fārsī, *Qalandar-nāma*, 60, 62.

148 Annemarie Schimmel, *Mystical Dimensions of Islam*, 416–418.

149 Khatīb-i Fārsī, *Qalandar-nāma*, 65.

150 *Abdāl* in this context is another term used to refer to a *qalandar*, see page 7, note 49.

151 Among the Persian meanings of the word *tajarrud* are being stripped, denuded; living in solitude; celibacy. Steingass, *A Comprehensive Persian-English Dictionary*, s.v. تجرد. The equivalent of the word *tajarrud* that would best correspond to the text of the *Qalandar-nāma* is perhaps 'renunciation'. However, the different connotations of the word in Persian and Arabic need to be present in mind when we encounter this term in the context of the *qalandarī* doctrine. Some of the connotations of the word in Persian overlap with the meanings of *tajarrud* in Arabic. However, the Arabic infinitives with the stem *jarad* yield connotations that have a fascinating connection with the implications of *tajarrud* as a core *qalandarī* concept: 1. inf. *jarad*, be naked, bare, hairless; lose the hair 2. inf. *tajrīd*, isolate; detach 3. inf. *tajarrud*, free one's self from; renounce worldly things; devote one's self entirely to; be separated, isolated. Steingass, The Student's *Arabic-English Dictionary*, s.v. جرد.

The explanation that Gowharīn gives for *tajrīd* can also clarify the Sufi conception of the term. According to him, *tajrīd* is a total state of detachment. This state has three stations: 1. The seeker is outwardly 'naked', (i.e. detached) from worldly intentions and desires. 2. S/he is inwardly detached from expectations of God's reward in the hereafter 3. S/he is detached from the thought that s/he has attained any spiritual state or station. The perfection of *tajrīd*, therefore, is when the seeker remains humble and detached from everything, except God. Sayyid-Ṣādiq Gowharīn, *Sharḥ-i iṣṭilāḥāt-i taṣavvuf*, vol. 3–4, s.v. تجرد.

152 Khatīb-i Fārsī, *Qalandar-nāma*, 66.

153 Khatīb-i Fārsī, *Qalandar-nāma*, 66–67.

154 *Javānmard* (lit. a young man) as a theme was included in Sufi works from the ninth to the twelfth century. The term refers to the embodiment of a complicated concept. Lloyd Ridgeon proposes to examine the manifestation of this concept in mediaeval times in relation to three categories, namely 'the felon, the faithful and the fighter'. The concept that comes close to that used in the context of *Qalandarnāma* is the second category, '*faqir*', which Ridgeon defines as 'faithful figure of religion'. However, Ridgeon does not elaborate on why he chooses this term for the term '*faqir*'. See Lloyd Ridgeon, 'Introduction: The Felon, the Faithful and the Fighter: The Protean Face of the

Chivalric Man (Javanmard) in the Medieval Persianate and Modern Iranian Worlds,' in *Javanmardi: The Ethics and Practice of Persianate Perfection*, ed., Lloyd Ridgeon. Gingko, 2018, pages 6, 3, 14.

155 Khatīb-i Fārsī, *Qalandar-nāma*, 67.

156 One of the meanings of the word *kashk* is sour milk dried or a sort of condiment made of butter-milk. Steingass, *A Comprehensive Persian-English Dictionary*, s.v. کشک.

157 The word *fann* has several meanings, such as manner, mode, and way. Steingass, *A Comprehensive Persian-English Dictionary*, s.v. فن

158 Farhad Daftari, in *The Encyclopaedia of Islam Three* s.v. Ahl al-Kisā'.

159 The expression عَلَى ٱلْأَرَآئِكِ is an allusion to the *Qur'ān*, 76:13 (sura al-Insān), which refers to the people who are rewarded with living in the paradise in the hereafter. Khatīb-i Fārsī, *Qalandar-nāma-yi Khatīb Fārsī* or *Sīrat-i Jamāl al-Dīn Sāvajī*, ed. Ḥamīd Zarrīnkūb (Tehran: Intishārāt-i Ṭūs, 1983), 67.

160 Annemarie Schimmel, *Mystical Dimensions of Islam*, 234.

161 Charles Lindholm, 'Prophets and Pirs, 214.

162 Christane Gruber, in *Encyclopaedia of Islam Three*, s.v. Mi'rājnāma.

163 Using the word *barādar* may imply Sāvī's invitation to Ṣafāhānī to join the *Qalandariyya* brotherhood.

164 Khatīb-i Fārsī, *Qalandar-nāma*, 68.

165 Probably, the hemistich must end with the word 'قسمست', which rhymes with 'اسمست' in the following hemistich. However, since Yazuci has the same citation, I have kept it as it appears in both editions. See Haṭīb Fārisī, *Manāqib-i Jamāl al-Dīn Sāvī*, ed. Tahsin Yazici (Ankara, Turk Tarih Kurumu Basımevi: 1972), 44.

166 Yazici's version is as follows: یکی موت طبیعی نام دارد. See Haṭīb Fārisī, *Manāqib-i Jamāl al-Dīn Sāvī*, ed. Tahsin Yazici (Ankara, Turk Tarih Kurumu Basımevi: 1972), 44.

167 Khatīb-i Fārsī, *Qalandar-nāma*, 68.

168 Khatīb-i Fārsī, *Qalandar-nāma*, 69.

169 For more see Margaret Malamud, 'The Politics of Heresy in Medieval Khurasan: The Karramiyya in Nishapur,' *Iranian Studies* 27, 1/4 (1994): 42–43.

170 This shows that there was already a hierarchical structure among the adherents of the *qalandarī* doctrine.

171 Khatīb-i Fārsī, *Qalandar-nāma*, 72.

172 Khatīb-i Fārsī, *Qalandar-nāma*, 73.

173 According to Zarrinkub, the original lines are as follows:

چو بشنیدند مردم حکم سلطان
از آن پس در دمشق او را نمانید

See Khatīb-i Fārsī, *Qalandar-nāma*, 75, n. 2 and 3.

174 Khatīb-i Fārsī, *Qalandar-nāma*, 73–75.

175 Khatīb-i Fārsī, *Qalandar-nāma*, 74–75.

176 Ibid., 77–78. This is where Khatīb-i Fārsī recounts how Sāvī receives the *jawlaq*, and assigns Balkhī the duty to ask for hair from the people, and to prepare two more garments (like Sāvī's garment), one in white for himself, and the other in black for Dargazīnī (pages 78–82). These couplets refer to Sāvī as founding the *Jawlaqiyya* movement. As the present study is focused on the Sāvī's codification of *Qalandariyya*, I do not include these couplets here.

177 Khatīb-i Fārsī, *Qalandar-nāma*, 83.

178 The word *kam-zan* means a low thrower at dice; unfortunate; one who does not entertain too high notions of his own excellence. The verb *kamzadan* means to diminish. Steingass, *A Comprehensive Persian-English Dictionary*, s.v. کمزن and کمزدن.

179 Khatīb-i Fārsī, *Qalandar-nāma*, 83.

[180] As mentioned before, this section is Sāvī's reiteration of the codification of the *Qalandariyya* doctrine. To avoid repetition in the body of the chapter, I move these lines and their translation to the appendix.

Works cited

Primary sources

Anṣārī, ʿAbd Allāh. *Risāla-yi Qalandar-nāma*, edited by Vaḥīd Dastgirdī. Tehran: Kitābfurūshi-yi Furūghī, 1970.

Bābā Ḥājī ʿAbd al-Raḥīm, *Qalandar-nāma-ʾī ba nām-i ādāb al-ṭarīq*, edited by Meharn Afshari, Tehran: Chishma, 2016.

Fārisī, Haṭīb, *Manāqib-i Jamāl al-Dīn Sāvī*, edited by Tahsin Yazici. Ankara, Turk Tarih Kurumu Basımevi, 1972.

Khatīb-i Fārsī. *Qalandar-nāma-yi Khatīb Fārsī* or *Sīrat-i Jamāl al-Dīn Sāvajī*, edited by Ḥamīd Zarrīnkūb. Tehran: Intishārāt-i Ṭūs, 1983.

Maqdasī, Muṭahhar bin Ṭāhir, *Āfarīnish-u tārīkh* (Vols. 4–6) translated and with an introduction by Muḥammad-Riżā Shafīʿī-Kadkanī, Tehran: Āgah, 1995.

Niẓāmī Ganjavī, *Laylī u Majnūn*, ed. W. Dastgirdī, Tehran: Armaghān, 1313/1934, second edition, ʿIlmī, 1363/1984.

Secondary sources

Al-Qārī, Mullā ʿAlī. *Encyclopaedia of Hadith Forgeries: Al-Asrār Al-Marfuʿa Fil-Akhbār Al-Mawżūʿa Sayings Misattributed to the Prophet Muḥammad.* Translated and with an introduction by Gibril Fouad Haddad. Rochdale UK: Beacon Books, 2013.

Ahmed, Shahab. *What Is Islam: The Importance of Being Islamic*. Princeton and Oxford: Princeton University Press, 2016.

Anvari, Hasan, *Farhang-i buzurg-i sukhan*, 8 vols., first publ. 1381, repr. Tehran: Intishārāt-i sukhan, 1382.

Arberry, Arthur J. *The Koran Interpreted: A Translation.* Oxford: Oxford University Press, 1983.

Bearman, P., T. Bianquis, C.E. Bosworth, E. van Donzel, and W.P. Heinrichs (eds.), *The Encyclopaedia of Islam*, Second Edition, Leiden: Brill, 1960–2007.

Bruijn, Johannes T.P. de, 'The *Qalandariyyāt* in Persian Mystical Poetry, from Sanāʾī onwards'. In *The Legacy of Mediæval Persian Sufism.* Edited by Leonard Lewisohn, 75–86. London and New York: Khaniqahi Nimatullahi Publications, 1992.

Fleet, Kate, Gudrun Krämer, Denis Matringe, John Nawas, Devin J. Stewart, Everett K. Rowson (eds.), *The Encyclopaedia of Islam Three*, Online, Leiden: Brill.

Gowharīn, Sayyid-Ṣādiq. *Sharḥ-i iṣṭilāḥāt-i taṣavvuf.* Tehran: Zavvār, 1382/ 2003–2004), vols 3–10.

Hodgson, Marshall G. S. *The Venture of Islam: Conscience and History in a World Civilization.* Vol II. Chicago and London: Chicago University Press, 1974.

Karamustafa, Ahmet T., 'Antinomian Sufis: Between Sublimation and Subversion: Divergent Attitudes Towards Social Norms and the Sharīʿa in Early Sufism (850–1200)'. In *The Cambridge Companion to Sufism*, edited by Lloyd Ridgeon, 101–124. Cambridge: Cambridge University Press, 2015.

Karamustafa, Ahmet T., *God's Unruly Friends: Dervish Groups in the Islamic Later Middle Period 1200–1550*. Salt Lake City: University of Utah Press, 1994.

Knysh, Alexander. *Sufism: A New History of Islamic Mysticism*. Princeton: Princeton University Press, 2017.

Lindholm, Charles, 'Prophets and Pirs: Charismatic Islam in the Middle East and South Asia'. In *Embodying Charisma: Modernity, Locality and the Performance of Emotion in Sufi Cults*, edited by Pnina Werbner and Helene Basu Werbner, 209–233. London: Routledge, 1998.

McAuliffe, J.D. (ed.), *The Encyclopaedia of the Qurʾān*, Leiden: Brill, 1960–2007.

Melchert, Christopher. 'Origins and Early Sufism'. In *The Cambridge Companion to Sufism*, edited by Lloyd Ridgeon, 3–23. Cambridge: Cambridge University Press, 2014.

Melchert, Christopher. *Before Sufism: Early Islamic Renunciant Piety*. Berlin, Boston: De Gruyter, 2020.

Nizami, Khaliq Ahmad, *Religion and Politics in India During the Thirteenth Century*, New Delhi: Oxford University Press, 2002.

Papas, Alexandre. *Thus Spake the Dervish: Sufism, Language, and the Religious Margins in Central Asia, 1400–1900*. Leiden and Boston: Brill, 2019.

Renard, John. *Friends of God: Islamic Images of Piety, Commitment, and Servanthood*. 1st ed. Berkeley: University of California Press, 2008.

Ridgeon, Lloyd. 'Introduction: The Felon, the Faithful and the Fighter: The Protean Face of the Chivalric Man (Javanmard) in the Medieval Persianate and Modern Iranian Worlds.' In *Javanmardi: The Ethics and Practice of Persianate Perfection*, edited by Lloyd Ridgeon, 1–27. Gingko, 2018. https://doi.org/10.2307/j.ctv75d0fs.4.

Ridgeon, Lloyd. 'Mysticism in Medieval Sufism'. In *The Cambridge Companion to Sufism*, edited by Lloyd Ridgeon, 125–149. Cambridge: Cambridge University Press, 2014.

Schimmel, Annemarie. *Mystical Dimensions of Islam*. Chapel Hill: The University of North Carolina Press, 1975.

Seyed-Gohrab, Ali-Asghar. 'My Heart is the Ball, Your Lock the Polo-Stick: The Development of Polo Metaphors in Classical Persian Poetry'. In *The Necklace of the Pleiades*. Eds. Franklin Lewis and Sunil Sharma, 183–205. Leiden: Leiden University Press, 2010.

Seyed-Gohrab, Ali-Asghar. *Laylī And Majnūn: Love, Madness and Mystic Longing in Niẓāmī's Epic Romance*. Leiden: Brill, 2003.

Suhravardī, Shihāb al-Dīn ʿUmar, *ʿAwārif al-maʿārif*, translated by Abū Manṣūr ʿAbd al-Muʾmin Iṣfahānī, edited by Qāsim Anṣārī. Tehran: Intishārāt-i ʿlmī farhangi, 1985.

Sviri, Sara. 'Ḥakīm Tirmidhī and the *Malāmatī* Movement in Early Sufism'. In *The Heritage of Sufism: Classical Persian Sufism from its Origins to Rūmī (700–1300)*, edited by Leonard Lewisohn, 583–613. Oxford, Oneworld Publications, 1999.

Trimingham J. Spencer. *The Sufi Orders in Islam*. Oxford: The Clarendon Press, 1971.

Yarshater, E., *Encyclopaedia Iranica*, Encyclopaedia Iranica Foundation, 1987–, http://www.iranicaonline.org/.

Moderate Level-Headed Antinomianism of Ḥāfiẓ and its Artistic Expression[1]

Majdoddin Keyvani

Abstract

This chapter examines a broad spectrum of motifs, themes, and metaphors employed by the celebrated Persian poet Ḥāfiẓ to critique the false piety exhibited by representatives of the Islamic hierarchy in Islamic society. The author analyses Ḥāfiẓ's utilisation of antinomian qalandari allusions to elucidate how the poet denounces hypocrisy. The deployment of these allusions is intricately linked to the societal perceptions of Islam in fourteenth-century Persia. Less than two centuries after its establishment, Islam faced numerous forms of opposition from various areas of the lands it had swept through, each with its own historical-cultural background, promoting its specific ideological, religious or political orientations. Over time, the increasing opposition led to factional rivalry, discordance and even physically bloody encounters among people who all professed Islam. The result was the creation of a good number of opposing denominations, and so-called heretical coteries and deviant orders, some minor and short-lived and others relatively powerful and persistent. They are mostly regarded as nonconformist or heretical by the Sunni Sharīʿa which, in Western Islamic studies, is generally considered "orthodox". However, for the sake of argument, we take the *Shiite* denomination as orthodox as well.

Keywords: Ḥāfiẓ; antinomianism; transgression; Sharia laws; piety; heresy.

Inconsistent interpretations

A substantial amount of discord came from the somewhat differing interpretations of Islam within the Muslim community and the way each group looked at the Sharīʿa and its role in the lives of its followers. Any one of these groups may regard the others as heretical and deviant and even accuse them of infidelity. Attention in this chapter is mostly focused on Sufi Orders and the lesser-known movements such as *Qalandarī* and *Malāmatī* that are counted as off-shoots of Sufism by some, and as partly independent socio-religious entities by others. Many of those deviating from orthodox Islam mainly targeted the excessive inflexibility of certain aspects of the new religion, arguably brought about by its staunch adherents and self-appointed custodians and exponents, some indisputably hypocritical with holier-than-thou attitudes.

Those coteries were not of the same mind regarding the areas of their conflict with orthodoxy, nor was their opposition of the same intensity. As a result, their reactions took multiple varying shapes. Thus, different designations, such as Shiism, Ismāʿīlīyya, Ṣūfīyya, Qalandarīyya, Malāmatīyya, and many others, appeared, each name pointing to their distinctive characteristics or major preferences and strategic approaches, their common denominator being non-conformity with the most rigid interpretation of so-called authentic Islam (*Islām-i Muḥammadī / Islām-i aṣīl*). Among these, Shiism and Ismailism have fundamental differences from orthodox Islam (*Sunna/Tasannun*). Sufism can be considered an "aberrant" sub-group of both orthodox *Sunna* and Shiism. That is, there are Sufis of a more Shiite persuasion and Sufis more inclined to *Sunna*.

Sufi position

Amongst all these denominations, Sufism seems to have represented the most immediate challenging opponent of both Shiism and *Sunna* in outlook, ritual practices and daily life. It is worth emphasising that such deviant individuals as *Malamātī*s and *Qalandarī*s are often deemed sub-groups either of *Sunna* or *Shiite*, not seriously committed to either though. At least a sizable number of Sufis were perhaps the most antinomian sub-community within Islam notwithstanding that they were rejected by some as disbelievers. As they grew more and more in size and fame, some ignorant commoners were attracted to them and were exploited by insincere, dishonest Sufi Sheikhs who assumed the appearance of true devout non-conformists but followed their own objectives, acting like some of the guileful and cunning influential figures in the Islamic Establishment such as *Muftī, Qāżī, Vāʿiẓ* and so on.

Ḥāfiẓ's perspective

Now the question is: where does Kh^{w}āja Ḥāfiẓ of Shiraz stand in this rather confused picture of the antinomian movement in Islam? Before we address this question, we must first determine to which of all the so-called deviant sub-groups described above and to what intellectual persuasions he belonged. An enormous amount of research has been done in this respect and many views, both resemblant and divergent, have been expressed as to Ḥāfiẓ's position among the numerous antinomian tendencies.

Personally, I am with those who believe that Ḥāfiẓ stands above all such tendencies while being very familiar with them but influenced only by the true and uncontaminated essence of each, always adhering to moderation and good judgement. For him morality comes first. What is important for Ḥāfiẓ is the kernel and not the shell. He lifts the deceitfully gilded cover and tries to see the core. He is a honey bee flying from one flower bush to another, sucking out the best of the best and refusing to accept any repellent and unhealthy smell or juice. There is no evidence whatsoever of his affiliation to any known conventional *Khānqāh* and his allegiance to any Sheikh or spiritual guide of historical reality. Nor is there any indication of the poet's presence in or active association with groups such as *qalandarīyya* or *malāmatīyya* in their intemperate, unrestrained vehemence. Nonetheless, as said, he is both influenced by and critical of them, because he has seen or read about good honest *qalandars* and bad and dishonest ones. So, one can observe both positive and negative remarks about this group in Ḥāfiẓ's ghazals (for extensive discussions on the rise and decline of the *qalandarī* movement throughout history, their origin, geographical distribution, changing outlooks, political positions since its inception in the mid-third to the ninth century, see: Shafīʿī-Kadkanī, especially chapters 3, 9. 11–14 and 49; Murtażavī, part 5).

Moreover, no sign of disrespect of true Islam can be spotted in Ḥāfiẓ's *Dīvān*, nor is there any indication of any rebellious outlook or negligence of religious obligations on his part. What he cannot stand is the abuse of any line of thought or ideology, whether it is of Islam, Sufism or *Qalandarī* convictions. For Ḥāfiẓ, a sanctimonious jurisprudent (*faqīh*) is as vicious and harmful as a false, insincere qalandar. Not every claiming Muslim is a true Muslim, nor is every pretending Qalandar a true Qalandar. It is not the outward appearance which makes one a true qalandar:

هزار نکتهٔ باریک تر ز مو اینجاست
نه هر که سر بتراشد قلندری داند

There are a thousand-minute points finer than a hair
Not everyone who shaved their head is aware of *qalandarī* [world]
(Ḥāfiẓ, 117/10)[2]

He looks at both sides, disdaining the side sullied with hypocrisy, fanaticism and excess. Some of his verses, whether construed as literal or figurative, advise moderation and proper timing even in drinking wine:

نگویمت که همه ساله می پرستی کن
سه ماه می خور و نه ماه پارسا می باش

I do not say that you fondly drink all the year through
Drink three months and be pious for nine months
(Ḥāfiẓ, 145/12)

صوفی ار باده به اندازه خورد نوشش باد
ور نه اندیشهٔ این کار فراموشش باد

If Sufi drinks in right proportion, then may he enjoy it!
If not, he'd better forget the idea of this altogether
(Ḥāfiẓ, 96/10)

Meanwhile, Ḥāfiẓ indirectly and tactfully reveals that some Sufis drink what is prohibited in Islam.

Middling attitude

Since our poet is a man of rectitude and morality, he just cannot stand any dishonest two-faced person. However, despite his criticising both the religiosity of the fanatic advocates of *Sharīʿa* and certain behaviours of extreme antinomians, he is neither anti-*Sharīʿa* nor free of some degree of antinomianism. Rather, he is a reasonable and sincere man of integrity and honesty execrating hypocrites no matter whether they are qalandars or hold high positions in the *Sharīʿa* establishment and ruling class. He loathes and condemns whoever double-deals and tries to deceive people by presenting himself as a righteous and trustworthy person, thus seeking his own gain (often illegitimate). When Ḥāfiẓ finds fault with the custodians of *Sharīʿa* and defies such influential officials as judges (*qāżī*), preachers and *muḥtasib*, he is naturally deemed to be disrespectful to the sacred. When it comes to casting doubt on areas considered to be fundamental and indubitable, he is charged with sacrilege. Here, in both cases Ḥāfiẓ has to some degree taken an antinomian position. Nonetheless, he is sensible enough not to go to extremes because he is by nature a man of peace and inclined to moderation; and this is supported by numerous verses in his *Dīvān*. Besides, contrary to some other protesting poets, such as ʿUbeyd of Zākān (d. circa 772/1370), he never adopts impolite language, let alone any obscene, lewd tone in criticising people he condemns.

Artistic expression of antinomianism

It may sound "un-English", but I choose this phrase to denote the way Ḥāfiẓ castigates those who are blameworthy for their immorality and devious acts. By "artistic expression of antinomianism" I mean the expression of one's strong displeasure, not in an ordinary conventional manner but in a creative fashion flavoured with a variety of rhetorical niceties and poetic devices often unattainable by non-artists. And this is what makes Ḥāfiẓ different from other critics, including many other poets. We may describe Ḥāfiẓ as being a great free thinker, a genuine nonconformist Sufi, a God-seeking knower (*ʿārif*), social critic and moral reformer pursuing high moral principles and ideals. Above all this, however, he is a poet, and I am inclined to consider him first and foremost an artist of exceptional creative ability more interested in the fine quality and elegance of his poetry. Khurramshāhī rightly observes that "From the dawn of Persian literature up to the $8^{th}/14^{th}$ century, Ḥāfiẓ was the most frequent user of figures of speech, especially the technique of *īhām*," or double entendre.[3] Despite the scholarly background evident from his historical, mythological, philosophical, Qurʾānic and jurisprudential references and allusions throughout his *Dīvān* (see, for example, Ḥāfiẓ, 10/8; 11/11, 20; 39/6; 41/ 9; 242/17; 255/6–9,12,13), he hardly compares himself to any philosopher or religious authority, but competes with such poets as Niẓāmī (Ḥāfiẓ, 233/2) and (at least in Furūghī's selected ghazals of Ḥāfiẓ,111/4) Żahīr Fārīyābī, Masʿūd Saʿd Salmān and Khʷājū of Kirmān. He never boasts about a wealth of knowledge of any kind. Indeed, he reprimands self-praise and insolence (see Ḥāfiẓ, 33/3; 69/ 5; 70/2; 173/14; 235/3; 237/10), but he does take pride in his superb poetic gift and command of the Persian language and its niceties and rhetorical nuances.

حافظ ار سیم و زرت نیست برو شاکر باش
چه به از دولت لطف سخن و طبع سلیم؟

O Ḥāfiẓ, if you have no silver and gold, go and be grateful
What is better than the fortune of fine speech and sound disposition?
(Ḥāfiẓ, 193/5)

ز شعر دلکش حافظ کسی شود آگاه
که لطف طبع و سخن گفتنِ دری داند

Aware of Ḥāfiẓ's fascinating poetry becomes he
who understands tender nature and *Dari* speech.
(Ḥāfiẓ, 117/18)

حسد چه می بری ای سست نظم بر حافظ؟
قبول خاطر و لطف سخن خداداد است

O you, writer of weak verses, why do you envy Ḥāfiẓ?
Public reception [of his poems]and grace of speech are God's blessings.

(Ḥāfiẓ, 19/11; also see: 11/7,12,1915/13; 22/11; 23/6; 35/4; 36 /13; 38/ 7; 90/15).

In fact, he draws on all he has studied of history, mythology, philosophy, theology, the Arabic language and literature, and bases his reflections and viewpoints on them to better drive his social and educational points home. He does not merely repeat what he has read, but recasts it in a rhetorically novel form and fresh poetical fashion. Although Ḥāfiẓ is greatly concerned about the socio-political irregularities and religious deviations around him and feels responsible for speaking out against them, for him the excellence of poetry comes first. His *Dīvān* contains a wealth of indications that reveal this preference. It is not unreasonable to claim that antinomianism is in the service of his art of poetry and not the other way round. Persian literary history has been fortunate to have Ḥāfiẓ, who is both a first-grade insightful social critic and a poet of superb artistic vision and linguistic ability all in one. Let me elaborate on this a little more.

Ḥāfiẓ is no doubt an antinomian, but he expresses this in such a way as to fit his poetical propensities. His admonishing of religious and socio-political digressions is not for the sake of sheer admonishment and limited to bare criticism; it is also to satisfy his artistic urges. So, he embellishes his criticism with artistic devices and various tropes to transform ordinary language into a far more effective and appealing expression. As far as his criticism of corruption and misbehaviour is concerned, Ḥāfiẓ makes use of satirical and sardonic language in the most effective, poignant and devastating manner without using a single indecent word or obscene expression. The reader of such poetry is not only impressed by Ḥāfiẓ's brave and responsible stance against misconduct and immorality but also derives a great deal of pleasure from the artistic way in which the poet articulates such matters.

Two techniques of criticism

The two dominant ways in which Ḥāfiẓ demonstrates his dislike of unjust and corrupt individuals are as follows:

1. When the objects of his criticism are politically and militarily powerful and arrogant and affluent men, he emphasises the value of spiritual self-sufficiency

(*istighnā*), the worthlessness of worldly authority and attachments, the danger of greed and, conversely, the inherent worth of poverty and spiritual uplift, thus demonstrating his contempt for despotism, unjust rule, earthly transient might and perishable possessions. Here are a few examples:

ما آبروی فقر و قناعت نمی بریم
با پادشه بگوی که روزی مقرر است

We do not disgrace poverty and contentment
Tell the king that our daily bread is predestined.
(Ḥāfiẓ, 15/9)

ز پادشاه و گدا فارغم بحمدالله
گدای خاک در دوست پادشاه منست

Thank God, I am free of both beggars and kings
The beggar at the beloved's doorway is my prince.
(Ḥāfiẓ, 43/6)

گدا چرا نزند لاف سلطنت امروز
که خیمه سایه ابرست و بزمگه لب کشت

Why does the destitute man not brag about his kingdom today?
While the shade of the clouds makes his canopy, and his banquet is set by the field.
(Ḥāfiẓ. 39/13)

مبین حقیر گدایان عشق را کاین قوم
شهان بی کمر و خسروان بی کلهند

Do not look down on the community of beggars of love who
are kings without belt and princes without crown.
(Ḥāfiẓ, 93/9)

گر چه گردآلود فقرم، شرم باد از همّتم
گر به آب چشمهٔ خورشیدْ دامن تر کنم

منِ که دارم در گدایی گنجِ سلطانی به دست
تنگ چشمم گر نظر بر چشمهٔ کوثر کنم

Even though I am covered with the dust of poverty, shame on my ambition (*himmat*), if I wet the skirt of my robe with the Sun's spring
I, having access to a king's treasure in poverty,
would be mean to look at the fountain of Kowthar.
(Ḥāfiẓ, 205/14,15)

It is worth remembering here that Ḥāfiẓ's opposition to the authorities was not motivated by political or religious ambition. In some of his ghazals, he makes it clear that he was not a man of war, nor even apt to conduct verbal disputes. His sole objective was the moral betterment of society.

غیرتم کشت که محبوب جهانی لیکن
روز و شب عربده با خلق خدا نتوان کرد

Jealousy killed me when I found you loved by the world, but
One cannot dispute with God's people all the time, day, and night
(Ḥāfiẓ, p 72/11)

یک حرف صوفیانه بگویم، اجازت است ؟
ای نور دیده صلح به از جنگ و داوری

Would you allow me to say a Sufi-like word?
O apple of my eyes, peace is better than war and contention.
(Ḥāfiẓ, 247/11)

ما قصهٔ سکندر و دارا نخوانده ایم
از ما بجز حکایت مهر و وفا مپرس

We have not read the story of Alexander and Dārā
Do not ask anything but the story of love and loyalty
(Ḥāfiẓ, 140/12; also see 274/8, 9, 12).

2. Ḥāfiẓ's second way of admonition is even more cutting and sardonic. It aims at two groups: (1) the too rigid, stern and often cantankerous ascetics (*zāhid*) who live a solitary life and avoid mingling with people and assuming social responsibilities. Of course, among this group can be found dishonest individuals who only feign austerity and piousness. (2) *Sharīʿa* guardians and those charged with law and order in the Muslim community who monitor the public to make sure that they strictly observe the *Sharīʿa* commandments and rites. They consist of Mullas of varying ranks, sheikhs, Imams (religious leaders), Imām-i jamāʿat ("prayer leaders"),

Imām-i shahr ("top cleric overseeing the strict practice of Islamic rules in a city"); muftī ("Muslim legal experts"), *vā'iẓ* ("preachers"), *qāżī* ("judges"), *muḥtasib* ("supervisors of bazaars in Medieval Islamic countries"), *asas* ("night guards") and *pāsbān* ("policemen").

Ḥāfiẓ does not fail to find faults with mosques, khānaqāhs, madrasas and sermon assemblies – ideal places for the display of domineering hypocritical clerics, preachers and Sheikhs whose main intention is to deceive the innocent suggestible people. Here are a few examples:

ز کنج مدرسه حافظ مجوی گوهر عشق
قدم برون نه اگر میل جست و جو داری

O Ḥāfiẓ, do not search for gem of love in the madrasa
Step out from there if you desire to explore.
(Ḥāfiẓ, 262/3; also see, 176/6,14).[4]

As mentioned earlier, Ḥāfiẓ's mere condemnation of hypocrisy, injustice and corruption, although very important in itself, is not as uniquely remarkable as the artistic manner in which he has articulated it, because this artistic manner makes his criticisms much more impressive and engaging to read. It enables the reader to become curious to know how people were dealt with by the ruling and religious authorities in the time of Ḥāfiẓ.

Before I address the artistic merits of Ḥāfiẓ's antinomianism, I want to emphasise the role of the criticisms by such open-minded and more tolerant thinkers as Ḥāfiẓ on the one hand, and their moderate, sensible and decent approach on the other, have had in helping to present a relatively milder, more refined, and agreeable version of Islam, at least in a theoretical or ideal form. Even though Ḥāfiẓ cannot be counted a typical, conventional and khānaqāh-affiliated Sufi,[5] he represents the unpolluted and bona fide Sufism of the kind taught by the likes of the eminent mystic Abū Sa'īd-i Abu 'l-Kheyr (d. 440/1048), who often denounced egoism and described Sufism as consisting of three components: "discarding whatever you have in mind, giving away anything you have in hand, and enduring what afflicts you."[6] It must be remembered that the main factor in differentiating the likes of Ḥāfiẓ from those exceedingly pious and khanaqah-bound Sufis is not necessarily one's physical presence in a khānaqāh or *ribāṭ*, but their broad-mindedness, tolerance and concern for others. Abū Sa'īd was the Sheykh of a khānaqāh, but he cared more about others than himself. He rejected the phony claims of some of the Sufis as *turrahāt* ("nonsense").[7] Contrary to the *faqih*s and self-appointed custodians of the *Sharī'a* who have unnecessarily turned a simple appealing Islam into a complicated network of mostly cumbersome, awkward rules and rituals, such free thinkers as Ḥāfiẓ have tried to make it less uncompromising and more agreeable and comprehensible. Ḥāfiẓ's Islam is friendlier and more forgiving than that of the *faqīh*'s which is too exacting and far less reconciling. The former inspires more hope, and confidence, whereas the latter emits more despair and fear. Ḥāfiẓ's God of clemency is in contrast with *faqīh*'s God of punishment. There is no single verse in his *Dīvān* that mentions, let alone confirms, any verdict issued by *faqīhs*, whereas he repeatedly refers to the Qur'ān as both his guide and source of inspiration. He clearly asserts that he owes to the Qur'ān whatever he has achieved (هر چه کردم همه از دولت قرآن کردم). The Qur'ān has had great influence on both the form and content of Ḥāfiẓ's poetry. There are quite a number of direct citations from the Qur'ān and numerous allusions to its verses.[8] However, to state his disagreement with the constant deceptive references by *faqīhs* to the Qur'ān and the Prophet's traditions, Ḥāfiẓ substantiates his statements by attributing them to people and things regarded as repulsive and untouchable (for more on this, see below).

More on Ḥāfiẓ's rhetorical criticism

Turning to Ḥāfiẓ's antinomian position and his rhetorically exquisite manner of demonstrating this position, let me first say that the second most frequent motif (after "love") in his ghazals is probably the denunciation of offices and positions either conventionally religious or somehow influenced and indirectly led by the Islamic establishment. For example, the judicial and endowments establishments were traditionally in the hands of the high-ranking clergy. Police forces, including *shahna*, *asas* and *muḥtasibs*, although officially government functionaries, were in the service of qadis who constituted part of the *Sharīʿa* authorities. There are relatively few ghazals in the *Dīvān* that make no mention of the oppression and misconduct of such offices and individuals. In the 30 pages I randomly selected (1–10, 100–110 and 200–210) from the *Dīvān*, Injavī edition, there are 52 references to the people and institutions that are the objects of some of Ḥāfiẓ's admonishments or ironic remarks.

An ingenious technique he employs to make his scornful observations more effective and bitter is the use of the names of people and places that are rejected and even prohibited by the *Sharīʿa* as sacrilegious and profane. A religion that regards the mere touching of wine as *najis* ("religiously unclean and impure") obviously bans the making and drinking of wine and even denounces the very favourable and sympathetic discussion of anything or anybody related to wine.[9] Against such an-ill-suited background, to talk about and encourage drinking could have put Ḥāfiẓ at risk. The way he talks about wine, wine-bearers, taverns, tavern masters, wine cups, *kharābāt* and so on cannot and must not be taken simply as "figurative," especially when used in combination with the religious hierarchy Ḥāfiẓ was critical of. In fact, he was challenging the insincere, self-seeking individuals in authority by praising exactly what they disapproved or often pretended to disapprove of. Ḥāfiẓ was commending things of which certain two-faced people had made a lucrative business by warning the community against them. In other words, Ḥāfiẓ advertised, as it were, the very profanity that the *Sharīʿa* guardians proscribed, not because our poet necessarily intended to entice people into an evil act. Rather, he wanted to remind the oppressive hypocrites that their pernicious mismanagement of society is far more wicked than indulging in drink and deserves more severe retribution. Drinking one cup of wine might adversely affect, if anybody, only the person who drinks it, but a biased venal qadi can ruin the lives of an entire family or a section of the community. When Ḥāfiẓ sings:

عنان به میکده خواهیم تافت زین مجلس
که وعظ بی عملان واجب است نشنیدن
مبوس جز لب ساقیَ و جام می حافظ
که دست زهد فروشان خطاست بوسیدن

We'll turn away from this congregation towards the tavern
Because it is incumbent not to listen to the sermons of those who do not act on their own words.
O Ḥāfiẓ, don't kiss anything but the cup-bearer's lip and the cup of wine
As it is wrong to kiss the hands of the do-nothings.
(Ḥāfiẓ, 217/ 3, 7)

He reveals that in such gatherings the *vāʿiẓ* urges his audience to do what he rarely does himself. To show his abhorrence to this hypocrisy, Ḥāfiẓ puts the tavern above religious assemblies. And this preference is a great blow to those whose benefits lie in the thriving of such meetings. Another place that our poet puts before any other sacred place is the *kharābāt*, a ruined, abandoned spot frequented by homeless drunkards, rogues and vagabonds. In the following verse:

حافظا روز اجل گر به کف آری جامی
یکسر از کوی خرابات برندت به بهشت

O Ḥāfiẓ if you grab a cup of wine on the day of your death
You will be carried from the kharābāt straight to heaven.
(Ḥāfiẓ, 38/18)

We see that, according to Ḥāfiẓ's judgement, drinking a cup of wine (a sinful deed) guarantees you heaven (a reward given only to the pious). Few contrasts can be this blasphemous. He intentionally juxtaposes some of the most sacrilegious with the most sacred notions. In the following verse, rather than resort to the sacred, Ḥāfiẓ adjures the cupbearer to bring him wine in the name of the spiritual contentment of the *rinds* so she/he (*sāqī*) can hear the singer utter the Qur'ānic verse: "*huva al-ghanī*" ("God is rich," i.e., wanting nothing).

ساقی به بی نیازِیِ رندان که می بیار
تا بشنوی ز صوت مغنّی هوالغنی

By the contentment of the rends, O Sāqī, I exhort you to bring wine
So that you will hear the singer recite: "He is rich."
(Ḥāfiẓ, 262/9)

Incidentally, remember that Ḥāfiẓ juxtaposes *mughannī* ("a singer," "musician") with *Ghanī* (one of God's Attributes), an utterly unacceptable statement in any *faqīh's* view.

سال ها پیروی مذهب رندان کردم
تا به فتوای خرد حرص به زندان کردم

For years did I follow the religion of rends
Until, upon the verdict of sound reason, I imprisoned avarice.
(Ḥāfiẓ,185/10)

Note that Ḥāfiẓ acted not on the *faqīh*'s *fatwa* ("verdict") but on that of reason, cleverly and implicitly denying the *faqīh*'s authority.[10]

مرید پیر مغانم، ز من مرنج ای شیخ
چرا که وعده تو کردیّ و او بجا آورد

I am a disciple of the doyen of the tavern (*Pīr-i Mughān*),
be not aggrieved with me, o Shaikh, because you promised, but he fulfilled it.
(Ḥāfiẓ, 64 / 8)

Consider the juxtaposition of the two (in the cleric's opinion) irreconcilably contrasting concepts of *mey* ("wine") and *raḥmat-i Khuda* ("God's Grace") in the following verse:

چو پیر سالک عشقت به می حواله کند
بنوش و منتظر رحمت خدا می باش

When the spiritual doyen instructs you to drink wine
Take it and wait for God's Grace.
(Ḥāfiẓ, 145/13)

Ḥāfiẓ and Sufism

Of the two trends in the Sufi movement, "devotional" and "erotic" (*ʿābidāna* vs. *ʿāshiqāna*), Ḥāfiẓ has rightly been described as belonging to the latter, reaching him from Abū Saʿīd Abu ʿl-Kheyr, ʿAṭṭār and Rūmī, because this branch of Sufism encourages much greater freedom and far fewer restrictions. Contrary to ascetic Sufism, it encourages healthy earthly pleasure, greater tolerance, social participation, avoiding bias and religious rigidity.[11] Therefore, despite his general praise of Sufism, this praise is not unconditional, dogmatic and prejudiced. So he can be critical of anybody and anything deviating from upright, ethical and moderate Sufism. Therefore, his negative tone about *ṣowmaʿa* ("Sufi cloister"), better known as khanaqah, is caused by his finding such meeting places not always free of hypocrisy, pretentious austerity and even immorality. Thus, he sings:

ز خانقاه به میخانه می رود حافظ
مگر ز مستی زهد و ریا به هوش آمد؟

Ḥāfiẓ goes from khānaqāh to the tavern
Perhaps, he has recovered from the intoxication of sanctimony and hypocrisy.
(Ḥāfiẓ, 95/7)

Since he finds sermons at the mosque too tedious and a waste of time, he leaves it for *kharābāt*:

گر ز مسجد به خرابات شدم خرده مگیر
مجلس وعظ دراز است و زمان خواهد شد

If I left the mosque for kharābat, don't blame me
The sermons there are long-winded and take much time.
(Ḥāfiẓ, 116/ 8)

An important Sufi topic Ḥāfiẓ takes issue with is the exaggerated claims made by many Sufi sheykhs, referred to as *ṭāmāt* and *shaṭḥ*. Such hyperbolic assertions imply that Sufi sheykhs can do spectacular mind-blowing things called "karāmāt". In fact, if not the sheykhs themselves, their disciples seem to equate *karāmāt* with miracles attributed to prophets.[12] We do not need to emphasise how infuriating the equation of *ṭamāt* with superstition would be to the arrogant sheikhs and their followers! Not only does Ḥāfiẓ criticise the insincere words and behaviour of Sufis, but he also utters negative remarks about whatever they wear or use to distinguish themselves as austere devotees: *Khirqa* ("a dervish's cloak of poor quality"), *ṭaylasān* ("the robe worn by judges and preachers"), *dalq* (another term for *khirqa*) and rosaries (*tasbīḥ*, *sabḥa*).[13] The enormous number of times that Ḥāfiẓ mentions *khirqa* and *dalq* demonstrates how deeply concerned he was about the insincerity and deceptiveness of Sufis and their sheikhs.

A theologically contentious issue Ḥāfiẓ takes a stance on is man's sin and its inconsistency with God's Clemency. He argues that unless man commits sin God's Mercy does not make sense.

سهو و خطای بنده چو گیرند اعتبار
معنیّ عفو و رحمت پروردگار چیست؟

If [God's] servant is to be accountable for his errors and sins
Then, what is the meaning of God's Forgiveness and Mercy?
(Ḥāfiẓ, 25/ 15)

نصیب ماست بهشت ای خدا شناس برو
که مستحقّ کرامت گناهکارانند

Heaven is ours o God-knower: go away
Because only the sinners need His Clemency.
(Ḥāfiẓ, 100/ 5)

Even more provocative is his assertion that infidelity is a necessity in God's creation, because it is the very ontological reason for God's retribution.

در کارخانهٔ عشق از کفر ناگزیر است
آتش کرا بسوزد گر بولهب نباشد

In the workshop of love, unfaithfulness is unavoidable
Should there be no Bū Lahab,[14] who should fire burn [in hell]?
(Ḥāfiẓ, 69/3)

Is Ḥāfiẓ not justifying – even giving some credit to – infidelity and Abū Lahab, both most hated in the Muslim community of his time? Demonstrating this degree of religious tolerance was far from acceptable, even deserving severe retribution. In the face of the *faqīh* who prescribes punishment for every single unorthodox act (even very trivial ones), Ḥāfiẓ sings:

هاتفی از گوشهٔ میخانه دوش
گفت ببخشند گنه، می بنوش

Yesterday, a heavenly messenger from the corner of the tavern
Said: sins are absolved, keep drinking!
(Ḥāfiẓ, 153/6)

فقیه مدرسه دی مست بود و فتوی داد
که می حرام ولی به ز مال اوقافست

Yesterday, while drunken, the seminary faqih issued this verdict:
Wine is forbidden, yet it is better than [income from] endowments.
(Ḥāfiẓ, 39/7)

ریا حلال شمارند و جام باده حرام
زهی طریقت و ملت، زهی شریعت و کیش

They consider hypocrisy legitimate, but a cup of wine forbidden
What a credo and religion, what a sharīʿa, and cult!
(Ḥāfiẓ, 145/8)

Of the two general doctrinal schools of Sufism, the school of piety and the school of love (*ʿābidāna* versus *ʿāshiqāna*) mentioned above, the former does not differ much from orthodox *Sharīʿa,* which stresses asceticism and rigid observance of religious requirements, hardly encouraging gaiety and cheerfulness. The difference seems to be the greater emphasis that pious Sufism places on self-abnegating, solitude and chastity. Ḥāfiẓ's proclivity is toward a broad-minded, tolerant and lenient Sufism invigorated by joy, merriment and jubilation, markedly evident in his ghazels. So, wherever he makes critical or satirical remarks about Sufis and Sufism he is generally aiming at the pious school that makes life more boring and sterner and less joyous and delightful. Ḥāfiẓ's most crushing attacks are directed against those who outwardly appear to be puritan and self-denying but privately indulge themselves even with evil acts. Their double-dealing comes into the open when the opportunity arises; so, they publicly commit what they have always frowned upon:

حافظ خلوت نشین دوش به میخانه شد
از سرِ پیمان گذشت، بر سرِ پیمانه شد
صوفی مجلس که دی جام و قدح می شکست
دوش به یک جرعه می عاقل و فرزانه شد

Yesterday, Ḥāfiẓ made his way from solitude to the tavern
He broke his covenant and engaged in drinking.
The Sufi who was smashing the wine cup and bowl,
by taking one sip of wine became sagacious and wise.
(Ḥāfiẓ, 64/ 11–12)

This opportunism is particularly depicted in one of Ḥāfiẓ's ghazals, where he includes himself among the apparent teetotallers who seize the chance brought about by the ruling prince. The poem apparently sets two groups apart: those who have publicly begun drinking and those who drink, but secretly and privately, hiding behind their extreme hypocrisy. The confused situation baffles Ḥāfiẓ, so he resorts to the master of the winehouse for an explanation and the shrewd master advises him to keep quiet.

Ḥāfiẓ is not necessarily unhappy because people, including himself, drink; what upsets him is the hypocrisy and sanctimony prevalent around him: a harmful practice deeply rooted in the community at large because of the politico-religious despotism that makes people fear candour and forthrightness and drives them into surreptitious activities:

در عهد پادشاه خطا بخشِ جُرم پوش
حافظ قرابه کش شد و مُفتی پیاله نوش
صوفی ز کنج صومعه در پای خُم نشست
تا دید محتسب که سبو می کشد به دوش
احوال شیخ و قاضی و شُرب الیهودشان
کردم سؤال صبحدم از پیر می فروش
گفتا نگفتنی است سخن، گر چه محرمی
در کش زبان و پرده نگه دار و می بنوش

In the reign of the forgiving and lenient prince
Ḥāfiẓ became a carboy-carrier and the mufti a wine drinker
Leaving the hermitage corner, the Sufi sat by the wine vat
when he saw the *muḥtasib* carrying a crock on his shoulder
About the shaikh and qadi and their stealthy drinking
did I ask the master of the winehouse early in the morning,
He said, "although you are an intimate, it is unspeakable

Speak no more; keep the secret and drink your wine"!
(Ḥāfiẓ, 147/1–4)

The following verse reveals the despicable outcome of constant suppression when temporarily stopped:

ز کوی میکده دوشش به دوش می بردند
امام شهر که سجاده می کشید به دوش

The city's prayer leader, who used to shoulder his prayer rug
Was seen being carried on others' shoulders.
(Ḥāfiẓ, 149/1)

The examples of Ḥāfiẓ's antinomian rhetorical remarks and beautifully worded satirical attacks on hypocrisy, double-dealing and the deceptive deeds of both the *Sharīʿa* hierarchy and Sufi network are too many all to be mentioned here. Suffice it to add here that Ḥāfiẓ's artistic voicing of his antinomianism forms part of his unique school of thought, generally known as "maktab-i rindī-yi Ḥāfiẓ."[15] As mentioned earlier, his obsession about the prevalence of insincerity and pharisaism in his time demonstrates that under authoritarian sway, both political and religious, society tends to choose hypocrisy as the most feasible way to survive. When people cannot live as they are or want to be, they put on a false face acceptable to the selfish authorities. And this was the root cause of Ḥāfiẓ's worry, leading to his artistic inimitable technique for expressing such an unhappy mood.

Conclusion

The period during which Ḥāfiẓ lived was a disturbed, insecure and morally degenerate time dominated by political despotism and religious dogmatism. This situation was squarely against Ḥāfiẓ's intellectual principles and ethical mores. Even though he was both a true broad-minded Muslim and a genuine moderate Sufi with Malāmatī and Qalandarī tendencies and had sympathy for them all, he had no reservations in censuring their shortcomings and deviations. He was especially sensitive to oppressive authoritarian rule and religious hypocrisy. In all this he was motivated not by unreasonable fanaticism but by his moral principles. He was far from biased in favour of any perspective and line of thought.

With all that said, Ḥāfiẓ was essentially a poet and artistically oriented. His *Dīvān* is not simply a collection of socio-political criticisms and religious disputes, but contains an artistic presentation of those criticisms and disputes. In other words, such topics, though of immense importance and sensitivity to Ḥāfiẓ, serve as a substantial portion of the themes of his poetry. In this way, his ghazals fulfil two purposes: (1) indicating some of the major problems and social interactions in fourteenth-century Iran and (2) showing Ḥāfiẓ's genius in exposing those problems in an exceptionally artistic fashion, while always taking an impartial and moderate position. So, it is not Ḥāfiẓ's sheer antinomian criticisms that make his poetry so uniquely likeable but, more importantly, the creative way in which he has expressed his antinomianism. I cannot help concluding my presentation with this question: is Ḥāfiẓ happy with the universe as it is? Has he no antinomian objection to the creation of the world and its habitants? What has he got in his mind when he says:

آدمی در عالم خاکی نمی آید به دست
عالمی دیگر بباید ساخت وز نو آدمی

No human can be found in this material world
There should be created another world and another man anew!
(Ḥāfiẓ, 260/14)

Notes

1 I would like to thank Dr Lloyd Ridgeon, of Glasgow University, for his careful reading of this chapter and making valuable suggestions.
2 Throughout this chapter, the two digits after Ḥāfiẓ's name refer respectively to the page and the verse in the poet's *Dīvān*.
3 for more on this see Khurramshāhī [1394] 1/186–197.
4 For more examples on this topic, see further below.
5 see Murtażavī, *Maktab*, pp. 72, 93, 131.
6 Abū Saʿīd, p. 297.
7 Ibid; also see Abū Saʿīd, pp. 330–31, for one of his definitions of those attending the khanaqah and the ten requirements to be called "Sufi".
8 For more on this see Khurramshāhī, (1386) II/ 651–4. On Qurʾānic sciences in Ḥāfiẓ's ghazals see Pakatchi, pp. 151–58.
9 For a fuller discussion on this ingenious technique see Keyvani, pp. 222–26.
10 Also see Ḥāfiẓ, 192/3; 193/7; 204/2–4;209/16; 243/14.
11 See Murtażavī, *Maktab*, pp. 88–89, 93.
12 For some examples of the verses in which Ḥāfiẓ negatively comments on those phony bogus claims and denounces them as "superstitious" see Ḥāfiẓ, 149/12; 170/4; 176/15; 177/1, 2, 4; 254/12,
13 See, for instance, Ḥāfiẓ, 4/7; 7/11; 35/19; 149/ 12; 165/ 13; 188/1, 10; 222/3, 6, 10 and many more.
14 The Prophet Muḥammad's uncle hostile to his nephew.
15 On this school see the comprehensive essay by Dādbih, chapter 2, pp. 28ff.

Works cited

Dādbih, Aṣghar, "Maktab-i Ḥāfiẓ, maktab-i rindī," in *Ḥāfiẓ (zindigī va andīsha)*, Tehran: GIE, 1391/2012.

Ḥāfiẓ-i Shīrāzī, *Dīvān*, ed., intr., and annotations by Abū al-Qāsim Injavī Shīrāzī, Tehran: Jāvidān Publishers, 1363 S./1984, 5th reprint.

Ḥāfiẓ-i Shīrāzī, *Ash'ār-i Guzīda az Dīvān-i Khwāja Ḥāfiẓ-i Shīrāzī*, by Muḥammad-ʿAlī Furūghi, Tehran: Quqnūs Publishers, 1364 S/ 1985, 5th reprint.

Keyvani, M. "Naqsh-i iḥsāsī-yi zabān va shīva-yi Ḥāfiẓ dar ibrāz-i nākhushnūdī-hā," in *Arj-nāma-yi Sādiq Kiyā, zindigī, āthār, justārhā-yi matn-pazhūhī*, ed. Askar Bahrāmī, Tehran: Markaz-i Mīrāth-i Maktūb, 1387 S/2008.

Khurramshāhī, Bahāʾ al-Dīn, "Muhtavā va ṣūrat dar ghazal-i Ḥāfiẓ," in *Dānishnāma-yi zabān-u adab-i Fārsī*, vol. II, ed. Ismāʿīl Saʿādat, Tehran, 1386/2007.

Khurramshāhī, Bahāʾ al-Dīn, "Īhām dar shiʿr-i Ḥāfiẓ," in *Hamayish-i beynalmilalī-yi Khwāja Shams al-Dīn Ḥāfiẓ* (The International Conference Commemorating Khʷāja Shams al-Dīn Muḥammad of Shīrāz), volume I, Tehran: 1394/2015.

Muḥammad b. Munavvar b. Abī Saʿīd, *Asrār al-towḥīd fī maqāmāt al-sheykh Abī Saʿīd*, ed. Zabīḥ-Allāh Ṣafā, Tehran: Amīr Kabīr, 1332/1953.

Murtażavī, Manūchihr, *Maktab-i Ḥāfiẓ, yā Muqaddama bar Ḥāfiẓ-shināsī*, Tehran: Tūs, 1365 S./1986, 2nd reprint.

Pākatchī, Aḥmad, "Ḥāfiẓ va Maʿārif-i Islāmī," *Ḥāfiẓ (zindigī va andīsha)*, Tehran: GIE, 1391/2012.

Shafīʿī-Kadkanī, Muḥammad-Riżā, *Qalandarīyya dar tārīkh, digardīsī-hā-yi yik īdiuluzhī*, Tehran: Sukhan, 1386 S./2007.

ʿUmar Khayyām's Transgressive Ethics and their Socio-Political Implications in Contemporary Iran[1]

A.A. Seyed-Gohrab
Utrecht University

Abstract
This chapter deals with the reception history of the Persian mathematician and astronomer ʿUmar Khayyām in twentieth century Iran. While examining the uneasy relationships between the provocative statements of Khayyām about the Creator, creation, death and the Hereafter and the religious beliefs of several Persian scholars, the chapter also elaborates on the processes and interpretations to make Khayyām's Bacchanalia acceptable for the Muslim audience. The chapter demonstrates how despite Khayyām's unorthodox ideology, scholars use the quatrains attributed to him and appropriate his ideas into Persian Islamic culture.

Keywords: Khayyām's philosophy; transgression; death and afterlife; wine poetry; antinomianism.

ابریق می مرا شکستی ربی
بر من در عیش را ببستی ربی
من می خورم و تو میکنی بدمستی
خاکم به دهان، مگر تو مستی ربی[2]

O Lord! you broke my wine jug;
O Lord! You barred the door of pleasure to me.
I am drinking wine while you like a drunkard behave badly
O Lord! May I perish [for asking], but are you drunk?

This quatrain is part of an anecdote relating to how God broke Khayyām's (ca. 1048–1131) wine jug when he wanted to drink. It is then said that Khayyām composed this quatrain extemporarily to protest against God.[3] Immediately after these blasphemous words, his face turned black. To apologise to God, he composed the next quatrain:

ناکرده گنه در این جهان کیست بگو!
آن کس که گنه نکرد چون زیست بگو!
من بد کنم و تو بد مکافات دهی
پس فرق میان من و تو چیست بگو!

Tell me, who in this world has not sinned?
Tell me, how does one who has not sinned live?
I do wrong while you punish wrongly,
Tell me, what is then the difference between you and me?[4]

God accepted his apologies, and his face returned to normal.

This is one of the dozen anecdotes in which Khayyām is associated with wine and blasphemy. It is cited by two eminent scholars of Persian literary history, Qāsim Ghanī (1892–1951) and Muḥammad-ʿAlī Furūghī (1877–1942) to highlight the problematic reception of Khayyām in Iran. They write,

> it is disappointing that although these quatrains have made Khayyām famous, our people, both learned and uninformed, have not appreciated his worth and have created imaginings about him. … Dry mystics and clerics have considered his words soaked with heresy, while people in general think of him as a wine drinker. They look at his poetry from the perspective of praising and prompting wine drinking. For the same reason, another group presuppose he has no beliefs in the soul's Origin (*mabdaʾ*) and the soul's Return (*maʿād*) and have, therefore, become his enthusiasts, while the divines discredit him for the same ideas.[5]

In this chapter, which is dedicated to my teacher, colleague and friend Dr Ahmad Karimi-Hakkak, I would like to examine several social implications of Khayyām's poetry. Dr Karimi-Hakkak's fascination with Persian poetry as a living tradition is a *leitmotiv* in his publications, examining the powerful artistic appeal of this millennium old tradition in modern times.[6] This chapter is just a droplet in the reception history of the Persian sage (*ḥakīm*) ʿUmar Khayyām, who has become a personification of transgressive ideas in Persian literary history. The fascination I share with Dr Karimi-Hakkak is due not only to Khayyām's poetic genius, (although he is not the author of the majority of quatrains attributed to him), but also to his problematic reception in twentieth century Iran and how he has been connected to the notion of modernity. Both religious and secular intellectuals have tried to position Khayyām in modern intellectual history of Iran in their own ways.

An exhaustive treatment of this topic would include a review of the ways in which influential figures in the modern cultural history of Iran have treated Khayyām's philosophy. Briefly, Khayyām's contemporary reception in Iran differs from the appreciation of other classical Persian poets such as Saʿdī (ca. 1210–1292),

Rūmī (1207–1273), Ḥāfiẓ (1315–1390), and even Ferdowsi (ca. 940–1029), although the last has also been connected to modern nationalism and Iranian identity. This chapter concentrates on two aspects of Khayyām's reception: first, it investigates how Khayyām's faith and ideas on life and the afterlife are perceived by Iranian intellectuals generally and by scholars such as ʿAbd al-Karīm Surūsh particularly. Second, it analyses how Khayyām's quatrains dealing with bacchanalian themes and motifs have been received by several Persian literary scholars who try to contextualise them in Islamic ethics. In articles on Khayyām and in introductions to his quatrains, they have sought to defend Khayyām's religiosity and mitigate his allusions to wine.

In today's Iran, Khayyām has the reputation of a cynical unbeliever. This reputation is constantly buttressed by both mediaeval Persian and modern Western evaluations of Khayyām. An example of the latter is a tourist guide about Iran by Maria O'Shea, published in the series Culture Shock! In one chapter, "The Language of Poetry and Sugar," the author examines the role of poetry in daily life in Iran, emphasising that Persian poets have confirmed "the Iranian concept of poetry as a necessity of life rather than an abstract art form."[7] She emphasises the "startling degree of erudition" in classical Persian poetry and names a few classical masters: ʿUmar Khayyām, followed by Saʿdī, Rūmī, Ḥāfiẓ, and Firdowsī. O'Shea describes Khayyām as follows: "Like many poets, his work protests against the established articles of faith and contains many possible blasphemies as well as exhortations to hedonism."[8] O'Shea is not simply repeating a Western appreciation of Khayyām; she is informing her potential travellers to Iran about the reactions they may receive if they mention Khayyām. This image of Khayyām as a blasphemous poet dates from the twelfth century.

Khayyām's reception in mediaeval Persia

In the mediaeval period, there is little criticism of wine in Persian poetry. Wine drinking, carpe diem, hedonism, and similar motifs and themes occur extensively in the works of other poets and authors. Bacchanalia is not only an indispensable part of Persian poetry, it was an essential part of Persian courtly culture and Persian Sufism, as chapters in the "mirror for princes" genre and mystical manuals testify.[9] Khayyām's name is heavily associated with wine and is included in several anthologies of quatrains. In this respect, there is no disapproval at all. Criticism is directed rather at Khayyām's philosophy concerning God, his creation, and the hereafter. These issues were also addressed by other Persian philosophers and poets before and after Khayyām, but their discussions did not generate such persistent condemnation. The criticism is directed at Khayyām as a philosopher who discusses thorny theological issues, planting doubts in the hearts and minds of Muslims. Jamāl al-Dīn Yūsuf Qifṭī (1172–1248) refers to Khayyām's deviant ideas in his poetry, characterising them as serpents for the Sharia.[10]

I limit myself here to two mediaeval authors who criticise Khayyām for his nonconformist opinions on God and as a materialist philosopher—namely, Farīd al-Dīn ʿAṭṭār (d.c. 1221) and Najm al-Dīn Dāya (1177–1256).[11] In his *Ilāhī-nāma*, ʿAṭṭār tells an anecdote about Khayyām in his grave. A seer comes to his grave and sees that the soul of the learned Khayyām is covered with perspiration, for he has realised that despite all his wisdom, he cannot rely on his philosophical knowledge in the hereafter. ʿAṭṭār's message is that any knowledge, especially intellectual discursive reasoning, that does not contain trust in God cannot save humankind in the hereafter, even if one is as learned as Khayyām. In ʿAṭṭār's opinion, intellect is part of the whole and can never fully understand the whole. He compares it to a person who by the aid of a candle wants to see the sun. The anecdote removes Khayyām from mysticism and connects him to philosophers who are characterised as *nātamām*, "incomplete," "deficient," or even "faulty":[12]

یکی بینندهٔ معروف بودی
که ارواحش همه مکشوف بودی
دمی گر بر سر گوری رسیدی
در آن گور آنچه می‌رفتی بدیدی
بزرگی امتحانی کرد خردش
بخاک عمر خیّام بردش
بدو گفتا چه می‌بینی درین خاک
مرا آگه کن ای بینندهٔ پاک
جوابش داد آن مرد گرامی
که این مردیست اندر ناتمامی
بدان درگه که روی آورده بودست
مگر دعویِ دانش کرده بودست
کنون چون گشت جهل خود عیانش
عَرَق می‌ریزد ازتشویر جانش
میان خجلت و تشویر ماندست
وزان تحصیل در تقصیر ماندست
بر آن دَر حلقه چون هفت آسمان زد
ز دانش لاف آنجا کی توان زد
چو نه انجام پیداست و نه آغاز
نیابد کس سر و پای جهان باز
فلک گوئیست و گر عمری شتابی
چو گویش پای و سر هرگز نیابی
که داند تا درین وادیِ مُنکَر

چگونه می‌روم از پای تا سر
سراپای جهان صد باره گشتم
ندیدم چارهٔ بیچاره گشتم
سراپای جهان درد و دریغست
که گر وقتیت هست آن نیز تیغست
مرا این چرخ چون صندوقِ ساعت
ز بازیچه رها نکند بطاعت

Once, there was a famous clairvoyant
to whom all souls were visible.
He had only to approach a tomb for a moment
to see what was happening in that tomb.
A great man tested the ability of this clairvoyant;
He brought him to the grave of ʿUmar Khayyām
and said to him: "What do you see in this grave?
O pure seer, make me aware."
The honourable seer gave him answer:
"Here lies a man who is incomplete,
because of the court to which he turned.
Although he claimed to have knowledge,
now, when his ignorance has become clear
he is perspiring out of shame for his own soul.
He is caught between sweating and shame.
The pursuit of knowledge has left him open to blame.
He made circles at the Gate like the seven revolving heavens.[13]
How could he boast of knowledge in the hereafter!
Since neither the beginning nor the end can be seen,
no one can solve the riddle of the world.[14]
The heavenly sphere is a ball, and like a ball,
A lifetime of haste won't ever discover its head or its foot."[15]

The second author is Najm al-Dīn Dāya, who cites two quatrains in his mystic manual *Mirṣād al-ʿibād* and uses them to criticise Khayyām for his materialist thoughts and his scepticism about the creation of the world. As a Ḥanafite, adhering to Ashʿarite rationalist theology, Daya was "an enemy of the philosophers because of their claim that the intellect (*ʿaql*) could reach gnosis."[16] Intellectual ratiocination fails to perceive the truth. Dāya cites Khayyām's quatrains to attack philosophers. The first is an example of Khayyām's agnosticism about human purpose, while the second is cited to condemn his doubt about God's purpose in creating humankind:

در دایره‌ای کامدن و رفتن ماست
او را نه بدایت نه نهایت پیداست
کس می نزند دمی درین عالم راست
کاین آمدن از کجا و رفتن به کجاست

We come and go in a circle
whose beginning and end is invisible
In this world, no one speaks a sincere word
About where we come from and where we are going.

دارنده چو ترکیب طبایع آراست
باز از چه قبل فکندش اندر کم و کاست
گر زشت آمد پس این صورعیب کراست
ورخوب آمد خرابی از بهرچراست

Why did the Owner who created the arrangement of nature
cast it to include shortcomings and deficiency again?
If it was ugly, who is to blame for these flaws forms?
And if it is beautiful, why does he break it again.[17]

The second quatrain is a popular one as it appears for the first time in Fakhr al-Dīn Muḥammad b. ʿUmar Rāzī's (d. 1209) exegesis of the Qurʾān and is cited in connection with the concept of *maʿād* or the place of the soul's return.[18] During Khayyām's time and later, there was a heated discussion as to whether the soul returns to the body on Resurrection Day. Philosophers generally believed that human beings would return to their original spiritual state after death.[19] The purpose of this temporal material life was to prepare oneself for eternal life in the hereafter. Humans were expected to purify themselves through ascetic training and to acquire knowledge of the world in order to know the Creator. The more one knows about the Creator, the more one knows about oneself, since the individual is created in the image of God and is a microcosmic representation of the universe. As De Bruijn explains, "according to this theory, life is to be conceived as a cyclical process which offers humans the opportunity to perfect their pre-eternal souls."[20] Theologians gave a different interpretation of *maʿād*, as "the idea of a separation between body and soul in the afterlife was unacceptable to them because it contradicted the dogma of the resurrection of the dead held to be one of the foundations of Islamic orthodoxy. In their view, *maʿād* could only mean the return of the souls to their resurrected bodies, which shall take place on the Day of Judgement."[21]

This difference of opinion between philosophers, Sufis, and orthodox theologians created the image of Khayyām the blasphemer, which has persisted to this day.

While the accusations made against Khayyām in his own time and soon after suggest that he may be the author of these quatrains, the unauthentic quatrains found in later collections, in which Khayyām defends himself against the accusation of heresy, show how a tradition was formed around his character. This tradition of accusing him of heresy also created a countermovement for those who identified with Khayyām to defend themselves. The authenticity of the apologia quatrains is most questionable:

دشمن به غلط گفت که من فلسفیم
ایزد داند که آنچه او گفت نیم
لیکن چو در این غم آشیان آمده‌ام
آخر کم از آنکه من بدانم که کیم

> The enemy wrongly accuses me of being a philosopher
> God knows that I am not what the enemy says
> But since I find myself in this house of sorrow
> The truth is, should not I know who I am?[22]

As previously noted, a reception history of Khayyām in the mediaeval Persian world is certainly a desideratum, as it would clarify the function of transgressive ideas in discussions of thorny theological issues. But that is beyond the scope of this research.

Khayyām in twentieth-century Iran

ʿAṭṭār and Dāya's evaluations of Khayyām have certainly contributed to his image among religious people in Iran. Even those religious people who furtively read him have mixed feelings. As the following anecdote shows, the first acquaintance of many Iranians from a traditional Islamic background with Khayyām is ambivalent. The prominent Persian scholar ʿAbd ʾl-Ḥuseyn Zarrīnkūb (1923–1999) recalls:

> I can never forget my first acquaintance with Khayyām. I was eleven years old when I was first introduced to this grey old man. I do not know which of my father's friends gave me a cheap edition of his quatrains with a lot of spelling mistakes, but I know very well that my father's strict and thorough approach to rearing and educating me could neither exclude this book (which is from end to end unbelief, scepticism and apostasy) from our house, nor withhold me from having the book and reading it. In those days, there was nothing else in our house but the sound of daily prayer and recitations of the Qurʾān. In those days, I was a frail child who sought pretexts [to go my own way] and I was just recovering from

a long illness. I do not know how many times I read the book, on that Friday at the end of February, but I do know that at the end of the day, many of the heart-ravishing, melodious poems had been engraved on the blank tablet of my mind. [. . .] I remember that one day I recited the quatrains for my grandmother. Tears filled her eyes, she cursed the poet, and then she went out of my room. Perhaps it was the same attitude [on her part] that had made my father an enemy of Khayyām.[23]

This candid recollection reveals several aspects of Khayyām's reception. Although Zarrīnkūb does not say so directly, it is clear that his father feared that the book would sow seeds of doubt and unbelief in the heart of his young son. On the other hand, his father allows a friend—someone who values the poems—to give a cheap edition to his son. The father perhaps feels a paradox: on one hand, Khayyām reminds his readers that life is brief and the world is vanity, while on the other, he problematises theological issues such as the role of the Creator, and the nature of the hereafter, in a way that disturbs readers with a religious disposition.

Another example of an ambivalent appreciation of Khayyām is ʿAbd al-Karīm Surūsh's discussion of death in his chapter "The Services and Benefits of Religion (*khadamāt va hasanāt-i dīn*)."[24] This is a long chapter covering several topics. In treating the question of human existence on earth, he says, "If we have come to this world as guests, what does the descending mean?" The author explains that humans are guests of God, both originally in paradise and now on earth. He contrasts the views of Jalāl al-Dīn Rūmī (1207–1273) to the philosophy of Khayyām by citing the following quatrain of Khayyām comparing humans with a cup of wine, a plaything of destiny:

جامی است که چرخ آفرین میزندش
صد بوسه مهر بر جبین میزندش
این کوزه‌گر دهر چنین جام لطیف
می‌سازد و باز بر زمین میزندش

It is a cup that is struck by the elevated Wheel
It gives the cup a hundred loving kisses on his forehead
the pot-maker of Time makes such an elegant cup
He makes it and smashes it again to the ground.[25]

Here God is depicted as a pot maker who creates humans and smashes them into pieces again. Surūsh rejects Khayyām's view, stating that those who consider the shortcomings and bitter experiences of this world as disappointments cannot see God and cannot have a loving relationship with God. Surūsh observes that it would be senseless to create such a convoluted creature as a human being only to break that creature into a hundred pieces. Rational reasoning can never find an explanation for this. Surūsh cites Rūmī, who, like many other Persian mystics such as ʿAṭṭār and Dāya, considers death as eternal life, a union between the lover and the beloved. He cites the following piece from Rūmī's *Mathnavī*, in which he depicts death as the soul's union with the Creator:

مرگ دان آنک اتفاق امتست
کاب حیوانی نهان در ظلمتست
همچو نیلوفر برو زین طرف جو
همچو مستسقی حریص و مرگ‌جو
مرگ او آبست و او جویای آب
می‌خورد والله اعلم بالصواب
ای فسرده عاشق ننگین نمد
کو ز بیم جان ز جانان می‌رمد
سوی تیغ عشقش ای ننگ زنان
صد هزاران جان نگر دستک‌زنان
جوی دیدی کوزه اندر جوی ریز
آب را از جوی کی باشد گریز
آب کوزه چون در آب جو شود
محو گردد در وی و جو او شود
وصف او فانی شد و ذاتش بقا
زین سپس نه کم شود نه بدلقا

Know death, as agreed among the Islamic community,
As the Water of Life hidden in the Land of Darkness.
Grow like the water-lily from this side of the river-bank,
Like one who suffers from dropsy be greedy and crave for death.
To him, the water is death, yet he seeks the water
He drinks it — and God best knows the right course.
O frozen lover, in the felt garment of shame,
Who, in fear of his life, flees the Beloved!
O you disgrace to women! Behold a hundred thousand souls
clapping their hands, [running] towards the sword of His love!
When you see a river, pour your jug in the river:
how could the water flee from the river?
When the jug's water is in the river-water,
it is dissolved in it, and the river becomes it.
Its attributes have disappeared, while its essence remains.
After this, it does not dwindle or become ill-favoured.[26]

Surūsh uses Rūmī's poem to argue that death is not like the pot that is fractured (*gusastan*), but like the water in it being united (*peyvastan*) with a flowing stream and then the ocean.[27] Surūsh observes that in this context, religion serves to reconcile humans with this world. As humans cannot do anything about death, religion offers a vision of the meaning of death. In this line of reasoning, religion comes to help when ratiocinating or intellectual deliberations fall short.

Surūsh appropriates the mystical philosophy of Rūmī for his political ideology, but whenever he feels that the philosophy of Khayyām's quatrains fit his own ideas, he cites him. Khayyām is so much part and parcel of Persian culture that even scholars and politicians who disagree with his philosophy on life, death, and the hereafter cite him as rhetorical buttressing. Discussing the topic of "Ideology and Worldly Religion" (*īdi'uluzhī va dīn-i dunyavī*), Surūsh posits that those who have not acquired the right perception of this world and the hereafter cannot claim to have fully understood the implications of religion for this world and the hereafter. He then demonstrates the relationship between this world and the hereafter through the metaphor of an embryo and the world, again citing Rūmī:

چون جنین بد آدمی بد خون غذا
از نجس پاکی برد مؤمن کذا
(...)
گر جنین را کس بگفتی در رحم
هست بیرون عالمی بس منتظم
یک زمینی خرمی با عرض و طول
اندرو صد نعمت و چندین اکول
کوهها و بحرها و دشتها
بوستانها باغها و کشتها
آسمانی بس بلند و پر ضیا
آفتاب و ماهتاب و صد سها
(...)
او بحکم حال خود منکر بدی
زین رسالت معرض و کافر شدی

When man was an embryo, his food was blood:
Likewise, a believer finds some purity in the "unclean" thing.
[...]
If anyone were to tell the embryo in the womb,
"Outside, there is a well-ordered world,
A pleasant earth, broad and long,
containing a hundred delights and so many things to eat,
with mountains and seas and plains,

fragrant orchards, gardens and sown fields.
A sky that's very lofty, full of light,
sun and moonbeams and a hundred stars."
[. . .]
The embryo would deny this, because of its present state, and
would reject this message and be an unbeliever.[28]

Surūsh cites these lines to explain humankind's position in this world, and the reasons for human birth and death. He develops a mystic interpretation, stating that a human is separated from the world of non-existence through a set of veils in the same way that a foetus is concealed in the womb. Before citing the second couplet of one of Khayyām's quatrains, Surūsh explains this metaphor:

> A foetus is both in the womb and in this world. This world has two phases: a prenatal and a postnatal phase. Only a veil separates these two phases. When we were still in the womb, we could not see the world and we did not know that we were in this world and that our mother was in this world and that our food was also from this world, etc. There was a veil between us and this world. We saw only the outward, i.e., we saw only ourselves, and the little world of the womb, but inside this embryonic world, which stands for this large and expanded world, was unknown to us and was veiled to us. As Khayyām says,[29]

[اسرار ازل را نه تو دانی و نه من
وین حرفِ معمّا نه تو خوانی و نه من]
هست از پس پرده گفت‌وگوی من و تو
چون پرده برافتد، نه تو مانی و نه من

[Neither you nor I could fathom the secrets of pre-eternity,
Neither you nor I can read these enigmatic letters.]
Our dialogue takes place behind the veil:
When the veil drops, neither you nor I remain.[30]

Although this quatrain shows a good deal more agnosticism about the hereafter than either Rūmī's poem or Surūsh's reading, Surūsh uses only the last couplet to emphasise the need for gnostic knowledge to understand the hereafter. Immediately after his citation, Surūsh adds:

> When this veil falls, we will enter into another world and the previous world falls away. At the moment we live in this world and [then] we are living in the Hereafter. We are the same embryos who are in the womb of this world, but this whole world and the embryos are together in the world of the Hereafter, which is the inner (*bāṭin*) of this world. But the

> people who see the outward (*ẓāhir-bīn*), only see the life in the outward world and are ignorant of its inside (*bāṭin*) which is the Hereafter. You know that God says to people, especially the Prophets, on the Resurrection Day, 'Certainly you were heedless of it, but now We have removed from your veil, so your sight today is sharp' (Qur'ān 50:22). When you had not experienced this situation, you were ignorant of this. We removed the veil from your eyes, we tore apart the veils. Today, your eyes are sharp and seeing. This means that your eyes were not seeing previously, because a veil and a curtain were put before them. It is just enough to tear them, and in that case, all our eyes will be opened, and see the inner world (*bāṭinī*) which we were barred from seeing.[31]

While in the previous example, Surūsh positions Khayyām and Rūmī in an oppositional binary, representing two mediaeval belief systems, here he is integrating Khayyām's poem entirely in a mystical and Qur'ānic context. For Surūsh, the idea of removing the veil (i.e., dying) is attractive and suits perfectly his argument, while Khayyām's doubt about the existence of the hereafter is ignored here; even the first couplet is not cited. In a literal interpretation of the last couplet, Khayyām observes that "when the veil drops, neither you nor I remain," which implies that it is not clear what happens with a human soul after death. As I have analysed elsewhere, the philosophy of this particular quatrain is not mystic, because in mysticism, the purpose of creation is defined.[32] God has created humankind out of love. In the first encounter between God and the souls of humankind, God asked Adam's souls, "Am I not your Lord?" to which the souls answered, "Yes, we witness you are." Mystics interpret this affirmative answer as the souls being spellbound by God's beauty. The souls had become drunk by the beauty, and therefore, they answered positively. It is this moment of union with the Creator that the human soul craves. Orthodox Muslims may read Khayyām's quatrain as sheer blasphemy, as the poet is claiming that humans cannot understand the reasons for God's creation. From an orthodox point of view, God's purpose for humankind on earth is evident: humans are temporarily on this earth to sow the seeds of good acts in order to harvest them in the eternal hereafter.

Even more provocative assertions are expressed in a series of quatrains attributed to Khayyām. In his prose work, Khayyām follows the critical ideas of Ibn Sīnā (Avicenna, about AD 980–1037) about God's knowledge of the particulars of what humans do and say, bodily resurrection on Judgment Day, and the existence of paradise and hell.[33] In several quatrains ascribed to Khayyām, he complains about a Creator who has dumped human beings in a deprived world with many responsibilities and without interfering with their affairs:

یارب تو گلم سرشته ایی من چه کنم
این پشم و قصب تو رشته ایی من چه کنم

چون خار بلا تو کشته ای من چه کنم
خود بر سر من نبشته ایی من چه کنم

O Lord, You have kneaded my clay, what can I do?
You have spun the wool and linen, what can I do?
When you've planted the thorn of affliction, what can I do?
You yourself have written my destiny on my forehead, what I can I do?[34]

The topic points at the heated debates between the Muʿtazilite and the Ashʿarite schools of theology during the poet's time, on theological issues such as God's unity, justice, reward, and punishment.[35] The Muʿtazilites rejected predestination and affirmed individual responsibilities, while the Ashʿarites took the opposite view.[36]

Some editors of Khayyām's quatrains, especially in the introductions of critical text editions, make these philosophical ideas more palatable in an Islamic context by framing them as part of Khayyām's inquisitive spirit and his longing to know God. For instance, the eminent Persian scholar Żīyāʾ al-Dīn Sajjādī writes: "Khayyām is not a pessimist, not a sceptic and also not a denier of God, he does not belong to Islamic mystics, Sufis, neither does he belong to Ismāʿīlī sect, and all these have their own arguments."[37] To prove Khayyām's sincere belief in God, Sajjādī refers to the report of Imam Muḥammad Baghdādī, one of Khayyām's sons-in-law, as reported by Abu'l Ḥasan ʿAlī ibn Zeyd Bayhaqī's *Tatimmā ṣivān al-ḥikmā*. When Khayyām was reading Ibn Sīnā's chapter "Theology" from his famous *Kitāb al-shifāʾ*, he was cleaning his teeth with a golden toothpick. When he came to the section "Unity and Multiplicity" (*al-wāḥid wa al-Kathīr*), he placed the toothpick in the book, asking for a pious person to come and write his will. After writing his will, he performed a prayer and started his fasting. Late in the evening, during his evening prayer, he knelt and directed his attention to God, saying:

یا رب به قدر قدر تو نشناختم تو را
در حد فکر کوته خود ساختم تو را
دردیست رنج غفلت و رنجیست درد جهل
افسوس با تو بودم و نشناختم تو را

O God! I have not known you in the degree you are worth.
I have made a 'You' within the small limit bounds of my thought.
My neglect is anguish, my ignorance is my grief.
Alas, I was with you but was unable to know you.[38]

After this prayer, Khayyām died. He had predicted that his grave would be in a place covered with blossoms in spring and autumn.[39] By citing the anecdote and emphasising that Khayyām did not have any religious or mystical affiliations, Sajjādī absolves Khayyām of heresy, presenting him as a pious believer, who used his knowledge to know God.

Another Persian literary scholar, Bahā' al-Dīn Khurramshāhī, defends Khayyām through an extensive commentary on controversial quatrains. He explains the quatrains within the Perso-Islamic framework, citing poetry from Khayyām's predecessors to explain that specific ideas and opinions knitted to Khayyām actually belong to the Persian cultural and literary heritage, as in the following quatrain:

گر می نخوری طعنه مزن مستانرا
بنیاد مکن تو حیله و دستانرا
تو غره بدان مشو که می مینخوری
صد لقمه خوری که می غلامست آنرا

If you're not drinking wine yourself, do not despise the drunk.
Do not prepare the ground for trickery and fraud.
Be not proud that you're not drinking wine,
You eat a hundred morsels, far, far, worse than wine.[40]

In Khurramshāhī's opinion, the reason the poet invites people to drink wine is not the wine itself; he wants to explain that hypocrisy is a sin.[41] Khurramshāhī conjectures that there are two types of wine in Khayyām's quatrains: grape wine (*bāda-yi angūrī*) and literary wine (*bāda-yi adabī*). He says:

> If we take Khayyām's allusions to, and themes of, wine, his praise of drunkenness, and his ignorance [of the hereafter] in his quatrains in a literal way, we will have a portrait of an irresponsible man, a vagabond, an alcoholic, a hedonist, a worshipper of wine, a waster of time, someone who throws away the fruits of his work and life, instead of a sagacious Khayyām who was an eminent sage and a mathematician, who was very possibly a student of Ibn Sīnā [and otherwise a follower of his philosophy].[42]

Khurramshāhī rejects such ideas and bases himself on Muḥammad ʿAlī Furūghī who interprets Khayyām's use of wine in the same vein as Ḥāfiẓ's. According to Furūghī, when Ḥāfiẓ refers to "two-year-old wine" (*may-yi du sāla*) and a "fourteen-year-old beloved" (*maḥbūb-i chahārdah sāla*), he is using metaphors: the former refers to the Qur'ān while the latter to the Prophet Muḥammad.[43]

Many contemporary Persian scholars try to contextualise Khayyām in a Persian mystic tradition. The eloquent Iranian scholar Ḥuseyn Ilāhī-Qumsha'ī defends Khayyām by placing him in Persian and Indian mystic traditions. In his opinion, the image of Khayyām as a heretic has been created in the West. He writes:

> It is a pity that in the opinions of many western readers he is a heretic, a lustful drunk, who has become a famous poet busy only with wine and worldly pleasures. This is the same current misinterpretation that people have about Sufism. The West looks at Khayyām from its own perspective. But if one wishes to appreciate the essence of Eastern literature, the reader should look at how indigenous readers interpret their own literature. It may be astonishing for the western public to hear that in Iran there is no discussion and difference of opinion about the true meaning of Khayyām's poems, and that everyone considers him as a great spiritual poet and a true believer.[44]

Although Qumshaʾī later admits that there are a wide range of opinions about the quatrains in Iran, he puts Khayyām's actual Persian quatrains aside and offers a purely mystical interpretation of Edward FitzGerald's (1809–83) version in Rubaiyat.[45] For Qumshaʾī, Khayyām's quatrains are so permeated by Islamic mysticism that even their English adaptations possess spiritual elements. To show this mysticism, he translates the English quatrains back to Persian and gives a commentary based on the philosophy of the Indian mystic and yoga master Paramahansa Yogananda (1893–1952). Afterwards, Qumshaʾī gives his own mystical interpretation. Here I give one example of Qumshaʾī at work:

> Awake! for Morning in the Bowl of Night
> Has flung the Stone that puts the Stars to Flight:
> And Lo! the Hunter of the East has caught
> The Sultan's Turret in a Noose of Light.[46]

Yogananda interprets this quatrain as follows:

> Awake and leave the sleep of ignorance and simple-mindedness, because the dawn of wisdom and knowledge has arrived. Rise and throw the hard stone of asceticism in the dark cup of ignorance, and make the faded light of the stars that manifest your desire and endless worldly lusts take flight.[47]

Qumshaʾī adds the following to this:

> O inhabitants of the city of deceit and imagination, awake, because my sun of the mystic and Gnostic message, which awakes the sleeping people, can be seen on the horizons of your towns. Rise and break the scales of ignorance with the spiritual stone of asceticism. Divest yourself of this worldly and ephemeral pleasure which shines only for one moment and is extinguished again.[48]

Khayyām and the antinomian movement

What is perhaps most intriguing about this brief reception history of Khayyām is why he in particular has been the locus of accusations of heresy, although other philosophers and poets expressed the same ideas in a philosophical context. For later mediaeval mystic poets, he was an example of a rational and materialist philosopher whose ideas opposed mystic views on the Creator, creation, and the hereafter. There was (and is) an adversarial relationship between theologians and philosophers: while the letter of the Qur'ān was enough for the religious scholars, philosophers problematised key notions of theology such as the soul's origin (*mabda'*), living in the material world (*ma'āsh*), and the return (*ma'ād*). Why then would mystic poets and religious scholars focus their critique on Khayyām? He formulated complex theological issues in a simple style comprehensible to people of all walks of life. He was quotable, and a poet to whom dozens if not hundreds of "heretical" quatrains were attributed from the thirteenth century onwards. While some of the quatrains narrated in anecdotes show him as remorseful, there are other contexts in which such quatrains are read in an antinomian context. But is this fair to Khayyām?

The antinomian qalandarī movement started to take shape gradually during Khayyām's life. Central motifs of the qalandarī poetry are wine, homoerotic love, and the censure of outward piety. To provoke religious scholars, these qalandars drank wine publicly and criticised the most sacred rites and rituals (such as the pilgrimage to Mecca), the mosque, and even Islam itself; they preferred winehouses, Zoroastrian temples or Christian churches, and unbelief (*kufr*). This antinomian poetry is deeply religious, reflecting a paradoxical piety that rejected any show of religiosity. While this poetry is a provocative response to the theologians, the strength of Khayyām's poetry lies in its personal tone, in which the poet wonders about the mysteries of the universe, who the Creator is, why the universe was created, what the purpose of humankind is, and what the destination of the soul in the hereafter is. Khayyām's wine poetry is a means to mitigate the pain and frustration of humankind's inability to perceive the imperceptible.

'Aṭṭār is one of the prominent qalandarī poets who criticise the holiest tenets of Islam, emphasising the individual's spiritual growth, but he does not take Khayyām as a qalandar; rather, as we have seen, he sternly criticises him. Much of the poetry of other Persian poets such as Ḥāfiẓ, Sa'dī, and Rūmī embodies a qalandarī philosophy, both in its emphasis on wine and in criticism of the holiest Islamic tenets. Yet even qalandarī poets such as 'Aṭṭār looked with a suspicious eye at Khayyām's ratiocinative worldview.

The growing body of heretic poetry attributed to Khayyām probably did not help to make his *Rubā'iyyāt* seem unequivocally spiritual. Any poet could write a quatrain and use Khayyām's name as a cover, making the corpus grow to some thousands of quatrains. Several qalandarī quatrains are attributed to Khayyām. One appears in the thirteenth-century collection of quatrains *Nuzhat al-majālis* by Jamāl Khalīl Shirvānī. In this collection of some 4,000 quatrains, he devotes a chapter to *dar maʿānī-yi ʿUmar Khayyām*. This heading is ambiguous because it may be understood as "On the Ideas of ʿUmar Khayyām," referring to a popular genre in which poets write on the same themes and motifs, such as carpe diem, bacchanalia, and complaints about fate. The heading can also be understood as "On the Meanings of ʿUmar Khayyām," which refers to the readings of his poetry. As the authorship of several of the poems cited in Shirvānī's chapter is unclear, Shirvānī is probably referring to poems with the themes and motifs for which Khayyām had become the personification. The chapter also includes quatrains by other poets, such as Sanāʾī, Sayfī, and Mujīr, which reinforces my interpretation of the chapter heading. Shirvānī also cites quatrains attributed to Khayyām elsewhere in the collection. The following quatrain on the qalandarī way appears in the first chapter "On Unity and Gnosis" (*towḥīd va ʿirfān*), but it is hard to accept it as authentic, based on the above line of reasoning:

تا راه قلندری نپویی نشود
رخساره بخون دل نشویی نشود
سودا چه پزی تا که چو دلسوختگان
آزاد به ترک خود نگویی نشود[49]

So long as you do not walk the path of qalandarī, it may not be;
So long as you do not wash your cheeks with the heart's blood, it may not be.
Why boiling your passion like those with burnt hearts,
unless you freely renounce your own ego, it may not be.

Raḥīm Riżāzāda Malik dismisses the attribution of this quatrain to Khayyām, stating, "the composer of this quatrain is so distanced from the logic of scholasticism and he is so unfamiliar from such tradition that he does not explain what it means to say [the lines above]."[50] Riżāzāda continues his criticism, stating that the composer of this poem is not at all clear about what he wants to say and the usage of the "gargantuan" word qalandar points to the author's vagabond (*qalandarī*) origin.

Conclusion

The popularity of Edward FitzGerald's adaptation of the quatrains in the West initiated a new evaluation of Khayyām and the quatrains in Iran. While influential intellectuals such as Ṣādiq Hidāyat (1903–1951) saw in Khayyām the rebellious Arian spirit who fought against Semitic beliefs, other less-well-known authors such as Ṣiddīqī Nakhjavānī published books and articles condemning Khayyām for giving unbridled advice to drink wine and disrespecting religion.[51] Surūsh's application of Khayyām's quatrains in modern religious-political contexts exhibits this oppositional binary. In one place, Surūsh cites Khayyām as an opponent of Rūmī, to convey the functionality of religion and how religion does help humankind understand death and the hereafter; in others, he simply cites Khayyām to strengthen his arguments about death, without going into Khayyām's views on the hereafter. In the latter cases, Khayyām's poetic memorability and popularity count more than his critical philosophy of the origins of creation.

Scholars such as Sajjādī, Khurramshāhī, and Qumsha'ī seek to create an Islamic context for both Khayyām's personality and his quatrains, so that his poetry can be viewed within the bounds of Islamic ethics. It remains fascinating that, despite all these heated discussions on the "Islamic" or "heretical" nature of Khayyām's quatrains, he has been among the best-selling authors in Iran, perhaps the most translated mediaeval poet in the world,[52] and a symbol of Persian spirits, philosophising the mysteries of the universe in poetry while drinking wine and loving his friends.

Notes

1 This chapter was previously published in *Iran-Namag*, Volume 5, Number 3, 2020, pp. 68–93. This chapter was written at Utrecht University as part of the ERC Advanced Grant project entitled *Beyond Sharia: The Role of Sufism in Shaping Islam* (www.beyondsharia.nl), funded by the European Research Council (ERC) under the European Union's Horizon 2020 research and innovation programme (Grant agreement No. 101020403).

2 *Rubāʿiyyāt-i Khayyām*, ed. M.ʿA. Furūghī & Q. Ghanī, republished by B.D. Khurramshāhī, Tehran: Nāhīd, 1373/1994, p. 54; also see Ṣādiq Hidāyat, *Tarāna-hā-yi Khayyām*, Tehran: Kitābhā-yi parastū, sixth print 1353/1974, p. 15. Also see Yār-Aḥmad Ḥuseyn Rashīdī Tabrīzī, *Rubāʿīyāt-i Khayyām: Ṭarab-khāna*, ed. Jalāl al-Dīn Humāʾī, Tehran: Humā, 1988, p. 137, quatrain 543. The phrase *khākam bi dahan* means literally "may dust be at my mouth," implying remorse. All translations are mine unless otherwise indicated.

3 On composing poems extemporarily in Persian literary tradition, see A.A. Seyed-Gohrab, "Improvisation as a Chief Pillar of the Poetic Art in Persian Literary Tradition," in *Images, Improvisations, Sound, and Silence from 1000 to 1800–Degree Zero*, ed. B. Hellemans and A. Jones Nelson, Amsterdam: Amsterdam University Press, 2018, pp. 131–144.

4 *Rubāʿiyyāt-i Khayyām*, p. 55. Also see Rashīdī Tabrīzī, *Rubāʿīyāt-i Khayyām: Ṭarab-khāna*, p. 255, quatrain 8. This quatrain with a different first couplet is also attributed to Rūmī. See Jalāl al-Dīn Muḥammad Rūmī, *Kulliyyāt-i Shams yā Dīvān-i kabīr az guftār-i Mowlānā Jalāl al-Dīn Muḥammad mashhūr bi Mowlavī, bā tashbīhāt va havāshī*, 3rd edition, ed. Badīʿ al-Zamān Furūzānfar, 10 vols. Tehran: Amīr Kabīr, AH 1378/AD 1999, 8, p. 266, quatrain 1579:

ای جان جهان جز تو کسی کیست بگو
بی‌جان و جهان هیچ کسی زیست بگو
من بد کنم و تو بد مکافات دهی
پس فرق میان من و تو چیست بگو

In English, it runs thus:
Tell me, O soul of the world! Who else is there?
Tell me! Could anyone live without a soul and the world?
I am doing bad and you punish badly,
Tell me, what is then the difference between you and me?

5 *Rubāʿiyyāt-i Khayyām*, p. 54.

6 See, for instance, Ahmad Karimi-Hakkak, "Continuity and Creativity: Models of Change in Persian Poetry, Classical and Modern," in *The Layered Heart: Essays on Persian Poetry, A Celebration in Honor of Dick Davis*, ed. A.A. Seyed-Gohrab, Washington, DC: Mage Publishers, pp. 25–54.

7 Maria O'Shea, *Culture Shock! Iran*, 1999, London: Kuperard, 2001, p. 88.

8 O'Shea, *Culture Shock*, 90. Chapter three is devoted to poetry, pp. 72–95. for a comprehensive study of Khayyām's reception history see Ghajarjazi, A., *Remembering Khayyām: Episodes of Unbelief in the Reception Histories of Persian Quatrains*, Berlin: De Gruyter, 2025 (forthcoming).

9 See, for instance, *Qābūs-nāma* in which chapters on *āʾin-i sharāb-khʷārī* ("rites of wine drinking") are elaborated. ʿUnṣur al-Maʿālī Kay Kāvūs, *Qābūs-nāma*, ed. G.H. Yūsufī, Tehran: ʿIlmī va Farhangī, AH 1371/AD 1992; ʿUnṣur al-Maʿālī Kay Kāvūs, *A Mirror for Princes*, trans. R. Levy, London: Cresset Press, 1951. Also see mystic manuals such as Shabistarī's *Gulshan-i rāz (The Secret Rose-Garden)*, which devotes chapters to the meaning and significance of wine, the winehouse, the cup, and the cupbearer. See Shabistarī's *Gulshan-i rāz*, ed. A. Mujāhid and M. Kiyānī, Tehran: Mā, AH 1371/AD 1992, pp. 184–190. For the consumption of wine in Islamic societies, see Shahab Ahmed, who conceptualises that wine is constitutive of Islam. Shahab Ahmed, *What Is Islam? The Importance of Being Islamic*, Princeton, NJ: Princeton University Press, 2016, pp. 36–38, 57–73; also see A.A. Seyed-Gohrab, "The Rose and the Wine: Dispute as a Literary Device in Classical Persian Literature," *Iranian Studies*, no. 1 (2013), pp. 69–85.

10 See A.A. Seyed-Gohrab, "Khayyām's Universal Appeal: Man, Wine, and the Hereafter in the Quatrains," in *The Great ʿUmar Khayyām: A Global Reception of the Rubaiyat*, Leiden: Leiden University Press, 2012, pp. 11–38, reference on p. 12; idem, "The Flourishing of Persian Quatrains," in *A History of Persian Literature: Persian Lyric Poetry in the Classical Era 800–1500: Ghazals. Panegyrics and Quatrains*, vol. 2, ed. E. Yarshater, London: I.B. Tauris, 2019, pp. 488–568.

11 Muḥammad-Amīn Rīyāḥī in *Encyclopaedia Iranica*, s.v. Dāya, Najm-al-Dīn Abū Bakr ʿAbd-Allāh. www.iranicaonline.org/articles/daya-najm-al-din. For an overview of these mediaeval critics on Khayyām, see Aminrazavi, *Wine of Wisdom*, pp. 40–66.

12 For an excellent study of ʿAṭṭār's philosophy, see H. Ritter, *The Ocean of the Soul: Man, the World, and God in the Stories of Farid al-Din Attar* (trans. of *Das Meer der Seele: Mensch, Welt und Gott in den Qeschichten des Fariduddin Attar*), ed. Bernd Radtke, trans. John O'Kane, Leiden: Brill, 2003.

13 This line can also be translated as "He knocked at the Door like the seven heavens." I have chosen the above translation to allude to the poet as an astronomer, drawing circles to measure heavenly bodies.

14 Literally, *sar-u pā-yi jahān*, "the head and the feet of the world," referring to the beginning and the end of the world.

15 Farīd al-Dīn ʿAṭṭār, *Ilāhī-nāma*, ed. H. Ritter, Tehran: Tūs, second print 1368/1989, p. 272, ll. 8–18.

16 Rīyāḥī in *Encyclopaedia Iranica*, s.v. Dāya.

17 Najm ad-Dīn Rāzī, *Mirṣād al-ʿibād min al-mabdaʾ ilaʾl-maʿād*, ed. M.A. Riyāḥī, Tehran: Scientific & Cultural Publications Company, 1992, p. 31. For an English translation of this book see *Razi: The Path of God's Bondsmen*, trans. H. Algar, Persian Heritage Series 35, New York: Caravan Books, 1982. The quatrain appears with some alterations in Khayyām, *Rubāʿiyyāt-i Khayyām*, ed. Furūghī and Ghanī, p. 112 (quatrain 34) and p. 108 (quatrain 31), respectively. For an analysis of this particular quatrain see Arash Ghajarjazi, *Remembering Khayyām*.

18 See my discussion of Khayyām's quatrains in the unique miscellaneous manuscript *Safīna*, which contains 209 works, copied between AD 1321 and AD 1323: A.A. Seyed-Gohrab, "Literary Works in Tabriz's Treasury," in *The Treasury of Tabriz: The Great Il-Khanid Compendium*, ed. A.A. Seyed-Gohrab and S. McGlinn, Amsterdam: Rozenberg Publishers and West Lafayette, IN: Purdue University Press, 2007, pp. 126–30. Also see Sayyid-ʿAlī Mīrafżalī, *Rubāʿiyyāt-i Khayyām dar manābiʿ-i kuhan*, Tehran: Nashr-i dānishgāhī, AH 1382/AD 2003, pp. 23–25.

19 See J.T.P. de Bruijn's discussion on this topic: J.T.P. de Bruijn, *Persian Sufi Poetry: An Introduction to the Mystical Use of Classical Poems*, Richmond, UK: Curzon Press, 1997, pp. 88–90.

20 De Bruijn, *Persian Sufi Poetry*, p. 89.

21 De Bruijn, *Persian Sufi Poetry*, p. 89.

22 Khayyām, *Rubāʿiyyāt-i Khayyām*, ed. Furūghī and Ghanī, p. 149, quatrain 129; Rashīdī Tabrīzī, *Rubāʿīyāt-i Khayyām: Ṭarab-khāna*, p. 245, quatrain 417. For Khayyām's reception history through the centuries see Ghajarjazi, *Remembering Khayyām*, forthcoming.

23 ʿAbd ʾl-Ḥusayn Zarrīnkūb, *Kitāb-i ḥowla*, Tehran: ʿIlmī, seventh print 1372/1993, pp. 127–128.

24 ʿAbd al-Karīm Surūsh, *Mudārā va mudīrīyat*, Tehran: Ṭulūʿ-i Āzādī, 1376/1997, pp. 227–276.

25 Surūsh, *Mudārā va mudīrīyat*, p. 268. Also see Khayyām, *Rubāʿiyyāt-i Khayyām*, ed. Furūghī and Ghanī, 143, quatrain 115; Rashīdī Tabrīzī, *Rubāʿīyāt-i Khayyām: Ṭarab-khāna*, p. 239, quatrain 13.

26 See Jalāl al-Dīn Muḥammad Rūmī, *The Mathnawí of Jalálu'ddín Rúmí*, ed., trans. and comm. R.A. Nicholson, Vol. 3, London: Gibb Memorial Trust, 1925–1940. My translation is based on R.A. Nicholson's with some alterations. I have used the critical Persian text by Jalāl al-Dīn Rūmī, *Mathnavī-yi Maʿnavī*, ed. M. Istiʿlāmī, Vol. III, Tehran: Zavvār, third print 1372/1993, p. 180, ll. 3909–3916.

27 ʿAbd al-Karīm Surūsh, *Mudārā va mudīrīyat*, pp. 268–269.

28 My translation is based on Nicholson's (p. 7), using Istiʿlāmī, *Mathnavī-yi Maʿnavī*, 11, lines 50, 53–56, 60.

29 ʿAbd al-Karīm Surūsh, *Mudārā va mudīrīyat*, pp. 184–85.

30 ʿAbd al-Karīm Surūsh, *Mudārā va mudīrīyat*, p. 185; Rashīdī Tabrīzī, *Rubāʿīyāt-i Khayyām: Ṭarab-khāna*, p. 250, quatrain 30.

31 ʿAbd al-Karīm Surūsh, *Mudārā va mudīrīyat*, p. 185.

32 A.A. Seyed-Gohrab, "There Was a Door to Which I Found No Key," There was a Door to which I found no Key – Beyond Sharia (accessed 15-11-2023); also Leiden Medievalists Blog, leidenmedievalistsblog.nl/articles/there-was-a-door-to-which-i-found-no-key (accessed 10 March 2020).

33 For a discussion about the Islamic nature of such provocative ideas, see Shahab Ahmed, *What Is Islam*, pp. 11–13.

34 This quatrain appears in neither Furūghī and Ghanī's nor in Mīrafżalī's edition of *Rubāʿiyyāt-i Khayyām*. The quatrain was probably written by Sharaf al-Dīn Shafarva of Isfahān (in the twelfth century) and later attributed to Khayyām. On Sharaf al-Dīn, see Ṣafā, *Tarīkh-i adabiyyāt dar Īrān*, vol. 2, Tehran: Firdows, AH 1368/AD 1989, pp. 740–743; Luṭf-ʿAlī Beyg Ādhar Bīgdilī, *Tadhkira-yi ātashkada ādhar*, ed. Sayyid Jaʿfar Shahīdī, Tehran: AH 1337/AD 1958, pp. 182–183. However, this quatrain is not mentioned in these sources, and I do not have Sharaf al-Dīn's *Dīvān* in my possession. The poem appears in a somewhat different reading in Rashīdī Tabrīzī, *Rubāʿīyāt-i Khayyām: Ṭarab-khāna*, p. 249, quatrain 21.

35 See M. Aminrazavi, "Reading the Ruba'iyyat as 'Resistance Literature,'" in *The Great 'Umar Khayyām: A Global Reception of the Rubaiyat*, Leiden: Leiden University Press, 2012, pp. 39–53. Aminrazavi gives many examples of quatrains attributed to Khayyām and reflecting the disputes between these schools.

36 D. Gimaret in *Encyclopaedia of Islam*, Second Edition, s.v. Mu'tazila.

37 Khayyām, *Rubā'iyyāt-i 'Umar Khayyām*, ed. Zīyā al-Dīn Sajjādī (Tehran: Kārūn, 1370/1991), p. 5.

38 This poem is not included in either Furūghī and Ghanī's or in Mīrafżalī's edition of *Rubā'iyyāt-i Khayyām*. Sajjādī summarises this poem in prose on p. 5, and the poem appears on several Internet pages, but the authenticity of this weak poem is questionable.

39 See Niẓāmī 'Arūżī, *Chahār-Maqāla*, ed. E.G. Browne, London: Gibb Memorial Series, Luzac & Co, 1921, pp. 71–72: "In the year A.H. 506 (A.D. 1112–1113) Khwaja Imam 'Umar-i-Khayyāmi and Khwaja Imam Muzaffar-i-Isfizari had alighted in the city of Balkh, in the Street of the Slave-sellers, in the house of Amir Abu Sa'd Jarrah, and I had joined that assembly. In the midst of our convivial gathering I heard that Proof of God *(Ḥujjatu'l-Ḥaqq)* 'Umar say, "My grave will be in a spot where the trees will shed their blossoms on me twice a year." This thing seemed to me impossible, though I knew that one such as he would not speak idle words. When I arrived at Nishapur in the year A.H. 530 (A.D. 1135–6), it being then four years since that great man had veiled his countenance in the dust, and this nether world had been bereaved of him, I went to visit his grave on the eve of a Friday (seeing that he had the claim of a master on me), taking with me one to point out to me his tomb. So he brought me out to the Ḥira Cemetery; I turned to the left, and found his tomb situated at the foot of a garden-wall, over which pear-trees and peach-trees thrust their heads, and on his grave had fallen so many flower-leaves that his dust was hidden beneath the flowers. Then I remembered that saying which I had heard from him in the city of Balkh, and I fell to weeping, because on the face of the earth, and in all the regions of the habitable globe, I nowhere saw one like unto him. May God (blessed and exalted is He!) have mercy upon him, by His Grace and His Favour! Yet although I witnessed this prognostication on the part of that Proof of the Truth 'Umar, I did not observe that he had any great belief in astrological predictions; nor have I seen or heard of any of the great [scientists] who had such belief."

40 Khayyām, *Rubā'iyyāt-i Khayyām*, ed. Furūghī and Ghanī, p. 99, quatrain 4. Rashīdī Tabrīzī, *Rubā'īyāt-i Khayyām: Ṭarab-khāna*, p. 202, quatrain 331.

41 *Rubā'iyyāt-i Khayyām*, ed. M.'A. Furūghī & Q. Ghanī, republished by B.D. Khurramshāhī, Tehran: Nāhīd, 1373/1994, p. 175.

42 Khayyām, *Rubā'iyyāt-i Khayyām*, ed. Furūghī and Ghanī, p. 11.

43 Ibid., p. 12.

44 *Rubā'iyyāt-i Khayyām-i Nayshābūrī*, Tehran: Khushrang, no date, introduction by Ḥusayn Ilāhī Qumsha'ī, p. 3.

45 Khayyām, *Rubā'iyyāt-i Khayyām-i Nayshābūrī*, ed. Qumsha'ī, 5, note 4.

46 P. Yogananda, *The Rubaiyat of Omar Khayyām Explained*, ed. J. Donald Walters, California: Crystal & Clarity, 1994, pp. 2–5.

47 These are not Yogananda's literal words but a summary made by Qumsha'ī.

48 Khayyām, *Rubā'iyyāt-i Khayyām-i Nayshābūrī*, ed. Qumsha'ī, 5.

49 Jamāl Khalīl Shirvānī, *Nuzhat al-majālis*, ed. M.A. Riyāḥī, Tehran: Mahārat, first edition 1366/1987, second edition, 1375/1996, p. 145, q. 33. The chapter on Khayyām appears in chapter 15, pp. 671–676. This chapter consists of 38 quatrains, 12 of which are attributed to Khayyām. Also see Sayyid-'Alī Mīrafżalī, *Rubā'īyāt-i Khayyām dar manābi'-i kuhan*, pp. 39–48. See also Rashīdī Tabrīzī, *Rubā'īyāt-i Khayyām: Ṭarab-khāna*, p. 126, quatrain 493.

50 Raḥīm Riżāzāda Malik, *'Umar Khayyām: Qāfila-yi sālār-i dānish*, Tehran: Mahārat, 1377/1998, pp. 125-26. Also Ṣādiq Hidāyat includes one of these qalandarī quatrains in his collection. See *Tarāna-hā-yi Khayyām*, p. 99.

51 Hidāyat, *Tarāna-hā-yi Khayyām*, 27; R. Siddīqī Nakhjavānī, *Khayyām-pindārī va pasukh-i afkār-i qalandarāna-yi ū*, Tabriz: Surūsh, AH 1320/AD 1931.

52 See Jos Coumans, *The Rubaiyat of Omar Khayyām: An Updated Bibliography*, Leiden: Leiden University Press, 2010. Coumans's bibliography lists 1,015 editions of the translations and is the first bibliography of the *Rubaiyat* since 1929, when A.G. Potter published his *A Bibliography of the Rubaiyat of Omar Khayyām*, London: Ingpen and Grant, 1994. Also see Jos Biegstraaten, in *Encyclopœdia Iranica*, s.v. "Khayyām, Omar xiv. Impact on Literature and Society in the West; A.A. Seyed-Gohrab, "Edward FitzGerald's Translations of *The Rubaiyat of Omar Khayyām*: The Appeal of Terse Hedonism," in *The Wiley Blackwell Companion to World Literature*, ed. Ken Seigneurie, John Wiley & Sons, 2019, pp. 2059–2070.

Works cited

Ādhar Bīgdilī, Luṭf-'Alī Beyg, *Tadhkira-yi ātashkada ādhar*, ed. Sayyid Ja'far Shahīdī, Tehran: 1337/1958.

Ahmed, S., *What Is Islam? The Importance of Being Islamic*, Princeton, NJ: Princeton University Press, 2016.

Aminrazavi, M., "Reading the Ruba'iyyat as 'Resistance Literature,'" in *The Great 'Umar Khayyām: A Global Reception of the Rubaiyat*, Leiden: Leiden University Press, 2012, pp. 39–53.

Aminrazavi, M., *The Wine of Wisdom: The Life, Poetry and Philosophy of Omar Khayyām*, Oxford: Oneworld, 2005.

'Aṭṭār, Farīd al-Dīn, *Ilāhī-nāma*, ed. H. Ritter, Tehran: Tūs, second print 1368/1989.

Biegstraaten, J., in *Encyclopœdia Iranica*, s.v. "Khayyām, Omar xiv. Impact on Literature and Society in the West.

Bruijn, J.T.P. de, *Persian Sufi Poetry: An Introduction to the Mystical Use of Classical Poems*, Richmond, UK: Curzon Press, 1997.

Coumans, J., *The Rubaiyat of Omar Khayyām: An Updated Bibliography*, Leiden: Leiden University Press, 2010.

Ghajarjazi, A., *Remembering Khayyām: Episodes of Unbelief in the Reception Histories of Persian Quatrains*, Berlin: De Gruyter, 2025 (forthcoming).

Gimaret, D., in *Encyclopaedia of Islam*, Second Edition, s.v. Mu'tazila.

Hidāyat, Ṣādiq, *Tarāna-hā-yi Khayyām*, Tehran: Kitābhā-yi parastū, sixth print 1353/1974.

Karimi-Hakkak, A., "Continuity and Creativity: Models of Change in Persian Poetry, Classical and Modern," in *The Layered Heart: Essays on Persian Poetry, A Celebration in Honor of Dick Davis*, ed. A.A. Seyed-Gohrab, Washington, DC: Mage Publishers, pp. 25–54.

Kay Kāvūs, 'Unṣur al-Ma'ālī, *Qābūs-nāma*, ed. G.H. Yūsufī, Tehran: 'Ilmī va Farhangī, AH 1371/AD 1992. (*A Mirror for Princes*, trans. R. Levy, London: Cresset Press, 1951).

Khayyām, 'Umar, *Rubā'iyyāt-i Khayyām*, ed. M.'A. Furūghī & Q. Ghanī, republished by B.D. Khurramshāhī, Tehran: Nāhīd, 1373/1994.

Khayyām, 'Umar, *Rubā'iyyāt-i Khayyām-i Nayshābūrī*, introduction by Ḥusayn Ilāhī Qumsha'ī, Tehran: Khushrang, no date.

Khayyām, 'Umar, *Rubā'iyyāt-i 'Umar Khayyām*, ed. Zīyā al-Dīn Sajjādī, Tehran: Kārūn, 1370/1991.

Mīrafżalī, Sayyid-'Alī, *Rubā'iyyāt-i Khayyām dar manābi'-i kuhan*, Tehran: Nashr-i dānishgāhī, 1382/2003.

Niẓāmī ʿArūżī, *Chahār-Maqāla*, ed. E.G. Browne, London: Gibb Memorial Series, Luzac & Co, 1921.

O'Shea, Maria, *Culture Shock! Iran*, London: Kuperard, (1999) reprinted 2001.

Potter, A.G., *A Bibliography of the Rubaiyat of Omar Khayyām*, London: Ingpen and Grant, 1994.

Rashīdī Tabrīzī, Yār-Aḥmad Ḥuseyn, *Rubāʿīyāt-i Khayyām: Ṭarab-khāna*, ed. Jalāl al-Dīn Humāʾī, Tehran: Humā, 1988.

Rāzī, Najm al-Dīn, *Mirṣād al-ʿibād min al-mabdaʾ ila'l-maʿād*, ed. M.A. Riyāḥī, Tehran: Scientific & Cultural Publications Company, 1992. (*Razi: The Path of God's Bondsmen*, trans. H. Algar, Persian Heritage Series 35, New York: Caravan Books, 1982).

Ritter, H., *The Ocean of the Soul: Man, the World, and God in the Stories of Farid al-Din Attar* (trans. of *Das Meer der Seele: Mensch, Welt und Gott in den Qeschichten des Fariduddin Attar*), ed. Bernd Radtke, trans. John O'Kane, Leiden: Brill, 2003.

Rīyāḥī, Muḥammad-Amīn, *Encyclopaedia Iranica*, s.v. Dāya, Najm-al-Dīn Abū Bakr ʿAbd-Allāh.

Riżāzāda Malik, Raḥīm, *ʿUmar Khayyām: Qāfila-yi sālār-i dānish*, Tehran: Mahārat, 1377/1998.

Rūmī, Jalāl al-Dīn, *Kulliyyāt-i Shams yā Dīvān-i kabīr az guftār-i Mowlānā Jalāl al-Dīn Muḥammad mashhūr bi Mowlavī, bā tashbīhāt va havāshī*, 3rd edition, ed. Badīʿ al-Zamān Furūzānfar, 10 vols. Tehran: Amīr Kabīr, 1378/1999.

Rūmī, Jalāl al-Dīn, *Mathnavī-yi Maʿnavī*, ed. M. Istiʿlāmī, Vol. III, Tehran: Zavvār, third print 1372/1993.

Rūmī, Jalāl al-Dīn, *The Mathnawí of Jalálu'ddín Rúmí*, ed., trans. and comm. R.A. Nicholson, Vol. 3, London: Gibb Memorial Trust, 1925–1940.

Ṣafā, Dhabīḥ-Allāh, *Tarīkh-i adabiyyāt dar Īrān*, vol. 2, Tehran: Firdows, AH 1368/AD 1989.

Seyed-Gohrab, A.A., "Edward FitzGerald's Translations of *The Rubaiyat of Omar Khayyām*: The Appeal of Terse Hedonism," in *The Wiley Blackwell Companion to World Literature*, ed. Ken Seigneurie, John Wiley & Sons, 2019, pp. 2059–2070.

Seyed-Gohrab, A.A., "Improvisation as a Chief Pillar of the Poetic Art in Persian Literary Tradition," in *Images, Improvisations, Sound, and Silence from 1000 to 1800 – Degree Zero*, ed. B. Hellemans and A. Jones Nelson, Amsterdam: Amsterdam University Press, 2018, pp. 131–144.

Seyed-Gohrab, A.A., "Khayyām's Universal Appeal: Man, Wine, and the Hereafter in the Quatrains," in *The Great ʿUmar Khayyām: A Global Reception of the Rubaiyat*, Leiden: Leiden University Press, 2012, pp. 11–38.

Seyed-Gohrab, A.A., "Literary Works in Tabriz's Treasury," in *The Treasury of Tabriz: The Great Il-Khanid Compendium*, ed. A.A. Seyed-Gohrab and S. McGlinn, Amsterdam: Rozenberg Publishers and West Lafayette, IN: Purdue University Press, 2007, pp. 113–136.

Seyed-Gohrab, A.A., "The Flourishing of Persian Quatrains," in *A History of Persian Literature* (Vol. 2): *Persian Lyric Poetry in the Classical Era 800–1500: Ghazals. Panegyrics and Quatrains*, ed. E. Yarshater, London: I.B. Tauris, 2019, pp. 488–568.

Seyed-Gohrab, A.A., "The Rose and the Wine: Dispute as a Literary Device in Classical Persian Literature," *Iranian Studies*, no. 1 (2013), pp. 69–85.

Seyed-Gohrab, A.A., "There Was a Door to Which I Found No Key," There was a Door to which I found no Key – Beyond Sharia (accessed 15-11-2023); also Leiden Medievalists Blog, leidenmedievalistsblog.nl/articles/there-was-a-door-to-which-i-found-no-key (accessed 10 March 2020).

Shabistarī, Maḥmūd, *Gulshan-i rāz*, ed. A. Mujāhid and M. Kiyānī, Tehran: Mā, 1371/1992.

Shirvānī, Jamāl Khalīl, *Nuzhat al-majālis*, ed. M.A. Riyāḥī, Tehran: Mahārat, first edition 1366/1987, second edition, 1375/1996.

Siddīqī Nakhjavānī, R., *Khayyām-pindārī va pasukh-i afkār-i qalandarāna-yi ū*, Tabriz: Surūsh, 1320/1931.

Surūsh, ʿAbd al-Karīm, *Mudārā va mudīrīyat*, Tehran: Ṭulūʿ-i Āzādī, 1376/1997.

Yogananda, P., *The Rubaiyat of Omar Khayyām Explained*, ed. J. Donald Walters, California: Crystal & Clarity, 1994.

Zarrīnkūb, ʿAbd ʾl-Ḥusayn, *Kitāb-i ḥowla*, Tehran: ʿIlmī, seventh print 1372/1993.

A Polemic on Knowledge: An Analysis of Two Persian Quatrains

Arash Ghajarjazi
Utrecht University

Abstract
This chapter deals with an intellectual dispute embedded within two Persian quatrains found in a manuscript from 644/1256, housed at the Shahīd ʿAlī Pashā library in Istanbul. Central to this debate are the terms *khabar* and *rāy*. These concepts are prevalent in Persian and Arabic thought yet their semantic complications and nuances have not been investigated. Typically, *khabar* denotes factual reports or narrative accounts, often associated with Islamic scholastic traditions. On the other hand, the term *rāy* holds broader usage across various literate communities, including scholars, poets, and Sufis. Among scholars, it signifies an opinion or idea formed through intellectual faculties, not always validated by Qurānīc scriptures or the *ḥadīth* tradition. In a broader context within fiction and poetry, *rāy* extends to meanings such as perspective, opinion, intention, mental image, thinking, deliberations, counsel, and occasionally, the general concept of mind. The clash between these terms represents a deeper philosophical divide within Persian-Arabic scholarship. The two quatrains in focus reflect this rift. The first is attributed to the rhetorician, poet, and scholar Aḥmad Ibn-i Manṣūr Samʿānī (d. 1140) while the second is given anonymously. The complex interplay between the two quatrains invites a closer investigation. The speakers in these two quatrains seem to compete over the ascendency of their preferred term: one stands on the side of *rāy* and the other on the side of *khabar*. One side rejects *rāy*, while the other favours it over *khabar*, even when it is considered unreliable. This chapter first maps out a literary context in the early Saljuq society where *rāy* circulated meaningfully among the literate members of the early Saljuq society. Subsequently, it dissects the disputing quatrains to reveal their semantic nuances. The chapter argues that the dispute uncovers an overlooked facet of Perso-Arab thought: a critical evolution in Persian thinking that expanded and pushed the boundaries of *rāy* beyond its Islamic scholastic strictures.

Keywords: Khayyām; quatrains; Zakarīyā al-Rāzī; heresy; intellectual history; concept of rāy.

Introduction

This chapter deals with a dispute between two Persian quatrains in a manuscript dated 644/1256 and preserved at Shahīd ʿAlī Pashā library in Istanbul. The dispute revolves around the tension between two words: *khabar* and *rāy*. Both terms are complicated and bring to mind a vastly complex semantic zone in Persian and Arabic.[1] The former is commonly used by Muslim scholars in the sense of a piece of information, a report, or a narrative account of the deeds and sayings of the Prophet.[2] A *khabar* is usually understood as evidence of an event exactly as it happened. In the context of *ḥadīth* tradition, if it can be authenticated, it is taken as evidence of the Prophet's actions and words undistorted by its transmission. The notion underscores a tendency in Muslim imagination to reconstruct the original way of the Prophet without modification or interpretation. In contrast and more broadly, the latter term, *rāy*, is used across different literate communities, from scholars to poets and Sufis. Among scholars, it may be used in the sense of an opinion, view, or idea that is produced by one's intellectual faculties and is not necessarily checked by the Qurʾānic scriptures or the *ḥadīth* tradition.[3] More broadly in fiction and poetry, it can also mean view, opinion, intent, mental image, thinking, deliberation, counsel, and sometimes as broad as mind.[4] Unlike *khabar*, which effaces its mediation and claims evidentiality, *rāy* does not conceal its constructed-ness. It is an image made up by the mind through its perceptual faculties. The two words came to represent a distinct clash between two traditions of thinking in Perso-Arab scholarship. The two contesting quatrains seem to reflect an incompatibility between these two terms:[5]

sunnat zi havā-yi bidʿat-ārā-yi tu bih
v-akhbār zi rāy-i tuhmat-afzā-yi tu bih
man az khabar-i rasūl gūyam, tu zi rāy
dānī khabar-i rasūl az rāy-i tu bih?

The tradition of Muḥammad is better than your heretical desire
and reports [of the Prophet] are better than your slandering *rāy*
I speak about the Prophet's reports and you of *rāy*
Do you know that the report of the Prophet is better than your *rāy*?

ilḥād zi madhhab-i muṭarrā-yi tu bih
Bū Jahl zi muqtadā-yi bī rāy-i tu bih
rāyī ki ṣavāb nāmad u ṣidq u mushīr[6]
az raqṣ u kachūl u az daf u nay-i tu bih

Heresy is better than your fawning creed
Abū Jahl is better than your *rāy*-less leader
A *rāy*, [even though it] is not sound, right and indicative
is better than your dance and jig and better than your daf and reed.[7]

As introduced by Sayyid ʿAlī Mīrafżalī, the first quatrain is quoted under the name "Samʿānī" and the second, which is a response to the first, is given anonymously. Mīrafżalī speculates that Samʿānī may be referring to the rhetorician, poet, and scholar Aḥmad Ibn-i Manṣūr Samʿānī (d. 1140), the author of a well-known commentary on the names of God, *The Spirit of Spirits in Explaining the Names of the Sovereign, the Opener* (*Rūḥ al-arwāḥ fī sharḥ asmāʾ al-malik al-fattāḥ*).[8] Mīrafżalī has moreover traced this first quatrain in a more Sufi-minded treatise *Unveiling the Mysteries and Preparing the Righteous* (*Kashf al-asrār wa ʿiddat al-abrār*) by the mystic and scholar Rashīd al-Dīn Abu 'l-Fażl Maybudī (alive in 1126).[9] Of the second poet, however, nothing is known. It can therefore be seen that the circulation of the first quatrain in the late twelfth-century Persianate societies can be tracked along a broad trajectory: it moves in between the Western side of Islamdom where the manuscript is preserved, through the middle territories in Yazd, where Rashīd al-Dīn Abu 'l-Fażl Maybudī was from, and to the East in Marv and Nayshābūr where Samʿānī and the author of the manuscript, who I will discuss later, was active.[10]

The dispute may even be backtracked to the ninth century in the person of Abū Bakr Muḥammad Ibn Zakarīyā al-Rāzī (d. 925), who was recorded to have unapologetically criticised prophecy in his lost works.[11] As Sarah Stroumsa translates from one of the few extant second-hand accounts of Rāzī's heresy as recorded by Abū Rayḥān al-Bīrūnī (d. 1050),

> He [i.e., Razi] said: "The followers of revealed religions have learnt their religion (*al-dīn*) by following the authority of their leaders. They reject rational speculation (*al-naẓar*) and inquiry about the fundamental doctrines [of religion]. They restrict [this inquiry] and forbid it. They transmit traditions (*akhbār*) in the name of their leaders, which oblige them to refrain from speculation (*al-naẓar*) on religious matters, and declare that anyone who contradicts the traditions (*akhbār*) they transmit must be branded an infidel.[12]

Similar to the speaker of the second quatrain above, Rāzī seems to stand against the logic of *khabar*. In Rāzī's opinion, this narrative transmission forbids the use of *al-naẓar*, which in Stroumsa's version is translated as speculation and may also be read as a synonym for *raʾy*. The first quatrain, moreover, uses the phrase "slandering *raʾy*", which comes quite close to how al-Bīrūnī paraphrases from Rāzī, when "He goes further to active slander, imputing to religion evil spirits, and the deeds of the demons".[13] In light of this preview, the two disputing quatrains show that the famous Rāzian critique of prophecy continued to be voiced in the Persian language – even though Rāzī's original ideas about Prophecy might not have been as strictly unaccommodating.[14]

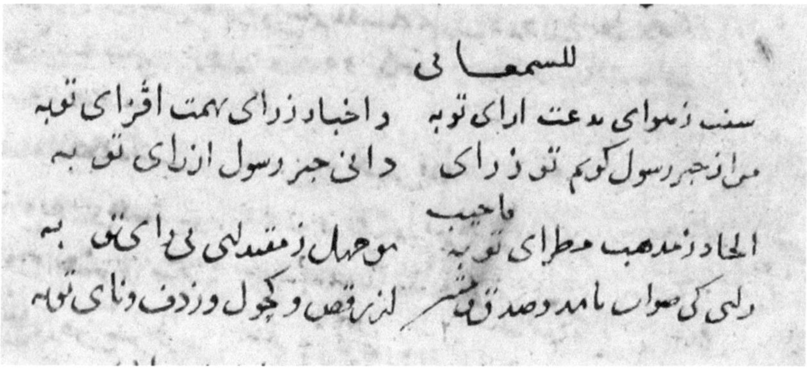

Figure 1. The two disputing quatrains as written in the original manuscript no. 598. fol. 363.

The complicated tension between the two quatrains and their broader historical resonance invites a closer analysis. The speakers in these two quatrains seem to compete over the ascendency of their preferred term: one stands on the side of *rāy* and the other on the side of *khabar*. Their respective views on the two terms are extreme. For the first, *rāy* is entirely rejected whereas, for the latter, it is preferred over *khabar* even if it "is not sound".[15] In this chapter, I will first map out a literary intellectual context in which the notion of *rāy* was meaningfully exchanged between the literate members of the early Saljūq society. Building on this, I will then analyse the two disputing quatrains and discuss their complicated semantic and conceptual frameworks. I argue that the dispute reveals a hitherto neglected aspect of Perso-Arab thought, namely, the existence of a critical genealogy of thought in Persian that extended and radicalised the notion of *rāy* beyond its jurisprudential stricture.

The manuscript and its intellectual context

The two quatrains appear at the end of the MS 598 in the form of an addendum. The main text is *Uṣūl al-fiqh* by the eleventh-century Ḥanafī scholar Muḥammad Ibn Aḥmad Ibn Abū Bakr al-Sarakhsī (d. probably 1096). Several pages are annexed to the main text and the quatrains appear on the first of these. The Persian quatrains are most likely added by the transcriber as they do not appear in other known manuscripts of Sarakhsī's *Uṣūl al-fiqh.*[16] As Norman Calder notes, Sarakhsī is known to have contributed to the Transoxianian jurisprudence as evidenced by a few extant works attributed to him, most importantly through his *Mabsūṭ*, the *Sharḥ al-siyar al-kabīr*, and the abovementioned *Uṣūl al-fiqh*. This latter work integrated elements from the distinct Transoxianian Ḥanafī tradition and the *uṣūl* writings of others such as Abul Ḥasan al-Karkhī (d. 951), Aḥmad Ibn Muḥammad al-Shāshī (d. 955), and al-Jaṣṣāṣ (d. 980).[17] Interestingly, Calder suggests that he dictated his *Mabsūṭ* while in prison, though the details regarding the rulership and reasons for his incarceration remain unclear. His theological background in the Ḥanafī school is important because it strengthens the hypothesis that the responding quatrain is quoted sympathetically to Sarakhsī's writing, most likely by a later scribe.

According to Willi Heffening and Joseph Schacht, Ḥanafī scholars were reportedly criticised for their reliance on *rāy* since the early eighth century.[18] This type of criticism was rooted in the emerging *ḥadīth* methodologies that continued well into the eleventh century when Sarakhsī wrote his *Uṣūl al-fiqh*. During those three centuries, Muslim scholars incorporated the retrospective methods of the so-called *ahl al-ḥadīth*, whereby it became incumbent on them to retrieve the Prophetic tradition from the scattered and indirect memories of Muḥammad's life and rulership.[19] D. W. Brown comments on the changing modality of making knowledge in this period:

> Thus *ʿilm* consisted of *sunnas* which had originated at the hands of pious forebears and which were eventually moulded into *ḥadīths*. *ʿIlm* seekers, *ʿulamāʾ* (pl. of *ʿālim*), were often antagonistic towards those who resorted to their *rāʾy*, the *ahl al-rāʾy*, and this gave way to an ongoing dialogue, or bitter dispute, between, on the one hand, a basically religious, precedent-centred point of view and, on the other hand, a somewhat secular stance with, according to some *ʿulamāʾ* far too little religion mixed in with it.

It was against this backdrop that during Niẓām al-Mulk's (d. 1092) premiership – the vizier of two Saljūq Sulṭāns, namely, Alp Arsalān (r. 1063–1072) and Malik Shāh (r. 1072–1092) – Ḥanafī and Shāfiʿī schools in Khurāsān included both *rāy*-based and *ḥadīth*-based methodologies. However, this was also the time in which Persian was re-emerging as a lingua franca and Persianate mysticism was in the air everywhere in Persian-speaking regions. It was during this period that Abū Ḥamid Muḥammad Ghazzālī (d. 1111) wrote his *Taḥaf al-falāsifa* (*Incoherence of the Philosophers*) in 1095, and figures such as Abū Saʿīd Abu ʿl-Khayr (d. 1049) and later Abu ʿl-Majd Ḥakīm Sanāʾī (d. 1131), and ʿAyn al-Qużāt (executed in 1131) became popular mystics in the Persianate world.[20] Also important to note is the astronomer and mathematician ʿUmar Khayyām (d. 1123/31) was the product of this period. The name Khayyām would become the main carrier of Persian quatrains in the Ilkhānīd era and was often associated with heresy in Perso-Arab thought.[21]

In this early Saljūq period, Muslims of various religious convictions often perceived different communities as heretics. Ḥanafīs and Shāfiʿīs viewed sects such as Karrāmis and Ismāʿīlīs as outright unbelievers.[22] Many mystics were quite commonly considered "*zandīq*s" and "*mulḥid*s" for their experiential anomalies by many Sunni orthodox thinkers as well as Shīʿīs.[23] The most notable victim of these harsh exchanges was the execution of ʿAyn al-Qużāt Hamadānī in 1131.[24] The Saljūq intellectual sphere was demonstrably intolerant of dissonance. As De Blois writes, "many of the Ṣūfīs, beginning with Ḥallāj, were accused of *zandaqa*, though their whole world outlook is diametrically opposed to Manichaean dualism".[25] Saljūqs' political life imposed and informed an urgency on thought to assimilate or silence non-conformist ideas. Every ideational or religious difference was perceived as a political and existential threat to various communities in the region. From a cultural-historical perspective, Christian Lange tracks this intolerance in the changing role of the moral police (*muḥtasib*) under the Saljuqs. *Muḥtasib*s were responsible for observing the Islamic moral code, howsoever vaguely understood, in the public sphere. As Lange observes, from the Būyīds to the Saljūqs, these morality officers were given more punitive freedom and were also allowed into the private spheres.[26] In this oppressive milieu, sects such as Ismāʿīlīs and earlier Karrāmiyya that might have seemed to have common ideas perceived each other as irreconcilable rivals. A different idea of God, death, or leadership was significant enough a reason to dismiss an entire community of believers as heretics. In these intellectual conflicts, the meanings of belief and unbelief became contested as each community of believers sought to formalise its political and intellectual sources into an ideological system.[27]

Moreover, during Niẓām al-Mulk's tenure, the Persian language became the dominant medium for bureaucracy and courtly affairs. The manual of political ethics and state management, *Siyāsat-nāma* (*The Book of Statecraft*), written by Niẓām al-Mulk himself, was among the most well-known texts in this respect.[28] This rising prominence of Persian was at the same time entangled in a milieu where religious differences were becoming more pronounced. Several textual pieces of evidence are extant from this period that evince how important religious differences were for the literate communities. Among the most canonical ones, *al-Milal wa al-niḥal* (ca. 1127), *Kitāb al-naqż* (ca. 1165), *Fażāʾiḥ al-rawāfiż* (ca. 1160), and *Tabṣirāt al-aʿwāmm* (ca. 1232) can be mentioned. These texts provided detailed, though often prejudiced, accounts of the existing religious sects and ideas in their times. *Kitāb al-naqż* was written by a Shīʿa scholar in response to the Sunni *Fażāʾiḥ al-rawāfiż*. What is immediately noteworthy about these works is the frequency of the various terms used to dismiss a community of (un)believers. The author of *Kitāb al-naqż*, Naṣir al-Dīn Abū al-Rashīd al-Qazvīnī, calls Sunnis who imagine God in anthropomorphic (*ahl-i shubha*) terms *mulḥid*. He also distinguishes his Shīʿism from that of Islamāʿīlīs.[29] On the other side of this textual conflict, *Fażāʾiḥ al-rawāfiż* views

Shīʿīsm as "the corridor to heresy (*ilḥād*)" and that Shīʿas are materialist (*dahrī*).[30] A few decades before these sources, Ghazzālī's *Incoherence of the Philosophers* shows even more fundamental cracks between the different fields of knowledge. Ghazzālī refutes not only Shīʿa ideas but also the entire philosophical tradition rooted in Ibn Sīnā on account of its leaning more towards personal opinion (*raʾy*).

In this varied climate, the literati and *ʿulamāʾ* sought court patronage for their intellectual livelihood. The more theologically oriented literati would gain the court's support for their jurisprudential and *kalāmī* texts, mostly in Arabic. In contrast, the more literary minds sought patronage for their poetry and belles-lettres, mainly in Persian. The more scientific minds could also find ways into the system. Finally, those with Sufi predilections would reach out to the court through the *khānqāh*s and the increasing social organisation of Sufism.

It is especially important to note that through the court patronage of Persian poets by the Saljūqs, a cast of *poeta doctus* emerged – learned poets characterised by their deep erudition and scholarly knowledge. These poets introduced conceptual schemes that had been hitherto external to Persian poetry, namely, medicine, botany, theology, occult sciences, astrology, and astronomy.[31] As a correlate, by the end of the twelfth century, Persian poets began to use more religious, and therefore Arabic, words in their poems. Prominent examples, Anvarī (d. 1189), Niẓāmī (d. 1209), and Khāqānī (d. 1190) were among the first poets who incorporated Arabic terms by borrowing from other fields, such as medicine, astrology and theology, ushering in the so-called poetic style of *ʿirāqī*.[32] It is as part of this augmented poetry that quatrains' popularity as well as mystical poetry increased. In contrast to the formal tone of court poets, with the dominance of panegyric and elegiac poetry, quatrains infused the informal and colloquial tone of everyday Persian thought into poetry.[33] Moreover, quatrains were increasingly used in prosimetrum as a tool to condense or elaborate on complex ideas in a concise format. Ḥamīd Balkhī's *Maqāmāt* (ca. 1156), and the celebrated Persian translation of *Kalīla va Dimna* by Naṣrullāh Munshī (d. before 1187) are among the most renowned examples of prose with a considerable number of poetic quotations.[34] The disputing quatrains I quoted above should be viewed within this emerging milieu. The informal register of Persian can be recognised in both, especially reflected in the two speakers' emotive attitudes.

Understandings of *rāy* in Persian thought

The term *rāy* has a wide semantic zone in eleventh-century Persian poetry. The following brief overview should give a general map of the different philosophical, theosophical, and theological connotations of the term. In the first instance, the panegyrics of Saljūq court poets should be mentioned. In both Manūchihrī (fl.

1031–1040) and ʿUnṣurī (d. 1039/40), the term is used as a positive attribute of kings. In some of Manūchihrī's panegyrics, the term is also associated with an anthropomorphised Spring. For instance, a panegyric addressed to Sulṭān Masʿūd Ghaznavī (r. 1030–1040), begins with the verse,

bar lashkar-i zimistān nawrūz-i nāmdār
karda ast rāy-i tākhtan u qaṣd-i kārzār

Upon the Winter-army, the famed New Year
Has set its intent to charge and sought the battlefield.[35]

Here, *rāy* is understood as the anthropomorphised power of the Spring to fight against Winter. In another instance, addressing an unnamed deceased dignitary, a panegyric verse reads,

bi jāygāh-i ʿazm, ʿazm ʿazm-i ū
bi jāygāh-i rāy, rāy rāy-i ū.[36]

In place of firmness, his firmness is the real firmness
In place of [showing] vision, his vision is the real vision.

And in praise of a Khwāja Ṭāhir, similar to above, a hemistich reads, "his firmness is the real firmness, his perfection is the real perfection, and his vision is the real vision". The word *rāy* in this verse can also be understood in the sense of opinion, view, and mental strength. I suggest the word vision as a way to capture all these possible connotations. However, this should not be taken as a denotation of the sense of sight. Although an association with visuality is certainly imaginable – especially given the Arabic verb *raʾaya* means to see – the way it is used in the lines above suggests a broader meaning for *rāy*. It is taken to mean one's intellectual power to form a prospective image of reality, such as a plan, a decision, a military strategy and so on. In another similar instance, Manūchihrī ascribes *rāy* to a man of high stature:

būḥarb-i bakhtiyār muḥammad, ki rāy-i ū
arkān-hā-yi mulk muʾakkad kunad hamī.[37]

Būḥarb-i Bakhtiyār Muḥammad, whose vision
strengthens the pillars of the kingdom

In most cases, Manūchihrī uses the term in the sense of intent, personal view, opinion, or mental power mostly associating it with kingly figures. It is generally understood as an effect of one's intellectual power, mediating one's righteous volition and intent in the world. This sense repeats the earlier poet ʿUnṣurī, whose panegyrics often praise kings such as Sulṭān Maḥmūd Ghaznavī (d. 1030) for their "enlightened vision" (*rāy-i rawshan*). Moreover, it is sometimes used as a surrogate for *khirad* as in *nishastast rāyash bi jāy-i khirad*, which may be translated as "his *raʾy* has sat in place of the intellect",[38] or as an effect of one's military intent in the phrase "*rāy-i ḥarb*".[39]

Another prominent poet of the late eleventh-century Saljūq court, Amīr Muʿizzī (d. 1125/7), repeats the same conception of *rāy* as that by ʿUnṣurī and Manūchihrī before him. For example, in the *maqṭaʿ* of a panegyric addressed to an unnamed Sulṭān, the poet uses the term *rāy* in a positive light:

bar har ṣifat ki bāshī rāy-i tu bād ʿālī
dar har vaṭan ki mānī mulk-i tu bād vālā

Whatever your traits are, may your opinion/vision be excellent
In any native lands you stay, may your kingdom be supreme.[40]

In another example, in a panegyric addressed to Sulṭān Sanjar, Muʿizzī praises the Sulṭān's intellectual power with an interesting reference to the word *khirad:*

hargiz khirad az rāy-i razīnash nakishad sar
gūʾī ki khirad sukhra shud ān rāy-i razīn rā

The intellect would never rebel against his weighty vision
As if the intellect became subdued by that weighty vision.[41]

In this verse, *rāy* acquires a meaning beyond reason, opinion, and mental percept. It becomes a transcendental psychological trait, closer to the divine realm and exclusive to the king. With the phrase weighty vision, I intend to underscore the divine intellectual capacity to see prospectively beyond one's immediate sensory field. This sense is central in the different Persian formulations of *raʾy*. As my brief review will further demonstrate, the concept of *raʾy* as a divine perspective power seems to be the most accepted and common way of thinking about it in Persian poetry.

As another example, the Ismāʿīlī poet and thinker Nāṣir(-i) Khusraw (d. 1072–8) should be mentioned. Unlike his contemporary panegyric poets, Nāṣir Khusraw has a much more critical take on the notion of *rāy*. As a particularly telling example, in a deeply introspective *qaṣīda*, he critiques the concept and casts it in a suspicious light. He begins the poem with the premise that one's desire should be subject to piety (*pārsāʾī*). Tapping into a diverse semantic zone, represented by terms like *āz*, *ārizū*, *murād*, and *kām*, which are used interchangeably for the notion of desire, he contends that faith (*dīn*) is essential for liberating one's self from the demons (*dīv*) of avarice (*āz*). He proposes that this faith (*dīn*) be understood as a school (*dabistān*), where a community (*ummat*) would be like children before the Prophet. However, in this school, people are not educated but convinced to accept doctrinal proofs (*ḥujjat*) without the use of reason (*rāy*) and analogy (*qiyās*):

bīsh az īn ay fitna gashta bar qiyās u rāy-i khwīsh
kardamī ẓāhir zi ʿaybat gar marā kardī kirā

More than this, O you who have been seduced and afflicted by your analogy and reason
I have revealed your flaw to you if you value me.[42]

Still more harshly in another *qaṣīda*, he writes,

mā bar athar-i ʿitrat-i payghambar-i khʷīshīm
awlād-i zanā bar athar-i rāy u havā-and

We follow the family of our Prophet
He, the child born out of adultery, following reason and lust.[43]

It must be noted that sometimes Nāṣir Khusraw changes his negative judgment against *raʾy* and allows himself to laud it as a pious virtue. For instance, in another *qaṣīda*, he writes

fakhr bi khūbī u zar u sīm zanān rāst
fakhr-i man u tu bi ʿilm u raʾy u vaqār ast

taking pride in beauty, gold and silver is for women
the pride of you and me is of knowledge, reason, and dignity.[44]

Yet on another occasion, his use of the word becomes more ambiguous, as in the hemistich

kār-i man guftār-i khūb u rāy-i ʿilm u ṭāʿat ast

My occupation is good speech, intent of knowledge and obedience to God.[45]

Whereas in ʿUnṣurī, Manūchihrī, and Amīr Muʿizzī, *raʾy* is consistently lauded as a kingly intellectual virtue that is capable of affecting and changing the world, with

Nāṣir Khusraw, it receives a negative meaning next to that positive one. In this way, he oscillates between two extreme views on the notion of *rāy*. When compared with faith and the Prophet, he rejects it entirely, but when references to the Prophet are lacking, he is willing to go as far as promoting it as a virtue.

Later in the early twelfth century, most notably with mystics such as Sanāʾī, *rāy* is absorbed into a mystic amatory poetic framework. Although he occasionally uses the term in the same manner as ʿUnṣurī, Manūchihrī, and Muʿizzī,[46] *rāy* is often referred to as a human intellectual or perceptual capacity, which can be both problematic and virtuous depending on the context of its use. The following verse showcases a virtuous understanding of *raʾy*:

mard ān buvad ki dānad har jāy rāy-i khwīsh
mardān bi kār-i ʿishq nabāshand sarsarī.[47]

Man is he who knows in every place his *rāy*
Chivalrous men do not occupy themselves with love carelessly.

In contrast, the following verse exemplifies a problematic *raʾy*:

pā-yi rāy-i nafs az tīgh-i sharʿī pay kunīm
pāy-i maʿnī az sipihr u akhtarān bartar nahīm.[48]

With the Sharia's blade, we cut off the foot of the lower soul's *raʾy*
we elevate the foot of meaning above the sky and stars.

In these latter lines, Sanāʾī subjugates *rāy* to faith, which is described metaphorically as a blade that cuts through one's perceptual faculty and can further sublimate meaning or Idea (*maʿnā*) to a higher status than that of the sky and the stars. But perhaps the following lines from the beginning of a *qaṣīda*, titled "On the union with the divine world (*dar vuṣūl bi ʿālam-i lāhūt*)" gives one of the most complicated uses of *rāy* by Sanāʾī.

chu mardān bishkan īn zindān yakī āhang-i ṣaḥrā[49] *kun*
bi ṣaḥrā dar nigar ān gah bi kām-i dil tamāshā kun

az īn zindān agar khʷāhī ki chu yūsuf burūn āʾī
bi dānish jān biparvar nīk u dar sar ʿilm[50] *rawʾyā kun*

mashu gumrāh u bīchāra chunīn andar rah-i sawdā
charāgh-i dānishat bifrūz u ān gah rāy-i sawdā kun

Like chivalrous men, break apart this prison and journey to the desert
Look then upon the desert and at that moment behold with the heart's desire

If you want to take leave of this prison, like Joseph
Foster your soul well with knowledge and dream interpretation in the head

Don't be lost and miserable in the path of passionate love
Light up the lantern of your knowledge first and then conceive of love.[51]

The poem prescribes a mystic path whereby one is expected to leave behind the realm of the bodily senses and seek inner knowledge with which to navigate the perilous path toward union. This gnostic knowledge further shapes and conditions one's *raʾy*, which I translated as "to conceive" in the last hemistich above. In this sense, the gnostic is advised to seek and perceive the path of love only through the lens of his inner knowledge. The term *raʾy* is therefore emptied of its connotation with and dependency on the human sensorium and becomes an incorporeal abstraction "broken" free from the "prison" of the body. *Raʾy* is thus re-conceptualised as a correlate of an immortal mind – or rather a mind that longs for immortality – which is capable of leaving the body behind and attaining an independent existence beyond the material world. This idea is further developed in the later lines of the same poem. In one line, this incorporeal *raʾy* is most emphatically formulated,

mulāqā chun kunī bā ʿaql zīr-i parda-yi ḥissī
nukhust az parda bīrūn āy u pas rāy-i mulāqā kun

How do you meet with the intellect from behind the sensory veil
First, take leave of the veil and then conceive of meeting.[52]

In his *Ḥadīqat al-ḥaqīqa*, Sanāʾī provides a similar perspective to the notion of *raʾy*, which comes much closer to the conflictual formulation in the two disputing quatrains. The couplets come in the third chapter, "In the Praise of Our Prophet Muḥammad Muṣṭafā (Peace Be Upon Him) and His Excellence among All Prophets". It opens with several lines in which the Prophet is admired for his superiority over human intellect (*ʿaql*) and towards the end of the poem, his religion (*sharʿ*) is compared to human *rāy*:

sharʿ-i ū rūḥ-i ʿaql-i rūḥānīst
raʾy-i tu yār-i dīv-i nafsānīst
[...]

har kujā shar' rūy-i khwīsh nimūd
rāy dar gard-i summ-i ū farsūd

'aql khud kār-i sarsarī nakunad
līk bā dīn barābarī nakunad

hast bā shar' kār-i ra'y u qiyās
hamchu pīsh-i kalām-i haqq vasvās

ra'y-i shar' ānka nafs rā sūzad
ra'y-i 'aql ānka shu'la afrūzad

His religion is the soul of the spiritual intellect
your mind is the companion of the demonic ego
[...]
Wherever the Sharia showed its face,
the mind worn out in the dust of its hoof

Intellect would not itself handle an affair carelessly
But it would not match faith

the affairs of *ra'y* and analogy are with the Sharia
like an evil temptation before God's words.[53]

The *ra'y* of Sharia is to burn the baser self,
the *ra'y* of the intellect is to kindle the flame

In these couplets, *ra'y* is uncomplicatedly subordinated to the Prophet's religion, or to use the terminology in the disputing quatrains, the Prophet's tradition (*sunnat-i rasūl*). Interestingly, Sanā'ī distinguishes between two types of *ra'y*, one religious and the other intellectual – the former removes the ego and the baser self, whereas the latter adds further noise to one's mind.

According to this overview, it can be said that as used in the Persianate sphere of the early Saljuq period, the notion of *ra'y* moved between two semantic zones. On the one hand, it is taken as a divine attribute that may be bestowed upon kings or mystics. In this meaning, *rāy* is a correlate of power and piety. It can change the world and open up new territories for a kingdom or enable a mystic to be better positioned in his quest for union. On the other hand, however, *rāy* may also be understood as an essentially flawed human trait. In this sense, it becomes a correlate of existential bewilderment and unbelief. It can divert a person from the right path and cause anxiety and grief. In this way, the term *ra'y* is caught in a tension between human flawed existence and the divine perfect being. For most poets and thinkers in this period, the problem is to recognise the right kind of *ra'y* and foster it.

This tension would be transformed and reshaped in the hands of later Persian poets and Sufi thinkers such as Niẓāmī, ʿAṭṭār, Najm al-Dīn Dāya, and Rūmī in the thirteenth century, and as late as Jāmī in the fifteenth century. It would require an extensive study to review the intricate nuances of the terms *ra'y* in these later poets. For the sake of the present study, it would be worth noting that this tension is radically subverted in a certain group of Persian quatrains that came to be associated with the name Khayyām. In what I term elsewhere Khayyāmcity, both the human-based and the divine *rāy* become the subject of criticism and suspicion. As three compelling examples, the following may be mentioned. The first is the very first quatrain quoted in Khayyām's name in the early thirteenth century, and the second and third are recorded in the mid-thirteenth century poetry collection *Nuzhat al-majālis*:

dāranda chu tarkīb chunīn khūb ārāst
bāz az chi sabab fikandash andar kam-u kāst?
gar khūb nayāmad īn banā ʿiyb-i kirāst?
var khūb āmad kharābī az bahr-i chirāst?

Why did the Owner who arranged the form so well
cast it again into shortcomings and deficiency?
If it was not good, who is to blame for these flaws in this construct?
And if it is good, why does he break it again?[54]

ān rā ki bi ṣaḥrā-yi ʿilal tākhta-and
bī u hama kārhā bipardākhta-and
imrūz bahāna'ī dar andākhta-and
fardā hama ān buvad ki dī sākhta-and

The one they have thrown into the desert of causes,
Without involving him/her, they have completed all affairs
Today, they have thrown in an excuse
Tomorrow, it will all be what they already made yesterday.

chun rūzī-yu ʿumr bīsh u kam natvān kard
dil rā bi chunīn ghuṣṣa dizham natvān kard
kār-i man u tu chunān ki ra'y-i man u tust
az mūm bi dast-i khʷīsh ham natvān kard

> As the length of one's lifespan cannot be shortened nor lengthened
> the soul cannot be afflicted by this sorrow.
> The affairs of you and me as based on our opinion,
> even with our own hands, we cannot mould wax.[55]

As I show elsewhere, the first quatrain continued to trouble the minds of many Muslim scholars spanning from Fakhr al-Dīn Rāzī (d. 1209) to Mullā Ṣadrā (d. 1641).[56] By posing a well-defined rhetorical question, the first four lines hint at the extremely heretical idea that God's intent may be flawed. The second quatrain expresses a deterministic view of life and considers God's creation arbitrary, which the term "excuse (*bihāna*)" intensifies. Cynically viewed, God's decision to make life the way it is is paradoxically seen as a slapdash and yet perfect event. Creation is slapdash because as the first hemistich in the quatrain puts it, a multiplicity of vague Divine agents – the subject of the third person plural – set forth creations into existence with haste (*tākhtan*) and carelessness. The verb *tākhtan* in Persian often means to rush and to hasten towards somewhere. God's *rāy* thus rushes creation into existence without much contemplation. In the third quatrain, however, it is the human *rāy* that is cast in a negative light – which is in this case explicitly mentioned. The speaker confesses an inability to alter or influence the world, using the imagery of moulding wax to illustrate this powerlessness. In essence, within this Khayyāmc framework, not only is human reason subject to critique but also divine reasoning is subjected to a critical deconstruction. While Sufis sought to safeguard the divine *rāy* from doubt and criticism, Khayyāmc poets aimed their precise critique at this protected conception of God.

In dialogue with and in counterpoint to this growing Khayyāmc poetry, many mystic apologetics struggled to re-sanctify the divine *rāy*. In the following example, the first quatrain in the disputing doublet is quoted to that end by Maybudī. This is an excerpt from his *Kashf al-asrār*:

> For the traditionist (*sunnī*) who seeks the path [to God], it is the path that drives him through the rein of the Truth. Along this path of righteousness, along the way of rightness, with the lantern of guidance, and Muṣṭafā's escort, [the seeker] turns his face towards salvation from realm to realm and from station to station until he is delivered at the seat of righteousness in the sovereign's company. But the innovator who lost the path of resignation and fell into the abyss of interpretation [by the use of reason] (*ta'wīl*), is not familiar with this because in his heart there is no light from the tradition: "It does not increase the unjust except in loss".[57] That destitute person who practices interpretation [by the use of reason] and avoids resignation (*taslīm*) does not know. Because the guarantor of understanding resignation is God whereas the guarantor of understanding interpretation (*ta'wīl*) is the reason (*rāy*). So whatever comes from interpretation [by the use of reason] would be on us, and whatever comes from resignation would be on God. Resignation is

an easy path and proximate to heaven and its stations are replenished. But interpretation [by the use of reason] is a difficult path, proximate to darkness, and its stations in ruin. Interpretation (*ta'wīl*) is to go after reason (*rāy*), which is more ominous than going after doubt (*shakk*). [In contrast,] resignation is to go after the Prophet, protect His tradition, rely on Him, accept its appearance, and leave the inner secret (*bāṭin*) to the Truth:

sunnat zi havā-yi bid'at ārā-yi tu bih
lafż-i nabavī zi lafż-i bad-rāy-i tu bih
man az sukhan-i rasūl gūyam tu zi rāy
ākhir sukhan-i rasūl az rāy-i tu bih

The tradition of Muḥammad is better than your heretical desire
the prophetic word is better than your ill-conceived word
I speak about the Prophet's speech and you of *rāy*
After all, the Prophet's speech is better than your *rāy*?[58]

The quatrain is only slightly different from the first one in the disputing doublet above. Maybudī's thoughts dismiss *rāy* entirely without entertaining the possibility of its usefulness, power, or virtuousness – in the manner panegyric poets such as 'Unṣurī and Manūchihrī imagined. Najm al-Dīn Dāya (d. 1247) would repeat this mystic argument almost a century after Maybudī in his *Marmūzāt-i Asādī*, where he frequently dismissed *rāy* as an illegitimate mode of knowing the world and the divine plan. In one interesting instance, Dāya manipulates the second Khayyāmc quatrain I quoted above by inserting the term *taslīm* in it:

kār-i man u tu bī man u tu sākhti-and
vaz nīk u bad man u tu pardākhti-and
taslīm kun imrūz ki fardā bi yaqīn
tukhmī rūyad ki dī dar andākhti-and

Our affair has been decided without you and me
They made you and me from both good and bad
Resign today as tomorrow for certain
The seed they sowed yesterday will sprout.[59]

Dāya's quatrain and the original Khayyāmc version creates disagreement regarding the notion of *rāy*. If for the Khayyāmc speaker, one is in awe of and has anxiety about the finality of life, the Sufi speaker in Dāya's version resigns himself to that finality and understands his death in terms of Muslim eschatological thought. While for the former, life ends with death, for the latter it "sprouts" in the afterlife.

The disputing quatrains

Returning to the two quatrains in dispute through the lens of the above semantic background, I wish to show how the two quatrains offer a unique perspective to the intellectual conflict between *ra'y* and *khabar* in the Persian sphere. The speaker in the first quatrain slanders his opponent with the term innovation (*bid'at*), a word that must have sounded all too familiar to the Perso-Arab literate societies as it frequently figured in heresiographies and polemics charged by traditionists. The core idea proposed in this offensive quatrain is not too complicated. The speaker considers every form of mental conception that is formed independent from, or indifferent to, the Prophetic tradition, a form of impiety and unbelief. It resonates with the piety of Nāṣir Khusraw, Sanā'ī, and Maybudī discussed earlier.

The complication arises in the second quatrain, which unapologetically supports *rāy*. The speaker contends that even an unsound *rāy* is better than *khabar*. There are three complications in this responding quatrain. First, the speaker's critique seems to be directed at not only the tradition and the epistemic mode of Prophetic *khabar*, but also certain aspects of Gnosticism. As formulated in the last hemistich, the first speaker's "dance and jig", and "daf and reed" are considered inferior to *rāy*, even though the latter would be an unsound one. The perceived piety that this hemistich refers to seems to be the ritualistic sessions famously organised and attended by Sufis and their followers. For instance, such activities could have commonly been witnessed in *samā'* sessions. In this way, the critique of *khabar* extends to that of Sufi practices as well. This viewpoint could well be directed at the anti-*rāy* ideas expressed by the ilks of Dāya and Maybudī.

The second complication is that the support for *rāy*, as formulated in the third hemistich, does not seem to resemble any of the intellectual loci I have briefly examined above. As I showed, the use of *rāy* is usually accepted or encouraged only if it regards a kingly figure or if it is already assimilable into a pious framework, whether Sufi or theological – as in Nāṣir Khusraw and Sanā'ī. Even in the Khayyāmc quatrains, *rāy* would not be promoted in such strong terms. One way to dismiss this complication is to allow Mīrafżalī's reading, "*ṣavāb bāshad u ṣidq u maṭīn*", where the verb "is not (*nāmad*)" is read as "is (*bāshad*)". With this reading, the verse would sound more familiar to its literary milieu. In my view, however, the typography of the word gives more credence to *nāmad*, given the downward indentation in the third letter, which cannot be read as the letter *sh*.

The third complication has to do with the fact that this quatrain is likely quoted by Sarakhsī himself or sympathetic to his treatise on *Uṣūl al-fiqh* – given the responding quatrain is quoted under the heading "(and I answer) *fa ujīb*". This is interesting because it suggests that the anti-*khabar* sentiment that is expressed in the second quatrain cannot be considered part of a *dahrī* atheism that many Sufis and theologians from Ghazzālī to Dāya refuted. Instead, it should be contextualised as part of an Islamic jurisprudential discourse that considers reasoning as a legitimate tool for the production of knowledge.

The two disputing quatrains reflect one of the most contrastive and yet unique conflicts in Perso-Arab thought. Although the disparity between the two is not necessarily representative of the quatrains' intellectual context, their harsh rhetorical tones suggest the existence of a rich discourse on epistemology – one that has been neglected by the intellectual historians of this period. My brief analysis suggests new avenues for research into the neglected genealogies of thought in the Persian sphere. Past scholarships on the notions of *rāy* and *khabar* have so far been limited to the Arabic milieu, where both terms were exclusively understood as part of Islamic jurisprudence. However, lacking is how Persian thinkers expanded the semantics of both terms beyond jurisprudential discourses. In this brief chapter, I have shown how the question of (political) power and piety are intertwined in the Persian thinking about *rāy* and *khabar*. The discussion will require a more comprehensive reading to further this initiatory study.

Notes

1 This chapter was written at Utrecht University as part of the ERC Advanced Grant project entitled *Beyond Sharia: The Role of Sufism in Shaping Islam* (www.beyondsharia.nl), funded by the European Research Council (ERC) under the European Union's Horizon 2020 research and innovation programme (Grant agreement No. 101020403). In Arabic, the vowel is short and follows a *ḥamza*: *ra'y*. However, in Persian, the word has a long vowel without a *ḥamza*. In this chapter, the transliteration of the word will be based on the Persian word unless the word is used as an Arabic term such as in the phrase *ahl al-ra'y*.

2 Arent Jan Wensinck. "Khabar". In *Encyclopaedia of Islam, Second Edition.*

3 Jeanette Wakin, and Aron Zysow, "Ra'y". In *Encyclopaedia of Islam, Second Edition.*

4 Steingass dictionary gives the following connotations for *rāy*: "Seeing; thinking, judging; knowledge, wisdom; opinion, belief, view, counsel; good pleasure".

5 Sayyid ʿAlī Mīrafżalī introduces these quatrains in his Telegram channel, "four-liner (*chahār khattī*)". According to him, the quatrain is quoted in the MS no. 598 and is dated 1256. I owe this reference to Asghar Seyed-Gohrab and Reza Pourjavadi.

6 Mīrafżalī reads the last three terms in the hemistich as "*ṣavāb bāshad u ṣidq u maṭīn*". However, he also provides two alternative readings by Hādī Akbarzāda and a colleague of his Ṭahirī. According to the first, the phrase reads, "*ṣavāb nāmad u ṣidq u munīr*" and very close to the first, the second reads, "*ṣavāb nāmad u ṣidq u mushīr*". The difference between these two alternatives with Mīrafżalī is significant as they make the dispute between the two terms far more contrastive. In my view, the last reading corresponds more accurately to the orthography. See below for a more detailed discussion.

7 I have deliberately left the complicated word *rāy* untranslated as no single English term can capture the complexity of its use in the two poems. The nuances of the term should become clearer towards the end of this chapter.

8 See Shahāb al-Dīn Aḥmad Samʿānī. *Rūḥ al-arwāḥ fī sharḥ asmāʾ al-malik al-fattāḥ*. For the only English translation of the work see Samʿānī. *The Repose of the Spirits: A Sufi Commentary on the Divine Names.*

9 See Annabel Keeler. "Meybodi, Abu'l-Fażl Rašid-Al-Din". In *Encyclopaedia Iranica*; *Sufi Hermeneutics: The Qurʾān Commentary of Rashīd Al-Dīn Maybudī.* Qurʾānic Studies Series, 3. Oxford: Oxford University Press, 2006.

10 For details of Samʿānī's life and work see the introduction in Samʿānī. *Rūḥ al-arwāḥ fī sharḥ asmāʾ al-malik al-fattāḥ.*

11 This well-known Razian heresy has been suggested by many scholars since the early twentieth century. In the Persian language, Ārāmish Dūstdār detailed it in Dūstdār. *Imtināʿ-i tafakkur dar farhang-i dīnī*, 297–359. For a review of mid-twentieth-century European Arabist Paul Kraus (d. 1944)'s works on the topic of a critical reevaluation of Rāzī's heresy in Islamic intellectual history see Hüseyin Güngör. "Razian Prophecy Rationalized", p. 2, note 1. For more recent studies, see Stroumsa. *Freethinkers of Medieval Islam: Ibn al-Rawāndī, Abū Bakr al-Rāzī and Their Impact on Islamic Thought*, pp. 87–120; Adamson. *Al-Rāzī*, pp. 1–24.

12 I have included some of the Arabic terms in Stroumsa's version to draw attention to the possible parallels between this excerpt and the disputing quatrains. Stroumsa. *Freethinkers of Medieval Islam*, p. 97.

13 Quoted in Ibid., p. 106.

14 That Rāzī might not have been as uncompromisingly against prophecy has been suggested most recently in Hüseyin Güngör. "Razian Prophecy Rationalized."

15 If Mīrafżalī's reading is considered, it can be seen that the second speaker aligns with a "sound, right and firm" *raʾy*, which implies a specific kind of *rāy* rather than the general concept. In this second quatrain, one can consider that there can also be a false *rāy*.

16 For the critical edition of the work see Abī Bakr Muḥammad Ibn Aḥmad Ibn Abī Sahl al-Sarakhsī. *ʾUṣūl al-Sarakhsī.* No poem is included in this edition.

17 Norman Calder. "al-SaraKhsī". In *Encyclopaedia of Islam, Second Edition.*

18 Willi Heffening and Joseph Schacht. "Ḥanafiyya". In *Encyclopaedia of Islam, Second Edition.* See also the entries to *ahl al-rāʾy* and *aḥl al-ḥadīth* in Peter C. Hennigan. "Ahl al-rāʾy". In *Encyclopaedia of Islam, THREE*; Joseph Schacht, "Ahl al-Ḥadīth". In *Encyclopaedia of Islam, Second Edition;* "Aṣḥāb al-Rāʾy". In *Encyclopaedia of Islam, Second Edition.*

19 For a detailed review of this development see Juynboll, and Brown. "Sunna". In *Encyclopaedia of Islam, Second Edition.*

20 Ghazālī's thoughts and career have been the subject of many scholarships. Less known is the extent to which his Persian works were received in the Saljūq period and beyond. Ali Asghar Seyed-Gohrab's recent monograph deals precisely with this aspect. See Seyed-Gohrab, *Of Heresy and Piety*, forthcoming.

21 For a recent study on how the name Khayyām evolved from the twelfth century to the present, see Arash Ghajarjazi. *Remembering Khayyām: Episodes of Unbelief in the Reception Histories of Persian Quatrains*, forthcoming.

22 See Malamud, "The Politics of Heresy in Medieval Khurasan".

23 For detailed explanations of these terms see Lewis, "Some Observations on the Significance of Heresy in the History of Islam"; Knysh, "'Orthodoxy' and 'Heresy'; Madelung, "Mulḥid"; De Blois, "Zindīḳ".

24 See, for instance, A.J. Arberry. *A Sufi Martyr*, pp. 50, 60, 70.

25 See De Blois, "Zindīḳ". For a recent discussion on the term *zandaqa* see Hughes. *An Anxious Inheritance: Religious Others and the Shaping of Sunnī Orthodoxy*, pp. 165–185.

26 Lange, "Changes in the Office of Hisba under the Seljuqs", pp. 157–9.

27 For a review of how notions of belief and unbelief changed in the period between the late seventh century to the ninth century, see Cornelia Schöck. "Belief and Unbelief in Classical Sunnī Theology". In *Encyclopaedia of Islam, THREE*.

28 For the English translation of this work see Nizam al-Mulk, *The Book of Government or Rules for Kings*. Translated by Hubert Darke, 1960. For a discussion on it, see Yavari, N., "Mirrors for Princes or a Hall of Mirrors: Niẓām al-Mulk's Siyar al-mulūk Reconsidered".

29 *Kitāb al-Naqż*, chapters 35, 40, 44.

30 Quoted in Bausani, A. "Religion in the Saljuq Period". In *Cambridge History of Iran*, vol. 5, 284–285.

31 This is observed by J.T.P. De Bruijn in his review of Anvarī, in which he writes, "Anvari used to boast of his great knowledge of music, the natural sciences, mathematics, astrology, logic, philosophy, and music", and continues to assert that in his poems, "traces of his learning can be found, through which he substantially extended the range of conventional themes and images". See *A History of Persian Literature*. Vol. 2, p. 129.

32 Ibid., p. 54.

33 Seyed Gohrab, "The Flourishing of Persian Quatrains after Omar Khayyam".

34 Ibid, 499. See also Joseph Harris, E. B. M Lottman, and Karl Reichl. *Prosimetrum: Crosscultural Perspectives on Narrative in Prose and Verse*. Suffolk: D.S. Brewer, 1997.

35 Manūchihrī Dāmghāni. *Dīvān*, p. 30.

36 Ibid., p. 85.

37 Ibid., p. 115.

38 Abulqāsim, ʿUnṣūrī Balkhī. *Dīvān*, p. 51.

39 Ibid., p. 88.

40 Amīr Muʿizzī. *The Complete Dīvān*, p. 22.

41 Ibid., 22.

42 Nāṣir Khusraw Qubādiyānī. *Dīvān*, p. 75.

43 Ibid., p. 153.

44 Ibid., p. 107.

45 Ibid., 223.

46 See for instance the twenty-fourth and fifth verses in the *qāṣīda* in praise of Khwāja Masʿūd ʿAlī Ibn Ibrāhīm in Abulmajd Sanāʾī Ghaznavī. *Dīvān*, p. 68–70, and in another *qaṣīda* in praise of Sulṭān Sanjar in Ibid., p. 85. For a critical discussion on Sanāʾī's Dīvān, see J. T. P. De Bruijn. *Of Piety and Poetry*, pp. 91–112.

47 Abulmajd Sanāʾī Ghaznavī. *Dīvān*, p. 654.

48 Ibid., p. 403.

49 In other versions of the poem. Instead of *ṣaḥrā* the word *bālā* (high) is used. Ibid., 492–3.

50 In at least another version of the poem, the phrase is inverted as *ʿilm dar sar*. Ibid.

51 Ibid.

52 Ibid., p. 494.

53 Sanāʾī. *Ḥadīqat al-ḥaqīqa va sharīʿat al-ṭarīqa*, p. 202–3.

54 Different versions of this quatrain are extant in various sources. The translation is based on Seyed-Gohrab's and De Bruijn's translations of a slightly different version of the same quatrain. See Seyed-Gohrab, *The Legacy of Khayyām*, pp. 12–13; De Bruijn, *Persian Sufi Poetry*, 12. For all the extant versions of this quatrain see the detailed work by Mīrafżalī, *Rubāʿiyyāt-i Khayyām dar manābiʿ-i*

kuhan, pp. 24, 28, 33, 46, 54, 119, 254. For the upcoming monograph on the broader intellectual history of Khayyāmic poetry, see Ghajarjazi. *Remembering Khayyām*. Forthcoming.

55 Shirvānī, Jamāl Khalīl. *Nuzhat al-majālis*, p. 672.

56 For a brilliant analytic essay on this topic see Jahāndīda Kūdahī and ʿAlīrizā Nikūʾi, *"Tawba va taṭhīr-i guftimānī dar Khayyāmiyyat-i pīshāmudern"*.

57 Taken from the Qurʾān 17:82. Fadel Soliman, Bridges' translation.

58 Abulfażl Rashīdī Maybudī. *Kashf al-asrār wa ʿiddat al-abrār*, pp. 561–2. My translation of the term *taʾwīl* is informed by Ismail Poonawala. "Taʾwīl". In *Encyclopaedia of Islam, Second Edition.*

59 Rāzī. *Marmuzāt*, pp. 144–145.

Works cited

Adamson, Peter. *Al-Rāzī.* New York: Oxford University Press, 2021.

Bausani, A. "Religion in the Saljuq Period". In *Cambridge History of Iran: The Saljuq and Mongol Periods.* Vol 5. Cambridge: Cambridge University Press,1968.

Blois, F.C. De. In *Encyclopaedia of Islam, Second Edition*, s.v. Zindīḳ.

Bruijn, J.T.P. de. *Persian Sufi Poetry: An Introduction to the Mystical Use of Classical Persian Poems.* Curzon Sufi Series. Richmond, Surrey: Curzon, 1997.

Bruijn, J.T.P. de. *Of Piety and Poetry: The Interaction of Religion and Literature in the Life and Works of Hakīm Sanāʾī of Ghazna*, Leiden: Brill, 1983.

Bruijn, J.T.P., de. "The Qaside After the Fall of the Ghaznavids 1100-1500 CE," in *Persian Lyric Poetry in the Classical Era, 800-1500: Ghazals, Panegyrics, and Quatrains*, Ed. E. Yarshater, 102-161. London: I. B. Tauris, 2019.

Calder, Norman. In *Encyclopaedia of Islam, Second Edition*, s.v. "al-SaraKhsī.

Dūstdār, Ārāmish. *Imtināʿ-i tafakkur dar farhang-i dīnī.* Paris: Khāvarān, 1991.

Encyclopaedia of Islam, THREE. Edited by Kate Fleet, Gudrun Krämer, Denis Matringe, and Everett Rowson. Leiden: Brill, 2007–. Online Publication.

Encyclopaedia of Islam, Second Edition. Edited by P. Bearman, Th. Bianquis, C.E. Bosworth, E. van Donzel, W.P. Heinrichs. Leiden: Brill, 1954–2004. Online Publication.

Ghajarjazi, Arash. *Remembering Khayyām: Episodes of Unbelief in the Reception Histories of Persian Quatrains*, forthcoming.

Güngör, Hüseyin. "Razian Prophecy Rationalized". *British Journal for the History of Philosophy*, 1–25 (2023).

Hamadānī, ʿAyn al-Quḍāt. *A Sufi Martyr: The 'Apologia' of 'ain Al-Quḍāt Al-Hamadhānī.* Translated by Arthur J. Arberry. London: Allen and Unwin, 1969.

Harris, Joseph, Lottman, E. B. M, and Reichl, Karl. *Prosimetrum: Crosscultural Perspectives on Narrative in Prose and Verse.* Suffolk: D.S. Brewer, 1997.

Hennigan, Peter C. In *Encyclopaedia of Islam, THREE*, s.v. Ahl al-rāʾy

Heffening, Willi, and Schacht, Joseph. In *Encyclopaedia of Islam, Second Edition*, s.v. Ḥanafiyya.

Hughes, Aaron W. *An Anxious Inheritance: Religious Others and the Shaping of Sunnī Orthodoxy.* New York: Oxford University Press, 2022.

Juynboll, G.H.A. and Brown, D.W. In *Encyclopaedia of Islam, Second Edition*, s.v. Sunna

Keeler, Annabel. In *Encyclopaedia Iranica*, s.v. Meybodi, Abu'l-Fażl Rašid-Al-Din.

Khusraw Qubādiyānī, Nāṣir. *Dīvān.* Edited by Ḥasan Taqī Zāda. Tehran: Mahārat, 1994.

Knysh, Alexander. "'Orthodoxy' and 'Heresy' in Medieval Islam: An Essay in Reassessment". *The Muslim World* 83, no. 1 (1993): 48–67.

Kūdahī, Jahāndīda, and Nikū'i, ʿAlīrizā. "*Tawba va Taṭhīr-i Guftimānī dar Khayyāmyyat-i Pīshāmudern*". *Nashriyya-yi Shiʿr Pajūhī*. no. 40 (2019): 77–100.

Lange, "Changes in the Office of *Ḥisba* Under the Seljuqs". In *The Seljuqs: Politics, Society, and Culture*. Edited by Christian Lange and Songül Mecit. Edinburgh: Edinburgh University Press, 2011: 157–181.

Lewis, Bernard. "Some Observations on the Significance of Heresy in the History of Islam". *Studia Islamica* 1 (1953): 43–63.

Madelung, W.. In *Encyclopaedia of Islam, Second Edition*, s.v. Mulḥid.

Malamud, Margaret. "The Politics of Heresy in Medieval Khurasan: The Karramiyya in Nishapur". *Iranian Studies* 27, no. 1–4 (1994): 37–51.

Manūchihrī Dāmghāni. *Dīvān*. Edited by Muḥammad Dabīr Sīyāqī. Tehran: Zavvār, 1959.

Maybudī, Abulfażl Rashīdī. *Kashf al-asrār wa ʿiddat al-abrār*. Edited by Aṣghar Ḥikmat. Tehran: Amīr Kabīr, 1992.

Mīrafżālī, Siyyid ʿAlī. *Kahyyām's Quatrains in Old Sources* (*Rubāʿīyāt-i Khayyām dar Manābiʿ-i Kuhan*). Tehran: Markaz-i nashr-i dānishgāhi, 2003.

Muʿizzī, Amīr. *The Complete Dīvān*. Edited by Nāṣir Hayyirī. Tehran: Marzbān, 1984.

Najm Rāzī, ʿAbdullāh Ibn Muḥammad. *Marmūzāt-i Asadī*. Edited by Muḥammad Riżā Shafīʿī Kadkanī. Tehran: McGill University Islamic Studies, 1973.

Nizām al-Mulk. *The Book of Government, or, Rules for Kings: The Siyasat-Nama or Siyar Al-Muluk*. Translated by H Darke. London: Routledge & Kegan, 1960.

Poonawala, Ismail. In *Encyclopaedia of Islam, Second Edition*, s.v. Taʾwīl.

Qazvīnī, ʿAbdul Jalīl. *Baʿż mathālib al-nawāṣib fī naqi 'baʿż fażāʾiḥ al-rawāfiż'*. Edited by Jalāl al-Dīn Muḥaddith. Qum: Dār al-ḥadīth, 2012.

Samʿānī, Aḥmad Ibn Manṣūr. *Rūḥ al-arwāḥ fī sharḥ asmāʾ al-malik al-fattāḥ*. Edited by Najīb Mayil Hiravī. Tehran: Shirkat-i intishārāt-i ʿilmī farhangī, 1989.

Samʿānī, Aḥmad Ibn Manṣūr. *The Repose of the Spirits: A Sufi Commentary on the Divine Names*. Translated by William C Chittick. New York: Suny Press, 2019.

Sanāʾī. Abu-'l-Majd Majdūd Ibn Ādam. *Dīvān*. Edited by Muḥammad Taqī Mudarris Rażavī. Tehran: Sanāʾī, 1984.

Sanāʾī. Abu-'l-Majd Majdūd Ibn Ādam. *Ḥadīqat al-ḥaqīqa va sharīʿat al-ṭarīqa*. Edited by Muḥammad Taqī Mudarris Rażavī. Tehran: Sipihr, date not available.

Sarakhsī, Abī Bakr Muḥammad Ibn Aḥmad Ibn Abī Sahl. *ʿUṣūl al-Sarakhsī*. Edited by Abulwafā Afghānī. 2 vols. Lāhūr: Dār al-Maʿārif al-Naʿmāniyya, 1981.

Schacht, Joseph. In *Encyclopaedia of Islam, Second Edition*, s.v. Ahl al-Ḥadīth.

Schacht, Joseph. In *Encyclopaedia of Islam, Second Edition*, s.v. Aṣḥāb al-Raʾy.

Schöck, Cornelia. "Belief and Unbelief in Classical Sunnī Theology". In *Encyclopaedia of Islam, THREE*. Edited by Kate Fleet, Gudrun Krämer, Denis Matringe, and Everett Rowson. Leiden: Brill, 2007–. Online Publication.

Seyed-Gohrab, Ali Asghar. *Of Piety and Heresy: Abū Ḥāmid Muḥammad Ghazzālī's Persian Treatises on Antinomians*. Berlin: de Gruyter, 2024.

Seyed-Gohrab, Ali Asghar. "The Flourishing of Persian Quatrains". In *A History of Persian Literature: Persian Lyric Poetry in the Classical Era 800–1500: Ghazals. Panegyrics and Quatrains*. Vol. 2. Edited by Ehsan Yarshater, London: I.B. Tauris, 2019: 488–568.

Seyed-Gohrab, Ali Asghar. (ed.) *The Great Umar Khayyām: A Global Reception of the Rubaiy*. Leiden: Leiden University Press: 2012.

Shirvānī, Jamāl Khalīl. *Nuzhat al-majālis*. Edited by Muḥammad Amīn Riyāḥī. Tehran: Mahārat, 1995.

Stroumsa, Sarah. *Freethinkers of Medieval Islam: Ibn al-Rawāndī, Abū Bakr al-Rāzī and Their Impact on Islamic Thought.* Islamic Philosophy, Theology, and Science, Vol. 35. Leiden: Brill, 1999.

ʿUnṣūrī Balkhī, Abulqāsim. *Dīvān*. Edited by Muḥammad Dabīr Sīyāqī. Tehran: Aḥmadi, 1985.

Wakin, Jeanette, and Zysow, Aron. In *Encyclopaedia of Islam, Second Edition,* s.v. Rāʾy.

Wensinck, Arent Jan.. In *Encyclopaedia of Islam, Second Edition,* s.v. Khabar.

Yavari, N., "Mirrors for Princes or a Hall of Mirrors: Niẓām al-Mulk's Siyar al-mulūk Reconsidered," *Al-Masāq: Islam and the Medieval Mediterranean*, 20, No. 1 (2008).

Omar Khayyām in German Reformulations: Translation between Politics, Scholarship and Belief

Amir Theilhaber
Universität Bielefeld

Abstract

The *Rubāʿiyyāt* attributed to Omar Khayyām were canonised in the German speaking world as *Die Sinnsprüche Omars des Zeltmachers* in a translation by the German diplomat and scholar of Oriental studies, Friedrich Rosen (1856–1935). These German engagements with Khayyām are an expression of transnational reformulations of bodies of knowledge under imperialism and nationalism. First exposed to the *Rubaiyat* at the court of the British viceroy in India in 1886, Rosen translated single quatrains along his later diplomatic stations in Tehran, Baghdad and Tangier, as a respite from his diplomatic chores. In Tehran, he was initiated into the Niʿmatullāhī order of Ṣafī ʿAlī Shah and Ẓahīr al-Dowla, and translated other bodies of Persian poetry. After presenting his translations and interpretations of the *Rubāʿiyyāt* at the International Orientalist Congress in Copenhagen in 1908, in the first edition of the *Sinnsprüche* in 1909 Rosen described the thought of Khayyām as characterised by free will and free thinking in opposition to religious orthodoxy. Despite Ignaz Goldziher challenging this dualism in Copenhagen, Rosen saw in Khayyām the Aryan-Indo-Germanic spirit that seeks cognisance, in a cultural war against the dogma of Semitic "Arabianness". Following a virulent antisemitic campaign that targeted Rosen when he became German foreign minister in 1921, a revised edition of the *Sinnsprüche* in 1929 lost the Aryan-Semitic dichotomy. At the time, Rosen collaborated with Taqī Arānī in Berlin on two Persian and one English Khayyām publications that emphasised the cultural-intellectual potential that Khayyām's intellectual heritage provided for the development of Iran.

Keywords: Omar Khayyām; *Rubāʿiyyāt*; reception history; Aryan myth; Friedrich Rosen.

Introduction

Lasting over five decades from the 1880s to the 1930s, the engagement of the scholar of Oriental studies, diplomat and German foreign minister, Friedrich

Rosen (1856–1935), with the *Rubāʿiyyāt* attributed to Omar Khayyām (1048–1131) occurred on three continents and spanned the era of European high imperialism and the rise of German and Iranian nationalism. Published first in 1909 as the *Sinnsprüche Omars des Zeltmachers*, Friedrich Rosen's selected translation of 93 of Khayyām's *Rubāʿiyyāt* ("quatrains") went through five editions by 1922, and a revised edition from 1928 with 152 quatrains remains in print today. Rosen's *Sinnsprüche* (aphorisms) became the canonical German translation of Khayyam's *Rubāʿiyyāt*. The paratexts of the Rosen translations of the Khayyām *Rubāʿiyyāt*, as well as the contexts in which the translations were made and published, portray a rich array of reformulations under the impression of thought categories from the realms of politics, scholarship and religion between Denmark, Germany, India, Iran, and Morocco. Rosen's translation of the Khayyām *Rubāʿiyyāt* came on the back of a longer German tradition of translating Persian poetry, as practiced by Johann Wolfgang von Goethe and Friedrich Rückert to name but a few German Persophilic savants.[1] But unlike many of these translations of poetry from languages conceived of as Oriental whose translators usually never visited "the Orient" or spoke Persian or other non-European vernacular languages, Rosen's translations were marked by an immediacy of experience in situ, language fluency and contemporary cultural literacy that influenced the translation process and the *Rubāʿiyyāt* and the Omar Khayyām Rosen crafted for his audiences. The different publications on Khayyām and the *Rubāʿiyyāt* that emerged out of Rosen's engagements were, however, far from stagnant. Sparked by a first encounter in British Indian circles, the bulk of Rosen's sources and interpretative frameworks came from literary circles in Iran and the work of European Orientalist acquaintances before the outbreak of the Great War. As the Hohenzollern and Qajar dynasties were abrogated and the two countries embarked on a tortured path into a post-imperial world, Rosen's labours on Khayyām and the *Rubāʿiyyāt* went through new reformulations in line with an emerging world of entangled nations.

Socialisation of a translator

In reference to the altercations surrounding the Dutch translation of Amanda Gorman's poem *The Hill We Climb*, the philosopher Souleymane Bachir Diagne noted that "translation does not take place against a background of identity. Translation takes place precisely between different languages and therefore different worldviews, and establishes a bridge between these different languages and worldviews." Following Diagne, it is not the individual experience of the translator that matters, but the "poetic experience".[2] If *The Author Is Dead*, to borrow from Roland Barthes, Friedrich Rosen's translation of the Khayyām *Rubāʿiyyāt* as *Die*

Sinnsprüche des Zeltmachers, a poetic work in its own right, and Rosen's other engagements with Khayyām and the *Rubāʿiyyāt* might be understood simply as literary texts. But in order to grasp the translation of Khayyām's *Rubāʿiyyāt* to German not just as translated text, but as reformulations of text and paratext and as such as a phenomenon in entangled global history, its author – the translator – and his horizons re-emerge. Not as a biography of the all powerful author, but showing the significance of individual experience, cognitive and emotional framing, personal relations, and acquired skill of the translator for what s/he seeks to bridge between Diagne's "different languages and worldviews".

So who was the translator of the *Rubāʿiyyāt*? Friedrich Rosen was born in Leipzig in 1856 as the son of Georg Rosen and Serena Rosen nee Moscheles. Serena was a pianist and the daughter of Ignaz Moscheles, a piano virtuoso from Prague, who had been baptised in the Anglican Church in London in the early 1830s. Georg was the son of Friedrich Ballhorn-Rosen, the chancellor of the principality of Lippe and a scholar of Oriental languages. Georg's older brother, Friedrich August Rosen (1805–1837), had been before his early death a well-known scholar of Sanskrit and Arabic at the University of London. Following the interests of his older brother, Georg became a scholar of Oriental languages. After an expedition to the Caucasus in 1843–4, Georg became dragoman (an interpreter with administrative tasks) at the Prussian embassy in Constantinople, before being appointed Prussian consul in Jerusalem in 1853.[3] Next to his consular tasks – at the time Jerusalem was not considered a politically important position – Georg Rosen continued with a series of scholarly activities, publishing dozens of works of history, archaeology, language and geography during the fourteen years he spent there. Shortly after Serena gave birth to Friedrich in Leipzig, she and her son travelled to Jerusalem to join Georg. Friedrich grew up trilingual German-English-Arabic. The Prussian consulate on Aqbat at-Takkiyah within the city walls lay in close proximity to the notable Khalidi family, that held high positions in the Ottoman administration. The Rosens entertained close family relations with the Khalidis. Friedrich, who went by the name of Suleiman (an accurate Arabic translation of the German word Friedrich) when interacting in Arabic, felt at home in Jerusalem. When he "returned" to Germany at the age of eleven, he felt out of place – a feeling that persisted throughout his youth, as can be gleaned from his narrative curriculum vitae that he submitted for his high school graduation in 1876.[4]

It was also in Detmold that Friedrich first started studying Persian. His father Georg had learned the language in Tbilisi with the bilingual poet and Sufi sceptical of orthodoxy Mirza Shafy Wazeh. A fellow student of Georg was Friedrich Bodenstedt, who later on published in German the poems *Die Lieder des Mirza-Schaffy*, which were in fact not poems or songs by Mirza Shafy Wazeh, as Russian Orientalists pointed out, but inventions by Bodenstedt. Georg Rosen on the other hand made more progress in Persian and Azeri-Turkish, as Bodenstedt noted in letters at the time. The Persian and Turkish skills he had acquired came in handy for social interactions in Ottoman Constantinople, for publishing a Persian language grammar in Latin and German, and for translating excerpts from Jalāl al-Dīn Rūmī's *Mathnawī* to German.[5] Although not a native speaker of the language, Friedrich's teacher in mid-century rural Germany could hardly have been more qualified.

Persian India: first encounters at the British viceregal court

Friedrich Rosen's passion for "the Orient" prevailed, leading him to study philology and Indian languages in Leipzig, Göttingen, Munich and Paris. After teaching at girls' schools and becoming the house teacher of a Prussian prince, during a visit to his mother's relatives in London in 1886, Rosen was offered to become the private tutor of the son of the British viceroy of India, Lord Dufferin (1826–1902). As letters between Rosen and the Dufferins show, Rosen's motivation was from the outset to use the opportunity to intensify his studies of the Persian language.[6] While attached to the Dufferins' viceregal court in 1886 and 1887, Rosen encountered a number of elevated Indian personalities for whom Persian was the language of culture, like the Maharajah of Benares, Ishwari Prasad Narayan Singh (1822–1889), who wrote his own diwan of Persian poetry. Music performances were put to Persian songs by Saʿdī and Ḥāfiẓ, and also in Hindustani literature Persian words, phrases, imagery and poetical styles played a significant role. Rosen was particularly interested in the blending of cultures, that he saw manifest in the theatrical production of Agha Hassan Amanat (1815–1858) *Indar Sabha*. First staged at the court of Wajid ʿAli Shah (1822–1887) – last king of Awadh and poet himself – in Lucknow in 1853, the *Indar Sabha* was paradigmatic for the composite culture of northern India. Rosen translated the piece to German and provided a literary and cultural analysis, which was accepted as his PhD thesis at Leipzig University in 1890.[7]

But it was also in India that Rosen became first acquainted with the poetry attributed to Omar Khayyām. Rosen and Dufferin shared an enthusiasm for Persian poetry, and the viceroy continued to update Rosen for many years about his progress in learning the Persian language. Dufferin had taken an interest in languages also in previous posts, but mastering a level of Persian was also important for the British administration of India. The British Indian administration relied on Indian regional rulers for support and local administration, and their language of culture was Persian, particularly in Northern India. Also in the British administration Persian played a large role, and entry exams for Indian applicants for the British service included a Persian test. Dufferin had struggled in the early years to learn the Arabic alphabet, and benefited from Rosen's more advanced skills. The two students of Persian would invite Indian singers to the viceregal lodge in Shimla to hear their recitals of Persian poetry, and it was also at Shimla that Dufferin published in 1887 a transliteration of *Rubaiyat of Omar Khayyām*.[8] At the time, this did not result in any noticeable deeper engagement of Rosen with Khayyām or the *Rubā'iyyāt*. Returning to Germany from India via Iran in the summer of 1887, on account of his good standing with the British, Rosen met Żill al-Sulṭān in Isfahan and Nāṣir al-Dīn Shah in Tehran for private audiences. These meetings as well as many other encounters and experiences, Rosen used upon his return to publish a Persian language guide for German travellers and merchants with the title of *Shuma Farsi härf mizänid? (Sprechen Sie Persisch?)*. Next to an introduction to Persian alphabet, pronunciation, grammar, and vocabulary, Rosen picked out several short texts for students to practice the language. Among these texts were newspaper articles, invented dialogues, and short stories, and translated excerpts from Nāṣir al-Dīn Shah's diary of his journey to Europe in 1873.[9] Omar Khayyām and poetry were notably absent.

Life and poetry of a German diplomat in Iran

After spending three years as a teacher for Hindustani and Persian at Berlin's newly established Seminar für Orientalische Sprachen, where Rosen became friends with the eminent scholar of Iranian studies of Armenian-Malay-German background, Friedrich Carl Andreas (1846–1930), Rosen joined the German foreign service. Grouped in the lowest rank, as dragoman (interpreter with administrative duties), Rosen was first posted to Beirut in 1890. Following an encounter with an Ottoman official in Beirut in which discussions quickly moved to Persian poetry, Rosen received from the Ottoman official a manuscript with excerpts from the *Maqūlāt-o andarzhā* by the Sufi polemicist and Hanbali commentator of the Quran, 'Abdullāh Anṣārī from Herat (1006–1089). The small collection became the first body of poetry Rosen translated from Persian to German.[10] Due to his Persian skills Rosen was posted in the same position as dragoman to Tehran in early 1891. In a time before Germany had developed stronger economic and geo-strategic interests in the region, the German legation in Tehran had a staff of three: envoy, dragoman and munshi (a local assistant). Rosen's significance rose quickly, as the envoy did not master the language and was largely ignorant of Iranian culture. When the envoy was recalled and posted to China, a replacement envoy was not sent for a year, leaving Rosen as charge d'affaires well into 1893. The Iran that Friedrich Rosen lived in during the 1890s was a country in crisis mode. Under pressure from Russia along its northern borders in the Caucasus for decades and under growing influence from the British in the south, the government of the long-ruling Nāṣir al-Dīn Shah struggled to combine modernising the country with the involvement and introduction of Western methods, while maintaining control over its territory and its political affairs. While at the German legation in the 1890s Rosen wrote several reports to the German foreign ministry detailing the various pressures the Iranian government dealt with: upheavals in various provinces, economic shortcomings and a taxing system prone to abuse, difficulties in reforming the military, resistance by the religious orthodoxy against social and educational reforms, and not least the political unrest surrounding the Tobacco concessions to the British in 1892. Although Germany had established diplomatic relations with Iran in 1873, German interests in Iran remained minimal until the late 1890s. While Russia and Britain held various assets in the country and maintained large embassies in Tehran, Germany was a minor player in the country. As such Germany appeared less menacing to Iranian decision-makers, with German officials often asked to increase their economic and military involvement in the country as a counter-weight to Russia and Britain. At the same time, German activities in Iran were often coordinated with the British for which Friedrich Rosen was particularly well suited.[11]

Friedrich Rosen was accompanied in Iran by his British-born wife Nina. With Friedrich's study book *Shuma Farsi härf mizänid?* Nina picked up Persian basics and became proficient through her social interaction in Tehran. A trained pianist, she listened attentively to local tunes and melodies, and struck up relationships and friendships with women in Tehran's society. Among them, many women attached to the Shah's Anduran, including several of the Shah's wives. As a series of letters in Persian addressed to her show, these relationships were conducted in Persian, and often times Nina had more access to Persian society than her husband, because as a European woman she was not confined to the Persian women's quarters but also interacted with male ministers.[12] Friedrich entertained a close working relationship with the Shah's prime minister, Mīrzā ʿAlī Aṣghar Khan Amīn al-Sultan (1858–1907), and a number of other political figures. Celebrating Kaiser Wilhelm II's birthday in 1893, a who's who of Iranian government officials attended. His relationship with Muḥammad Ḥuseyn Mīrzā Badīʿ al-Mulk ʿImād al-Dowla, also a politician, was different in the sense that the basis of their interactions was less political than a joint interest in questions of philosophy. ʿImād al-Dowla, himself a student of philosophy in the vein of Mullā Ṣadrā Shīrāzī (1572–1635) with a significant library of Iranian philosophical treaties, wrote in a letter to Rosen that he considered the German diplomat to be a "highly esteemed philosopher" who was in Tehran "the centre, emanating rays of light into the surrounding circle."[13] Another, even more profound relationship bound Friedrich to the son-in-law of the Shah and ceremonial master of the court, ʿAlī Kan Qajar Ẓahīr al-Dowla (1864–1924). Exchanging frequent letters and visiting each other in their studies, Rosen and

Ẓahīr al-Dowla became friends, helping each other politically, but also with more mundane services. They travelled together, went hunting, and enjoyed parlaying and studying poetical and philosophical texts together.[14] Through the introduction of Ẓahīr al-Dowla, Rosen was also introduced in the Niʿmatullāhī order of the "illustrious and anti-conformist" last major Iranian Sufi, Ṣafī ʿAlī Shah (1835–1898). Born as Mīrzā Ḥasan Iṣfahānī, Ṣafī ʿAlī Shah was a reform-minded Sufi scholar, who had spent several decades in India, before attaching himself to the Shah's court and gaining a significant following among the court's princes. How far along Rosen progressed on his path to *ʿirfān* ("Gnosis") is not clear, but a later publication shows his firm understanding of the functioning of the order, its *silsila* ("chain of descent"), and the order's practices. After the passing of Ṣafī ʿAlī Shah, Ẓahīr al-Dowla took over the leadership and transformed the order into a more formal organisation for education and socialisation, the Anjuman-i Ukhuvvat. From among its ranks many members became important figures in Iran's Constitutional Revolution, not least Ẓahīr al-Dowla himself, who was responsible as governor of Hamadan for convening the first Iranian regional parliament in 1906 – a month before the national assembly.[15]

The library of Ẓahīr al-Dowla, in which Rosen spent many hours, held vast tomes covering different topics. Among them also various poetic oeuvres. Rosen wrote in his memoirs: "The most precious of his books was a copy of the Gulistan ... purported to have been written in the lifetime of that great poet by the famous calligrapher Yāqut Mustaʿṣimī for the use of the Caliph Mustaʿṣimī", the last ʻAbbasid caliph. Travelling across Iran, Rosen would frequently encounter people of all social strata quoting verses or entire bodies of poetry, as he noted time and again. Persian poetry also played an elevated role in the Sufi order Rosen and Ẓahīr al-Dowla frequented. Their spiritual leader Ṣafī ʿAlī Shah had – under the influence of Jalāl al-Dīn Rūmī and Muḥyi al-Dīn Ibn ʿArabī – authored several collections of mystical prose. His masterpiece was a versified exegesis of the Quran in over 32,000 rhyming couplets, the *ʿIrfān al-Ḥaqq* ("The Gnosis of Reality/Truth"). Written in Persian, it was intended to make understanding the Quran easier for a broader Persophone population, provoking orthodox opposition that called for Ṣafī ʿAlī Shah's expulsion from Iran. Poetry was political and played an important role in society and culture. Sitting for exams to join the consular corps (a level up from the dragoman service) in 1897, Rosen wrote a 200 page long essay on Iranian society, economy and politics, ending on the note that amid Germany's prevailing political weakness in the country, it would be advisable for German merchants and others living in Iran to learn Persian and in particular become acquainted with Persian, as this would be the best protection against adverse situations in the country. Not surprising then that Rosen began to compile his own collection of Persian poems while in Iran. In one of several poetry books that survive in the Rosen collection,

Tarjemah Ash'ar Farsi binyan Almani az Suleiman Rosen, he had compiled Persian poems on the left and German versified translations on the right by Saʿdī, Rūmī, Nāṣir Khusrow, Khwāja Shams al-Dīn Muḥammad Ḥāfiẓ, ʿAbdullāh Anṣārī, and also his first *Rubāʿiyyāt* by Omar Khayyām.[16]

Rubāʿiyyāt translations and Khayyām studies at the turn of the century

E. Denison Ross first acquaintance with rising field of Khayyām studies was through Gertrude Bell, a family friend of Nina, who had stayed with the Rosens in Tehran. Ross helped Rosen have his *Shuma Farsi härf mizänid?* appear in a revamped English edition in 1898. At the time Denison Ross was working on Khayyām and questions of wandering quatrains (*Rubāʿiyyāt* that appear in poetic collections attributed to Khayyām but also in collections attributed to other poets) that the Russian Orientalist Valentin Zhukovskii had problematised.[17] This Western reception of the Khayyām *Rubāʿiyyāt* in the aftermath of Edward FitzGerald and his genre-setting translations was an important factor in how Rosen conceived of the *Rubāʿiyyāt* and his own translations. The *Rubāʿiyyāt* had become an important literary and cultural phenomenon in Europe and North America, and was hotly discussed in Orientalist academia as well. But the Khayyām craze had vastly passed by the German speaking lands. Persophilic infatuation had focused on Johann Wolfgang Goethe's "twin in spirit" Ḥāfiẓ and the ghazel rhyme form popularised by Joseph von Hammer-Purgstall and Friedrich Rückert. Until Rosen's translation, renderings by Friedrich Bodenstedt and others were either re-translations via French or English, and/or did not reproduce the typical rhyme structure of the *Rubāʿiyyāt* (aaba) but were prose translations.[18] Rosen saw an opportunity to fill this gap with his own reading of the *Rubāʿiyyāt*. Friends of Rosen in Germany, to whom he had shown translations of his Persian poems, encouraged him to publish the poems.

The sources of the quatrains that Rosen chose for translation cannot be clearly reconstituted. Some may have derived from Sheikh Hassan, a teacher of the Persian language to Friedrich Rosen, Gertrude Bell, Friedrich Carl Andreas and others in Tehran. Bell recounted in her memories that he had his students read Persian poetry including Khayyām's *Rubāʿiyyāt* in his language lessons. Perhaps some poems stemmed from the story teller in Shimla in 1886, or derived from the same collection that Lord Dufferin drew on for his transliteration. After all, the *Rubāʿiyyāt* enjoyed popularity at the Mughal courts and across northern Indian literate society well into the nineteenth century.[19] Several *Rubāʿiyyāt* in German translation were included in letters Rosen wrote to his family from a one-year posting as German consul in Baghdad in 1898. Further quatrains clearly derive from the bilingual Persian-English edition of E.H. Whinfield *The Quatrains of Omar Khayyām* from 1883, as a copy of the book in the Rosen collection shows Persian quatrains earmarked for translation to German, with Rosen writing in the margin in Persian "no tarjemeh" ("new translation").[20] The visible sources show on the one hand the importance of the arteries of the British Empire in which Rosen moved. FitzGerald's translation had made the *Rubāʿiyyāt* and Omar Khayyām a literary sensation and even a brand.[21] Rosen's engagement with the *Rubāʿiyyāt* was framed by this global attention to the poetry of the mediaeval Iranian philosopher. On the other hand, Rosen perceived that beyond the Western craze, Khayyām and the *Rubāʿiyyāt* held their own significance in a Persophone world, in which the role of poetry was an integral part of culture, society, scholarship, religion and politics. Rosen thought that an accurate direct translation of the *Rubāʿiyyāt* from Persian to German and an introduction of the philosopher Omar Khayyām was a good opportunity to transmit part of the Persian culture, that he had experienced for many years, to a German audience.

Rosen's thematic selection of *Rubāʿiyyāt* for his 1909 *Die Sinnsprüche Omars des Zeltmachers* ("epigrams of Omar the tentmaker") was in keeping with the collections of FitzGerald, Jean-Baptiste Nicolas, Ambrose Potter, Whinfield and others: the transience of life, the question of theodicy (how evil can exist in a world created by god, who is good), and a sense of carpe diem and (metaphysical) wine drinking.[22] Present also in other collections but more pronounced in Rosen's *Sinnsprüche* is the rejection of orthodoxy and often religion outright. Rosen included a number of quatrains that poke fun at god, religious beliefs and figures of organised religion. Most of these quatrains are interdenominational in their derision of religion. Islam, Christianity, Judaism and Zoroastrianism are all rejected as nonsensical and repressive. Emblematic is the ruba'i that Rosen renders as follows in German:

> Kaaba und Götzenhaus bedeuten Knechtung
> Der Christen Glocken, hört sie läuten Knechtung
> Kirche und heil'ge Schnur und Rosenkranz und Kreuz
> Wahrlich, sie alle nur bedeuten Knechtung.[23]

> Ka'ba and idol house mean subjugation,
> The bells of the Christians, hear, they ring subjugation.
> Church and holy cord and rosary and cross
> Truly, they all mean subjugation.

"Heretical" notions are not absent from the overall corpus of the over one thousand *Rubāʿiyyāt* attributed to Khayyām. But as Michelle Kaiserlian has pointed out that the *Rubāʿiyyāt* can be "infinitely transformed to suit ones desires", Rosen's anti-clericalism constitutes a leitmotif for his *Sinnsprüche*.[24] In Tehran, Rosen had been appalled by the passivity which he found in a large part of the city in response to an outbreak of cholera in 1892, which killed over 10,000 people. He blamed religious leaders for the fatalism spread among the population. But this rejection of religious figures and mores was not confined to Islam. In an autobiographical account of his childhood in Jerusalem, he decried the Protestant priest from Germany his father had hired as a house teacher as an ignorant and condescending philistine, and expressed his bewilderment over the fanaticism of the Christian churches fighting over the Holy Sepulchre.[25] Similar to many German scholars of Oriental languages from often liberal bourgeois milieus, who perceived themselves in the tradition of the enlightenment, for Rosen the church and organised religion had lost its monopoly over meaning and belief. For Rosen this was not exclusively a European phenomenon. Having grown up in Jerusalem and encountered many learned personalities in India, Iran, Syria and elsewhere considered Oriental at the time, Rosen thought that a scientific spirit might be more developed in Europe, but that the basis for free inquiry and criticism was also present in the cultures of the Islamicate world. If only free will was not thwarted by religious clergy. As such, Rosen's thought was similar to Iranian modernist nationalists, such as Mīrzā Fatḥ-ʿAlī Ākhu2ndzāda (1812–1878), Mīrzā Āqā Khan Kirmānī (1854–1896) and Mīrzā Malkum Khan (1834–1908). Also Rosen's interlocutors in Tehran in the 1890s at the court and in the Niʿmatullāhī order struggled with how to combine Persian culture and Islamic mores with modernity and the pressures of global integration of economies emanating from European imperialism.

Next to these "Oriental" thought collectives that Rosen had engaged with, the second important forum of interaction, that shaped his knowledge production of Persian culture for a German speaking audience, was the world of European Orientalist scholarship. Familiar with Ross's and Zhukovskii's scholarly work on Khayyām, Rosen presented a selection of his German translations of the *Rubāʿiyyāt* at the International Orientalist Congress in Copenhagen in 1908. At the time, Rosen was German envoy in Morocco, where he sought to prop up Moroccan sovereignty amid overwhelming French dominance. An impossible task, as he wrote to his superiors in Berlin time and again. As a respite from his political travails, he worked on his translations of the *Rubāʿiyyāt*. Rosen was the political representative of the German Reich at Copenhagen's gathering of the most reputable Orientalist scholars of the day. Under the eyes of the Danish royal family, Rosen led a large delegation of German scholars into the halls of Copenhagen's university, and in a speech during the opening ceremony praised the Danish contributions to Orientalist scholarship throughout the ages.[26]

His own scholarly contribution to the field of Omar Khayyām studies Rosen made in the Islam section, presided over by the British scholar of Iranian studies Edward Granville Browne and the Hungarian scholar of Islam Ignaz Goldziher. In his presentation, Rosen presented several of his translations of the *Rubāʿiyyāt* together with a description of Omar Khayyām's life, his philosophical and mathematical treatise, and situating him in the political and intellectual currents of eleventh century Iran. Rosen posited a continuity of a supposed Persian spirit, reminiscent of the notion of the "Volksgeist" much discussed in liberal-national circles in Germany at the time, encapsulated in the philosopher Omar Khayyām and the *Rubāʿiyyāt* attributed to him throughout the ages. At the same time Khayyām, in Rosen's reading, was also relevant beyond the Persianate world:

> "In the great, the only and eternal culture clash, which man has always fought, the fight between the seekers and those, who believe to have found, he embodies the direction restlessly striving for knowledge (Erkenntnis). Omar Khayyām is the Aryan, who does not want to go under in the dogma and tradition of Arabianness so prevalent in his country at the time. 400 years of Islam's rule had not sufficed to eradicate the Indo-German spirit of Persianness."

For Rosen, the scholar Khayyām was one among Persian scholars, who:

> "despite the rigidity of Mohammedan orthodoxy... albeit in Arabic language and form – very gradually dared to reassert the teachings of Plato, Aristotle, Euclid.... It was **Aryan spirit in Semitic garb** [Rosen's emphasis]. In this they made use of movements which seem to have originated in part in Islam itself."[27]

Rosen's interest in Khayyām and in relaying Khayyām and the *Rubāʿiyyāt* was to convey a work of a free spirit against the odds. He also posited that this spirit derived from an Indo-German spirit, which was synonymous with the Aryan spirit. Like Rodinson has observed of other European scholars looking eastward at the time, they posited a commonality with the countries in which Indo-European languages were spoken, and blamed the monotheistic religions at large for dogmatism, fatalism and stagnation.[28] In Khayyām and the *Rubāʿiyyāt* Rosen found an example to show that in Oriental countries there was a potential for development from its own sources, that was based on a common spirit of free thinking and seeking knowledge. To illustrate his contemplations to the scholars present in the Islamic section at the Orientalist Congress, Rosen presented his translation of the aforementioned quatrain that saw in all religions only subjugation. The quatrain drew the interest of the presiding Ignaz Goldziher.[29] A member of the Jewish community in Budapest, Goldziher, like many Jewish Orientalists, had developed a stronger interest in Islam, also due to what Susannah Heschel described as the "uncanny recognition" many Jewish scholars experienced when they began to study Islam. Goldziher saw himself in Islam, and entertained close relations with a series of Islamic reformers, such as Jalal ed-Din al-Afghani. Like for Judaism, the question for Islam was how it could maintain its religious and cultural role, while modernising.[30] Thus, Goldziher was not only sceptical when it came to promulgations of supposed Aryan qualities in Khayyām, because that relegated the Islamic-Semitic to insignificance, which had in the aftermath of the German "Antisemitismusstreit" in the late 1870s clear ramifications for Jews. But Goldziher also questioned the anti-religious impetus that Rosen strengthened in his argument. Goldziher did not know Persian well, so it is doubtful that, when Goldziher requested to see the quatrain in question in the Persian original, he could grasp the consequential interpretation that Rosen had made in his rendering.

بتخانه وکعبه خانهٔ بندگیات
ناقوس زدن ترانهٔ بندگیات
زنّار و کلیسیا و تسبیح و صلیب
حقّا که همه نشانهٔ بندگیات

Kaaba und Götzenhaus bedeuten Knechtung,
Der Christen Glocken, hört, sie läuten Knechtung.
Kirche und heil'ge Schnur und Rosenkranz und Kreuz
Wahrlich, sie alle nur bedeuten Knechtung.

Rosen chose to render the Persian word *bandagiyyat* as Knechtung, from Knecht, a servant. Roughly this translates into subjugation in English. Other ways to translate *bandagiyyat* would be piety or devotion, which alters the meaning of the quatrain significantly. Rosen was well aware of the different meanings of the word in Persian. On the seating arrangements for the Kaiser's birthday celebrations with Iranian grandees in 1893, he had marked his own seating position with the Persian word *banda*, a polite way to describe oneself as a servant. He knew that Persian words had different meanings, and as he wrote in an introduction to poems by Ḥāfiẓ, he translated, precisely these double-meanings made Persian poetry so strong and important in social and political interactions.[31] Finding an accurate word in German that conveyed the different meanings is difficult. So Rosen had to make a choice, and he chose a translation that aligned with his opinions and with those of many other anti-clerically motivated Orientalists at the time.

But not with Goldziher. In the following years, Rosen and Goldziher corresponded frequently, and the admittance that some of these developments of free will and inquiry originated in Islam was a result of this correspondence with Goldziher, who struggled with many of his Orientalist colleagues, who he thought were giving Islam a bad name.[32] But it was not only Jewish Orientalists like Goldziher who rejected the Aryan-Semitic myth. Also Iranists like Rosen's friend Friedrich Carl Andreas had questioned the Aryan origins even of ancient Iran, and Browne, who had in earlier works popularised the idea that Sufi mysticism was essentially the Aryan dimension of Islam, distanced himself from his earlier writings in the late 1890s.[33] In 1903 the Orientalist Martin Hartmann of the Berlin's Seminar für Orientalische Sprachen in a 1903 review of the Danish Iranist Arthur Christensen's PhD thesis *Omar Khajjâms Rubâijât: En litteraerhistorisk undersøgels* praised:

> "And here we are dealing with a people, in which, despite the blood mixing, always lived a potency, that stands highly elevated above the neighbouring Semites, and of course even higher above the neighbours, the Turks, and whose influence on all of Asia cannot be judge highly enough ... The ruba'i is not a minor moment in the path that the Persian course of victory has taken, but rather one of its sharpest weapons."[34]

But Christensen had made do without the Aryan myth completely. Rather, as correspondences in the aftermath of the congress between Christensen and Rosen show, Rosen came to base some of his interpretations on the Christian, who conceived of a great rather timeless Persian spirit living in Khayyām, which was, however, no longer so much a transnational phenomenon as Friedrich Rosen had experienced between Beirut and India, but as something closer related to Iranian nationalism and at the same time part of world literature and thus cosmpolitanised.[35] By the time Rosen published his next book on Persian poetry, a new edition of his father's translation of Rūmī's *Mathnawī* with a lengthy introduction to Sufi Islam based on his experiences in the Niʿmatullāhī order of Ṣafī ʿAlī Shah in Tehran, the Aryan was no longer a factor. As Rosen wrote in a manuscript that was edited out of the final publication: "Especially by Goldziher it has strikingly been proven, that among the oldest appearance of Sufism in Islam certainly as many Arabs as Persians are found. We thus win the impression that Sufism is Islam itself and has not necessarily its roots in the Aryan ethnic affiliation."[36]

Transnational reformulations of Khayyām after the Great War

Friedrich Rosen's *Sinnsprüche Omars des Zeltmachers* quickly became the standard translation of Khayyām's *Rubāʿiyyāt* in German. It helped that Rosen's public profile began to rise with his rise in the German diplomatic corps, into the circles of Kaiser Wilhelm II, and with the attention the press paid to the ongoing altercations in Morocco, where Rosen was German envoy. An article a journalist of the conservative *Norddeutsche Allgemeine Zeitung* wrote about his visit to the holiday home of German chancellor Bernhard von Bülow in late 1908 ended with a laudatory discussion of Rosen's *Sinnsprüche* and quoting several of the quatrains. As an employee of the state, Rosen had needed to receive approval of his publication. Bülow approved and endorsed Rosen's book with free advertising before its publication.[37] Until 1922, the

Sinnsprüche went through five unaltered editions, with a luxury edition reproducing the style of an original Persian manuscript in Rosen's possession, and already in 1914 music was being set to Rosen's translations.[38] Rosen's translation of the *Rubāʿiyyāt* became canonical when it was picked up by the publishing house Insel-Verlag, renowned for high literature, in 1929. It remains in print in unaltered form. The 1929 edition, however, differed significantly from the 1909 edition. Rosen expanded the selection of quatrains from 93 to 152, which corresponded thematically to the ones he had selected before. The three essays about Omar Khayyām, his work and his times, that had served as a lengthy afterword in 1909 made way for a shorter introduction. Notably absent in this introduction were any references to Semitic or Aryan qualities. What remained was the celebration of the great Persian spirit in a nationalist vein, the assertion that the *Rubāʿiyyāt* of Khayyām belonged to world literature and a thicker description of the intellectual currents between Greek and European, Islamic, Zoroastrian and Indian influences that had shaped Iranian culture, the "chain mesh human spiritual/intellectual labour", as Rosen had written about Rūmī.[39]

What had happened? Part of the answer is that Rosen had already shortly after the publication of the *Sinnsprüche* in 1909 parted with the Aryan myth. He had accepted Goldziher's argument that there was little to substantiate a particular Aryan spirit as a driving force for Iranian greatness, which the philosopher-poet Khayyām supposedly symbolised. Something else accelerated Rosen's departure from the Aryan myth: the antisemitic campaigns against him, first by German colonialist circles before the war, and then by the monarchist and revisionist right-wing in the Weimar Republic, when Rosen became German foreign minister in 1921. Although Rosen was not Jewish and it had been nearly a century since his grandfather Ignaz Moscheles and his wife Charlotte Embden were baptised, in 1921 the revanchist "völkische" and mostly protestant press clamoured that Rosen was one of supposedly four Jewish ministers in the government of the left-wing Catholic Joseph Wirth and that Germany was now in the hands of the Jews, who were faulted for Germany's defeat in the war and the upheavals that had befallen Germany since. A vicious campaign ensued. The only actual Jew of the cabinet was Walther Rathenau. When he succeeded Rosen as foreign minister in 1922, he was assassinated by a right-wing terrorist organisation.[40]

Another factor that influenced Rosen's engagement with Khayyām and the *Rubāʿiyyāt* was the arrival of many Iranian intellectuals and students in Berlin during and after the war. The centre of Berlin's Iranian circles became the publishing house Kaviani in upscale Charlottenburg. Set up during the war with support from the foreign ministry as part of the propaganda war effort, Kaviani continued publishing several newspapers after the war and a wide array of Persian and Arabic books ranging from textbooks for chemistry, dictionaries, theatre plays, the Quran, instructions for constructing telegraphic lines, children's books, academic publications on economics and poetry. Kaviani supplied its books to bookshops in

London, Istanbul, several cities in Iran and in India.[41] One of the young students moonlighting at the Kaviani publishing house during his studies in physics and chemistry at Berlin's university was Taqī Arānī. The young man of Azeri origin, who would later become famous as a figurehead of Iran's socialist Tudeh Party, was under the influence of his experiences in tumultuous Weimar Berlin and his engagements with the German Communist party, abandoning his prior chauvinist Iranian nationalism.[42] Rosen was one of a few German Iranists who frequented the Iranian Kaviani circles, and Rosen's house in Willmersdorf became a spot for Iranian students to visit and spend time with the elderly Persian-speaking couple that enjoyed their company.[43] Already before the war, Rosen had written in his introduction to the translation of Rūmī's *Mathnawī* that the Islamic world was well capable to develop on its own, if it tapped into the potential of philosophical inquiry and free will rooted in Sufism. In Rosen's view European involvement was not conducive to development and was often even counterproductive. Needed was "organic development".[44] Arānī would in many ways have been the proof of his argument. A young man, interested in the natural sciences, and like him interested in Omar Khayyām. Only, Arānī's interest in Khayyām derived less from the poetry attributed to the philosopher, but in his mathematical and scientific works. Rosen assisted Arānī in gaining access to an Omar Khayyām *Commentary of Euclid's Elementa* held at Leiden University, on which Arānī based his 1936 Tehran publication *Discussion of Difficulties of Euclid by Omar Khayyām*. Published a year after Rosen passed away in 1935, Arānī commemorated in the introduction his "old friend" and thanked him for supplying him with manuscripts from Leiden and his own collection.[45] With Arānī Rosen had also worked on a Persian language edition of *Rubāʿiyyāt* attributed to Khayyām, based on a manuscript that surfaced in Berlin in the early 1920s. It was speculated to be a particularly old manuscript of Khayyām quatrains, but was in due course discarded as bringing new light to the question, if there were any *Rubāʿiyyāt* that were likely to have been written by Khayyām himself.[46]

In Rosen's engagements with Iran and Persian literature the Aryan myth had disappeared – to the extent that in a series of articles in Persian and German in 1933 and 1934 on the occasion of the 1000 year Firdowsī celebrations and after the rise to power by the National-Socialists, he attacked the Aryan myth as fanciful altogether.[47] But the wide reception of his initial publication of the *Sinnsprüche* in 1909 caused the initial Aryanisation to stick. The renowned Iranian fiction author Sadeq Hedayat, who spent the 1920s mostly in Paris but also visited Berlin on several occasions, characterised Khayyām in his 1934 *Tarānahā-yi Khayyām* ("Songs of Khayyām") as an "Aryan spirit" with "Semitic thought" amid a number of demeaning comments about Islam.[48] In Germany, a young scholar of Iranian studies at Tübingen University, Christian Rempis, perceived Khayyām in 1934 to be constitutive of the "Aryan-Indo-Germanic spirit". A spirit, Rempis wrote, "that does not stop in the face of the last conclusions and suns itself in the possibilities of its strength. Even though Rempis sought to present himself and his Khayyām studies to Sol Gittleman as oppositional to National-Socialism in the aftermath of the war, his publication record from the period and his involvement with convinced national-socialist Orientalists, such as Hans-Heinrich Schaeder and Jakob Wilhelm Hauer, show that Khayyām and those studying the *Rubāʿiyyāt* could also be made pliable to fascism.[49]

Conclusion

The case of Friedrich Rosen's engagement with Persian poetry and his translation of the *Rubāʿiyyāt* attributed to Omar Khayyām to German as *Sinnsprüche Omars des Zeltmachers* shows the reformulations that were taking place in the process of interpretation and translating poetic texts from one language to another. These reformulations did not appear in an empty space, but were carried out by a translator who was socialised in a particular way and who combined due to his upbringing in a multilingual household between Jerusalem and Germany, and along the way of his diplomatic career that traversed the realms of politics, scholarship and culture an interplay of thought categories that shine through his selection of Persian *Rubāʿiyyāt*, his interpretation of their meaning and their translation to German. In the process, the author placed Khayyām and the *Rubāʿiyyāt* in new thought categories. But the *Rubāʿiyyāt* did not stay in these categories. While Hedāyat and Rempis continued along the way of promulgating an Aryan-Semitic divide with different but in both cases decidedly chauvinistic motivations, Rosen himself left the Aryan myth behind, helped the young Iranian scholar Arānī reconnect to an important source of (Iranian) science, and shaped a new German *Rubāʿiyyāt* that is thoroughly Persophilic in a traditional German way and that holds a humanist vision in a confusing and often cruel world.

Notes

1 Andrea Polaschegg, *Der andere Orientalismus. Regeln deutsch-morgenländischer Imagination im 19. Jahrhundert* (Berlin: De Gruyter, 2005); Hamid Dabashi, *Persophilia. Persian Culture on the Global Scene* (Cambridge: Harvard University Press, 2015).

2 David Tabourier and Laura Raum, *Peut-on Tout Traduire? Les Idées Larges avec Souleymane Bachir Diagne.*, Laura Raim and Souleymane Bachir Diagne, Arte (UPIAN:COM, 2023).

3 Amir Theilhaber, *Friedrich Rosen. Orientalist Scholarship and International Politics* (Berlin: De Gruyter, 2020), 42–48; Agnes Stache-Weiske and Frank Meier-Barthel, *Georg Rosen. Notizen von einer Reise durch Serbien, Anatolien und Transkaukasien in den Jahren 1843 und 1844* (Berlin: eb-Verlag, 2020); Rosane Rocher and Agnes Stache-Weiske, *For the Sake of the Vedas: The Anglo-German Life of Friedrich Rosen, 1805–1837* (Wiesbaden: Harrassowitz, 2020).

4 Theilhaber, *Friedrich Rosen*, 39–69.

5 Theilhaber, *Friedrich Rosen*, 73; Stache-Weiske and Meier-Barthel, *Georg Rosen. Notizen von einer Reise durch Serbien, Anatolien und Transkaukasien in den Jahren 1843 und 1844*, 68–73; Friedrich Bodenstedt, *Die Lieder des Mirza-Schaffy* (Berlin: Deckerschen Geheimen Ober-Hofbuchdruckerei, 1851); Arthur F.J. Remy, "The Influence of India and Persia on the Poetry of Germany" Doctoral Dissertation (Columbia University, 1901), 64–71; Georg Rosen, *Elementa Persica. "Hekayat Farsi" id est narrationes Persicae. Ex libro manuscripto edidit, gloassario explanavit, grammaticae brevem adumbrationem praemisit* (Berlin: Veith, 1843); Georg Rosen, *Mesnevi oder Doppelverse des Scheich Mewlānā Dschelāl ed dīn Rūmi* (Leipzig: Fr. Chr. Wilh. Vogel, 1849).

6 Friedrich Rosen to Frederick Hamilton-Temple-Blackwood, 6 September 1887, 19, Vol 108 Neg 4332, British Library – India Office Records (BL IOR). On the joint learning and teaching of Persian of Rosen and the Dufferins see also the correspondence between Friedrich Rosen, Lord Dufferin, and his son Terence between 1887 and 1900, D72 Rosen-Klingemann Nr. Zugang 77/2022, Karton 8, Landesarchiv NRW – Abteilung OWL, Detmold.

7 Nina Rosen, *Acht orientalische Weisen aus dem Munde des Volkes in Teheran und Fez aufgezeichnet und bearbeitet* (Hannover: Orient-Buchhandlung, 1926); Friedrich Rosen, "Briefe aus Indien. Benares," *Frankfurter Zeitung* 311 (7 November 1886); Friedrich Rosen, *Die Indarsabhā des Amānat. Ein Beitrag zur Kenntnis der Hindustani-Litteratur. Inaugural-Dissertation der Hohen Philosophischen Fakultät der Universität Leipzig zur Erlangung der Doktorwürde.* (Leipzig: F.A. Brockhaus, 1891); Rosie Llewellyn-Jones, *The Last King in India. Wajid 'Ali Shah, 1822–1887* (London: Hurst & Company, 2014); M. Aslam Qureshi, *Wajid Ali Shah's Theatrical Genius* (Lahore: Vanguard Books, 1987).

8 Frederick Hamilton-Temple-Blackwood to Arthur Nicolson, 14 June 1886, F130-23, BL EM – Dufferin Collection; Frederick Hamilton-Temple-Blackwood to Arthur Nicolson, 16 September 1886, F130-23, BL EM – Dufferin Collection; Arthur Nicolson to Frederick Dufferin, 10 June 1886, F130-26, BL EM – Dufferin Collection; Health and Lands. Government of India Department of Education, Notification, 7 November 1927, R/15/2/1458, BL IOR; Friedrich Rosen, *Modern Persian Colloquial Grammar: Containing a Short Grammar, Dialogues and Extracts from Nasir-Eddin Shah's Diaries, Tales, Etc. and a Vocabulary.* (London: Luzac & Co, 1898), V; Frederick Hamilton-Temple-Blackwood, *Rubáiyát of Omar Khayyam* (Shimla: Self-Published, 1887).

9 Arthur Nicolson to Frederick Dufferin, 3 March 1887, F130-27, BL EM – Dufferin Collection; Gustav Schenck zu Schweinsberg, Empfehlungsschreiben. Friedrich Rosen, 24 May 1887, I 10076, Personalakten 012577, Politisches Archiv – Auswärtiges Amt (PA AA); Friedrich Rosen, *Shumā Farsī härf mīzänīd (Sprechen Sie Persisch?): neupersischer Sprachführer, für die Reise und zum Selbstunterricht enthaltend eine kurze Grammatik, Wörtersammlung, Gespräche und Lesestücke* (Leipzig: Koch, 1890).

10 Suleiman Rosen, "Tarjemah Ash'ar Farsi Binyan Almani [in Persian]," 1890s, Agnes Stache Weiske Personal Collection, Grafing (ASWPC); Friedrich Rosen, *Oriental Memories of a German Diplomatist* (New York: Dutton, 1930), 103.

11 Friedrich Rosen, *Oriental Memories*, 122–63; Friedrich Rosen, "Bericht", 4 October 1892, 8948, R 18984, PA AA; Friedrich Rosen, "Bericht", 2 December 1892, A 31, R 18977, PA AA; Nikolaus von Wallwitz, "Bericht", 10 November 1893, A 35, R 18977, PA AA; Friedrich Rosen, "Bericht", 20 March 1893, A 11, R 18977, PA AA; Günther von Gaertner-Griebnow, "Bericht", 19 October 1896, 11998, R 18978, PA AA; Rudolf Nadolny, "Bericht", 11 May 1896, A 5063, R 19072, PA AA; Bradford G. Martin, *German-Persian Diplomatic Relations. 1873–1912* ('S-Gravenhage: Mouton & Co, 1959); Jennifer Jenkins, "Experts, Migrants, Refugees. Making the German Colony in Iran, 1900–1934," in *German Colonialism in a Global Age.*, Bradley Narranch and Geoff Eley (Durham and Lonon: Duke University Press, 2014), 147–69; Abbas Amanat, *Pivot of the Universe. Nasir al-Din Shah Qajar and the*

Iranian Monarchy, 1831–1896 (London: I.B. Tauris Publishers, 1997); Rose Greaves, "Iranian Relations with Great Britain and British India, 1798–1921," in *The Cambridge History of Iran*, vol. 7, Peter Avery, Gavin Hambly, and Charles Melville (Cambridge: Cambridge University Press, 1991), 374–425; Firuz Kazemzadeh, *Russia and Britain in Persia: Imperial Ambitions in Qajar Iran* (London: I.B. Tauris, 2013).

12 Marie Dickens, *Mumsey's Recollections. Eighty-Four Years Ago* (London: Printed for Private Circulation, 1936), 53; Nina Rosen to Lou Salomé-Andreas, 9 September 1891, 362 1 Cod. Ms. F. C. Andreas, Staats- und Universitätsbibliothek Göttingen (SUBG); Mohtaram ed-Dowleh to Nina Rosen, March 1896, D72 Rosen-Klingemann, Nr. Zugang 77/2022, Karton 12, Landesarchiv NRW – Abteilung OWL (LAV NRW OWL); Monir es-Saltaneh to Nina Rosen, 1890s, D72 Rosen-Klingemann, Nr. Zugang 77/2022, Karton 12, LAV NRW OWL.

13 Mohammad Hossein Mirza 'Emad ed-Dowleh to Friedrich Rosen, 1890s, D72 Rosen-Klingemann Nr. Zugang 77/2022, Karton 12, LAV NRW OWL; Mohammad Hossein Mirza 'Emad ed-Dowleh to Friedrich Rosen, 1892, D72 Rosen-Klingemann Nr. Zugang 77/2022, Karton 12, LAV NRW OWL.

14 Friedrich Rosen, *Oriental Memories*, 136–39; ʿAlī Khan Qajar Ẓahīr al-Dowla and Iraj Afshar, *Khāṭirāt va asnād-i Ẓahīr al-Dowla [in Persian]. Memoirs and Documents of Ẓahīr-al-Dowleh* (Tehran: Intishārāt-i Zarrīn, 1988), 6; Ẓahīr ed-Dowleh to Friedrich Rosen, 1896, D72 Rosen-Klingemann Nr. Zugang 77/2022, Karton 12, LAV NRW OWL; Ẓahīr ed-Dowleh to Friedrich Rosen, 7 April 1893, D72 Rosen-Klingemann Nr. Zugang 77/2022, Karton 12, LAV NRW OWL; Ẓahīr ed-Dowleh to Friedrich Rosen, December 1892, D72 Rosen-Klingemann Nr. Zugang 77/2022, Karton 12 LAV NRW OWL; Friedrich Rosen, Bericht, 28 January 1893, A1805, R 18977, PA AA; Friedrich Rosen, *Persien in Wort und Bild. Mit 165 Meist Ganzseitigen Bildern und einer Landkarte*, (Berlin: Franz Schneider Verlag, 1926), 130.

15 Lloyd Ridgeon, "Revolution and a High-Ranking Sufi: Ẓahīr al-Dowleh's Contribution to the Constitutional Movement," in *Iran's Constitutional Revolution. Popular Politics, Cultural Transformations and Transnational Connections*, H.E. Chehabi and Vanessa Martin (London: I.B. Tauris, 2010), 143–62; Thierry Zarcone, *Secret et sociétés secrètes en Islam. Turquie, Iran et Asie centrale. XIXc-XXc siècles. Franc-Maçonnerie, Carboneria et Confréries soufies* (Milan: Archè, 2002), 159–61; Nile Green, trans. and ed., "A Persian Sufi in the Age of Printing: Mirza Hasan Safi 'Ali Shah (1835–99)," in *Religion and Politics in Modern Iran: A Reader*, Lloyd Ridgeon (London: I.B.Tauris, 2005), 99–112; Nile Green, "A Persian Suf'i in British India: The Travels of Mīrzā Ḥasan Ṣafī 'Alī Shāh (1251/1835–1316/1899)," *Journal of Persian Studies* 42 (2004): 201–18; Friedrich Rosen, "Entwürfe zu Mesnevi," notebook, 1912, D72 Rosen-Klingemann Nr. Zugang 77/2022, Karton 15, LAV NRW OWL; Zarcone, *Sociétés secrètes*, 159–61; Ahmad Kasravi, trans. and ed., Lloyd Ridgeon, "The Detrimental Consequences of Sufis: Extracts from Sufism," in *Religion and Politics in Modern Iran: A Reader*, Lloyd Ridgeon (London: I.B.Tauris, 2005), 114.

16 Friedrich Rosen, *Oriental Memories*, 138; Theilhaber, *Friedrich Rosen*, 153, 168; Friedrich Rosen, Poem, 1892, D72 Rosen-Klingemann Nr. Zugang 77/2022, Karton 12, LAV NRW OWL; Friedrich Rosen, *Der Ratgeber für den Umgang mit Menschen. Achtes Buch des Gulistan nebst einigen anderen Stücken von Muslih ed din Saadi aus Shiras 1189–1291* (Berlin: Georg Stilke, 1921), 25–28; Friedrich Rosen, "Wissenschaftliche Arbeit zum Konsulatsexamen," 1897, I 16292, Personalakten 012570, PA AA; Suleiman Rosen, "Tarjemah Ash'ar".

17 Firuza Abdullaeva, "Zhukovskiĭ, Valentin Alekseevich," *Encyclopædia Iranica*, 15 August 2009. http://www.iranicaonline.org/articles/zhukovskii-valentin-alekseevich; E. Denison Ross, "Some Side-Lights Upon Edward FitzGerald's Poem, 'the Ruba'iyat of Omar Khayyam.' Being the Substance of a Lecture Delivered at the Grosvenor Crescent Club and Women's Institute," lecture, 22 March 1898,

Grosvenor Crescent Club, London; Friedrich Rosen, *Modern Persian Colloquial Grammar*, VIII; Gertrude Bell, *Persian Pictures. With a Preface by Sir E. Denison Ross* (London: Ernest Benn, 1928).

18 Joachim Wohlleben, "Omar Chajjam, das Rubai und die deutsche Literatur. Ein Fall glückloser Begegnung," typed manuscript with handwritten corrections and comments by author., 149/1136, GSA (New York, 1968), 28–39; Remy, "India and Persia on the Poetry of Germany," 66; Theilhaber, *Friedrich Rosen*, 348–52; Sol Gittleman, "The Reception of Edward FitzGerald's Rubaiyat of Omar Khayyam in England and Germany," Doctoral Dissertation (University of Michigan, 1961), 165.

19 Juan Cole, "The Rubaiyat of Omar Khayyam and Muslim Secularism," *Studies in People's History* 3, no. 2 (2016): 138–50.

20 Bell, *Persian Pictures*, 97–101; Friedrich Rosen to Hareth Rosen, 31 June 1898, 3 NL Müller-Werth 1199/34, Hessisches Hauptstaatsarchiv Wiesbaden (HHStAW); Friedrich Rosen to Friedrich Carl Andreas, 20 October 1912, 361 1 Cod. Ms. F. C. Andreas, SUBG; E.H. Whinfield, *The Quatrains of Omar Khayyam* (London: Trübner & Co, 1883), 23.

21 A.A. Seyed-Gohrab, "Khayyām's Universal Appeal: Man, Wine and the Hereafter in the Quatrains," in *The Great 'Umar Khayyām: A Global Reception of the Rubáiyát*, A.A. Seyed-Gohrab (Leiden: Leiden University Press, 2012), 11–38; Jos Coumans, "An 'Umar Khayyām Database," in *The Great 'Umar Khayyām: A Global Reception of the Rubáiyát*, A.A. Seyed-Gohrab (Leiden: Leiden University Press, 2012), 245–52; Esmail Z. Behtash, "The Reception of FitzGerald's Rubáiyát of 'Umar Khayyám by the Victorians," in *The Great 'Umar Khayyām: A Global Reception of the Rubáiyát*, A.A. Seyed-Gohrab (Leiden: Leiden University Press, 2012), 203–14.

22 Theilhaber, *Friedrich Rosen*, 345–53.

23 Suleiman Rosen, "Tarjemah Ash'ar".

24 Michelle Kaiserlian, "The Imagined Elites of the Omar Khayyám Club," in *FitzGerald's* Rubáiyát of Omar Khayyám. *Popularity and Neglect*, ed. Adrian Poole, Christine van Ruymbeke, and William H. Martin, Sandra Mason (London: Anthem Press, 2011), 172.

25 Hanns-Peter Fink, "Kindheit und Jugend des Diplomaten und Orientalisten Friedrich Rosen (1856–1935)," *Lippische Mitteilungen aus Geschichte und Landeskunde* 76 (2007): 129–50; Friedrich Rosen to Friedrich Carl Andreas, 16 September 1892, 361 1 Cod. Ms. F. C. Andreas, SUBG.

26 Theilhaber, *Friedrich Rosen*.

27 Friedrich Rosen, *Die Sinnsprüche Omars des Zeltmachers. Rubaijat-i-Omar-i-Khajjam* (Stuttgart: Deutsche Verlagsanstalt, 1909), 85, 107–8.

28 Maxime Rodinson, *Europe and the Mystique of Islam*, Roger Veinus (London: I.B. Tauris, 2006), 66–70.

29 Friedrich Rosen to Ignaz Goldziher, August 1908, GIL/36/06/04, Oriental Collection-Magyar Tudományos Akadémia, Budapest (OC MTA).

30 Susannah Heschel, "German Jewish Scholarship on Islam as a Tool for de-Orientalizing Judaism," *New German Critique* 39, no. 3 (2012): 91–107; Susannah Heschel, *Jüdischer Islam: Islam und jüdisch-deutsche Selbstbestimmung*, Dirk Hartwig, Moritz Buchner, and Georges Khalil, Fröhliche Wissenschaft (Berlin: Matthes & Seitz, 2018); Susannah Heschel, "The Philological Uncanny: Nineteenth-Century Jewish Readings of the Qur'an," *Qur'anic Studies* 20, no. 3 (2018): 193–213.

31 Friedrich Rosen, *Harut und Marut und andere Dichtungen aus dem Orient verdeutscht durch Friedrich Rosen* (Berlin: Verlag von Georg Stilke, 1924), 68; Friedrich Rosen, trans., "Ode von Hafiz (Inschrift auf seinem Grabe)," 1920s, D72 Rosen-Klingemann Nr. Zugang 77/2022, Karton 12, LAV NRW OWL.

32 Friedrich Rosen to Ignaz Goldziher, 8 January 1913, GIL/36/06/03, OC MTA; Ludmila Hanisch, ed., *"Machen Sie doch unseren Islam nicht gar zu schlecht". Der Briefwechsel der Islamwissenschaftler Ignaz Goldziher und Martin Hartmann, 1894–1914* (Wiesbaden: Harrassowitz Verlag, 2000); Friedrich Rosen to Ignaz Goldziher, 21 November 1910, GIL/36/06/02, OC MTA.

33 Edward Granville Browne, *A Literary History of Persia: From Firdawsi to Sa'di* (Cambridge: Cambridge University Press, 1956), 246–59; Edward Granville Browne, "Sufiism," in *Religious Systems of the World Religious Systems of the World: A Contribution to the Study of Comparative Religion* (London: Swan Sonnenschein, 1889), 315; Edward Granville Browne, *A Year Amongst the Persians: Impressions as to the Life, Character, & Thought of the People of Persia. Received During Twelve Months' Residence in That Country in the Years 1887–1888. With a Memoir by Sir E. Denison Ross* (Cambridge: Cambridge University Press, 1893), 123; Theilhaber, *Friedrich Rosen*, 289.

34 Martin Hartmann, "Christensen, Arthur. Omar Khajjâms Rubâijât," *Wiener Zeitschrift für die Kunde des Morgenlandes* 17 (1903): 366–74.

35 Arthur Christensen to Martin Hartmann, 10 July 1909, I 1 Utilg. 578, Det Kongelige Bibliotek, Copenhagen (KB HA); Arthur Christensen, *Omar Khajjâms Rubâijât: En litteraerhistorisk undersøgelse* (Copenhagen: Siegfried Michaelsens Efterfølger, 1903); Arthur Christensen to Friedrich Rosen, 1 July 1909, I 1 Utilg. 578, KB HA.

36 Georg Rosen, Friedrich Rosen, *Mesnevi oder Doppelverse des Scheich Mewlānā Dschelāl ed dīn Rūmi*, (Munich: Georg Müller, 1913); Friedrich Rosen, "Entwürfe zu Mesnevi," 123–5.

37 "Beim Reichskanzler in Norderney," *Norddeutsche Allgemeine Zeitung* 994 (23 November 1908): 1–2.

38 Friedrich Rosen, *Die Sinnsprüche Omars des Zeltmachers. Rubaijat-i-Omar-i-Khajjam*, 2 (Stuttgart: Deutsche Verlagsanstalt, 1912); Friedrich Rosen, *Die Sinnsprüche Omars des Zeltmachers. Rubaijat-i-Omar-i-Khajjam*, 5 (Stuttgart: Deutsche Verlagsanstalt, 1922); Hans Hermann, *Sinnsprüche des Omar Khajjam. Deutsch von Friedrich Rosen. Für eine tiefe Stimme mit Klavier komponiert* (Berlin: Kommissionsverlag Albert Stahl, 1914).

39 Georg Rosen, Friedrich Rosen, *Mesnevi*, 28; Friedrich Rosen, *Die Sinnsprüche Omars des Zeltmachers. Rubaijat-i-Omar-i-Khajjam*, 6 (Leipzig: Insel-Verlag, 1929); Friedrich Rosen, "Der Einfluß geistiger Strömungen auf die politische Geschichte Persiens," *ZDMG* 76 (1922): 101–25.

40 Theilhaber, *Friedrich Rosen*, 486–7.

41 The "Kaviani" Art Printing Press, *List of Publications & Books for Sale* (Berlin: Kaviani, 1924); Afshin Matin-Asgari, "The Berlin Circle: Iranian Nationalism Meets German Countermodernity," in *Rethinking Iranian Nationalism and Modernity*, Kamran Scot Aghaie and Afshin Marashi (Austin: University of Texas Press, 2014), 49–66; Kamran Arjomand, "Die Buch- und Kunstdruckerei Kaviani und die iranischen Intellektuellen in Berlin um die Zeit des Ersten Weltkrieges," in *Fremde Erfahrungen: Asiaten und Afrikaner in Deutschland, Österreich und in der Schweiz bis 1945*, vol. 4, Gerhard Höpp, Zentrum Moderner Orient (Berlin: Das Arabische Buch, 1996), 169–84; Keivandokht Ghahari, *Nationalismus und Modernismus in Iran in der Periode zwischen dem Zerfall der Qāǧāren-Dynastie und der Machtfestigung Reżā Schahs. Eine Untersuchung über die intellektuellen Kreise um die Zeitschriften Kāweh, Īrānšahr und Āyandeh* (Berlin: Klaus Schwarz Verlag, 2001).

42 Younes Jalali, *Taghi Erani, a Polymath in Interwar Berlin: Fundamental Science, Psychology, Orientalism and Political Philosophy* (Cham: Palgrave Macmillan, 2019).

43 Carla von Urff, "Friedrich Rosen," *Die Post* 42 (12 July 1971): 4–5.

44 Georg Rosen, Friedrich Rosen, *Mesnevi*, 28.

45 Taqi Arani, *Discussion of Difficulties of Euclid by Omar Khayyam* (Tehran: Sirousse, 1936), I–V.

46 Friedrich Rosen, *Ruba'iyat Hakim 'Omar Khayyam [in Persian]* (Berlin: Kaviani, 1925).

47 Friedrich Rosen, "Jashn-e Hezar Saleh-Ye Ferdawsi," *Iran-e Bastan* 2: 28 (18 August 1933): 2–3; Friedrich Rosen, "Zur Tausendjahrfeier Firdousis," *Deutsche Allgemeine Zeitung* 257 (6 June 1934).

48 Sadek Hedayat, *Taranye-hay Khayyam [in Persian]* (Tehran: Darmatabai Roshnaii, 1934), 23, 32.

49 Christian Rempis, *Die Vierzeiler 'Omar Chajjāms in der Auswahl und Anordnung Edward FitzGeralds aus dem Persischen verdeutscht* (Tübingen: Verlag der Deutschen Chajjām-Gesellschaft, 1933); Christian Rempis, *Beiträge zur Ḫayyām-Forschung* (Leipzig: Deutsche Morgenländische Gesellschaft

in Kommission bei F.A. Brockhaus, 1937); Christian Rempis, "Die Überlieferung der 'Umar-i Ḫayyām zugeschriebenen Vierzeiler im 13. bis 16. Jahrhundert", Doctoral Dissertation (Friedrich-Wilhelms-Universität zu Berlin, 1937); Christian Rempis, *Neue Beiträge zur Chajjām-Forschung* (Leipzig: Otto Harrassowitz, 1943); "Rempis, Christian," Entnazifizierung. Spruchkammerakten, 27 June 1949, Nr. 2669/151, Wü 13 T 2 Staatskommissariat für die politische Säuberung / 1945–1952, Landesarchiv Baden-Württemberg. Staatsarchiv Sigmaringen; Gittleman, "FitzGerald's Rubaiyat of Omar Khayyam in England and Germany"; Ekkehard Ellinger, *Deutsche Orientalistik zur Zeit des Nationalsozialismus 1933–1945* (Edingen-Neckarhausen: Deux mondes, 2006), 182–84, 314–19; David Motadel, "Iran and the Aryan Myth," in *Perceptions of Iran: History, Myths and Nationalism from Medieval Persia to the Islamic Republic*, Ali M. Ansari (London: I.B. Tauris, 2014), 127; Dirk Schuster, *Die Lehre vom "arischen" Christentum. Das wissenschaftliche Selbstverständnis im Eisenacher "Entjudungsinstitut"* (Göttingen: V&R unipress, 2017), 237–41; Horst Junginger, *Von der philologischen zur völkischen Religionswissenschaft. Das Fach Religionswissenschaft an der Universität Tübingen von der Mitte des 19. Jahrhunderts bis zum Ende des Dritten Reiches* (Stuttgart: Franz Steiner Verlag, 1999), 230–47.

Works cited

Abdullaeva, Firuza. "Zhukovskiĭ, Valentin Alekseevich." *Encyclopædia Iranica*, 15 August 2009. http://www.iranicaonline.org/articles/zhukovskii-valentin-alekseevich.

Amanat, Abbas. *Pivot of the Universe: Nasir al-Din Shah Qajar and the Iranian Monarchy, 1831–1896*. London: I.B. Tauris Publishers, 1997.

Arani, Taqi. *Discussion of Difficulties of Euclid by Omar Khayyām*. Tehran: Sirousse, 1936.

Arjomand, Kamran. "Die Buch- und Kunstdruckerei Kaviani und die iranischen Intellektuellen in Berlin um die Zeit des Ersten Weltkrieges." In *Fremde Erfahrungen: Asiaten und Afrikaner in Deutschland, Österreich und in der Schweiz bis 1945*, vol. 4, Gerhard Höpp. Zentrum Moderner Orient, Berlin: Das Arabische Buch, 1996, 169–84.

Behtash, Esmail Z. "The Reception of FitzGerald's Rubáiyát of 'Umar Khayyám by the Victorians." In *The Great 'Umar Khayyām: A Global Reception of the Rubáiyát*, A.A. Seyed-Gohrab, Leiden: Leiden University Press, 2012, 203–14.

"Beim Reichskanzler in Norderney." *Norddeutsche Allgemeine Zeitung* 994 (23 November 1908): 1–2.

Bell, Gertrude. *Persian Pictures. With a Preface by Sir E. Denison Ross*. London: Ernest Benn, 1928.

Bodenstedt, Friedrich. *Die Lieder des Mirza-Schaffy*. Berlin: Deckerschen Geheimen Ober-Hofbuchdruckerei, 1851.

Browne, Edward Granville. *A Literary History of Persia. From Firdawsi to Sa'di*. Cambridge: Cambridge University Press, 1956.

Browne, Edward Granville. "Sufiism." In *Religious Systems of the World Religious Systems of the World: A Contribution to the Study of Comparative Religion*, London: Swan Sonnenschein, 1889, 314–32.

Browne, Edward Granville. *A Year Amongst the Persians. Impressions as to the Life, Character, & Thought of the People of Persia. Received During Twelve Months' Residence in That Country in the Years 1887–1888. With a Memoir by Sir E. Denison Ross*. Cambridge: Cambridge University Press, 1893.

Christensen, Arthur. *Omar Khajjâms Rubâijât: En litteraerhistorisk undersøgelse*. Copenhagen: Siegfried Michaelsens Efterfølger, 1903.

Cole, Juan. "The Rubaiyat of Omar Khayyām and Muslim Secularism." *Studies in People's History* 3, no. 2 (2016): 138–50.

Coumans, Jos. "An 'Umar Khayyām Database." In *The Great 'Umar Khayyām. A Global Reception of the Rubáiyát*, A.A. Seyed-Gohrab, Leiden: Leiden University Press, 2012, 245–52.

Dabashi, Hamid. *Persophilia: Persian Culture on the Global Scene.* Cambridge: Harvard University Press, 2015.

Dickens, Marie. *Mumsey's Recollections: Eighty-Four Years Ago.* London: Printed for Private Circulation, 1936.

Ellinger, Ekkehard. *Deutsche Orientalistik zur Zeit des Nationalsozialismus 1933–1945*. Edingen-Neckarhausen: Deux mondes, 2006.

Fink, Hanns-Peter. "Kindheit und Jugend des Diplomaten und Orientalisten Friedrich Rosen (1856–1935)." *Lippische Mitteilungen aus Geschichte und Landeskunde* 76 (2007): 129–50.

Ghahari, Keivandokht. *Nationalismus und Modernismus in Iran in der Periode zwischen dem Zerfall der Qāǧāren-Dynastie und der Machtfestigung Reżā Schahs. Eine Untersuchung über die intellektuellen Kreise um die Zeitschriften Kāweh, Īrānšahr und Āyandeh.* Berlin: Klaus Schwarz Verlag, 2001.

Gittleman, Sol. "The Reception of Edward FitzGerald's Rubaiyat of Omar Khayyām in England and Germany." Doctoral Dissertation. University of Michigan, 1961.

Greaves, Rose. "Iranian Relations with Great Britain and British India, 1798–1921." In *The Cambridge History of Iran*, vol. 7, Peter Avery, Gavin Hambly, and Charles Melville, Cambridge: Cambridge University Press, 1991, 374–425.

Green, Nile. "A Persian Suf'i in British India: The Travels of Mīrzā Ḥasan Ṣafī 'Alī Shāh (1251/1835–1316/1899)." *Journal of Persian Studies* 42 (2004): 201–18.

Green, Nile. "A Persian Sufi in the Age of Printing: Mirza Hasan Safi 'Ali Shah (1835–99)." In *Religion and Politics in Modern Iran: A Reader*, Lloyd Ridgeon, London: I.B.Tauris, 2005, 99–112.

Hamilton-Temple-Blackwood, Frederick. *Rubáiyát of Omar Khayyām.* Shimla: Self-Published, 1887.

Hanisch, Ludmila, ed. *"Machen Sie doch unseren Islam nicht gar zu schlecht". Der Briefwechsel der Islamwissenschaftler Ignaz Goldziher und Martin Hartmann, 1894–1914*. Wiesbaden: Harrassowitz Verlag, 2000.

Hartmann, Martin. "Christensen, Arthur. Omar Khajjâms Rubâijât." *Wiener Zeitschrift für die Kunde des Morgenlandes* 17 (1903): 366–74.

Hedayat, Sadek. *Taranye-hay Khayyām [in Persian]*. Tehran: Darmatabai Roshnaii, 1934.

Hermann, Hans. *Sinnsprüche des Omar Khajjam. Deutsch von Friedrich Rosen. Für eine tiefe Stimme mit Klavier komponiert.* Berlin: Kommissionsverlag Albert Stahl, 1914.

Heschel, Susannah. "German Jewish Scholarship on Islam as a Tool for de-Orientalizing Judaism." *New German Critique* 39, no. 3 (2012): 91–107.

Heschel, Susannah. *Jüdischer Islam: Islam und jüdisch-deutsche Selbstbestimmung*. Dirk Hartwig, Moritz Buchner, and Georges Khalil. Fröhliche Wissenschaft. Berlin: Matthes & Seitz, 2018.

Heschel, Susannah. "The Philological Uncanny: Nineteenth-Century Jewish Readings of the Qur'an." *Qur'anic Studies* 20, no. 3 (2018): 193–213.

Jalali, Younes. *Taghi Erani, a Polymath in Interwar Berlin: Fundamental Science, Psychology, Orientalism and Political Philosophy.* Cham: Palgrave Macmillan, 2019.

Jenkins, Jennifer. "Experts, Migrants, Refugees. Making the German Colony in Iran, 1900–1934." In *German Colonialism in a Global Age*, Bradley Narranch and Geoff Eley, Durham: Duke University Press, 2014, 147–69.

Junginger, Horst. *Von der philologischen zur völkischen Religionswissenschaft. Das Fach Religionswissenschaft an der Universität Tübingen von der Mitte des 19. Jahrhunderts bis zum Ende des Dritten Reiches.* Stuttgart: Franz Steiner Verlag, 1999.

Kaiserlian, Michelle. "The Imagined Elites of the Omar Khayyám Club." In *FitzGerald's Rubáiyát of Omar Khayyám: Popularity and Neglect*, Adrian Poole, Christine van Ruymbeke, and William H. Martin, Sandra Mason, London: Anthem Press, 2011, 147–74.

Kasravi, Ahmad, trans. and ed., Lloyd Ridgeon. "The Detrimental Consequences of Sufis: Extracts from Sufism." In *Religion and Politics in Modern Iran: A Reader*, Lloyd Ridgeon, London: I.B.Tauris, 2005, 113–38.

Kazemzadeh, Firuz. *Russia and Britain in Persia: Imperial Ambitions in Qajar Iran*. London: I.B. Tauris, 2013.

Llewellyn-Jones, Rosie. *The Last King in India. Wajid 'Ali Shah, 1822–1887*. London: Hurst & Company, 2014.

Martin, Bradford G. *German-Persian Diplomatic Relations. 1873–1912*. 'S-Gravenhage: Mouton & Co, 1959.

Matin-Asgari, Afshin. "The Berlin Circle: Iranian Nationalism Meets German Countermodernity." In *Rethinking Iranian Nationalism and Modernity*, Kamran Scot Aghaie and Afshin Marashi, Austin: University of Texas Press, 2014, 49–66.

Motadel, David. "Iran and the Aryan Myth." In *Perceptions of Iran: History, Myths and Nationalism from Medieval Persia to the Islamic Republic*, Ali M. Ansari, London: I.B. Tauris, 2014, 119–45.

Polaschegg, Andrea. *Der andere Orientalismus. Regeln deutsch-morgenländischer Imagination im 19. Jahrhundert*. Berlin: De Gruyter, 2005.

Qureshi, M. Aslam. *Wajid Ali Shah's Theatrical Genius*. Lahore: Vanguard Books, 1987.

Rempis, Christian Herrnhold. *Beiträge zur Ḫayyām-Forschung*. Leipzig: Deutsche Morgenländische Gesellschaft in Kommission bei F.A. Brockhaus, 1937.

Rempis, Christian Herrnhold. *Neue Beiträge zur Chajjām-Forschung*. Leipzig: Otto Harrassowitz, 1943.

Rempis, Christian Herrnhold. "Die Überlieferung der 'Umar-i Ḫayyām zugeschriebenen Vierzeiler im 13. bis 16. Jahrhundert." Doctoral Dissertation. Friedrich-Wilhelms-Universität zu Berlin, 1937.

Rempis, Christian Herrnhold. *Die Vierzeiler 'Omar Chajjāms in der Auswahl und Anordnung Edward FitzGeralds aus dem Persischen verdeutscht*. Tübingen: Verlag der Deutschen Chajjām-Gesellschaft, 1933.

Remy, Arthur F.J. "The Influence of India and Persia on the Poetry of Germany." Doctoral Dissertation. Columbia University, 1901.

Ridgeon, Lloyd. "Revolution and a High-Ranking Sufi: Ẓahīr al-Dowleh's Contribution to the Constitutional Movement." In *Iran's Constitutional Revolution: Popular Politics, Cultural Transformations and Transnational Connections*, H.E. Chehabi and Vanessa Martin, London: I.B. Tauris, 2010, 143–62.

Rocher, Rosane, and Agnes Stache-Weiske. *For the Sake of the Vedas: The Anglo-German Life of Friedrich Rosen, 1805–1837*. Wiesbaden: Harrassowitz, 2020.

Rodinson, Maxime. *Europe and the Mystique of Islam*. Roger Veinus. London: I.B. Tauris, 2006.

Rosen, Friedrich, *Ruba'iyat Hakim 'Omar Khayyām [in Persian]*. Berlin: Kaviani, 1925.

Rosen, Friedrich, "Briefe aus Indien. Benares." *Frankfurter Zeitung* 311 (7 November 1886).

Rosen, Friedrich, "Der Einfluß geistiger Strömungen auf die politische Geschichte Persiens." *ZDMG* 76 (1922): 101–25.

Rosen, Friedrich, *Harut und Marut und andere Dichtungen aus dem Orient verdeutscht durch Friedrich Rosen*. Berlin: Verlag von Georg Stilke, 1924.

Rosen, Friedrich, *Die Indarsabhā des Amānat. Ein Beitrag zur Kenntnis der Hindustani-Litteratur. Inaugural-Dissertation der Hohen Philosophischen Fakultät der Universität Leipzig zur Erlangung der Doktorwürde*. Leipzig: F.A. Brockhaus, 1891.

Rosen, Friedrich, "Jashn-e Hezar Saleh-Ye Ferdawsi." *Iran-e Bastan* 2: 28 (18 August 1933): 2–3.

Rosen, Friedrich, *Modern Persian Colloquial Grammar. Containing a Short Grammar, Dialogues and Extracts from Nasir-Eddin Shah's Diaries, Tales, Etc. and a Vocabulary*. London: Luzac & Co, 1898.

Rosen, Friedrich, *Oriental Memories of a German Diplomatist*. New York: Dutton, 1930.

Rosen, Friedrich, *Persien in Wort und Bild. Mit 165 Meist Ganzseitigen Bildern und einer Landkarte.* Berlin: Franz Schneider Verlag, 1926.

Rosen, Friedrich, *Shumā Farsī härf mīzänīd (Sprechen Sie Persisch?): neupersischer Sprachführer, für die Reise und zum Selbstunterricht enthaltend eine kurze Grammatik, Wörtersammlung, Gespräche und Lesestücke.* Leipzig: Koch, 1890.

Rosen, Friedrich, "Zur Tausendjahrfeier Firdousis." *Deutsche Allgemeine Zeitung* 257 (6 June 1934).

Rosen, Friedrich, *Der Ratgeber für den Umgang mit Menschen. Achtes Buch des Gulistan nebst einigen anderen Stücken von Muslih ed din Saadi aus Shiras 1189–1291.* Berlin: Georg Stilke, 1921.

Rosen, Friedrich, *Die Sinnsprüche Omars des Zeltmachers. Rubaijat-i-Omar-i-Khajjam.* Stuttgart: Deutsche Verlagsanstalt, 1909.

Rosen, Friedrich, *Die Sinnsprüche Omars des Zeltmachers. Rubaijat-i-Omar-i-Khajjam.* 2. Stuttgart: Deutsche Verlagsanstalt, 1912.

Rosen, Friedrich, *Die Sinnsprüche Omars des Zeltmachers. Rubaijat-i-Omar-i-Khajjam.* 5. Stuttgart: Deutsche Verlagsanstalt, 1922.

Rosen, Friedrich, *Die Sinnsprüche Omars Des Zeltmachers. Rubaijat-i-Omar-i-Khajjam.* 6. Leipzig: Insel-Verlag, 1929.

Rosen, Georg. *Elementa Persica. "Hekayat Farsi" id est narrationes Persicae. Ex libro manuscripto edidit, gloassario explanavit, grammaticae brevem adumbrationem praemisit.* Berlin: Veith, 1843.

Rosen, Friedrich, *Mesnevi oder Doppelverse des Scheich Mewlānā Dschelāl ed dīn Rūmi.* Leipzig: Fr. Chr. Wilh. Vogel, 1849.

Rosen, Georg, Friedrich Rosen. *Mesnevi oder Doppelverse des Scheich Mewlānā Dschelāl ed dīn Rūmi.* Munich: Georg Müller, 1913.

Rosen, Nina. *Acht orientalische Weisen aus dem Munde des Volkes in Teheran und Fez aufgezeichnet und bearbeitet.* Hannover: Orient-Buchhandlung, 1926.

Ross, E. Denison. "Some Side-Lights Upon Edward FitzGerald's Poem, 'the Ruba'iyat of Omar Khayyām.' Being the Substance of a Lecture Delivered at the Grosvenor Crescent Club and Women's Institute." Lecture. Grosvenor Crescent Club. London, 1898.

Schuster, Dirk. *Die Lehre vom "arischen" Christentum. Das wissenschaftliche Selbstverständnis im Eisenacher "Entjudungsinstitut".* Göttingen: V&R unipress, 2017.

Seyed-Gohrab, A.A. "Khayyām's Universal Appeal: Man, Wine and the Hereafter in the Quatrains." In *The Great 'Umar Khayyām. A Global Reception of the Rubáiyát,* A.A. Seyed-Gohrab, Leiden: Leiden University Press, 2012, 11–38.

Stache-Weiske, Agnes, and Frank Meier-Barthel. *Georg Rosen. Notizen von einer Reise durch Serbien, Anatolien und Transkaukasien in den Jahren 1843 und 1844.* Berlin: eb-Verlag, 2020.

Tabourier, David, and Laura Raum. *Peut-on Tout Traduire? Les Idées Larges avec Souleymane Bachir Diagne.* Laura Raim and Souleymane Bachir Diagne. Arte. UPIAN:COM, 2023.

The "Kaviani" Art Printing Press. *List of Publications & Books for Sale.* Berlin: Kaviani, 1924.

Theilhaber, Amir. *Friedrich Rosen. Orientalist Scholarship and International Politics.* Berlin: De Gruyter, 2020.

von Urff, Carla. "Friedrich Rosen." *Die Post* 42 (12 July 1971): 4–5.

Whinfield, E.H. *The Quatrains of Omar Khayyām.* London: Trübner & Co, 1883.

Ẓahīr al-Dowla, ʿAlī Khan Qajar and Iraj Afshar, *Khāṭirāt va asnād-i Zahīr al-Dowla [in Persian]. Memoirs and Documents of Ẓahīr-al-Dowleh.* Tehran: Intishārāt-i Zarrīn, 1988.

Zarcone, Thierry. *Secret et sociétés secrètes en Islam. Turquie, Iran et Asie centrale. XIXc–XXc siècles. Franc-Maçonnerie, Carboneria et Confréries soufies.* Milan: Archè, 2002.

The Boy Sheikh: The Trial of an Ottoman Heretic

Colin Imber
Manchester University

Abstract

From the early sixteenth century, the Ottoman sultans saw themselves as the pre-eminent upholders of Sunni Islam, whose rule was a necessary precondition to the rule of the shariah. In these circumstances, any renunciation of the shariah could be seen as a rebellion against the sultan's rule. Nonetheless, groups holding antinomian beliefs were widespread throughout his realms but, in reality, posed no serious threat. The problem for the authorities was to identify and suppress those groups that presented a political as much as a theological danger. To this end, the Ottoman authorities drew on the centuries-old traditions of fiqh to define the borders of Islamic orthodoxy, and the classical works on heresiography by al-Ghazali (d.1111) and others. It was these works that guided the authorities in their efforts to identify and bring to trial heretics, such as Oğlan Şeyh – "the Boy Sheikh" – executed in Istanbul in 1539.

Keywords: heresy; Ottoman Empire; jurisprudence; Oğlan Şeyh; orthodoxy and heterodoxy.

Unbelief, apostasy and *zandaqa*

In his preamble to the Law-Book of Buda of 1541, the Ottoman jurist and mufti Ebu's-u'ud (1490–1574) described the reigning sultan Süleyman I (r.1520–1566) as: "The one who prepares the path for the precepts of the manifest sharīʿa and upholds the articles [of faith] of the firm religion."[1] The effect of Ebu's-u'ud's statement is to identify the Ottoman sultan with the sharīʿa and the dogmas of orthodox Islam. The sultan's rule is a pre-condition to the maintenance of Islam and the sharīʿa, and the sultan himself gains his legitimacy from his role as defender and guardian of the faith. In the world of politics, therefore, a rejection of the faith or a deviation from Sunni orthodoxy was tantamount to a rejection of the sultan's rule, while a rebellion against the sultan was tantamount to a repudiation of the true faith. In principle, therefore the Ottoman sultans demanded of their subjects not only loyalty to the dynasty but also – from their Muslim subjects – adherence to orthodox Sunni Islam.

In pursuit of this ideal, the sultans maintained a network of courts administering Muslim law, a network of mosques where their subjects practised the Sunni rites, and a network of madrasas that trained the personnel to staff these institutions. By the sixteenth century, a well-educated body of ʿulamā had come into existence to oversee these institutions and to regulate the practice of religion and law. Nonetheless, uniformity of religion was impossible to achieve. The population of the Ottoman Empire was heterogeneous. In its European provinces Christians outnumbered Muslims; and among its Muslim populations, popular religion often diverged from formal Muslim dogma. Above all, there was a proliferation of Sufi sects whose beliefs and ceremonies differed wildly from the prescriptions of orthodox Islam. For a sultan who claimed to be the promulgator of the sharīʿa and defender of Sunni Islam the problem was to determine who, among many charismatic religious figures, and which, among a multiplicity of sects, was "heretical" and what their punishment should be. The solution to the problem fell to the ʿulamā who, by the sixteenth century, were the recognised arbiters in all matters of religion and law, and guardians of the boundary between faith and unbelief. Even in cases where religious dissenters openly rebelled against the rule of the Ottoman sultan, the sultan might still ask the mufti of Istanbul for a ruling justifying their execution or war against them. In the sixteenth century, for example, the detailed fatwas of Ebu's-suʿud and other muftis refuting the beliefs of the *kızılbaş*[2] served to justify Ottoman wars against the Safavid shahs and the violent suppression of their followers in the Ottoman realms.

The *kızılbaş*, however, were a special case. As an anti-Sunni sect that rejected Ottoman rule and expressed their political and religious adherence to the Safavid shah, they presented a real danger to the dynasty and state. Other heretics were less easy to recognise, since their practices and beliefs were hard to distinguish from those of the many unorthodox but tolerated groups that flourished in the Ottoman realms. It was a duty of the ʿulamā to differentiate heretics from believers, and to determine the fate of anyone whom they pronounced guilty of unbelief. In reaching a judgement the Ottoman ʿulamā had at their disposal the resources of Ḥanafī *fiqh* and a centuries-old tradition of Muslim heresiography.

To condemn a Muslim as a heretic required first making a distinction between faith (*īmān*) and unbelief (*kufr*). Unbelief, in the definition of al-Ghazālī (d. 1111) is to "deny the Prophet in everything he brought [to mankind]' while faith is 'to believe him in everything he brought".[3] The articles of faith that al-Ghazālī identified as fundamental were belief in God, belief in the Prophet and belief in the Last Day.[4] In law, anyone who abandons these beliefs is an apostate (*murtadd*) and, to become an apostate, a person has to do no more than to "utter on their tongue words [denoting] unbelief (*kalimat al-kufr*)".[5] Their intention in speaking those words is legally irrelevant: even if they spoke them in jest or unintentionally, the consequence is the same. It is, for example, unbelief to use the expression "God's arm is long" since, if taken literally, the words anthropomorphise God. It was not only careless words that could lead to a judgement of apostasy, but also any action deemed to resemble the behaviour of infidels. For example, to refuse to go to the sharīʿa court to settle a lawsuit is unbelief, as it implies contempt for the sharīʿa.[6] It required, in fact, no more than a misplaced word or an ill-considered action to become an apostate. To return to the faith an apostate must "free himself of all religions other than Islam".[7] They can achieve this through an act of sincere repentance, which al-Bābartī (d. 1384) defines as follows: "He should say, 'I repent and return to the religion of Islam, and I am free from all religions except the religion of Islam.' However, it is said that this is after he has twice pronounced the affirmation of the faith; and [additionally] an affirmation of [belief in] the Resurrection and the Last Day are recommended." Beyond this, the law imposes an additional requirement. During the period of their apostasy, an apostate loses all the privileges and protections of the law, including the right to contract a valid marriage. In consequence, their existing marriage dissolves and must be renewed on their return to the faith. If the apostate is obdurate and does not repent, he should be imprisoned for three days, and if he does not repent within this period, he should be executed. A female apostate escapes the death penalty but, if she does not repent, she remains in prison until she dies. Bābartī, however, recommends that "If the apostate (*murtadda*) is a woman in possession of her senses, she should be killed, not for her apostasy but because here she is fomenting corruption on earth."[8]

The laws of apostasy shaped how the ʿulamā understood heresy and heretics. The basic principle is that it is not a person's intention in speaking "profane words" (*alfāẓ al-kufr*) or acting in a way that "resembles the actions of infidels" that determines whether or not they had committed apostasy. A person's inner beliefs – "what is in their heart" – is legally irrelevant. Profane words spoken, for example, in jest or under duress are no different from the same words spoken with sincere intent. An apostate, in short is judged on externalities. The penalty for apostasy is death, and here the only source of contention is whether an apostate should be given the chance to repent. Arguments on this point often centred around the term with which the ʿulamā chose to label the offender.

More heinous than simple apostasy was *zandaqa*, the condition of a *zindīq*. The term *zindīq* was traditional in Islamic heresiography but, unlike *murtadd* had no clear definition. al-Ghazālī, in one passage, gives a maximalist definition, describing a *zindīq* as one who "denies the Next World and the Creator, and does not profess to the prophethood [of Muḥammad]; who maintains that death is utter extinction; that the world does not pass away, but is self-existent. They do not believe in God or the Last Day".[9] Other authorities gave other definitions. For al-Taftazānī (d. 1390), for example, a *zindīq* is someone who is inwardly an unbeliever while outwardly professing belief.[10] All agree that the punishment for *zandaqa* is death but opinions differ as to whether a *zindīq* should be given the chance to repent and, if so, whether their repentance is acceptable after arrest, before arrest, or whether it is acceptable at all. For those responsible for the arrest, investigation and sentencing of heretics, the term was particularly useful as the multiplicity of definitions could fit a multiplicity of cases. The same was true of a number of other terms, such as *mulḥid*, which appear among the charges laid against heretics.

A term particularly useful to the authorities in identifying heretics and bringing them to trial is *ibāḥa*. It may, in some cases, have served simply as a label to discredit anyone suspected of unorthodox beliefs, but – unlike *zandaqa* – it does in fact have a precise meaning. To profess *ibāḥa* is to ignore the distinction between licit (*ḥalāl*) and illicit (*ḥarām*) and to declare what the *sharīʿa* makes *ḥarām* to be permitted (*mubāḥ*), and what the sharīʿa makes obligatory (*wājib*), such as prayer (*ṣalāt*), to be voluntary. By thus declaring the forbidden to be licit, and the obligatory to be voluntary, the *ibāḥī* is symbolically rejecting the sharīʿa and Islam. The penalty for *ibāḥa* is death. In al-Ghazālī's words: "[The *ibāḥī*s] destroy all the laws (*sharāʾiʿ*) of the Prophets, and it is incumbent on the sultan of the age to spill their blood and to cleanse them from the face of the earth."[11] Two offences in particular – wine-drinking (*shurb al-khamr*) and fornication (*zinā*) – became emblematic of activities that are *ḥarām* and feature prominently in accusations against heretics. This fatwa of Ebu's-suʿud is typical:

> Question: While they are drinking wine, a group of Semavetlüs, with one another's permission, have disposal of each other's wives. What should be done to them?
> Answer: Execution is required (*lāzım*).[12]

The Semavetlüs were a group in north-eastern Bulgaria whom the Ottoman authorities suspected of heresy. Here the accusation against them is almost certainly fabricated, but serves to show the utility to the Ottoman authorities of accusations of wine-drinking and fornication in constructing cases against heretics. It was not, however, the actual commission of these offences that led to charges of heresy and the imposition of the death sentence: the formal, and rarely imposed, penalty for wine-drinking was eighty lashes and not death. The offence was to declare openly the belief that wine-drinking and fornication, or indeed anything that was *ḥarām*, to be *ḥalāl*.

Centuries before Ebu's-suʿud, al-Ghazālī had identified and described a particular type of *ibāḥī*. This is one who proclaims himself to be a Sufi and believes that "he has attained such a position with God Most High that [his obligation] to perform prayer has lapsed, and wine-drinking, sin and consuming the sultan's property are permitted to him. In such a case, there is no doubt about the obligation to kill him ... Killing someone like this is more meritorious than killing a hundred infidels."[13] Here al-Ghazālī is describing those Sufis who believe themselves to be in direct communion with God and therefore absolved both from the obligations of the sharīʿa and from obedience to the secular authority. Sufis of this kind who had found God within themselves, appeared to threaten the rule of the sharīʿa, the ʿulamā and the sultan, in short to overthrow Islam. Hence Ghazālī's violent reaction.

The Boy Sheikh and his teachings

It was also the reaction of the Ottoman authorities in the sixteenth century when they discovered heretical Sufis of the kind that had troubled Ghazālī. Like him, they found that the key to identifying such heretics was to examine their views on *ḥalāl* and *ḥarām*. In a letter, probably from the 1550s, Ebu's-suʿud instructed the authorities examining a certain Gazanfer Dede to question the suspect on *ḥalāl* and *ḥarām*, in order to establish whether or not he was in fact a *zindīq* and a *mulḥid.*[14] Gazanfer was acquitted, but some others suffered the fate that Ghazālī had had in mind for heretics of this sort.

The most famous of these was Ismāʿīl-i Maʿşukī, remembered as Oğlan Şeyh ("the Boy Sheikh"), executed in 1539, aged about twenty.[15] Ismāʿīl was the son of Pīr ʿAlī of Aksārāy, the leader – or *quṭb* – of one branch of the Bayrāmī *ṭarīqa*. After the death of the *ṭarīqa*'s founder, Hacci Bayram, in 1429, his followers had split, with one branch embracing unorthodox beliefs and adopting, or at least acquiring, the epithet of *melāmī*, traditional in some circles for those Sufis who seek blame rather than respect. For almost a century after the death of Hacci Bayram, the *bayramiyye-i melametiyye* – to give the movement its formal designation – was an Anatolian sect with a membership drawn largely from urban craftsmen. Aware that their beliefs would lead to persecution, its members wore no distinctive clothing and practised no public rituals. This was until, at some point in the 1530s, Pīr ʿAlī's teenage son, seemingly against his father's wishes, left Aksaray for Istanbul where he began to preach in public even, apparently, from the pulpits of the city's mosques. His activities and the size of his following led, in 1539, to his arrest, trial, and execution alongside twelve of his acolytes. With Ismāʿīl's execution the Ottoman *melāmī*s had gained their first martyr.

Ismāʿīl-i Maʿşukī had attracted a large following during his lifetime and inspired continuing devotion after his death. Nonetheless, records of his doctrines and beliefs are limited to a handful of poems – five ghazals and a qasida – and the statements of witnesses at his trial. In addition to these, a fatwa of Ebu's-suʿud refuting the arguments of "the Sufi Zeyd" was almost certainly issued as an answer to Ismāʿīl's claims.

Ismāʿīl's verse draws largely from the language and conventions of Sufi verse that were commonplace in literary circles. The following couplet, for example, uses the story of Yūsuf and Zuleikhā as a metaphor for the beauty of divine love:

> It is Your beauty, o Lord, that is manifest in Yūsuf,
> It is Your love, o Lord, that appears from Zuleikhā[16]

This was a Sufi commonplace and, despite seeming to express the idea of God appearing in an idealised human form, was acceptable to all except the strictly orthodox. Ismāʿīl, however, went beyond the metaphorical and, in places, appears to enunciate the doctrine that God is literally visible in the human form:

> We plainly saw God's form (*Hakkın sureti*) in your form.
> The ascetic's fables cannot hold us back from God.[17]

The acetic (*zāhid*) here is a conventional trope, referring to the orthodox believer, and particularly to the ʿulamā who reject Sufism. Further verses take us more directly to the doctrines that Ismāʿīl professed. God's beauty is present in all creation, but the creator himself becomes manifest in human form. The human is the "name" (*ism*) and God is the "named" (*musammā*):

> Although all things give news of your beauty,
> You whose name (*ism*) is 'human' gives [us] a sign of the named (*müsemma*).[18]

Similarly, a beautiful human – expressed in a conventional literary form as "moon" – is equated to the Creator (*mükevvin*):

> Because your heart is Allah, your form is the Merciful (*Rahman*),
> Because your name is Creator (*mükevvin*), O moon, it is the creator of the universe (*halik-i ekvan*).[19]

In one couplet which recalls an instruction, reported at his trial, to his followers to look at him as they perform their prayers, Ismāʿīl goes so far as to suggest that it is God in the human figure before which worshippers should prostrate themselves:

> It is your person before whom prostration is made; before it all perform prostration,
> Whether lovers (*ʿaşık*) in the mosque or monks in church.[20]

The doctrine that God is visible in human form also appears in poems by Aḥmed the Camel Driver (*sārbān*), a successor to Oğlan Şeyḫ's father, Pīr ʿAlī, as *quṭb* of the *melamī*s. He too wrote using the conventions of Sufi literature, and most of his verse, however shocking it might have been to some orthodox believers, nonetheless remained within acceptable limits. The following couplet, for example, compares a non-Sufi, conventionally described as an "ascetic" (*zāhid*) to blind bats who cannot see God in the world around them:

> What does it matter if the ascetic closes his eyes to you, the heart-adorning light?
> The bat's eye cannot see the shining sun.[21]

Or:

> Those who do not sometimes drink the wine of unity from the beloved's hand
> Are like fish who do not know where the ocean is.[22]

These lines compare with a similar couplet by Aḥmed's contemporary, the poet Hayālī (d. 1557) who, despite a disreputable early life as a *kalender*, enjoyed the patronage of Sultan Suleyman:

> The world-adorner is in the world; they do not know how to look,
> Like fish in the sea who do not recognise the sea.[23]

In some places, however, Aḥmed clearly did cross the bounds of what was acceptable. He was, above all, quite open about finding God in the human form:

> O lover who wishes to behold the beloved,
> Look carefully at every human you see.[24]

Or, more explicitly:

> Know that the mirror of man is the form of the Merciful.
> Come to the mirror, look and see the Sultan there![25]

These lines express the belief that God is visible in the human figure. Unlike Oğlan Şeyḫ, however, he was careful to stress that this truth must remain hidden from the world at large:

> O Aḥmed, do not reveal the secret word to the ignorant.
> Do not imagine that the wellspring of life is fitting for animals![26]

To make it public was to invite arrest and execution.

While much of Ismāʿīl's and Aḥmed's verse adheres to the conventions of Sufi poetry, the idea that the divine appears in human form, inherent in the concept of "the name and the named" clearly goes beyond the boundaries of what is acceptable. It also points to the source of *melami* doctrine. The notion of the human face as the visible form of the divine is a commonplace of *ḥurūfī*-ism, evident most clearly in the poetry of Nesimi. For example:

> The deity (*ilāh*) saw His light in your face on the day of the eternal past (*ezel güni)*
> And said: 'I witness that there is no Deity (*ilāh*) but Allāh.[27]

Or:

> Your eyebrows, your lashes and your musky locks are the Mother of the Book ...[28]

It seems, therefore, that *ḥurūfī*-ism was a source of the doctrines found in the verses of Ismāʿīl and Aḥmed. Whether they accepted the whole panoply of *ḥurūfī* doctrine including a belief in a cabalistic interpretation of the letters of the Arabic alphabet or the idea, expressed in Nesimi's couplet above, that the lines on the human face are a representation of the "Mother of the Book", that is the *fātiḥa*, is less certain. Perhaps not, but a surviving poem by ʿAlaeddin of Vize, an acolyte of Aḥmed the Camel-Driver, does suggest an interest in the hidden significance of the letters of the Arabic alphabet:

> The purpose of the *alif* is that you should be [one] with God
> May you expect blessings through the *ba* of *bismi'llah* ...
> *Shin* tells [you] to beware of doubt (*shekk*), so that it does not deceive you ...
> *ʿAyn* is grace (*ʿināyet*). May you find it through God's favour ....[29]

However, some lines of Ismāʿīl's verse are by themselves enough to place him in Ghazālī's category of heretics who "have become so close to God" that all obligations to the Almighty have lapsed. Indeed, they have become so close that they believe themselves to be manifestations of the divine.

Further evidence of Ismāʿīl's doctrines comes from the statements of the witnesses at his trial in 1539.[30] These are uncorroborated, and the court register does not record how he answered the accusations but, as presented, they more than satisfy Ghazālī's definition of *kufr* and *zandaqa*. Ghazālī defines unbelief (*kufr*) as "refuting the Prophet and anything that he brought [to mankind]", amounting to a refutation of the revelation and the sharīʿa. The beliefs of Oğlan Şeyh, if we believe the witnesses at his trial, more than satisfied this definition. According to one witness, while not explicitly denying Muḥammad's prophethood, he seems to have denied any relevance it might have to the present time, stating: "In place of Muḥammad, there is someone in person. Let us show this with our affirmation and with our love". This is perhaps a suggestion that the revelatory role of the *quṭb* had superseded the role of the Prophet, since two witnesses, and also "his followers", testified in his presence that he had said: "My father [Pīr ʿAlī of Aksaray] is the *quṭb* and I am the *mahdī*. The Faith of anyone who does not follow us is unsound."

These statements amount to a disavowal of the revelatory role of the Prophet and, by implication, a rejection of the sharīʿa. This is abundantly confirmed in several of Ismāʿīl's reported statements on the question of *ḥarām* and *ḥalāl*. As Ghazālī had emphasised, an acceptance of the distinction between the two served as a test of faith and Ismāʿīl, if we are to accept the evidence of his trial, openly proclaimed that what the *sharīʿa* forbade was licit. Two witnesses claimed that he had said: "What the *sharīʿa* says is *ḥarām* is *ḥalāl*", and much of the evidence at his trial exemplifies this statement. The usual test of whether a person accepted the distinction was to question them on their view of wine-drinking and illicit sexual intercourse (*zinā*). To proclaim that either was *ḥalāl* amounted to rejection of the *sharīʿa*. Ismāʿīl's views on the matter were clear: "Wine," he is reported to have said, "is the pitcher of love. It is divine rapture (*cezbe-i ilahi*)," and "There is nothing in *zinā* and sodomy. Earth penetrates earth. These are the pleasures of love." One of the witnesses went further in suggesting that Ismāʿīl preached an unbridled licentiousness, available at least to himself: "When some dissolute persons (*fesaka*) said: 'Our wives and sons follow your path,' he said: 'Your wives, slave-boys (*oğlan*) and slave-girls are *ḥalāl* to you, and all of them are *ḥalāl* to men of God (*ehlu'llah*)'" Furthermore, Ismāʿīl denied not only the prohibitions of the Holy Law, but also its obligations, the acts of worship (*ʿibadat*) which are incumbent on all Muslims, declaring: "Fasting, *zakat* and Pilgrimage are like a fine (*cürm*)[31] on us. There is nothing in them."

If we are to believe the evidence of his trial, Ismāʿīl's public utterances more than satisfy Ghazālī's definition of *kufr*. Ghazālī, however, separately described the form of unbelief which he categorised as "absolute *zandaqa*", which he defined as the denial of the Creator and the Hereafter and, by this definition, Ismāʿīl was certainly a *zindīq*. He not only openly disavowed God, but his first recorded statement: "Mankind is pre-existent (*qadīm*)" strongly suggests that this was the case, and the final witness-statement from a certain Muhiyeddin, the most prolific of his accusers, reinforces this impression. Ismāʿīl, Muhiyeddin claims, said: "It is you who create sons and daughters. You come to a woman and make one, and then you say: 'God created it.'" Humans, therefore, create the human body, but the body acquires a soul by the process of metempsychosis: "The soul leaves one body and migrates to another." A belief in metempsychosis or *tanāsukh* implies the immortality of the soul in this world and, consequently, a denial of an afterlife in the Next. It is also contrary to fundamental dogma: anyone professing *tanāsukh* is an apostate (*murtadd*). Ismāʿīl, the witnesses report, not only denied fundamental beliefs about life after death – "There is no torment of the grave. There is no Questioning and Reckoning" – he even subjected them to mockery. According to a certain Hacci Turaḳ: "He said to people performing prayer: 'Aren't you doing this so you'll see Paradise? We wouldn't tie our donkey to what you call Paradise.'"

The words which the witnesses at his trial attribute to Ismāʿīl fit neatly into Ghazālī's categories of *kufr* and *zandaqa*. Ghazālī, however, went further, identifying the category of Sufis who "believe themselves to be so close to God that [the obligation] to perform prayer has lapsed, and wine-drinking, sin and consuming the sultan's property are permitted." These people, he stated, do greater harm to religion than do infidels, and "through them the gate of licentiousness is opened". A specific danger that these Sufis posed was their rejection of *ʿilm* – that is, knowledge of God and God's law embodied in the sharīʿa – and, with it, the rejection of the authority of the ʿulamā. Satan, Ghazālī wrote, has convinced Sufis that *ʿilm* is a veil concealing the truth, but that the matter is too great for the ʿulamā who do not understand that *dhauq*, the knowledge of God that comes from direct experience, is superior to *ʿilm*, the knowledge of God acquired through learning. Sufis such as these proclaim: "It is not a matter for *ʿilm*. It is a matter for *dhauq* ... They [the ʿulamā] remain in the fetters of the sharīʿa while to you the way of Truth (*ḥaqīqat*) is open." These Sufis in fact treat the word *danishmand* (learned man') as a term of abuse.[32]

It is here, perhaps, that Ghazālī comes closest to characterising Ismāʿīl's fundamental beliefs that led him to reject orthodox belief in the Creation, the Afterlife, the distinction between *ḥarām* and *ḥalāl* and other fundamentals of Sunni Islam. In the court record of his trial, the testimony of Muhiyeddin provides the clearest statement of what appears to be Ismāʿīl's underlying belief: "Every person is God," he is reported as saying. "It is He who appears in every [person's] form (*ṣūret*)." It seems, however, that God was manifest most clearly in the form of Ismāʿīl himself. After denying that a believer (*muʾmin*) need perform more than two *bayram* prayers a year, he tells his followers: "In those two *bayram* prayers, instead of prostration, look at me (*beni görün*)," hinting that God is manifest in his form and that the sight of God removes the need for formal prostration.

If the witness statements at his trial are to be credited, Ismāʿīl preached in public doctrines that laid him open to condemnation as an unbeliever, an apostate, a *zindīq* and as one who believed that divinity resided within himself. There is no record as to whether or how he defended himself against these charges. The only account of what seems to be his defence appears in a fatwa of Ebuʾs-suʿud which does not refer to the accused by name, but only to "the Sufi Zeyd". However, the Zeyd in question is, in all probability, to be identified with Ismāʿīl. Again, no evidence exists to corroborate the contents of the fatwa, and Ismāʿīl's statement appears in a form re-written either by Ebu'ʾs-suʿud himself or by an official in the fatwa-office. Furthermore, the fatwa addresses an issue that does not appear in the witness statements or in Ismāʿīl's own verse. This is the question of the legality of the whirling dance (*deveran*) that Ismāʿīl performed with his followers.

The opening statement of the fatwa presents the crux of the problem: "A leader of the Sufis, the preacher Zeyd, stands in mosques and pulpits and calls out in public: 'It is *ḥalāl* to dance in the circle of *zikr* with the intention of [performing] an act of worship [*ʿibāda*].'" Now the term *ʿibāda* refers to the obligatory "acts of worship" – *ṭahāra, ṣalāt, ṣaum, ḥajj, zakāt* – which the worshipper must perform with sincere intent (*niyya*). Without *niyya*, they are invalid. Here "the preacher Zeyd" is equating the *deverān* of his Sufis with a canonically required act of worship. This is the charge against the "Sufi Zeyd": the questioner then continues by laying out "Zeyd's" defence.

In claiming that the whirling *deverān* dance is an "act of worship" (*ʿibāda*) whose validity requires sincerity of intent, Ismāʿīl is mimicking the sharīʿa. His defence of this view is also in effect a pastiche of the orthodox mode of argument. He begins by quoting an *āya*: "Remember God (*faʾdhkurūʾllah*) when standing, sitting and lying on your sides" (Qurʾān 4.104), and arguing that it means "Remember God in all situations" and that "standing" includes dancing (*raqṣ*). From the Qurʾān, he moves to the *ḥadīth*, quoting from the *Sunan* of Abū Dāʾūd: "Whoever resembles a people is one of them." In *fiqh*, this *ḥadīth* serves to justify the rule that Muslims should distinguish themselves from non-Muslims not only in religious belief but in mundane matters such as appearance and dress. The "Sufi Zeyd", however, understands it differently. The *deverān*, he claims, resembles "the angels performing *deverān* around the Throne [of God]." Furthermore, he says, the Prophet himself danced (*raqṣ*), and "his blessed cloak fell from his shoulders." For Zeyd, therefore, the Qurʾān, *ḥadīth* and the *Sunna* of the Prophet all justify *deverān* as a legitimate, and even angelic activity. Then, after quoting the words of God and the Prophet in his defence, he moves to the next level of authority, contending that "of the great masters and noble sheikhs", men such as Shāfiʿī and Ghazālī had upheld this view, and that *deverān* had been practised "until our times." So far, Zeyd's sources of authority have been impeccable, however unorthodox his interpretations of them may have been. His final line of defence, however, was clearly unacceptable to his accusers. The questioner tells us that a "learned man" (*ʿālim*) had told Zeyd: "Muftis have on many occasions issued fatwas forbidding [*deverān*]," to which he had replied: "This is a state of *zevk* (*dhauq*). It is said: 'He who does not taste, does not know (*man lam yadhuq lam yaʿrif*).' They can tell us it is *ḥarām*, but we will not abandon what is *ḥalāl* for us." Here, by declaring what is *ḥarām* to be *ḥalāl*, Zeyd is effectively condemning himself, since failure to recognise the distinction is the hallmark of unbelief. He justified his rejection of the distinction between *ḥarām* and *ḥalāl* by citing the aphorism common to most Sufi groups: "He who does not taste does not know." In other words, the direct experience of the divine (*dhauq*) gives Sufis a knowledge (*ʿurf*) of God that is beyond the knowledge (*ʿilm*) of the ʿulamā encapsulated in the sharīʿa. Therefore, Ismāʿīl argues, *ḥarām* and *ḥalāl* do not apply to his followers. "Let them tell us it is forbidden: we will not abandon what is *ḥalāl* for us."

These, the questioner says are the arguments that Ismāʿīl brought in his defence and, having laid them out, asks Ebuʾs-suʿud: "Is Zeyd's reasoning from these proofs valid, and is it permissible to credit his opinion?" In reply Ebuʾs-suʿud demolishes Ismāʿīl's arguments one by one. In the first place, he argues, he has perverted the sense of the *āya*: "There is absolutely no indication in the noble *āya* that dancing is permitted. Anyone who uses the āya to claim that those ugly deeds are *ḥalāl* must renew their faith and marriage, because they have perverted the sense (*maʿnā*) of the Word of God and followed their own whim [and thus become apostates]". Here Ebuʾs-suʿud not only refutes Ismāʿīl's interpretation of the *āya*, he also states that allowing such a blasphemy to cross the tongue amounts to apostasy, making the speaker an unbeliever. To return to Islam from a state of unbelief, he must renew his faith and also renew his marriage which would have dissolved when he spoke the offending words. Ismāʿīl's next line of defence was the *ḥadīth* quoted from the *sunan* of Abū Dāʾūd: "Whoever resembles a people is one of them". Ebuʾs-suʿud in response admitted that the *ḥadīth* was sound, but denied that it could ever be a command to compare the actions of men to the actions of angels. Rather than resembling angels, the dancing of Sufis resembles the dancing of infidels, so by their actions they become unbelievers. Furthermore, he says, to attribute dancing to the Apostle of God is unbelief, since dancing is the action of the frivolous and: "It is written in books of fatwas that to attribute frivolity to one of the Prophets is unbelief (*kufr*), and to believe that the Noble Companions would perpetrate such an ugly deed is a lie and a slander (*iftirā*)." Ebuʾs-suʿud next discredits Ismāʿīl's claim that Shāfiʿī and Ghazālī had permitted dancing. He does this by distinguishing the dancing (*raqṣ*), such as Ismāʿīl performed with his followers from *samāʿ*. No *mujtahid* – such as Shāfiʿī – had said that *raqṣ* was *ḥalāl*: their disagreement was about *samāʿ*, the distinction between "dancing" and "*samāʿ*" being essentially one of their acceptability or non-acceptability to the ʿulamā. Ceremonial dancing of which the religious authorities approved was *samāʿ*: all other dancing was *raqṣ* and could lead to accusations of unbelief. Nor was it permissible to rely on the opinions of "Imam Ghazālī and such people in matters of *ijtihād*." Only the opinions of *mujtahids*, that is the founders of the *madhhabs*, were valid. Up to this point, Ismāʿīl has argued from impeccably orthodox sources: the Qurʾān, the *ḥadīth* and the opinions of the great Imams. He had, in Ebuʾs-suʿud's judgement abused these sources to arrive at a false conclusion, but worse still was his final assertion that he and his followers had a direct knowledge of God that exempted them from the observance of *ḥarām* and *ḥalāl*.

It now remained only to specify what penalty Ismāʿīl should receive, and in this Ebu's-suʿud follows Ḥanafī guidelines by specifying what penalty should follow what level of unbelief, and whether or not repentance would be accepted. Ismāʿīl was, in the first place, guilty of unbelief (*kufr*): "People who act satanically and preach to the people with devilish delusions and falsehoods are both erring (*ḍall*) and leading astray (*muḍill*), and have been declared infidels by the consensus of *mujtahids*. They should be restrained by imprisonment and the most severe *taʿzīr*." "Erring and leading astray" is a standard designation that al-Ghazali and others used for any Muslim who has strayed from the paths of righteousness. Anyone so convicted is guilty of unbelief, but repentance and punishment are enough to bring him or her back to the fold. *Taʿzīr* is a punishment, usually understood as a flogging, imposed at the discretion of the judicial authorities. Ismāʿīl however, by declaring that "the ʿulamā are not privy to the mysteries of the people of spiritual bliss (*ehl-i zevk*)' went far beyond merely 'erring and leading astray' and this, Ebu's-suʿud declares, makes him worse than an unbeliever: 'If he persists in this abomination, he is a *zindīq*. His execution is obligatory." Finally, Ebu's-su'ud answers a question which had exercised his juristic predecessors: "His repentance is not accepted after his arrest." A *zindīq* must repent before his arrest: if he does not do so, his execution is mandatory.[33]

Ismāʿīl, however, refused to repent and persisted in his claim that he possessed knowledge that transcended the knowledge of the ʿulamā, and that the obligations of *ḥalāl* and *ḥarām* did not apply to him and his followers. Since a refusal to recognise the distinction between *ḥalāl* and *ḥarām* was the hallmark of heresy, Ismāʿīl's failure to recant rendered his execution inevitable. So heinous was his offence in the eyes of the authorities that in future anyone declaring that Ismāʿīl's execution was unjust or professing allegiance to his sect should themselves suffer the same fate. This Ebu's-suʿud makes clear in a fatwa issued sometime after the event:

> Question: What should happen to Zeyd who says: 'The person known as Oğlan Şeyh who was previously executed was killed unjustly'?
> Answer: If he belongs to his sect, he should be executed.[34]

The execution of Ismāʿīl-i Maʿşūkī did not halt the progress of the Ottoman *melamis*. From the mid-sixteenth century, the sect spread from its birthplace in central Anatolia to the western Balkan peninsula where it became particularly strong in Bosnia. It was Bosnia, too, that furnished the movement with its second martyr, Ḥamza Bali, executed in Istanbul in 1561, and in Bosnia that the Ottoman authorities carried out extensive investigations and arrests of suspected *melamis* in the early 1580s. Persecution, however, did not eliminate the sect, and its leaders remained under suspicion into at least the early seventeenth century.

Summary

The Ottoman Empire rose to power in the fourteenth and fifteenth centuries in Anatolia and the Balkan peninsula. At this time, Islam had long been established as the dominant religion in the Iranian and Arab worlds but, in Anatolia, it was a recent import, and it reached the Balkan peninsula only with the Ottoman conquest from the mid-fourteenth century. The largely Turkish-speaking Muslim populations of Anatolia and the Balkans were evidently uneducated in the rudiments of the religion, as also, it seems, were many of the elite. From the fourteenth century, texts on Islamic law, ethics and other matters began to appear in Turkish to instruct the few who were literate, but could not read the Arabic or Persian texts necessary for learning and understanding the religion. Popular Islam, meanwhile, expressed itself in oral tales of saints, heroes and miracles, and was evidently receptive to antinomian doctrines within Islam – such as *ḥurūfī*-ism – coming into Anatolia from the east. In the century after 1400, however, the creation of a network of schools and madrasas in the Ottoman realms supported the growth of an educated corps of ʿulamā and the firm establishment of Islamic orthodoxy. By 1500, the Ottoman elite had assimilated the legal, theological, institutional, literary and cultural traditions of the old Islamic world. Finally with the conquest, in 1516–17, of the Mamluk Empire in Syria and Egypt and, with it, the annexation of the Holy Cities of Mecca, Medina and Jerusalem, the Ottoman sultan could claim to be the supreme leader of the Islamic world and the defender of Sunni orthodoxy. In his role as "the one who prepares the path for the precepts of the manifest sharīʿa and upholds the articles [of faith] of the firm religion", it became the duty of the sultan to protect the "true faith" from heresy, the more so since by the sixteenth century, the repudiation of orthodox Islam had become synonymous with the rejection of the rule of the Ottoman sultan.

This presented a problem. While unorthodox beliefs and practices flourished among Ottoman Muslims, only a few sectarian groups – most notably the *kızılbaş* who professed allegiance to the Safavid shah rather than to the Ottoman sultan – presented a political danger or a threat to established religion so serious that it appeared to undermine the rule of the dynasty. When a sect or person suspected of heresy came to the attention of the authorities, it was the duty of the ʿulamā to establish which side of the boundary between heresy and religious and political orthodoxy they fell; if condemned, whether they should be given the opportunity to repent; and what their punishment should be. In performing this task, they called on the centuries-old traditions of *fiqh*, and the heresiographies of Ghazālī and others.

The trial of Ismāʿīl Maʿşūkī demonstrates the procedure. It seems that the religious and judicial authorities in Istanbul initially tolerated his activities even – if we are to believe the records of the case which are all hostile to Ismāʿīl – when he preached in the city's mosques. What alarmed them most was quite probably the size and enthusiasm of the congregation that he attracted. This by itself would make him appear as a threat to public order. It was, however, the evidence of his trial that made his execution inevitable. The witness statements suggest that he abjured fundamental tenets of Islamic belief and that, in particular, he rejected the distinction between *ḥalāl* and *ḥarām*. This alone was sufficient proof that he did not recognise the authority either of the sharīʿa or of the sultan who claimed legitimacy as the defender and promulgator of the sharīʿa.

There is, however, no direct evidence that Ismāʿīl and the *melamis* declared their opposition to the Ottoman sultan in particular rather than simply to the sharīʿa and orthodox Islamic belief in general. There are, however, some tiny scraps of evidence that this was the case. Ismāʿīl's father was a *quṭb* of the Ottoman *melamis*, a sect whose members hid their identities in the knowledge that recognition would lead to persecution. It was Ismāʿīl's insistence, against his father's wishes, on preaching in public that led to his trial and execution. Furthermore, in addressing a poem to a human figure in whom he finds the divine, the *melami quṭb* Aḥmed the Camel-Driver hints at his rejection of Ottoman rule: "If I were to find one atom of the tidings from your ruby lips / I would not buy the Kingdom of Solomon (Süleyman) for the smallest coin".[35] Süleyman was the name of a Prophet, but it was also the name of the ruling sultan, Süleyman I. Finally, in Bosnia in June, 1582, witnesses testified against a group of suspected *melamis*, claiming that they belonged to "the sect of the heretic (*mulḥid*) called Ḥamza, who was previously executed after his heresy was proven." These, the witnesses stated, declared that "The sultanate is ours' and that one of them was 'known as the sultan (*sultan namına olub*)". This was a certain Mehmed b. Ḥasan whom the witnesses reported as saying: "I have become Sultan Mehmed in place of Sultan Ḥamza". A later document, dated August/September, 1582, seeks rewards for the men who had arrested these heretics (*mulḥid*) "who claimed the sultanate and had appointed a sultan, vizier, kadiʿasker, kadi, defterdār and çavuş from among their number."[36] Vizier, kadiʿasker, kadi, defterdār and çavuş are the titles of officers of state serving under the Ottoman sultan, and their appearance in the witness statements suggests that – unless these are complete fabrications – the *melamis* really did forswear allegiance to the Ottoman sultan and imagined their own little conclaves, meeting in secret, as the legitimate government.

Notes

1 Ö.L. Barkan, *Kanunlar*, Istanbul: Bürhaneddin Matbaası (1943), 296, pl. XXXV (autograph).

2 Elke Eberhard, *Die Osmanische Polemik gegen die Safawiden im 16. Jahrhundert nach arabischen Handschriften*, Freiburg-im-Breisgau: Klaus Schwarz Verlag (1970); Colin Imber, 'Ottoman propaganda against the *kızılbaş*: Sarı Görez, Ebū's-suʿūd and Celālzāde' in Robert Gleave and István Kristó-Nagy (eds.), *Legitimate and Illegitimate Violence in Islamic Thought*, Edinburgh: Edinburgh University Press (2018), 204–214.

3 Al-Ghazali, *Faiṣal al-Tafriqa bain al-Islām wa al-Zandaqa*, Cairo: Maṭbaʿa al-Saʿāda (1907), 4.

4 Al-Ghazali, *Faiṣal*, 15.

5 Al-Kāsānī, *Badāʾiʿ al-Ṣanāʾiʿ fī Tartīb al-Sharāʾiʿ*, Beirut: Dār al-Kitāb al-ʿArabī (1982), vol. 7, 134.

6 These and numerous further examples of 'expressions of unbelief' can be found in any work of Hanafi *fiqh*, under *Alfāẓ al-kufr*.

7 Ibn Humām, *Fatḥ al-Qadīr*, Cairo: Maṭbaʿa Muṣṭafā al-Bābī al-Ḥalabī (1972) vol. 6, 70

8 Al-Bābartī, *Sharḥ al-ʿInāya ʿalā al-Hidāya*, Cairo: Maṭbaʿa Muṣṭafā al-Bābī al-Ḥalabī (1972) vol. 6, 72.

9 Al-Ghazali, *Faiṣal*, 15.

10 Quoted in Kemālpaşazāde, *al-Risāla fī mā yataʿallaqu bi-lafẓ al-zindīq*, trans. A.Y. Ocak in *Osmanlı Toplumunda zındıklar ve mülhidler*, Istanbul Tarih Vakfı Yurt Yayınlar (1998), 350–351

11 Al-Ghazālī, ed. and trans: Otto Pretzl, *Die Streitschrift des Gazālī gegen die Ibāhīja*, Munich: Bayerische Akademie der Wissenschaften (1935), 26/50.

12 M.E. Düzdağ (ed.), *Şeyhülislâm Ebussuud Efendi Fetvalar Işığında 16. Asır Türk Hayatı*, Istanbul: Enderun Kitabevi (1972), 970.

13 Al-Ghazali, *Faiṣal*, 16.

14 Nevʿīzīde ʿAṭāʾī, *Dhail Shaqāʾiq al-Nuʿmāniyya*, Istanbul: Matbaʿa-i ʿĀmire (1851/20), 87–88.

15 A.Y. Ocak in *Osmanlı Toplumunda Zındıklar ve Mülhidler*, Istanbul: Tarih Vakfı Yurt Yayınları (1998), 274–290. Professor Ocak provides the most detailed examination of heresies and heretics in the Ottoman Empire between the fifteenth and seventeenth centuries. His account of the career and execution of Ismaʿil-i Maʿşuki/Oğlan Şeyh is particularly important, as his discovery of a dated court record relating to his trial has enabled him to correct the traditionally accepted chronology of the event and to provide an insight into Ismaʿil's doctrines. I am especially grateful for his inclusion in the book of a facsimile and transliteration of this document, alongside other important archival records.

16 Abdülbakî Gölpınarlı, *Melâmilik ve Melâmîler*, Istanbul: Devlet Matbaası (1931), 51.

17 Abdülbakî Gölpınarlı, *Melâmilik*, 52.

18 Abdülbakî Gölpınarlı, *Melâmilik*, 51.

19 Abdülbakî Gölpınarlı, *Melâmilik*, 53.

20 Abdülbakî Gölpınarlı, *Melâmilik*, 52.

21 Abdülbakî Gölpınarlı, *Melâmilik*, 59.

22 Abdülbakî Gölpınarlı, *Melâmilik*, 59.

23 E.J.W. Gibb, *A History of Ottoman Poetry*, London: Luzac (1909), vol. 6, 131

24 Abdülbakî Gölpınarlı, *Melâmilik*, 59.

25 Abdülbakî Gölpınarlı, *Melâmilik*, 59.

26 Abdülbakî Gölpınarlı, *Melâmilik*, 59.

27 K.E. Kürkçüoğlu, *Seyyid Nesîmî Divanından Seçmeler*, Istanbul: Millî Eğitim Basımevi (1973), 90.

28 E.J.W. Gibb, *A History*, vol. 6, 37

29 Abdülbakî Gölpınarlı, *Melâmilik*, 208–209.

30 For a facsimile and transliteration of the document recording the witness statements, see A.Y. Ocak, *Osmanlı Toplumunda*, appendix V, 354–357.

31 In Ottoman administrative usage, *cürm* ('crime, offence') sometimes acquires the sense of 'fine for a misdemeanour', as in the expression *cürm ü cinayet*. That is perhaps its meaning here.

32 Al-Ghazali, *Die Streitschrift*, 15/36,

33 M.E. Düzdağ (ed.), *Şeyhülislâm Ebussuud Efendi Fetvaları Işığında 16. Asır Türlk Hayatı*, Istanbul: Enderun Kitabevi (1972), 85–86.

34 M.E. Düzdağ (ed), *Şeyhülislâm Ebussuud*, 196.

35 Abdülbakî Gölpınarlı, *Melâmilik*, 59.

36 A.Y.Ocak, *Osmanlı Toplumunda*, 369.

Works cited

Bābartī, al-, *Sharḥ al-'Ināya 'alā al-Hidāya*, Cairo: Maṭba'a Muṣṭafā al-Bābī al-Ḥalabī (1972) vol. 6.

Düzdağ, M.E (ed.), *Şeyhülislâm Ebussuud Efendi Fetvalar Işığında 16. Asır Türk Hayatı*, Istanbul: Enderun Kitabevi (1972).

Ghazālī, al-, ed. and trans: Otto Pretzl, *Die Streitschrift des Gazālī gegen die Ibāhīja*, Munich: Bayerische Akademie der Wissenschaften (1935), 26/50.

Ghazali, al-, *Faiṣal al-Tafriqa bain al-Islām wa al-Zandaqa*, Cairo: Maṭba'a al-Sa'āda (1907).

Gibb, E.J.W, *A History of Ottoman Poetry*, London: Luzac (1909), vol. 6.

Gölpınarlı, Abdülbakî, *Melâmilik ve Melâmîler*, Istanbul: Devlet Matbaası (1931)

Kāsānī, al-, *Badā'i' al-Ṣanā'i' fī Tartīb al-Sharā'i'*, Beirut: Dār al-Kitāb al-'Arabī (1982), vol. 7.

Kemālpaşazāde, *al-Risāla fī mā yata'allaqu bi-lafẓ al-zindīq*, trans. A.Y. Ocak in *OsmanlıToplumunda zındıklar ve mülhidler*, Istanbul Tarih Vakfı Yurt Yayınlar (1998), 350—351.

Kürkçüoğlu, K.E., *Seyyid Nesîmî Divanından Seçmel*er, Istanbul: Millî Eğitim Basımevi (1973).

Nev'īzīde 'Aṭā'ī, *Dhail Shaqā'iq al-Nu'māniyya*, Istanbul: Matba'a-i 'Āmire (1851/).

Ocak, A.Y., *Osmanlı Toplumunda Zındıklar ve Mülhidler*, Istanbul: Tarih Vakfı Yurt Yayınları (1998).

Islam's Margins: Ahl-i Haqq, Angels and Peacocks, and the Marginal Scholars who Loved Them

Martin van Bruinessen
Utrecht University

Abstract
This chapter is a tribute to my late friend Peter Lamborn Wilson, aka Hakim Bey (d. 2022), and to the late Vladimir A. Ivanow (d. 1970), two marginal scholars who spent years in self-chosen exile in Iran and shared a fascination with Ismāʿīlism and the small heterodox communities that might be influenced by it, and who in different ways contributed to my motivation to carry out field research among the Ahl-i Haqq of Gūrān, reputedly the most antinomian community that could be found in Iran. I have often had reason to revisit Ivanow's writings, especially his book *The Truth-Worshippers of Kurdistan*, while over the years I have kept corresponding with Wilson about the place of Satan and the Peacock Angel in the cosmology and anthropology of the Ahl-i Haqq and the Yezidis. I shall focus on two aspects of the Ahl-i Haqq religion: the place in their pantheon of seven angelic beings (*haft tan*) who appear in human incarnations in each cycle of history, and the social and ritual role of holy lineages (*khānadān*) in Ahl-i Haqq communities. Both suggest similarities or perhaps historical connections with other communities such as Yazidis and Alevis, as well as a possible connection with pre-Islamic Iranian religions. Some authors have claimed that the Ahl-i Haqq religion is, beneath a thin Islamic veneer, essentially a survival of Zoroastrianism or a "popular" variant of Iranian religion. I shall argue that there is a much more pervasive influence of early Islam in the Ahl-i Haqq religion (as well as Yezidism and Alevism) than these scholars are willing to admit.

Keywords: Ahl-i Haqq; Kurdistan; Yezidism; Alevism; heterodoxy; Vladimir Ivanow; Peter Lamborn Wilson.

A Satanic shrine in southern Kurdistan

The Gūrān district in western Iran, immediately north of the Baghdad-Kermanshah highway, is the location of some of the most important shrines and holy sites of the Ahl-i Haqq.[1] The shrine of Bābā Yādegār at Sarāne in this district is, in fact, the one most frequently visited by the devotees of this religion from all over Iran. It attracts even more pilgrims than the shrine of the religion's reputed founder Soltān Sahāk at Nosūd in the Hawramān district further north. Bābā Yādegār, who flourished in the early sixteenth century, seems to have been Soltān Sahāk's successor to the leadership of the new sect, and quite possibly it was he who institutionalised the new dispensation. There are *kalāms*, religious poems of the Ahl-i Haqq, relating his miraculous birth from the mouth of his virgin mother, but he was definitely a historical person, for we have a document recording a quite material grant of land in his name (Mokri 1963). Bābā Yādegār is the object of great veneration, not for his role in organising the religion but because he is believed to have been the incarnation of a high spiritual being emanated from and almost indistinguishable from the Divine Essence, which had Itself been incarnate in Soltān Sahāk.

On the way to Sarane, near the village of Zarde where the Dālāhū mountains begin to rise, the pilgrims pass by another grave. It has no domed shrine erected over it; it is marked by a rectangular raised platform around three meters in length, covered with dark green glazed tiles, in an enclosure surrounded by low walls. This is said to be the grave of Dāwūd, another companion of Soltān Sahāk. Some of the pilgrims from far away may pause here to offer *niyāz* (an offering of sweetmeats and/or pomegranates), for all sub-sects of the Ahl-i Haqq recognise Dāwūd as the incarnation of one of the four archangels who accompany the Deity in each of his successive earthly manifestations.[2] Others prefer not to linger here, for they know of the peculiar popularity of this grave among some of the local people, who identify Dāwūd with Satan, and who visit this grave to request the Disobedient Angel's assistance in their worldly affairs.

I first heard of this "devil-worshipping" sub-sect of the Ahl-i Haqq (henceforth: AH) from a member of the group around the Tehrani AH master Bahram Elahi (the grandson of the reformer Hājjī Niʿmatullāh Jayhūnābādī). This man gave me an adventurous account of his pilgrimage to Bābā Yādegār, claiming that the area was infested by devil-worshipping robbers and bandits, who left no one unharmed but those belonging to the AH religion, whom they considered as brothers. Later I was to hear similar stories from other AH and from Twelver Shiʿi Muslims in Kermanshah province. Bahram Elahi even claimed that he had watched a group of Qalkhānī tribesmen (who have a well-established reputation for robbery) say prayers at Dāwūd's grave and had heard them promise Satan a part of the spoils if he would assist them in their exploit. Other informants made much of a few murders that had taken place at the holy places in the Gūrān district several years before.

Once I became acquainted with the Gūrān, I found the evil reputation that they have, even in the eyes of their co-religionists, to be highly exaggerated. In reality, robberies were not so frequent and most of the Qalkhānī, though resisting government interference in their affairs, made their living in other ways. And murders were, in fact, very rare, although they are a recurrent theme in the mythology of these AH. The real reason for the bad reputation of the Gūrān is probably their heterodoxy, embarrassing especially to those AH who prefer to present their religion as an esoteric sect within Twelver Shiʿi Islam.

Most of the other AH sub-sects claim that the Gūrān's heterodox beliefs and practices, such as the veneration of Satan and other elements to be discussed below, are recent developments, deviations from and corruptions of the original doctrine. S.C.R. Weightman, who was in contact with the reformed branch in Tehran and who also visited the town of Kerend in the Gūrān district, attributed the remarkable veneration for Satan to the influence of a pocket of Yezidis whom he found living in the neighbourhood (Weightman 1964). I myself could not find those Yezidis, nor had any of my informants ever heard of them. Weightman probably mistook a sub-sect of the Gūrān AH who are even greater partisans of Dāwūd than the others for Yezidis because they call Satan by his Yezidi name of Malak Tāwūs. Both this name, however, and some of the beliefs objected to by the other AH groups are occasionally referred to in the scriptures of the sect, and therefore cannot be dismissed as very recent borrowings. There is reason to believe, as I shall try to show below, that at least some of the heterodox beliefs of the Gūrān, not shared by the other AH, represent an older layer of religious ideas that had been suppressed for some time but survived in oral tradition and later surfaced again. The most striking instance of this, to be discussed below, is the dualistic cosmology that has over the past century come to be embraced by some sections of the Gūrān, and in which we may perceive the echo of an older Iranian religion.

An apology of Satan

My first contact with the Gūrān AH was accidental. I spent some time in Kermanshah for other reasons in the winter of 1975–76, but my bushy, untrimmed moustache drew the attention of some AH villagers from the Gūrān district, who enquired whether I belonged to their religion – the long moustache is the major exterior sign by which the AH recognise each other, like the Yezidis and the Qizilbash (Alevis). They took me to the Kermanshah *jamkhāne*, the AH equivalent of a mosque or *khānaqāh*, where I was very hospitably received although I told my hosts that I was nothing but a curious outsider. One of the persons whom I met there, a young man whom I shall call ʿAlī Kāka'ī, volunteered to take me to Bābā Yādegār and the other holy places. Although still young, ʿAlī appeared to be respected by people who were much older because he knew many *kalāms*, the religious hymns in which AH doctrine is contained. Moreover, he was an excellent musician on the *temmūr* (tanbur), the two-stringed long-necked lute that is played to accompany the singing of

AH kalāms. The *kalām-khwān,* singer of kalām, is something of a religious authority among the AH because of his supposedly great knowledge and understanding of doctrines. A kalām-khwān of ʿAlī's accomplishment is moreover often believed to be inspired by a higher spirit. ʿAlī therefore was the ideal person to introduce me to his community, and we set off that very day.

On one of the first occasions that we were alone, I asked ʿAlī what precisely was the attitude of his people towards Satan. Muslims in Kermanshah, pointing at my moustache, had jokingly asked if I was a *shaytānī,* so I inferred that this was a pejorative name for (some of) the AH. I also had the impression that the AH were not exactly pleased to be called by that name, and I therefore put my question as carefully and indirectly as I could. To my surprise, however, ʿAlī proudly told me that yes, certainly, he was a *shaytān-parast,* a devil-worshipper. This did not imply that he paid homage to the evil principle, however: he insisted that it is only the calumny of mankind, especially the *ahl-i sharīʿat,* that proclaims Satan to be the Lord of Evil. To explain this, ʿAlī told me a radical variant of the well-known tale of Satan's fall:

> When God desired to manifest Himself, He first created, out of His own light, the major angels. One of His most beloved angels was Malak Tāwūs, the Peacock Angel, whom mankind now calls Shaytān. Malak Tāwūs was always in God's immediate company, a close witness to the entire process of Creation. When God had completed his great work by moulding, out of clay, the first man, he ordered all His other creatures to kneel before this Adam. Malak Tāwūs, as is well known, refused to do so, and with good reason. For, ʿAlī asked rhetorically, isn't it absurd for an angel, whose substance is of the Divine Light, to prostrate himself before one created out of base matter? God's order was clearly unjust, and Malak Tāwūs was right in disobeying ("If your king gave you an unjust command", another Ahl-i Haqq friend later remarked to me, "wouldn't you also refuse to obey?").

ʿAlī suspected, in fact, that God's order had been a test, which all the other angels, obedient but uncritical, had failed, while only Malak Tāwūs had shown himself worthy of God's love. Opinion among the AH was divided, ʿAlī added, as to whether Malak Tāwūs had ever been punished by God for his disobedience; he himself belonged to those who believed that this was just slander invented by man. Man, of course, resented the Peacock Angel's refusal to recognise him as superior. One man (was it Adam himself?) even attempted to achieve by deceit what God's command had not accomplished. He invited the angel to a meal in his house, and made the door opening so low that the angel would have to bend low upon entering. Malak Tāwūs, however, saw through this stratagem and reprimanded man for his arrogance. Ever since, men have resentfully called him Shaytān and Lord of Evil, and accused him of tempting mankind to sin. Thereby they do him great injustice. In reality, God has appointed precisely this Peacock Angel as the overseer of all affairs of this world. God himself does not directly intervene in the world (except when He manifests Himself

> in another human incarnation), leaving this to Malak Tāwūs, "whom we know as Dāwūd". Any person seeking supernatural assistance should therefore, logically, direct himself to Malak Tāwūs.

This version of the Iblīs theme is reminiscent of Sufi re-interpretations of the Qur'anic story but it is more radical than any of them: Satan's association with evil is denied, and his lordship over the world is positively appreciated.[3]

The Peacock Angel is considered as one of the embodiments of a pure spiritual being that accompanied the Deity in all of His earthly manifestations. In the time of Soltān Sahāk, this spirit was incarnate in Dāwūd, and the Gūrān most commonly refer to him by that name, even in his other manifestations: "In the time of Hazrat-i 'Alī, Dāwūd was ['Alī's groom] Qanbar".[4] Dāwūd was also Emām Reżā, the eighth imam, as well as Shams-i Tabrīzī, and a spark of Dāwūd's spiritual essence manifested itself in Iran's great king, Nādir Shah (reigning 1736–47). Some of the Gūrān (as well as other AH) also identify Dāwūd with the Hebrew prophet David, the bringer of the second holy book, the *Zabūr* (the Psalms of David). One collection of kalāms much beloved of these Dāwūd-worshippers is therefore called *Zabūr-i ḥaqīqat*, "the Psalms of Truth". This name connects these kalāms with Dāwūd and therefore, among others, with Satan. Most of the kalāms that 'Alī was to sing for me were from these, Satan's songbooks.

The veneration of Shaytān (or rather, his identification with Dāwūd, who had long been venerated) and his disassociation from evil seems to be a relatively recent development, and one about which there is as yet no full unanimity even among the Gūrān themselves. It seems to be correlated with another development in the cosmology of one faction among the Gūrān, by which certain other spirits in the AH pantheon are being propelled into the role of dark and evil forces, opposed to the spirits of light. The result is a world-view strongly reminiscent of older Iranian dualism. This development in AH cosmology has sown division among the Gūrān, for both groups of spiritual beings are associated with concrete social groups. Those Gūrān whose initiatory affiliations are with the second group of spirits can do little but deny the evil aspect of the latter and de-emphasise the dualism. We thus find among the Gūrān two rival cosmologies, one with dualist, the other with monotheist overtones.

Incarnation in Ahl-i Haqq doctrine

One of the central tenets of the AH religion is the belief in a succession of divine incarnations. In each of His manifestations, the Deity is at least accompanied by the four Archangels who were His first emanations or creatures and usually by a number of less clearly defined secondary emanations as well. The very first manifestation of the Divine Essence and Its four Companions was as God the Creator (called Khawandagār in the AH tradition) and the four Archangels known to Islam. The subsequent manifestations took place in the world and in historical time.

The AH recognise various different forms or degrees of manifestation, from the full incarnation to the temporary indwelling in an otherwise ordinary human being. In the case of incarnation proper, the Deity or Angel assumes the form of a human being (or occasionally an animal, or even an inanimate object) just like one might don a garment. This is, in fact, the metaphor explicitly used: the human manifestation is called the Deity or Angel's *jāma* or *dūn*, both of which mean "garment." Another popular metaphor, referring to the succession of manifestations, is that of a duck diving under water and resurfacing elsewhere. For this process of successive incarnations, the AH use the terms *dūna dūn* or *tanāsukh*, the latter being the common Arabic term for the transmigration of souls. It is, incidentally, not only the Deity and the higher spirits who continually re-appear. All human souls are subject to a similar process of transmigration, which is referred to by the same terms. Opinions on the modalities of the process of reincarnation (e.g. the possibility of reincarnation in lower and higher classes of beings, the time span between successive incarnations, the number of incarnations each soul has to pass through) diverge widely between the various sub-sects of the AH and even between members of the same sub-sect. My Gūrān informants all gave conflicting answers when my questioning became too detailed, and hardly any of them showed an interest in such questions at all.

The second type of manifestation is that in which otherwise normal human beings are temporarily (or even permanently) inhabited by the Deity or an Angel. These have thus an ordinary human soul, but "are" in a way also the Deity or Angel that has invaded them. Such persons are, appropriately, called Shāh-mehmān, Dāwūd-mehmān, etc.: "host to the King (i.e., the Deity)", "host to Dāwūd"; the corresponding terms for proper incarnations are Shah-maẓhar, "manifestation of the King", etc. The process of indwelling is also referred to, among the literate AH, by the term *ḥulūl*, well known from Muslim speculative philosophy and often associated with the mystic al-Ḥallāj (executed in 309/922). Not surprisingly, the AH interpret al-Ḥallāj's well-known utterance *anā 'l-ḥaqq* as meaning that he was Shāh-mehmān. There are again various interpretations of what precisely *ḥulūl* is and how it works. It seems to be generally accepted that in this case, as opposed to incarnation proper, only a spark (*zarre*) of the Divine Essence establishes itself in its human vehicle.

Many of the written texts seem to assume implicitly that the indwelling is permanent. Among the Gūrān, on the other hand, I heard cases described where the divine presence only manifested itself in moments of spiritual rapture. In at least one case, the manifestation might be better described in terms of spirit possession. The dervish and poet Nowrūz used to enter trance states and then dictate poetry of which he remembered nothing after returning to his normal state. The poems were believed to be inspired by the spirit that took temporary possession of Nowrūz's body, in this case Dāwūd, alias the angel Mīkā'īl. Perhaps we should regard such spirit possession as a third, distinct type of manifestation.

Four Angels, *haft tan*, and Satan's ambivalence

In the cosmology and sacred history of the AH, not *allhaft tan* (the main seven angelic beings) receive equal prominence. The Deity himself and the four archangels (*chār malak*) are unambiguously identified by name in each of the cycles of history, but the identity and role of the others is often not clear. Some scholars have wished to perceive in the *haft tan* none other than the seven Zoroastrian angels, the Amesha Spenta, a theory that is much favoured by Iranian nationalists.[5] The prominence of the *chār malak*, even in the most elaborately developed myths of the cycle of Soltān Sahāk, as well as their names (Binyāmīn, Dāwūd, Pīr Mūsī, and Mustafā-i Dāwūdān, identified with Jibrīl, Mīkā'īl, Isrāfīl, and ʿAzrā'īl) clearly indicate the AH angels' derivation from Muslim cosmology. Unambiguous traces of Iranian religion are less easy to identify.

It is only the Gūrān and some of their southern neighbours who identify Shaytān with Dāwūd. None of the other AH communities do this, and for most of them Shaytān remains the Fiend. At first sight it might seem strange that Dāwūd, who is after all one of the Archangels (Mīkā'īl), could also be identified with Shaytān (whose angelic name is, in the Muslim tradition, ʿAzāzil). The Gūrān never make an explicit identification of Shaytān and Mīkā'īl; these angels belong to different sets of myths, which have not yet been unified and made consistent. This could mean that the adoption of Shaytān as one of the avatars of Dāwūd is a relatively recent development.

As said before, the Gūrān sometimes call Shaytān by the name of Malak Tāwūs, which is also the name by which the Yezidis know him (though usually in the form Tāwūs-ē Malak). This name, although not often occurring in writing, can be attested among the Gūrān from at least the second half of the nineteenth century.[6] In the early twentieth century, one sub-sect among the Gūrān was reportedly called Tāwūsī, another (or perhaps the same subgroup?) Dāwūdī; the former, or "Peacock sect" were said to venerate Satan. The missionary Stead, to whom we owe this piece of information, does not mention the name of Malak Tāwūs but quotes, as an explanation of the latter appellation, the well-known tale that the Peacock was the guardian of Paradise, who let Satan in so that he could meet Adam and Eve (Stead 1932).

For lack of unambiguous evidence, we cannot decide whether the AH borrowed the name of Malak Tāwūs from the Yezidis; there is some evidence that the spiritual leaders of the Gūrān AH sent envoys to various other heterodox communities as far as Asia Minor. However, it is more likely that both derived the concept of the Peacock Angel from mediaeval Islamic cosmology rather than some unidentified pre-Islamic Iranian tradition. The widely read cosmography*ʿAjā'ib al-makhlūqāt* ("Marvels of Creation") by the thirteenth-century author Zakariyā Qazwīnī has a long chapter on the various angels, in which the angel Gabriel (Jibrīl) is given the honorific title of *tāwūs al-malā'ika*, "peacock of the angels." Here the peacock appears to have unambiguously positive connotations, but when the title was adopted by the AH it became attached to another angel and was given more ambiguous, Satanic connotations.[7]

The earliest scholarly works in which the name of Malak Tāwūs occurs in connection with the AH rather than the Yezidis, are V. Ivanow's two annotated editions of Persian-language AH texts (Ivanow 1948, 1953). Unlike the kalām themselves, which did not circulate outside the AH community because they were typically in the Gūrānī language, these texts were simple renderings of AH myths in Persian prose, indicating that there had been contacts between the "popular" dervish milieu and AH communities. Ivanow comments on a passage in which Malak Tāwūs appears in an eschatological context as a Satanic being, king of the creatures of fire. None of his Persian AH interlocutors, Ivanow notes, knew Satan by this peacock name; he was usually referred to as Dāwūd-i Rash, "Black Dawud."[8]

More than other scholars, it was the Ismaʿili specialist V. Ivanow who insisted on the origins of the AH religion in heterodox Islam rather than pre-Islamic Iranian religion. Although he acknowledged possible influences of Mithraism and heterodox Christianity as well, he was convinced that the major formative influence had been from post-Alamut Ismāʿīlism. He pointed specifically to the Central Asian Ismāʿīlī text *Umm al-kitāb*, in which he found very similar cosmological concepts, as well as passages on the insurrection of the disobedient angels and the struggle between Adam and Satan.[9] My reading of Ivanow's *Truth-Worshippers of Kurdistan* with its fascination for ordinary people's heterodox religiosity was, more than Minorsky's more dispassionate scholarly articles on the AH religion (Minorsky 1920, 1921), a major factor that pushed me towards my own field work among the AH of western Kermanshah.

Vladimir Ivanow

Ivanow (St Petersburg 1886–Tehran 1970) prepared for life as an armchair orientalist but revolution and war propelled him into the rather more adventurous life of the itinerant scholar, in close contact with the people about whom he was to write.

When I lived intermittently in Tehran myself in the years 1974–76, preparing for fieldwork in Kurdistan or briefly retiring from the field, I first became acquainted with Ivanow's work, thanks to the rich library of the British Institute of Persian Studies. Having travelled among the Kurds of Khurasan myself, I found Ivanow's articles on the Kurds and other ethnic groups of Khurasan and on the Kurdish dialect spoken in Khurasan (Ivanow 1926, 1927) particularly impressive, and I got the impression from his work on the AH that he had been something of a wandering dervish himself, collecting scraps of knowledge wherever fate took him. I heard stories of his final years as a lonely, aging man living in bare quarters at Tehran University, and I regretted not having had the occasion to meet him. Only later did I learn more about his life, from the bio-bibliographical tributes written by Farhad Daftary, from Ivanow's own posthumously published autobiography, and from Ivanow's correspondence with Henry Corbin, published by Sabine Schmidtke.[10]

Ivanow had spent several periods in Iran, at the beginning and end of his career. Between 1912 and 1914 he worked as a young employee at several branches of the Russian Imperial Bank in Persia, at first in Birjand and later in Kermanshah. His articles on the Kurds and other ethnic groups of Khurasan were based on his stay in Birjand, when he met many dervishes and carried out linguistic fieldwork on various Persian and Kurdish dialects. In Kermanshah he may have had his first encounters with Ahl-i Haqq, or at least have heard stories about them. Returning to Russia, he spent the war years as assistant keeper of manuscripts at the Academy of Sciences in St Petersburg. This was where he first became acquainted with Ismāʿīlī literature. He was twice sent to Bukhara to collect more Arabic and Persian manuscripts. His first mission was very successful, but by the time of his second mission it was 1918, Russia was in the grip of revolution and civil war, and in Bukhara the Basmachi uprising against Russian rule made his work impossible.

Unable to return to St Petersburg he travelled to Mashhad, where he found employ in the service of the British General W.E.R. Dickson, who had commanded the Anglo-Persian forces in East Persia during the Great War. When Dickson and his troops left Persia, Ivanow joined them to India, where he was to spend four decades.

He found modest employ cataloguing the Persian manuscript collection of the Asiatic Society of Bengal, collected manuscripts in various parts of India himself, and also made trips to Persia, where he visited and investigated Alamut, the Ismāʿīlī fortresses of Ḥasan Ṣabbāḥ (d. 518/1124). In 1930 Ivanow resettled in Bombay, where he had contacts in the Ismāʿīlī Khoja community. From 1931 onward he was employed by the [Third] Āqā Khān for research on literature, history and doctrine of the Ismāʿīlīs. The Ismaili Society, which he helped establish and of which he was the honorary secretary as well as the editor of the book series, published many of his editions and translations of Ismāʿīlī texts. In 1959, with the consent of the new [Fourth, since 1957] Āqā Khān, he moved to Tehran, where he lived very frugally in a guest room at the university, and where he died in 1970.

Ivanow loved manuscripts and philological work, and he was fascinated by Ismāʿīlism, but he was certainly not a believer; his interest was purely intellectual, and sceptical. He must have been a lonely and increasingly bitter man, as becomes clear from his letters to Henry and Stella Corbin (edited by Schmidtke 1999). That correspondence is worth quoting from. It begins with a letter by Henry Corbin, who had recently, in 1946, established the Department of Iranology in the Institut Franco-Iranien. Corbin wrote to Bombay to introduce himself and his new Department which, he announced, was to focus on the study of Perso-Islamic mysticism. Therefore he was much interested in the Ismāʿīlī Society (which was also established in 1946) and wished to subscribe to all its publications. Ivanow answered in the blunt style we also find in some of his publications. He enquired what other departments the French Institute had and whether they were also engaged in more interesting things than mysticism: "I believe the study of mysticism, unless it is merely silly talk, can only be done by qualified psychiatrists, by clinical methods. It is a pity that while the East is changing with such tremendous speed, and many old forms decay and pass away almost incessantly, no more urgent and important matter is found meriting study than mystic nonsense. Pity to waste time on this" (Schmidtke 1999, 21).

When Ivanow published *Truth-Worshippers*, his edition and analysis of "popular" AH texts in Persian, Corbin sent him a letter full of praise (but in a somewhat haughty and hollow, French rhetorical style), congratulating him on noting the possible influence of Mithraism and Christian sects on the AH.[11] In that same year, Corbin himself published his edition and analysis of Nāṣir-i Khusrow's (d. between 465/1072 and 471/1078) *Jāmiʿ al-ḥikmatayn*, a work of which he was quite proud. Ivanow responded by sending Corbin his draft of an as yet unpublished book review that lacked the polish and praise of Corbin's style. Ivanow basically wrote that he found this a useless book, for Nāṣir-i Khusrow was not an original thinker but an unsophisticated epigone of the classical Ismāʿīlī literature of the Fātimid period. It would have been better to spend all that effort, he asserted, on more serious works such as those by Ḥamīd al-Dīn al-Kirmānī, which still awaited study.

Ivanow was himself very productive in collecting and making available numerous Ismāʿīlī texts. His commentaries were not the product of a highly cultured and imaginative mind as Corbin's but were based on his extensive fieldwork and reading of manuscripts. He had explored Alamut on foot, making its history tangible and locating the graves of its rulers; and he was used to interacting with people at the grassroots level in a way the urbane Corbin could not.

In all his letters, Ivanow showed respect for Corbin's philosophical scholarship and that of his teacher Massignon (unlike the work of many other orientalists, about whom he was scathing in his criticism), but there was always an unspoken subtext of irritation at Corbin's display of erudition and his verbose French style. Ivanow's brusque style must have been deliberate, as if demonstrating the different style of philology that distinguished his work from Corbin's. He was very proud of his own work on unsophisticated "popular" texts from the dervish milieu, as in *Truth-Worshippers*. In 1958 he wrote to Corbin:

> I have authorisation [from the living Imam] to edit several Persian Nizārī texts, but they are not *philosophical*, being mostly of the *vulgar* variety, productions of little educated authors. Of course, from my point of view such works are far more interesting than outstanding works of highly qualified individuals, because such *popular* works stand nearer to the common ideas and beliefs of the masses. ... .[12]

I can't help being in sympathy with that statement. Of Ivanow's publications, those that I have found most helpful were his edition and thoughtful annotation of precisely such "vulgar" works, the Ahl-i Haqq *risālas* that had once belonged to dervishes. I have also been fascinated, though never entirely convinced, by his speculations that the AH religion was shaped by Ismāʿīlī influences, besides those of Mithraism and heterodox brands of Christianity, mediated and "Suficised" by unsophisticated dervishes who transmitted them to Kurdish and Gūrān peasant and nomad communities.

Daftary ends his biographical note on Ivanow in *Encyclopaedia Iranica* with the sentence "Largely thanks to his pioneering research and numerous contributions, the Nezāri Ismaʿilis of the Alamut period are no longer judged on the basis of medieval crusader legends and Marco Polo's fantasies as a band of drugged assassins led by a fanatical 'Old Man of the Mountain'" (Daftary 2007).

Peter Lamborn Wilson

Ḥasan-i Ṣabbāḥ was again romanticised, but this time as a counter-culture hero, the anti-Caliph, the model of an anarchist revolutionary fighting against the powerful state, in the writing of William S. Burroughs and Peter Lamborn Wilson. Wilson devotes long chapters of his books *Scandal* (1988) and *Sacred Drift* (1993) to his vision of Ḥasan al-Ṣabbāḥ as the ultimate revolutionary. In an interview given not long after 9/11, he remarked:

> The only thing that really occurs to me that I can say on this is to point out how fascinating it is that the Hasan Al-Sabbah archetype keeps turning up over and over again. If only Burroughs were alive now, what a kick he would get out of this. He did realize that Khomeini was the sort of Hasan Al-Sabbah type, which he was. And of course Osama is also, even though he's a Sunni which makes the comparison a little weird. Nevertheless, that's the archetype. He disappears up into the mountains and is never seen again. Believe me, he'll never be seen again. He'll live forever because of that. With the long white beard and sending out the Fedayeen to sacrifice themselves. It's an archetype that apparently just keeps popping up in Islam. (Abdou and Habele 2009)

I met Peter L. Wilson in Tehran in 1974; we frequently met in the library of the British Institute of Persian Studies and gradually became friends. Peter was then living in Tehran and earning some money as an editor at one of the English-language newspapers and a translator of Sufi poetry. He was in contact with Javād Nūrbakhsh' branch of the Niʿmatullāhiyya but also with Seyyed Hossein Nasr (who, he told me, was not much liked by the Sufis). When Nasr received lavish patronage from the *shahbānū* (the Empress, Farah Diba) to establish the Imperial Iranian Academy of Philosophy, Peter chose to follow Nasr rather than stay with Nūrbakhsh as his *murshid* – I suspect the patronage Nasr had to offer played a part in that decision. Peter then worked for several years at the Academy, as an editor of its journal Sophia Perennis, while continuing his translations of Sufi poetry. He came to conceive great admiration for Henry Corbin, who was a frequent visitor at the Academy.

The first book Peter got published – by the Imperial Academy of Philosophy – was a translation of poems by the Ismāʿīlī author Nāṣir-i Khosrow about whom Ivanow had been so dismissive but to whom Corbin had devoted much work (Wilson and Aavani 1977). This was soon followed by translations of Awḥad al-Dīn Kirmānī's Sufi quatrains (Weischer and Wilson 1978), a substantial book on the Niʿmatollāhiyya that he co-authored with Nasrollah Pourjavady (Pourjavady and Wilson 1978) and, a few years after the revolution, translations of the poetry of Fakhruddīn ʿIrāqī (Chittick and Wilson 1982).

Peter was a convert to Islam, though hardly an average one. He had in fact joined a Black American Muslim sect, the Moorish Orthodox Church, along with other members of the 1960s psychedelic movement, before dropping out of university and travelling to the Muslim world: Morocco, Lebanon, Turkey, India, Pakistan, Iran. In retrospect, he explained his attraction to Islam because this religion was the ultimate enemy of the Western establishment. Peter had spent two years in India on the hippie trail, seeking out Hindu gurus and Muslim murshids, and establishing a relationship with Inayat Khan's Sufi movement that he was later, after his return to the US, to continue in collaboration with Zia Inayat Khan, Vilayat Khan's son and the grandson of the founder of the movement.

Peter's interest in the Ismāʿīlīs and especially Ḥasan Ṣabbāḥ must have begun at Columbia University in the 1960s, listening to the beat poets Allan Ginsberg and William S. Burroughs (of *Naked Lunch* and *Junkie* fame). In Tehran, he often spoke of Ginsberg and Burroughs as sources of inspiration. Burroughs, who lived for years in Tangiers and used more hard drugs than any of the other beat poets, had developed an obsession with Ḥasan-i Ṣabbāḥ and his alleged use of cannabis to make his warriors fearless, and he referred to him in several of his later novels, notably in *Cities of the Red Night*.[13] In Tehran, at the Academy, Wilson came under the influence of Henry Corbin, learning more about Ismāʿīlism and especially the visionary and imaginal dimensions of Sufi literature that loomed large in Corbin's reading. It appears that Burroughs in turn learned more about Hasan-i Sabbāh from conversations with Peter Wilson after his return to the USA, for he thanked him in the dedication of his next novel, *The Western Lands*, and wrote a blurb for Peter's *Scandal*.[14]

Reading the Ivanow-Corbin correspondence, I was often reminded of my own conversations with Peter Wilson. Peter was by that time growing into a real scholar, and we had both come to our current interests in the course of extensive travelling rather than academic study. He was working on high literature in the capital, and I was spending most of the time in villages interviewing simple peasants and nomads. Peter took me to meet urban middle class Sufis and pontificated on Islamic esotericism, whereas I told him of my encounters with dervish story-tellers and village Ahl-i Haqq, and professed to be an agnostic in spite of my interest in popular religiosity. Once, when I challenged him and asked why someone of his background would convert to Islam, his answer was, "what do you accept as an argument? Is beauty a proof?" He was an aesthete, and he perceived beauty especially in the heterodox margins of Islam. Much of his published work was an effort to make that beauty visible to others.

When he had drifted into Nasr's orbit, Peter urged me to read Fritjof Schuon's *Transcendental Unity of Religions*, which he then believed to be the most important book written in the twentieth century. René Guénon's *The Reign of Quantity*, and the works by Titus Burckhardt and Martin Lings on Sufism were also of fundamental importance, he asserted. I do not believe he actually followed Nasr in joining Schuon's Maryāmiyya, but he spoke of this conservative Western intellectual Sufi order with fascination and was generally in agreement with their fiercely anti-modern attitude.[15] Nasr was his patron, but he found Henri Corbin and Toshihiko Izutsu, who were also affiliated with the Academy, closer to his heart. Corbin especially stimulated Peter's interest in the esoteric and heterodox. Corbin's fascination with angels and the survival of Mazdean angelology in esoteric Shiʿism no doubt strengthened his already existing interest in the Yezidis and Ahl-i Haqq and especially in veneration of Satan.[16] At the Academy, both helped Nasr prepare a translation of Ḥallāj's apology of Satan, his *Ṭawāsīn*.

Peter never travelled to the Gūrān region himself but was fascinated by what I could tell him after my first visits – although I fear he kept reading things in my oral reports and later in my publications that were not really there. His major sources of information were books and people in Tehran, but also other cultural artefacts such as pictorial carpets. He wrote the texts for a lavishly illustrated book on such carpets that included representations of dervishes, *jinns*, demons, and other mythological themes besides the more common animals and kings (Schlamminger and Wilson 1980). One spectacular carpet, which he also reproduced on the back cover of his 1988 book *Scandal*, represents what appears to be a black demon leading a blue horse. Corbin, who had seen the carpet, suggested that it must have originated with one of the surviving Satan-worshipping (*shaytān-parast*) communities in Iran.[17] Watching the photos of this carpet again, after re-reading Ivanow, it evokes the name of Black Dāwūd by which Ivanow's interlocutors knew the disobedient angel. And now I remember more: the most common epithet of Dāwūd in the Gūrānī kalām is *Kō-suwār*, of which the most literal translation is "rider of the blue horse" – which might explain the blue horse represented in the carpet.[18]

The Peacock Angel was the reason why Peter re-established contact with me after his return to the US – he had left Iran at the time of the Revolution, when Nasr fled to the US, and he had travelled in Asia, including in Indonesia before finally resettling in New York. We kept corresponding irregularly through the years. His final book, initially titled *Cauda Pavonis* (Latin for "The Peacock's Tail") but finally published as *Peacock Angel* (2021), concerns the religion of the Yezidis, which he attempts to show to have originated in a long esoteric tradition.

The Yezidis and Ahl-i Haqq were but two of the heterodox traditions that excited Peter's aesthetic admiration. Another heterodox Sufi practice on which he spoke and thought and published much was *shāhid-bāzī*, the contemplation of God's beauty by gazing upon the faces of beardless young boys. It was probably no coincidence that two of the Sufi poets whose work he translated, Awḥad al-Dīn Kirmānī (d. 1237 or 1238) and Fakhraddīn ʿIrāqī (d. 1289) were especially known as *shāhid-bāz*.[19] In their commentaries, Wilson and his colleagues, still working in Iran, held back from interpreting this apparent love of young boys literally and emphasised its allegorical meaning.

Back in America, and not constrained by more cautious colleagues any more, Peter insisted that he took this love of boys more literally. In his first major book on Islamic heresy, *Scandal* (1988), he reproduced some of his translations of Kirmānī in a chapter titled "the witness game: imaginal yoga and sacred pedophilia in Persian

Figure 1. "The Black Div," a rare carpet of unknown origin, published and discussed by Peter Wilson in Schlamminger and Wilson 1980, pp. 30-37: "On the mountaintop, at the focus of the composition, the Black Div strides or prances. He leads a wild blue stallion, and a minor blue djinn or monkey hangs to his tail. A hand, or an ebony cock's comb, protrudes from his forehead. A red goat lifts its hooves in a gesture of worship towards the satanic figure."

Sufism." (ʿIrāqī re-appeared in another chapter, devoted to wine-drinking.) A few years later Peter was to bring out, as Hakim Bey, his re-creations of the frankly homoerotic poetry by the early Arab poet Abū Nuwās (d. 814) under the explicit title *O Tribe That Loves Boys* – which was published, of all places, in Utrecht (Hakim Bey 1993). The book was dedicated to Allen Ginsberg, and the first poem sets the tone:

> A pound of meat, a few loaves of bread,
> A jug of wine, at least one willing boy,
> A pipe of hashish. Now the picnic's spread
> My garden beggars paradise's joy.

Hakim Bey was a pseudonym that Peter started using in the 1980s – initially, it seems, for publications that might bring him into trouble with the law. The name first appears on the cover of a fantasy novel with lots of willing boys, *Crowstone*, which is set on a different planet, where conditions are reminiscent of the European middle ages (Hakim 1983). Vaguely reminiscent of William S. Burrough's experiments with science fiction and obsession with ejaculations, the novel is about two men who meet in a brothel with enslaved dancing boys and after sharing the same boy's favours for one night set out on a mystical quest, the search for a holy grail, the crowstone. In one of the protagonists, a former scholar-monk turned professional thief with great swordsman skills and a deep knowledge of esoteric traditions, I believe I recognise Peter's image of himself, projected to a different time and place. Pederasty remained for Peter, I believe, primarily a literary trope and one of the last taboos not broken down by the counter-culture movement, not something he actually wanted to advocate.[20]

Heterodox Islam, heresies, and controversial Sufi practices – wine drinking and gazing at beardless boys, the ingestion of hemp in its various forms – remained at the core of Peter's broad interest in the esoteric traditions of the world. And he transmitted that interest to widening circles in the US after his return. He reconnected with the beat poets Ginsberg and Burroughs whom he so admired, and lectured occasionally at the Jack Kerouac School of Disembodied Poetics at the Naropa Institute in Boulder, which had been founded by Anne Waldman and Allen Ginsberg. Through this network he also came into contact with the French avant-garde in cultural studies and co-operated with their journal *Semiotext(e)*, of which he also co-edited a special issue.[21] An after-midnight show on a Manhattan local radio station, where he spoke on Sufism and esotericism, read from underground magazines, recited poetry, played cassette tapes with music collected on his travels, and took calls from listeners, gave him a growing audience.[22]

When I visited Peter in New York around 1990, he told me he had moved on spiritually and become an anarcho-Ismāʿīlī. His alter ego Hakim Bey (of whom I was not aware then) had already become a veritable cult figure through his concept of "poetic terrorism" as a form of resistance to capitalism, imperialism and the cultural establishment. He collected his evocative calls to resistance in what became the ultimate text of lifestyle anarchism, *T.A.Z., The Temporary Autonomous Zone* (Hakim Bey 1991). By the new millennium he had become one of America's most prominent and most widely read anarchists – along with the social anarchist Murray Bookchin, who was fiercely critical of Wilson.[23]

The transmission of Islamic heterodoxy in the New World

In his book *Scandal*, which surveys the broad range of Wilson's heretical and heresiological interests, he writes:

> "Heresies" are often the means of transfer of ideas and art-forms from one culture to another. Persia could not have become Islamic, despite its military conquest by the Arabs, were it not for the heterodoxies of Shiism and Sufism, or outright heresies such as Nizari Ismailism, Hurufism and the Ghulat. (Wilson 1988, p. 13).

Historians may take issue with the confident claim, but I have gradually come to realise that Peter himself exemplified that process. Initially converted to the self-invented Islam of the Black Moorish Orthodox Church, he gradually absorbed much Muslim culture through his travels and reading. Back in the US he became, to his own surprise, a guru of the counterculture to many people one or two generations younger than himself, who embraced his mixture of Islamic ideas, Sufi poetry, psychedelics and anarchism.

Transferred to the US, Peter's multiple heresies, like his anti-establishment attitude, found a following among young white men (and perhaps a few women) who like him embraced an imagined Islam as the ultimate counter-culture. Some of them followed up their conversion by joining one or another of the globalised Sufi movements operating in North America or by travelling to the Muslim world and studying textual Islam.

This is exemplified by the novelist and essayist Michael Muhammad Knight, who came from the Islamo-punk scene and who for some time was one of Peter's most dedicated followers. Peter helped Knight to get his first novel *Taqwacores* published by Peter's own publisher, with a recommendation by Peter on the back cover: "Sooner or later Punk and Islam were fated to meet and produce strange offspring. This excellent novel represents the first blast of the trumpet – loud and utterly unique" (Knight 2004). In Knight's second book, *Blue-Eyed Devil*, in which he travels through North America in search of the identity of the mysterious W.D.

Fard, the founder of the Nation of Islam, Peter Wilson appears as a knowledgeable teacher and guide:

> It was January and New York State came under an arctic blast as I drove four hundred miles to meet a brilliant writer who, while not Muslim per se, goes a long way in exposing the real richness and depth of Islam. No, it wasn't John Esposito. Peter Lamborn Wilson has been described somewhere as an 'Anarcho-Sufi.' I don't know what that means but it sure as hell sounds cooler than 'Progressive.' (...) He has become something of a living myth and modern-day Hassan bin Sabbah in anarchist circles.[24]

Knight then continues to paraphrase Peter's theory of Islamisation through heterodoxy:

> According to Peter, Islam has followed the same patterns on this continent as many religions when they arrive in new societies; entering first as heresy mingled with native culture (i.e., the Nation of Islam), followed by a phase of strict orthodoxy as converts struggle to learn the proper traditions. Made sense; four of Muslim America's biggest heroes had started out in the Nation of Islam, only to later go completely Sunni: Malcolm X, Warith Deen Mohammed, three-time heavyweight champion Muhammad Ali and Imam Siraj Wahhaj. I never thought to ask Peter what comes after the strict orthodoxy phase.[25]

Knight later started work on an authorised biography, travelling with Peter to many meetings and events, but gradually became estranged and broke with Peter over the latter's unapologetic defence of his writing on paedophilia as not just a Sufi metaphor but a possible physical act. The failed biography is still embedded in Knight's unusual but fascinating book (Knight 2012).

Peter Lamborn Wilson was but one of a broader circle of American Muslim anarchists, about whom recently a serious study appeared (Abdou 2022). He was probably the most outrageous of them, but also likely the most cultured and eloquent, and certainly the most productive. He was also very much aware of standing in an American tradition of religious dissent and romantic rejection of modernity. The last years of his life he spent as a hermit far from the city, living frugally in a simple house in upstate New York, a cross between Henry David Thoreau and the Old Man of the Mountain.

Notes

1 The description of the AH religion that follows here is drawn from my unpublished paper "Satan's Psalmists: Some Heterodox Beliefs and Practices among the Ahl-e Haqq of the Guran District," written on the basis of two ten-day visits and conversations with kalam-khwans in 1975 and 1976 and revised many times in the following years.

2 See the analysis of a kalām dedicated to Dāwūd in Mokri 1974. Mokri lists attributes of Dāwūd and persons in whom he manifested himself on pp. 63–4. There is no reference to Satan or Malak Tāwūs in this kalām, but Mokri cites another AH text that does make the identification of Dāwūd and Malak Tāwūs.

3 Awn 1983; Nurbakhsh 1986. More on AH beliefs concerning Satan in Bruinessen 2014.

4 AH sacred history consists of a series of cycles, in which angels and other spirits manifest themselves in the world (Bruinessen 2009). The cycle of the birth of Islam is not named for Muhammad, who plays an unimportant role in AH cosmology, but for ʿAlī (ibn Abī Tālib), Muhammad's cousin and son-in-law and the first Shiite Imam.

5 See Tabibi 1975, Hamzeh'ee 1990.

6 Mohammad Mokri (1974, p. 90) quotes the Gūrānī text *ʿĀlam-i Haqīqat* (after a manuscript in his possession) that explicitly identifies Dāwūd with Malak Tāwūs.

7 For an extensive discussion of peacock symbolism in creation myths and its transfer between different religious communities, see Bruinessen 2020. On various interpretations of Satan among the AH, see Bruinessen 2014.

8 References to Malak Tāwūs: Ivanow 1948: 167, 177, 184; Ivanow 1953: 46, 169. Dāwūd-i Rash: Ivanow 1948: 167. The concept of Black Dawud appears to be illustrated by an amazing Persian carpet showing a black demon (see Fig. 1), to which Peter L. Wilson has drawn attention and that is reproduced in Schlamminger and Wilson 1980, p. 35 and 37 and discussed ibid. pp. 30–32.

9 Ivanow 1932; Ivanow 1953: 46, 49, 74.

10 Daftary 2007; Daftary (ed.) 2015; Schmidtke (ed.) 1999; see also Baiza 2020.

11 Ivanow 1953. Corbin wrote: "Votre analyse met admirablement en valeur les traces des autres croyances religieuses. Vous dégagez celles du Mithraïsme de façon très heureuse (...). Tout à fait d'accord avec vous sur l'opportunité de rechercher les traces des sects chrétiennes; vous touchez juste avec les Pauliciens. De mon côté je suis très préoccupé par l'intérêt du docétisme (...)" See Schmidtke (ed.) 1999, 101.

12 Schmidtke 1999, 158. His referring tot the Āqā Khān as "the living Imam" was no doubt ironical, for Ivanow was a sceptic, not a believer.

13 In his excellent Burroughs biography, Ted Morgan notes that "the author's point of view (in *Cities of the Red Night*) is that of the Old Man of the Mountain, Hassan i Sabbah: Nothing is true, everything is permitted. Every taboo that is broken, every act of outrage that is committed, is a justifiable act of insurrection against a bankrupt system of morality. Whatever his characters are doing, Burroughs seems to be saying, the actual conditions on the planet, created by the villains and morons in power, are worse" (Morgan 1988, 567).

14 "Fascinating material on the Ismaili sect and on Hassan I Sabbah ... the only spiritual leader who has something significant to say in the Space Age." Burroughs on the back cover of Wilson 1988.

15 On Schuon, Guénon, Burckhardt, Nasr and Lings, see the excellent study by Mark Sedgwick 2004.

16 Corbin 1976. After his return to the USA, Peter Wilson wrote a book on angels that is essentially a summary explanation of Corbin's views on the subject (Wilson 1994).

[17] See Fig. 1, one of the two large reproductions and Peter Wilson's analysis of the possible meanings of this representation in Schlamminger and Wilson 1980, pp. 30–7. The same text, in which I recognise some of my own reports, reappears in Wilson 1988, pp. 177–82.

[18] Gūrānī *kō*, like Persian *kabūd*, refers to the colour of the sky, i.e. blue or grey. Mokri 1974 interprets the epithet *kō-suwār* as indicating Dāwūd's riding on the winds and cites local beliefs in the Kermanshah region that attribute turbulent winds to demonic activity.

[19] On these poets: Safa 1987, Yar-Shater 1998. Translation and commentary: Chittick and Wilson 1982, Weischer and Wilson 1978.

[20] It appears that the North American Man/Boy Love Association (NAMBLA) considered Hakim Bey as one of theirs, and several former admirers broke with him over the association with paedophilia, including his would-be biographer Michael Muhammad Knight (2012). Friends who had been closely associated with him over a long period insisted that the accusations of actual rather than literary pederasty were unfounded (Foye 2022, Green 2022).

[21] Rucker, Wilson and Wilson 1989. On *Semiotext(e)* see the chapter "L'aventure de Semiotext(e)" in Cusset 2005, pp. 81–85.

[22] See the recollections of Raymond Foye and many others collected after Peter's death in Foye 2022.

[23] Bookchin 1995; see also the interviews Abdou & Haberle 2009 and Versluis 2010. Both Peter L. Wilson and Hakim Bey contributed many articles to *Fifth Estate*, "The Anarchist Review of Books." (https://www.fifthestate.org/fe_author/peter-lamborn-wilson/ and https://www.fifthestate.org/fe_author/hakim-bey/). In spite of their political differences, Wilson/Hakim Bey later wrote with great sympathy on Abdullah Öcalan and the Rojava Revolution of Syria's Kurds, who were strongly influenced by Bookchin's ideas (Dirik et al. 2016).

[24] Knight 2006, p. 55.

[25] Knight 2006, p. 58.

Works cited

Abdou, Mohamed. *Islam and Anarchism: Relationships and Resonances*. London: Pluto Press, 2022.

Abdou, Mohamed, and Sean Haberle. "Affinity Project Interview with Peter Lamborn Wilson," 2009. Online at https://theanarchistlibrary.org/library/affinity-project-interview-with-peter-lamborn-wilson.

Awn, Peter J. *Satan's Tragedy and Redemption: Iblīs in Sufi Psychology*. Leiden: Brill, 1983.

Baiza, Yahia. "Wladimir Ivanow and Ismailism: The Rise of Modern Ismaili Studies and Historiography." In *Proceedings of the International Congress on Historiography and Source Studies of Asia and Africa, St Petersburg University, 19–21 June 2019*, 81–98. St Petersburg, 2020.

Bookchin, Murray. *Social Anarchism or Lifestyle Anarchism: The Unbridgeable Chasm*. Edinburgh and San Francisco: AK Press, 1995.

Bruinessen, Martin van. "When Haji Bektash still bore the name of Sultan Sahak. Notes on the Ahl-i Haqq of the Guran district." In *Bektachiyya: études sur l'ordre mystique des Bektachis et les groupes relevant de Hadji Bektach*, edited by Alexandre Popovic and Gilles Veinstein, 117–138. Istanbul: Éditions Isis, 1995.

Bruinessen, Martin van. "Ahl-i Haqq." In *The Encyclopaedia of Islam*, Third Edition, Part 2009-2, 51–58. Leiden: Brill, 2009.

Bruinessen, Martin van. "Veneration of Satan among the Ahl-e Haqq of the Gûrân region." *Fritillaria Kurdica, Bulletin of Kurdish Studies* No. 3–4: (2014) 6–41.

Bruinessen, Martin van. "Between Dersim and Dalahu. Reflections on Kurdish Alevism and the Ahl-e Haqq religion." In *Islamic Alternatives: Non-Mainstream Religion in Persianate Societies*, edited by Shahrokh Raei, 65–93. Wiesbaden: Harrassowitz, 2017.

Bruinessen, Martin van. "The Peacock in Sufi Cosmology and Popular Religion: Connections between Indonesia, South India, and the Middle East." *Epistemé: Jurnal Pengembangan Ilmu Keislaman* 15(2) (2020) 177–219. doi: https://doi.org/10.21274/epis.2020.15.02.177-219.

Burroughs, William S. *Cities of the Red Night*. London: Picador, 1981.

Burroughs, William S. *The Western Lands*. London: Viking Penguin, 1987.

Chittick, William C. and Peter Lamborn Wilson, eds. *Fakhruddin 'Iraqi, Divine Flashes*. [Classics of Western spirituality]. London: SPCK, 1982.

Corbin, Henry. *Spiritual Body and Celestial Earth: From Mazdean Iran to Shī'ite Iran*. Princeton: Princeton University Press, 1976.

Cusset, François. *French Theory: Foucault, Derrida, Deleuze & Cie et les mutations de la vie intellectuelle aux États-Unis*. Paris: La Découverte, 2005.

Daftary, Farhad. "Bibliography of the publications of the late W. Ivanow." *Islamic Culture* 45(1) (1971) 55–67.

Daftary, Farhad, ed. *Mediaeval Isma'ili History and Thought*. Cambridge, 1996.

Daftary, Farhad. "Ivanow, Vladimir Alekseevich." *Encyclopaedia Iranica* Vol. XIV, Fasc. 3, pp. 298–300, 2007. URL: https://iranicaonline.org/articles/ivanow-vladimir-alekseevich.

Daftary, Farhad, ed. *Fifty Years in the East: The Memoirs of Wladimir Ivanow*. London: I.B.Tauris, 2015.

Dirik, Dilar, David Levi Strauss, Michael Taussig, and Peter Lamborn Wilson, eds. *To Dare Imagining: Rojava Revolution*. Brooklyn, NY: Autonomedia, 2016.

Foye, Raymond, ed. "In Memoriam: A Tribute to Peter Lamborn Wilson (1945–2022)." *The Brooklyn Rail*, October 2022. URL:
https://brooklynrail.org/2022/10/in-memoriam/A-Tribute-to-Peter-Lamborn-Wilson.

Green, Penelope. "Peter Lamborn Wilson, Advocate of 'Poetic Terrorism,' Dies at 76." *New York Times*, 11-06-2022. URL: https://www.nytimes.com/2022/06/11/us/peter-lamborn-wilson-dead.html.

Hakim. *Crowstone: The Chronicles of Qamar*. Amsterdam: Spartacus, 1983.

Hakim Bey. *T.A.Z.: The Temporary Autonomous Zone, Ontological Anarchy, Poetic Terrorism*. Brooklyn: Autonomedia, 1991; 2003.

Hakim Bey. "The Lemonade Ocean & Modern Times." *Hermetic Library*. Online at: https://hermetic.com/bey/lemonade, 1991.

Hakim Bey. *O Tribe that Loves Boys: The Poetry of Abu Nuwas. Translated (with a Biographical Essay)*. Amsterdam and Utrecht: Entimos Press / The Abu Nuwas Society, 1993.

Hamzeh'ee, M. Reza. *The Yaresan: A Sociological, Historical and Religio-Historical Study of a Kurdish Community*. Berlin: Klaus Schwarz, 1990.

Ivanow, W. "Notes on the Ethnography of Khorasan." *Geographical Journal* 67 (1926)143–158.

Ivanow, W. "Notes on Khorasani Kurdish." *Journal and Proceedings of the Asiatic Society of Bengal* 23 (1927)167–236.

Ivanow, W. "Notes sur l'Ummu 'l-kitab des Ismaëliens de l'Asie Centrale." *Revue des études islamiques* 6:4 (1932) 19–481.

Ivanow, W. "An Ali-Ilahi fragment." In *Collectanea vol I*, edited by W. Ivanow, 147–184. Leiden: Brill for the Ismaili Society, 1948.

Ivanow, W. *The Truth-Worshippers of Kurdistan*. Leiden: Brill for the Ismaili Society, 1953.

Knight, Michael Muhammad. *The Taqwacores*. Brooklyn, NY: Autonomedia, 2004.

Knight, Michael Muhammad. *Blue-Eyed Devil: A Road Odyssey Through Islamic America*. Brooklyn: Soft Skull Press, 2006.

Knight, Michael Muhammad. *William S. Burroughs vs. the Qur'ān*. Berkeley, CA: Soft Skull Press, 2012.
Minorsky, Vladimir F. "Notes sur la secte des Ahlé Haqq." *Revue du monde musulman* 40–41 (1920)19–97.
Minorsky, Vladimir F. "Notes sur la secte des Ahlé Haqq – II." *Revue du monde musulman* 44–45 (1921) 205–302.
Mokri, Muḥammad. "Étude d'un titre de propriété du début du XVIe siècle provenant du Kurdistan." *Journal Asiatique* 251 (1963) 229–256.
Mokri, Mohammed. "Le kalam gourani sur le cavalier au coursier gris, le dompteur du vent." *Journal Asiatique* 262 (1974) 47–93.
Morgan, Ted. *Literary Outlaw: The Life and Times of William S. Burroughs*. New York: Avon Books, 1988.
Nurbakhsh, Javad. *The Great Satan "Eblis."* London: Khaniqahi-Nimatullahi Publications, 1986.
Pourjavady, Nasrollah, and Peter Lamborn Wilson. *Kings of Love: The History & Poetry of the Ni'matullahi Sufi Order of Iran*. Tehran: Imperial Iranian Academy of Philosophy, 1978.
Rucker, Rudy, Peter Lamborn Wilson, and Robert Anton Wilson, eds. *Semiotext(e) SF*. Brooklyn: Autonomedia, 1989.
Safa, Z. "Awḥad-al-Dīn Kermānī." *Encyclopædia Iranica*, Vol. III, Fasc. 2: 118–119, 1987. URL: https://www.iranicaonline.org/articles/awhad-al-din-kermani-hamed-b.
Schlamminger, Karl, and Peter Lamborn Wilson. *Persische Bildteppiche: Geknüpfte Mythen*. München: Callwey Verlag, 1980.
Schmidtke, Sabine, ed. *Correspondance Corbin-Ivanow. Lettres échangées entre Henry Corbin et Vladimir Ivanow de 1947 à 1966*. Paris: Institut d'études iraniennes / Peeters, 1999.
Sedgwick, Mark J. R. *Against the Modern World: Traditionalism and the Secret Intellectual History of the Twentieth Century*. Oxford: Oxford University Press, 2004.
Stead, F. M. "The Ali-Ilahi sect in Persia." *The Moslem World* 22 (1932)184–189.
Tabibi, Heshmatollah. "Influences of the Seven Amshasepand on the Religious Beliefs of the Ahl-e Haqq Kurds." *Barrasiha-ye Tarikhi / Historical Studies of Iran* no. 3, (1975) 95–100.
Versluis, Arthur, and Peter Lamborn Wilson. "A Conversation with Peter Lamborn Wilson." *Journal for the Study of Radicalism* 4(2) (2010)139–165.
Weightman, S. C. R. "The Significance of the Kitab Burhan ul-Haqq." *Iran* 2 (1964) 83–103.
Weischer, Bernd Manuel, and Peter Lamborn Wilson, eds. *Heart's Witness: The Sufi Quatrains of Awḥaduddīn Kirmānī*. Tehran: Imperial Iranian Academy of Philosophy, 1978.
Wilson, Peter Lamborn, and Gholam-Reza Aavani, eds. *Nasir-i Khusraw: Forty Poems from the Divan. Translated with Introductions and Notes*. Tehran: Imperial Iranian Academy of Philosophy, 1977.
Wilson, Peter Lamborn. *Scandal: Studies in Islamic Heresy*. Brooklyn: Autonomedia, 1988.
Wilson, Peter Lamborn. *Sacred Drift: Essays on the Margins of Islam*. San Francisco: City Lights Books, 1993. [some parts available on Google Books.]
Wilson, Peter Lamborn. *Angels: Messengers of the Gods*. New York: Thames and Hudson, 1994.
Wilson, Peter Lamborn. *Spiritual Journeys of an Anarchist*. Brooklyn: Autonomedia, 2014.
Wilson, Peter Lamborn. *Peacock Angel: The Esoteric Tradition of the Yezidis*. Rochester, Vermont: Inner Traditions, 2022.
Yarshater, Ehsan. "'Erāqī, Fak̲r-al-Dīn Ebrāhīm." *Encyclopaedia Iranica*, Vol. VIII, Fasc. 5 (1998) 538–540. URL: https://iranicaonline.org/articles/eraqi.

A Persian Essay in Defence of Suhrawardī Against the Accusation of Supporting Metempsychosis (*tanāsukh*)

Cornelis van Lit
Utrecht University

Abstract

This chapter edits and studies a Persian (mixed with Arabic) essay by a certain Muḥammad Bāqir Jīlānī, defending Suhrawardī against the accusation of advocating for the doctrine of metempsychosis (*tanāsukh*) instead of affirming bodily resurrection (*ma'ād jismānī*). It can be traced back to the Safavid milieu of the early eighteenth century, and has a link with previous comments by Mīr Dāmād. The author does not situate Suhrawardī's (admittedly ambiguous) ideas on resurrection in an esoteric context, but rather explains it using traditional, exegetical, philosophical, and theological sources, mostly from Sunni authors of the twelfth to fourteenth centuries. The notion of a "world of image" (*'ālam al-mithāl*) is also invoked, to come to a carefully crafted defence of Suhrawardī.

Keywords: *tanāsukh*; bodily resurrection; Muḥammad Bāqir Jīlānī; Mīr Dāmād, Safavid philosophy; Ḥikmat al-ishrāq.

Introduction

The impact of the twelfth century philosopher Suhrawardī (d. 587/1191) on Safavid era thinkers, philosophers, theologians, and mystics alike, is generally assumed to be big. For example, Shahab Ahmed, when considering the Persianate world of what he termed the Balkans-to-Bengal complex, claims that Suhrawardī is one "of the most socially-pervasive and consequential thought-paradigms in the history of societies of Muslims."[1] Of course, only with actual evidence can we turn that claim into a credible statement from which to synthesise a narrative of Islamic intellectual history. I previously investigated how many commentaries were written on Suhrawardī's works. I concluded there to be 58 in total, 31 of which are extant.[2] In the article, I also outlined how previous scholarship has been enormously divided on the issue of Suhrawardī's importance, especially for Safavid thinkers, and how both camps work mostly on the basis of assumptions rather than evidence-based analyses. Granted, the onus is on those who argue in favour of the importance of Suhrawardī, as it is hardly fair to ask for evidence when the very thesis is that there is no evidence.

This chapter picks up one of the unpublished commentaries, presenting a small but important piece of evidence related to this discussion. The text in question is a Persian essay, defending Suhrawardī against the accusation of advocating for the doctrine of metempsychosis (*tanāsukh*) instead of affirming bodily resurrection (*maʿād jismānī*). This is an exciting piece of evidence to consider. As it can be traced back to the Safavid milieu of the early eighteenth century, it shows the continuation of debates on Suhrawardī's thinking, which were apparently heated enough to warrant written statements. It also shows which subjects were interesting for these intellectuals, in this case the theory of metempsychosis on which Suhrawardī is admittedly ambiguous, and the notion of suspended images and the world of image (*ʿālam al-mithāl*), an innovation brought forth by Suhrawardī and expanded by his commentator Shahrazūrī (d. about 687/1288) to argue for some form of bodily afterlife without being physical. Further, this essay shows *how* Suhrawardī was discussed: although our author, Muḥammad Bāqir Jīlānī, relates the discussion to a highly esoteric part of Suhrawardī's writings, he does not at all push it that way but rather embeds it in a mainstream discussion on resurrection, citing traditional, exegetical, philosophical, and theological sources, mostly from Sunni authors of the twelfth to fourteenth centuries. Lastly, the essay is a typical example of the formal aspects of intellectual writings from the early-modern era. Instead of writing *in abstracta* about a claim that Suhrawardī supported metempsychosis, the essay is styled as a gloss on a sentence from Suhrawardī's *Ḥikmat al-ishrāq*. Also, the essay exemplifies the perfect interweaving of Persian and Arabic in the writing practice of early-modern intellectuals, as well as the practice of using earlier sources to their own advantage.

The essay is by a certain Muḥammad Bāqir Jīlānī, who I have not been able to identify with anyone in major Shīʿī biobibliographical works. Mustafa Dirayati, in his *Fihristgān: Nuskhah-hā-yi khaṭṭī-i Īrān*, writes that this essay is "a commentary on the fifth chapter of the second part of *Ḥikmat al-ishrāq*," and he dates the manuscript he considered to the twelfth century hijri.[3] Since the essay is basically an extension of a letter by Mīr Dāmād on the same matter, who died in 1040/1631, Mūhammad Bāqir Jīlānī most probably lived in the late eleventh/seventeenth or early twelfth/eighteenth century. Jīlānī's reference to Mīr Dāmād, his mentioning of the concept of the Imamate, the infallible Imams, and his reference to *Amir al-muʾminīn*, presumably ʿAlī, as well as his *nisba*, all indicate our Muḥammad Bāqir should be considered part of Shīʿī, Safavid circles. This corroborates the notion that Suhrawardī's philosophy was well received in the Shiʿi world, as first argued by Henry Corbin.[4] It is possible that our Jīlānī actually lived in Mughal India and wrote this essay there. This wouldn't change the strong relations with the Shīʿī, Safavid world and it could hardly change the era it was written in. A slightly later date is possible, but the dating of manuscripts related to Jīlānī have him no later than the twelfth/eighteenth century. One argument in favour of geographically relating this essay to Mughal India is that metempsychosis enjoyed greater popularity over there.

Dirayati explains that the essay focusses in particular on one sentence in *Ḥikmat al-ishrāq* that says "[God] has decreed to the Faithful Spirit that He will answer the prayers of all who are weighed down with gloom, of all who are pure yet seek to be darkened, and that He will aid the patient against the evils of the sons of the devils, that He will clothe the evildoers in shirts of tar."[5] This may seem bewildering (it did for me), as this sentence seems hardly related to metempsychosis, *tanāsukh*, meaning in particular the transmigration of the soul to another body in the sub-lunar world. *Ḥikmat al-ishrāq* is, when taken as a whole, a book of philosophy, in which Suhrawardī lays out some of his most intricate thoughts. This includes both criticism against certain ideas and ways of thinking that philosophers of his time were want to, as well as the proposal and detailing of his most innovate contributions to philosophy. A treatment of metempsychosis is part of this philosophical discussion, albeit occupying only a minor place. The part from which the sentence comes which Jīlānī quotes is not the proper part on metempsychosis. Rather, in it Suhrawardī discusses spiritual and mystical practices in order to draw closer to God and His angels, while also evocatively describing eschatological punishments for those who go against such practices. This comes in the very last pages of the book and is qua style and content in marked contrast with the rest of the book. The end of *al-Talwīḥāt*, another book on philosophy, has a similar ending in terms of content.[6] The better comparison, though, are Suhrawardī's "devotional and occult" prayers and litanies, which have largely been left unedited.[7] The sentence in itself, therefore, is an odd choice and is, as we learn from Jīlānī's essay, really only chosen because a popular commentary on *Ḥikmat al-ishrāq*, by polymath Quṭb al-Dīn Shīrāzī (d. 710/1310), glosses the term "shirts" with the remark "that is, black skins which belong to species of animals."[8] It is this explanation of "shirts" that apparently opponents latched on to, arguing that Suhrawardī and Quṭb al-Dīn Shīrāzī here suggest that "evildoers" are to reincarnate as animals.

Suhrawardī on metempsychosis

Metempsychosis found support in the early centuries of Islamic history.[9] Its influence on Islamic thinkers is usually traced back to ancient Greek philosophers and Indian culture. Of the two, Greek culture made a bigger impact on Islamic intellectual discourse, and Ibn Sīnā's refutation of metempsychosis seems to have been important in neutralising the positive remarks on metempsychosis among Greek philosophers.[10] As such, metempsychosis was not a significant issue of discussion in later centuries, and an accusation thereof strikes more of defamation than an opening for a serious discussion. Exceptions, of course, can always be found, such as with the *ahl-i ḥaqq*, an esoteric branch (or offshoot) of Islam that emerged in sixteenth century Western Persia.[11] There is no indication that the existence of the *ahl-i ḥaqq* was a contributing factor for writing this essay.

The case of Suhrawardī, however, merits closer attention. He, too, related Ibn Sīnā's arguments against metempsychosis. For example, the argument that since every material body that comes to be requires the Active Intellect to bestow it a soul made just for it, meaning transmigration is impossible, because one body would end up with two souls, the transmigrating soul and the newly made soul, is related in nearly every of Suhrawardī's philosophical works.[12]

There are, however, also passages that are much more ambiguous. Foremost are passages in *al-Talwīḥāt* and *Ḥikmat al-ishrāq*. In *al-Talwīḥāt*, Suhrawardī says, countering those who would allow all human beings to move beyond the physical world after death:[13]

> How can they allow the wretched to separate from their body, when this would leave no veil between them and the celestial souls, thereby [allowing them] to connect with them and [share in their] delight? Where would misery be [in that]? [...] It ought to be that the wretched souls transmigrate to something among the agonized animals, according to their character, habits, and attachment to bodies.

The paragraph out of which this passage comes starts with "I say" (*aqūlu*), which is evidence for Suhrawardī's personal commitment to this view. The argumentation strategy, with its use of rhetorical questions, suggests a personal commitment to it. Having exhausted the *pathos* of his rhetoric, by invoking a sense of justice with his readers, he moves on to *ethos*, proposing arguments from authority. Thus, he says that the ancient philosophers, prophets, and even the Koran agree to this. He finishes with the *logos* of his rhetorics, spending more than two pages on critiquing the most popular philosophical arguments against metempsychosis. For example, against the two-souls-one-body argument he says that one soul will be more suitable for it, and that is the soul which will take the body, denying the other. In slightly schizophrenic fashion, he starts to counter his own criticism mid-paragraph, for example writing that the soul that is made just for that body is always more suitable. This counter-critique runs for half a page before he breaks off his discussion by saying "this book is not the place to elaborate further."[14]

Since this chapter is not the place to elaborate on it either, I shall refrain from minutely going over all of his argumentation. Instead, I wish to draw attention to the solution that Suhrawardī introduces a few pages later in *al-Talwīḥāt*, for souls that fall short of perfecting themselves in order to be absorbed into the intelligible world, after death. This solution is, essentially, to provide a way for deceased people to imagine things even though they do not have a body anymore. In this manner, people can imagine all the eschatological promises, whether good or bad. Suhrawardī argues that these souls could use celestial bodies as their faculty of imagination. This idea may sound odd at first, but Suhrawardī (and before him Ibn Sīnā) arrives at it by insisting that the human imagination is a bodily function reducing the candidates to stand in for a body. Physical bodies, such as of animals are technically not rejected, but this seems implied. What gets ample attention is a specific kind of material body, made of vapour and smoke. This too is rejected, and so Suhrawardī (and Ibn Sīnā) have to look beyond the sublunar world. In the celestial bodies they find their ideal candidate.[15] Within this discussion of allowing imagination for people after death, Suhrawardī makes a soteriological division, related to different celestial bodies that can offer different degrees of pleasure. As such he has to discuss once more those people who have been the worst during their Earthly life. He says:[16]

> As for the wretched, their attachment is not with these noble [celestial] bodies who possess luminous souls and the power that requires bodily imagination. It is not impossible that there is a spherical body under the orbit of the moon and above the sphere of fire, unpierced [by either], being a species by itself, a barrier between the ethereal and material world, functioning as the substrate for their imaginations.

The first step of reasoning is an acknowledgment of the previous passage, pointing out that wretched humans do not deserve to be elevated to the same level as angels. Another similarity is his strategy, which suggests he is aware of the unconventional, almost heretical, nature of his thinking. In the previous passage, we saw him walk back on his statement by giving counterarguments and shutting down the discussion before it was resolved. In this second passage he softens his tone by introducing it with "it is not impossible." What decisively binds the two passages is a statement he makes in a sentence after the second passage, when he says "and with this, the remaining resemblance with the supporters of metempsychosis is warded off."[17] This above all shows that Suhrawardī was aware that his thinking is tantamount to metempsychosis, which he insists it is not. The difference with metempsychosis is supposed to come out in the conclusion that Suhrawardī draws. Before, he declared openly that these people deserve to reincarnate as an animal. Now he says that they might attach to a special body that is neither part of the material world nor of the ethereal world. Technically, they stay in the sublunar world, but do so in a way that removes them altogether from Earthly life. The two conclusions are not entirely conflicting; in the first he speaks of what *ought* to happen, in the second he speaks of what *actually* happens. A charitable reading, then, may conclude that Suhrawardī was attracted to the ethical dimension of metempsychosis but agreed with the many arguments against it. Perhaps he saw some room for upward transmigration, and thereby posited a new spherical body in between the ethereal and material world. A less charitable reading concludes that Suhrawardī is definitely arguing for metempsychosis and his feeble attempt to cover this up only makes him dishonest.

A strong argument in favour of the second reading is a passage in *Ḥikmat al-ishrāq*, which can be seen to refer to both passages translated above. There, Suhrawardī says:[18]

> As for the wretched [...], [it does not matter] whether transference is true or wrong, since arguments for either side are weak. When they leave their barrier fortresses [i.e. their bodies] they will have shadows of suspended images according to their character.

The two sides alluded to can be interpreted to refer to the two passages from *al-Talwīḥāt*. At the very least it shows the indecisiveness of Suhrawardī on this issue. Even though he concludes here in *Ḥikmat al-ishrāq* that they will have suspended images, meaning that they use their imagination, he does not side with the second passage of *al-Talwīḥāt* entirely, since he does not mention the new spherical body. In fact, he does not refer to this new body in any of his writings.[19]

Lastly, then, we need to consider the subchapter in *Ḥikmat al-ishrāq* actually dedicated to metempsychosis. As Sabine Schmidtke already called attention to, this subchapter is not entitled "on the impossibility of metempsychosis" (*fī imtināʿ al-tanāsukh*), as it is titled in other writings of Suhrawardī, but bears the heading "in explanation of metempsychosis" (*fī bayān al-tanāsukh*).[20] This chapter is not the place to dwell in detail on this subchapter, but anyone comparing it with the above translated passage of *al-Talwīḥāt*, will notice that Suhrawardī copied and appropriated the passage from *al-Talwīḥāt* to fit into his *Ḥikmat al-ishrāq*. Two differences stand out. Firstly, in *Ḥikmat al-ishrāq* he places most of the positions in the mouth of "Buddha and other sages of the East" (*Būdhāsaf wa-man qabluhu min al-ḥukamāʾ al-mashriqiyīn*), in what seems as a way to distance himself from it. Secondly, of the counter-counter-arguments mentioned in *al-Talwīḥāt*, he only includes the one about the two-souls-one-body argument in *Ḥikmat al-ishrāq*, and emphasises twice that this is what "the Peripatetics" think. Notably, he mentions this in the middle of his sub-chapter, not at the end, thereby reducing the importance of it.

These passages from *al-Talwīḥāt* and *Ḥikmat al-ishrāq*, then, easily lent themselves to interpreting them as advancing the doctrine of metempsychosis. Indeed, Shahrazūrī, the most devoted of all commentators on Suhrawardī, unreservedly supports the idea of metempsychosis and uses the passages in *al-Talwīḥāt* and *Ḥikmat al-ishrāq* to his advantage.[21] Quṭb al-Dīn Shīrāzī, who based his commentary of *Ḥikmat al-ishrāq* on Shahrazūrī's commentary, sees no other way out than to admit that the plain meaning of the text points in the direction of metempsychosis. Outside of these commentaries, however, I have been unable to find those who appreciate the *Ḥikmat al-ishrāq* (*al-Ishrāqiyūn*) identified as supporters of metempsychosis. We may note ʿAbd al-Razzāq Kāshānī (d. 730/1329), who does identify them as such in passing, in his *Sharḥ al-Fuṣūṣ al-ḥikam*,[22] but clearly this identification was not widespread.

The Safavids discussing Suhrawardī

A few centuries later, we find Muḥammad Bāqir Jīlānī's essay, which clearly shows that at that point there definitely was some discussion about Suhrawardī's position on metempsychosis. The background for Jīlānī's essay is a stray remark made by Mīr Dāmād (d. 1041/1631), in a letter to a man named Amīr Abū 'l-Ḥusnā al-Farāhānī. The letter is edited and published as "taʿlīqa ʿalā Ḥikmat al-ishrāq,"[23] but the letter actually consists of two remarks, one on Suhrawardī and one on Ibn Sīnā's *Ḥayy ibn Yaqẓān*.[24] *Ḥayy ibn Yaqẓan* is an allegorical tale, which people after Ibn Sīnā commented upon to explain the allegory by means of giving philosophical interpretations of different terms mentioned in the story. Mīr Dāmād expands in the letter on such an interpretation as found in Quṭb al-Dīn Shīrāzī's *Durrat al-tāj*,[25] which he finds to be superficial. The majority of the letter is devoted to this topic, while Suhrawardī receives only one paragraph. This paragraph reads:

> In the course of merry discussion and happy exchanges of letters, a veil has been removed [for me] from the secret of the remark made by the reviver of the works of the stoics, the sheik of the followers of the Illuminationists, in the seventh part of the fifth chapter of *Ḥikmat al-ishrāq*, which reads:[26] "God has inscribed in the Book and decreed to the Faithful Spirit, that He will answer the prayers of all who are weighed down with gloom, of all who are pure yet seek to be darkened for the good pleasure of God, and that He will aid the patient against the evils of the sons of the devils, that He will clothe the evildoers in shirts of fire."[27] The reflection they made, interpreting the previous sentence through metempsychosis, has come to be seen as correct and pertinent.[28] [However,] the context of the last part of the remark is a pointer to that in the Noble Revelation, in the blessed sura *Ḥajj*, which relates: "for them garments of fire shall be cut",[29] and in the venerable sura *Ibrāhīm*: "of pitch their shirts, their faces enveloped by the Fire", and in the prayer for ablution, which relates: "I seek refuge in You from the garments of the Fires." In no way does the method of metempsychosis have a relation with [these] narrations, and the

> same counts for the sheik, the author of this book, towards the doctrine of the adherents of metempsychosis. A pure and innocent heart can come up with the correct understanding of that [sentence], according to the writings of him with which we are befallen and the statements of him which have reached us. And God, the Knower, exalted is His power, knows best.

Mīr Dāmād informs us, then, that it was commonly asserted that this sentence by Suhrawardī should be understood as supporting metempsychosis. Mīr Dāmād thinks that this does not need to be the case. The sentence reminds him of certain passages in revelation, and just as these passages do not mean to promote metempsychosis, so does Suhrawardī's sentence not promote it. An actual explanation of what the sentence really means is purposely not given. He leaves it at that as the "pure of heart" will understand.

It seems then, that our Muḥammad Bāqir Jīlānī took it upon himself to fill this void left by Mīr Dāmād. I would argue that Jīlānī's main effort was to create an interpretation of Suhrawardī's sentence that was unassuming, to make the sentence sound as innocent as possible. He did so in several ways which we can organise in a similar fashion as how we earlier read Suhrawardī's passage, in the rhetorical categories of *ethos*, *pathos*, and *logos*. Firstly, he constructed his essay out of quotations of other sources. Nearly two-thirds of the essay comes from other sources, and he acknowledges each source. These sources are invariably mainstream thinkers, mostly from the twelfth to fourteenth century. Jīlānī thus makes an argument from authority (*ethos*), suggesting that Suhrawardī's thought is no different from these well-respected thinkers. Secondly, he included a great amount of traditional sources, both Revelation and its traditional interpretation. By not discussing their compatibility with Suhrawardī's sentence, it is assumed that Suhrawardī's sentence is perfectly compatible with the Koran and its traditional interpretation. I find this a *pathos* argument, as it evokes an agreeable sentiment in the reader. The *logos* of his rhetoric comes last and is the most misleading. He cites an argument against metempsychosis from Suhrawardī's *al-Mashāriʿ*, to convince his readers that Suhrawardī was patently against it. Meanwhile, he leaves the truly problematic passages from *al-Talwīḥāt* and *Ḥikmat al-ishrāq* out of the essay.

Jīlānī's main argument is that Suhrawardī is not speaking of a metempsychosis, as he is not speaking of the soul returning to a material body in this world, but returning to an imaginable body in another world. Jīlānī argues that from the time of death until the moment of resurrection, human beings stay in "the world of image" (*ʿālam-i mithāl*), known by the *Ishrāqiyūn* as "Hurqalya" and by traditional Muslim thinkers as the "barzakh". Why Suhrawardī would be speaking here of imaginable bodies is only asserted and not argued for. The exploration of how metempsychosis can be distinguished from resurrection is, however, interesting in its meticulous construction of a definition of metempsychosis that carefully delimits what is and what is not considered metempsychosis. The summary provided below will shed more light on his argumentation.

In spirit, Jīlānī's interpretation comes close to what was argued for by Shaykh Bahāʾī (d.1020/1631), an important Shīʿī scholar who was good friends with Mīr Dāmād.[30] Shaykh Bahāʾī was one of the first to use the notion of the world of image to give philosophical meaning to the traditional notion of the *barzakh*.[31] From the same time we have Mullā Ṣadrā (d. 1045/1635), who also discusses these issues. Importantly, he does not invoke the traditional notion of the *barzakh* when interpreting imaginable bodies. He does not acknowledge that we connect to *an* imaginable body, meaning, some different body, but rather that we stay the same as our soul and its accrued lifetime experience becomes the matter on which the imaginable body is shaped.[32] He contrasts this with the followers of Suhrawardī, the *Ishrāqiyūn*, who consider any imaginable to be possible.[33] As such, by considering Jīlānī's essay we get the sense of a lively debate surrounding resurrection, metempsychosis, and the world of image, in seventeenth century Safavid Iran.

Sources

To understand the discursive context of Jīlānī's essay, we can consider his sources. He draws from fourteen sources in order to construct his essay, which together take up more than two-thirds of the text. They can be divided roughly into three groups: a) philosophical texts that situate the problem, b) theological texts that explicate the underlying discussion, and c) revelation, traditional sources, and literary sources that exemplify how the discussion is embedded in mainstream Islamic thinking. The cited sources tell us that Suhrawardī's ideas were discussed as part of a sober, theological-philosophical discourse. The generous use of traditional sources such as Koran, Hadith, and *tafsīr*, tell us in addition that this discussion was conceived to be in full agreement with Islamic dogma, at the centre rather than the periphery of Islamic thinking. Here follows a list of the sources.

Illuminationist Sources

First there is the sentence from Suhrawardī's (d. 587/1191) *Ḥikmat al-ishrāq* around which this essay is structured. Compared to the original, Jīlānī has dropped a few words and changed one singular into a plural (evils instead of evil). Its equivalent can be found in Suhrawardī, *The Philosophy of Illumination* [= Ḥikmat al-Ishrāq], transl. by J. Walbridge and H. Ziai, Provo: Brigham Young University Press, 1999, p. 158 (§ 268).

At the end of the epistle is another excerpt from Suhrawardī. This is the entire section of *imtināʿ al-tanāsukh* from his *al-Mashāriʿ wa-l-muṭāraḥāt*. To be found in Suhrawardī, *Opera Metaphysica et Mystica* [= Œuvres Philosophiques et Mystiques / Majmūʿa fī al-ḥikma al-ilāhiyya], ed. by H. Corbin, Orig. publ. 1945–1970, 4 vols., Tehran: Institut franco-iranien, 2009, vol. 1, pp. 499–500.

Then there is Quṭb al-Dīn Shīrāzī's (d. 710/1310) explanation of this sentence. It can be found in Shīrāzī, Quṭb al-Dīn, *Sharḥ Ḥikmat al-ishrāq* [= Commentary on Illuminating Wisdom], ed. by A. Nourani and M. Mohaghegh, Tehran: Mu'assasah-i muṭālaʿāt al-islāmī, 2001, p. 524.

Finally, in this category we may include Mīr Dāmād's (d. 1041/1631) discussion of this very sentence. The correspondence in question has survived and has been published in Mīr Dāmād, "Taʿlīqa ʿalā Ḥikmat al-ishrāq," in *Muṣannafāt-i Mīr Dāmād*, ed. by A. Nourani, Tehran: Anjuman-i āthār wa mufākhir-i farhangī, 2003, pp. 523–527.

Philosophical Sources

The next group includes the polymath Taftāzānī (d. 793/1390), whose cited passage comes from a discussion on eschatology in Taftāzānī, Saʿd al-Dīn, *Sharḥ al-Maqāṣid*, ed. by A.R. Umayra, 5 vols., Beirut: ʿĀlam al-kutub, 1989, vol. 5, pp. 89–90.

Another passage is from the theologian Fakhr al-Dīn Rāzī (d. 606/1209). The closest equivalent can be found in a chapter on the difference between spiritual and bodily resurrection in *Nihāyat al-ʿuqūl*. The passage in Jīlānī's essay, however, is in comparison only a paraphrase, and I have therefore refrained from giving precise alternative readings in the apparatus. Compare Rāzī, Fakhr al-Dīn, *Nihāyat al-ʿuqūl fī dirāyat al-uṣūl*, ed. by S. Fouda, 4 vols., Beirut: Dār al-dhakhā'ir, 2015, vol. 4, pp. 144–145.

Samarqandī (d. 701/1302),[34] best known as an astronomer, is also cited, again from a chapter on eschatology. In fact, we are concerned here with two distinct passages: Samarqandi, Shams al-Dīn, *al-Ṣaḥā'if al-ilāhiyya*, ed. by A.A. al-Sharif, Kuwait: Maktabat al-falāḥ, 1985, pp. 437–438, 441–443.

The last member of this group is Iṣfahānī (d. 749/1348). Like the others in this group, he is a polymath-theologian. An entire paragraph from the discussion on eschatology is taken: Iṣfahānī, Maḥmūd ibn ʿAbd al-Raḥmān, and ʿAbd Allāh Bayḍāwī, *Matāliʿ al-anẓār ʿalá Ṭawāliʿ al-anwār*, ed. by U. H. al-Khishab, Cairo: al-Maṭbaʿa al-khayriyya, 1323 (1905) [Reprint Cairo: Dār al-kutbī, 2008], pp. 217–218.[35]

Traditional Sources

Among non-philosophical sources, the Koran is cited ten times, with the following verses: Ibrāhīm 14:50, al-Ḥajj 22:19, al-Najm 53:47, Ya-Sīn 36:78–79, al-Qiyāma 75:3-4, al-Nāziʿāt 79:11, Fuṣṣilat 41:21, al-ʿĀdiyāt 100:9, al-Qaṣaṣ 28:88, and al-Naba' 78:18.

Hadith are used too, but without a rigorous reference. There is a Hadith on ablution, one about the cutting of lips of transgressors with fiery scissors, and a long one on how people will gather at the Day of Resurrection in different forms according to their behaviour during their Earthly lives.

Prose is used twice. One time, a proverb is cited without attribution. It can be related back to Māwardī (d. 450/1058), compare Māwardī, *Adab al-dunyā wa-l-dīn*, Beirut: Dār al-kutub al-ʿilmiyya, 1987, p. 305. Additionally, a verse is used, again without attribution. It is commonly attributed to Imam al-Shāfiʿī (d. 204/820), compare Shāfiʿī, *Dīwān al-imām al-Shāfiʿī*, ed. by I.B. Yaqub, Beirut: Dār al-kitāb al-ʿarabī, 1996, p. 165.

In this category, I also wish to include two citations from Koran commentaries. The first comes from the famous *al-Kashshāf* by Zamakhsharī (d. 538/1143). The end of the commentary on Sura Ibrāhīm is included, Zamakhsharī, Abū l-Qāsim, *al-Kashshāf ʿan ḥaqāʾiq ghawāmiḍ al-tanzīl wa-ʿuyūn al-aqāwīl fī wujūh al-taʾwīl*, ed. by A.A. Abd al-Mawjud and A.M. Mu'awwad, 6 vols., Riyadh: Maktaba al-ʿubaykān, 1998, vol. 3, p. 394.

The second is a *tafsīr* fragment on al-Nabaʾ 78:18. Jīlānī does not attribute it to anybody, but it can be found nearly verbatim in Fakhr al-Dīn Rāzī, *al-Tafsīr al-kabīr* [= Mafātiḥ al-ghayb], ed. A.R. Muhammad, Cairo: al-Maṭbaʿa al-bahiyya, n.d., vol. 31, p. 10. It should be noted, however, that with the exception of the first sentence, this explanation can already be found in Zamakhsharī, *al-Kashshāf*, vol. 6, pp. 298–299. As such, it became a popular interpretation and it could be that Jīlānī actually took this excerpt from another work of *tafsīr*.

Summary

Jīlānī explicitly divides his essay into three parts, an introduction (*muqaddima*), investigation (*tabṣira*), and conclusion (*takhtima*). It seems that the conclusion is missing, although the way the essay ends now works just as well. Before this "introduction" there is a paragraph which we can call a preface. In total, if we follow the rhetorical flow of the text, we can identify thirteen paragraphs, which may be summarised as follows.

1. Preface. The author, Jīlānī, explains how a sentence from Suhrawardī's *Ḥikmat al-ishrāq* stood out to some people, who thought it smacked of metempsychosis (*tanāsukh*). They were strengthened in this by the commentary of Quṭb al-Dīn Shīrāzī on this sentence. Suhrawardī's sentence is the following: "[God] has decreed to the Faithful Spirit that He will answer the prayers of all who are weighed down with gloom, of all who are pure yet seek to be darkened, and that He will aid the patient against the evils of the sons of the devils, that He will clothe the evildoers in shirts of tar."[36] A snippet from Quṭb al-Dīn Shīrāzī's commentary is mentioned in explanation of the "shirts of tar." He says: "that is, black skins which belong to species of animals." This mention of animals is enough, for some, to accuse Suhrawardī and Quṭb al-Dīn Shīrāzī of adhering to metempsychosis. Jīlānī says he finds this strange, "as no other place has such a statement about metempsychosis." He then announces, in a humble manner, that he will absolve Suhrawardī in this essay.

2. *Introduction.* Jīlānī says he found out about this issue while reading correspondence (*murāsila*) from Mīr Dāmād, who cites this sentence from Suhrawardī and says that some scholars have used it as an indication of metempsychosis. Mīr Dāmād thinks this is not the case.

3. *The answer of Mīr Dāmād.* Jīlānī quotes directly from Mīr Dāmād, who says that while exchanging letters, he came to a new insight on this sentence from Suhrawardī's *Ḥikmat al-ishrāq*. Mīr Dāmād thinks it should be seen in the context of verses from Sura Hajj and Sura Ibrahim. He specifically thinks of verse 50 of Ibrahim, which reads "of pitch (*qaṭirān*) their shirts, their faces enveloped by the Fire." He also reminds the reader of a Hadith about ablution which reads "I seek refuge in you from the garments of flames." These traditional sources speak of clothing, as Suhrawardī did, but they do not intend to mean metempsychosis, and likewise Suhrawardī's sentence should be read not to mean metempsychosis. Jīlānī gives another Koran verse and a Hadith to support Mīr Dāmād's use of the ablution-Hadith.

4. *Zamakhsharī's explanation of the Koran verse which Mīr Dāmād referred to.* In the next paragraph, Jīlānī argues why Mīr Dāmād's use of the Koran verse is apt. He cites Zamakhsharī's commentary on the verse, who explains how the word "qaṭirān" refers to a particular berry from which an intense black dye can be cooked. It is this dye that is supposed to be used to paint the people of Hell.

5. *Investigation.* This is the heart of Jīlānī's essay, in which he sets forth his defence of accusations of metempsychosis mounted against Suhrawardī. He starts by giving definitions of metempsychosis (*tanāsukh*) and resurrection (*ḥashr wa-maʿād*), which are nearly the same. In both cases the human soul is returned to a material body in order to undergo punishment or reward in accordance with its actions. However, with metempsychosis the human soul is returned to a body in *this* genesis (*nash'a*, i.e. this world) whereas for resurrection the human is returned to a body in *another* genesis. Jīlānī then explains the function of the different parts of the definition. Humans *need to return* so that they may undergo punishment and reward. This is

necessary because punishment and reward are necessary. They are necessary, in turn, because there needs to be justice. As Jīlānī says, life can only be considered fair if an oppressor receives retribution for what they did against the oppressed. According to Jīlānī, the function of Suhrawardī saying "He will aid the patient against the evils of the sons of the devils," is to refer to this principle of justice. Next, to include in the definition that a human returns to an *elemental* body is done in order to exclude imaginable bodies. Jīlānī is basically pointing out that when souls connect to imaginable bodies, neither the term metempsychosis nor resurrection is applicable to it. Continuing, that the soul *connects* is said so that metempsychosis in a general meaning is included in this discussion, that is to say, transmigration to animals, plants, and inanimate objects. *Punishment and reward* is part of the definition so that other cases of people returning to this genesis are excluded, as is the case for several prophets such as Uzair and Imam Ali,[37] and as is also the case for the state in the grave, when Munkir and Nakir interrogate a human being.[38] Jīlānī concludes that what Suhrawardī meant with the sentence in question is a connection with an imaginable body in the intermediate state between death and resurrection. These souls are in what is called the world of image (*ʿālam al-mithāl*), which is also called *Hūrqalyā* by the Illuminationist philosophers, in which these people experience pain and pleasure. Jīlānī says this state is known as the *barzakh* in traditional Islamic sources and is mentioned by philosophers, Christians, and the infallible Imams. Muslim intellectuals also support this interpretation. For example Ghazālī and Ghiyāth al-Dīn Dashtakī agree with this notion, according to Jīlānī. In this sense, Suhrawardī's sentence has nothing to do with metempsychosis which is explicitly and only the return to an elemental body for the purpose of punishment and reward [in this genesis].

6. An excerpt from Taftāzānī. Jīlānī immediately follows his own explanation with a string of citations. The first is from Taftāzānī. In this passage, Taftāzānī explains how different factions have understood resurrection. Some say it is bodily only, others spiritual only. A last group thinks it is both, which includes Ghazālī, "the majority of Sufis and Shi'is," and also those who support metempsychosis.

7. An excerpt from Fakhr al-Dīn Rāzī. The passage from Fakhr al-Dīn Rāzī more or less continues the train of thought of the excerpt from Taftāzānī. Rāzī says that for Muslims, souls come to be at a certain time and are returned to a body in a different abode, whereas supporters of metempsychosis claim that souls have always existed and are again and again returned to bodies in this world. They thereby deny the afterlife, heaven and hell, and for this are to be avoided.

8. An excerpt from Samarqandī. The passage which Jīlānī chose from Samarqandī rehashes what Taftāzānī and Fakhr al-Dīn Rāzī have been saying, with an emphasis on affirming that the Koran promotes a bodily resurrection. The reader is also introduced to the principle that the nonexistent cannot be brought back; therefore, in order to have a resurrection, something needs to remain in existence.

9. An excerpt from Iṣfahānī. A passage from Iṣfahānī explains that death and destruction, such as indicated by the well-known Koran verse from al-Qasas "All things perish, except His Face," does not mean going out of existence, but means the division of a body into pieces that disperse over the world.[39]

10. Moving on to Quṭb al-Dīn Shīrāzī. Jīlānī writes that we now know that Suhrawardī means that the soul lives on to connect with an imaginable body. Furthermore, this does not imply metempsychosis, which is specifically connecting with an elemental body. As for Quṭb al-Dīn Shīrāzī's interpretation on Suhrawardī's sentence, this too can be connected with Koran verses and Hadith, such as the Koran verse from al-Naba "the day the Trumpet is blown, and you shall come in troops."

11. A Quran commentary explaining the verse. Jīlānī cites a Koran commentary to show the connection between the verse and Quṭb al-Dīn Shīrāzī's statement. The commentary explains that the term "troops" (*afwāj*^{an}) here mean "different groups." In a Hadith, the prophet gave examples of them. One group, those who engage in slander, will resurrect in the form of monkeys. Another in the form of pigs, for those who have illegal possessions. Others, who take interest on loans, will be inverted with their feet up and their head dragging on the floor. And so forth. As such, Quṭb al-Dīn Shīrāzī's comment on "[different] species of animals" is an innocent remark that can be related to how Muhammad spoke about the different groups in the Hereafter.

12. Conclusion. Jīlānī does not use the word for conclusion, *takhtima*, as he announced at the beginning of his essay, at this point in the essay. Even so, the essay is nearing the end and at this point he states in three sentences what we have learned from the argumentation that he presented. He says that the foregoing confirms that to speak of a certain form (such as a monkey, a pig, or an inverted body) does not imply metempsychosis, and this is how Suhrawardī's and Quṭb al-Dīn Shīrāzī's sentence should be understood.

13. Suhrawardī himself argues against metempsychosis. In the last paragraph of the essay as it has survived to our day, Jīlānī says that Suhrawardī himself argued against metempsychosis, and gives a passage from *al-Mashāriʿ*. Suhrawardī there argues that when a body comes to be, a suitable soul is created for it. When a human soul separates from the body at death, and it would go to a new body, it would find that this body already has a soul, namely, the one which was suitably created for it. This means that this body now has two souls, the one created for it and the one transmigrated to it, and this is impossible. This is, of course, the two-souls-one-body argument discussed before, and its inclusion here by Jīlānī without any discussion of its precarious nature in Suhrawardī's writings is, for us as outside observers, highly problematic. Jīlānī simply continues to cite *al-Mashāriʿ*, and has Suhrawardī argue that if transmigration would work downward, then it is easily seen that this cannot add up. The number of animals greatly exceeds the number of human beings, and similarly plants outnumber animals, so there would be more carriers for souls than souls, which is impossible. If transmigration would work upwards, then the number of souls would exceed the number of carriers for a soul. Transmigration is therefore not correct, "although," says Suhrawardī, "there is a discussion about this for which you will have to look elsewhere in my writings." Jīlānī does not elaborate on this enigmatic last statement but simply says "here ends the interpretation of his statement," and with that the essay itself ends too.

Conventions

I have based the edition on digital photos of two manuscripts, National Library of Iran 166792, ff. 29b–33a, and Marʿashī 11619, ff. 119b–123a. Initially I only knew of the Marʿashī manuscript, and I thank Dr. Muḥammad Javad Esmaeili for bringing the other manuscript to my attention and supplying me with photographs of both manuscripts. The photos were of bad quality but adequate enough for the job at hand. Of the Millī manuscript, one page per photo was visible. The photos are about 1100 × 1700 in pixel size, and 180kb in file size. Colour balance and lighting are okay, but the cut is too tight, meaning that the edges of the manuscript are not visible. The text under consideration is in the text block of the manuscript and is as such entirely visible. The Marʿashī manuscript shows a page spread per photo, at 1178 ×1210 in pixel size and about 330kb in file size. The colour balance is okay though the lighting could be brighter. The cut is slightly too tight, as the edges of the manuscript fall just outside the photos.

Since I only have photos of the relevant folios, I cannot give a full codicological description. The pages of the Marʿashī manuscript are much longer than they are wide. They have 22 lines per page, using red ink for rubrication. Red ink is also used for overlining but this is done inconsistently. What is more interesting is the use of script. The essay is in principal written in Persian, but with the extensive citations more than half of the essay ends up being in Arabic. This is reflected in the script; Persian parts are in *nastaʿlīq*, Arabic parts are in *naskh*. The essay is properly introduced at the top of a new page with a *basmala* and white space. The essay ends two lines from the bottom of a page and leaves those two lines blank. This, I think, shows a deliberate end to the essay and indicates that the place the essay ends now is likely the place the essay ended in the manuscript which the copyist used. The manuscript shows catchphrases and occasional corrections in the margin.

The pages of the Millī manuscript are unusually white. The line number seems to differ from page to page, but is about 19. The text is written in a somewhat sloppy *nastaʿlīq*, with a few rubrics in red. There are a few corrections in the margin but no catchwords. Like the other manuscript, this one introduces the essay properly with a *basmala* at the head of the page with white space. It ends about a third of the way down a page and leaves the rest open.

In editing, I have not given preference to either of the manuscripts. I do not note difference in eulogies, nor conjugation of verbs. Where the essay cites a source but differs from it, I have followed the essay and indicated the difference in the apparatus. For example, in Māwardī's saying, the last word is written *al-mutafarriq* in both manuscript copies of the essay, while in the printed edition it is written *al-muftariq*; in the body of the text I edited *al-mutafarriq*. For distinguishing the manuscripts and the different sources, I use the following abbreviations.

المخطوطات الأصلية	
ق	كتابخانه عمومى حضرت آية الله لطفى مرعشى نجفى، قم، رقم ١١٦١٩، صص. ١١٩ظ-١٢٣و
ط	كتابخانه ملى ايران، طهران، رقم ١٦٦٧٩٢، صص. ٢٩ظ-٣٣و

المصادر الإشراقية	
س ح	السهروردي، حمكة الإشراق
س م	السهروردي، المشارع والمطارحات
ق د	قطب الدين الشيرازي، شرح حكمة الإشراق
م د	مير داماد، تعليقة على حمكة الإشراق

المصادر العقلية		المصادر النقلية	
ت	التفتازاني، شرح المقاصد	{}	القرآن الكريم والأحاديث النبوية
ف ن	فخر الدين الرازي، نهاية العقول	م	الماوردي، أدب الدنيا والدين
ص	السمرقندي، الصحائف الإلهية	ش	الشافعي، ديوان الإمام الشافعي
إ	الإصفهاني، شرح الطوالع	ز	الزمخشري، الكشاف
		ف م	فخر الدين الرازي، مفاتح الغيب

Edition

***

بسم الله الرحمن الرحيم
الحمد لله حق حمده والصلوة على نبيه محمد وآله الذين هم هداه طريق الحق من بعده

أما بعد[40] چنين گويد معتصم بلطف عميم ربانى محمد باقر جيلاني كه بعضى از اخوان عقلانى وخلّان روحانى استكشاف واستعلام فقره از كلام شيخ اتباع الرواقيه محيى مراسم اشراقيه الشيخ الجليل الالهى شيخ شهاب الدين السهروردى روّح الله روحه نموده بودند كه در[41] مقاله خامسه از قسم ثانى حكمت اشراق كه باين عبارت فرموده وقضى إلى الروح الأمين ليجيب دعوة كل مظلوم[42] بانظلامة وكل ذي نظافة يطلب التظلم[43] ولينصر الصابرين بأساء[44] أنباء الشياطين وليلبس الفاجر سربال القار جمله أخيره را قطب فلك تحقيق علامه شيرازى شرح وبيان چنين[45] كرده كه أى الجلود السود التي لأنواع الحيوانات واين كلام روى بمذهب تناسخ وارد و شيخ الهى و هم شارح علامه را نسبت بتناسخ نمودن بعيد وغريب است چه سخنان او در هيچ مواضع ديگر به تناسخ ندارد هر چند امثال اين قليل البضاعه را جراة اقدام در حلّ كلام اساطين حكماى عظام نمودن در عرضه سهام اغراض وملال[46] در آمدنست امّا بموجب كلام اكابر كه وإنما حظّ الاخير جمع الشارد وحفظ المتفرق[47] طرفى از كلام حكماى عظام وعلماى اعلام بحسب مناسبت مقام در سلك انتظام در آورده شد
مترصد از صاحبان طبع قويم وذهن مستقيم آنكه اگر بر هفوتى وزلتى كه لازمه طبيعت انسانيست مطلع كردند در اصلاح[48] كوشند نه در افضاح

وعين الرضا عن كل عيب كليلة ولكن عين السخط تبدي المساويا

واين مساله مرتب است بر مقدمه وتبصره وتختمه
ومنه الاستعانة في البدأة والخاتمة

مقدمه بعضى از علماى[49] فارس استكشاف اين فقره كلام بطريق مراسله از خاتم الحكماء المتالهين باقر علوم الاولين والآخرين قدّس الله نفسه واوطن في خطائر القدس رُمْسَهُ نموده بودند باين عباره كه راى زرين وخرد خرده بين نوّاب مستطاب حكمت مآب ثالث[50] المعلمين جامع الحكمتين استاذ البشر العقل الحادى عشر فخر الحكما وارث الانبيا[51] وسمَى مولانا لا زال كاسمه باقرا چه ميفرمايند در حلّ اين فقره از كلام شيخ مقتول در مقاله خامسه از قسم ثانى حكمت اشراق كه وقع الله في السفر وقضى إلى[52] روح الأمين إلى قوله وليلبس الفاجر سربال القار[53] علماى فارس حمل جمله اخيره بر تناسخ نموده اند ومخلص را نسبت تناسخ شيخ تامل است
جواب كه از حضره قدسيه وسدهٔ فيلسوفيه سمت اصدار يافته بود در بيان اعضال[54] باين عبارت بود كه در طى مفاوضه مبتهجه[55] ومكاتبه بهيجه استكشاطى رفته بود از سر آنچه محيى آثار رواقيه[56] شيخ اتباع الاشراقيه در سابع خامسه[57] حكمت اشراق بهذه العبارة گفته است وقع الله في السفر وقضى إلى الروح[58] الأمين[59] ليجيب دعوة كل مغلوب بانظلامة وكل ذي نظافة يطلب التظلم[60] ولينصر الصابرين[61] بأساء أنباء الشياطين وليلبس الفاجر سربال القار[62] تاملى كه در[63] جمله اخيره بر[64] تناسخ نموده اند[65] در موضع استقامت[66] ومحزّ اصابت واقع آمده است سياق ساقت عبارت

اشارتست بآنچه در تنزیل کریم در سورهٔ مبارکه حج[67] ودر سورهٔ مکرمه ابراهیم است که ﴿سرابیلهم من قطران وتغشی وجوههم النار﴾ ودر حدیث دعای[68] غسل شمال واردست ﴿وأعوذ بك من مقطعات النیران﴾ بهیچ وجهی نسبت[69] بحکایت[70] تناسخ ندارد وهمچنین شیخ مصنف[71] کتاب از اعتقاد[72] تناسخ[73] بريء الساحه وناصح الجیب می نماید علی ما وقع إلینا من زبره بلغنا من أقاویله انتهی کلامه اعلی الله مقامه بعبارته وألفاظه واز استفادات حضرت قدسیه وسده فیلسوفیه می باشد که لفظ مقطعات النیران را بکسر عین الفعل وبفتح[74] هر دو متیوان خواندن امّا فتح اشارتست بآیه کریمه ﴿فالذین کفروا قطّعت لهم ثیاب من نار﴾ که استعاذه از آن می باشد وآنچه توجیه کسر است اشارتست[75] بآنچه در احادیث از طریق معصومین صلوات الله علیهم اجمعین آمده است که ﴿دست وپای عاصیانرا بمقراض آتشین ومنشار خواهند برید﴾
وصاحب کشاف در تفسیر آیه کریمه ﴿سرابیلهم من قطران وتغشی وجوههم النار﴾ ذکر کرده که القطران ما یتحلّب من شجر یقال له[76] الأبهل فیطبخ ویتهنأ[77] به الإبل الجربي فیحرق الجرب بحرّه[78] وقد تبلغ حرارته الجوف ومن شأنه أن یسرع فیه اشتعال النار وقد یستسرج[79] وهو أسود اللون منتن الراحة[80] فیطلی به جلود أهل النار حتی یعود طلاؤة لهم کالسرابیل وهي القمیص[81] فیجمع[82] علیهم الأربع لذع القطران وحرقته وإسراع النار في جلودهم واللون الوحش والریح[83] المنتن[84] والتفاوت بین القطرانین کالتفاوت بین النارین وکلما[85] وعد[86] الله سبحانه وأوعد[87] به في الآخرة فبینه وبین ما نشاهد من جنسه تفاوت[88] لا نقادر قدره وکأنه ما عندنا منه لیس[89] إلا الأسامي انتهی عبارته
تبصرة بدانکه تناسخ عبارتست از عود روح انسانی که عبارت از نفس ناطقه است[90] ببدن عنصری مطلقا بجهه مجازات ومکافات اعمال درین نشاه وحشر ومعاد عبارتست از عود روح ببدن اول عنصری بجهه مجازات ومکافات اعمال در نشاۀ دیگر چنانکه حق سبحانه وتعالی در قرآن مجید[91] میفرماید ﴿وأن علیه النشأة الأخری﴾ چون انتصاف مظلوم از ظالم بنابر قاعدۀ عدل بر متمکن لازم وواجب است شرعا وعقلا چنانکه شیخ فرموده که[92] وینصر الصابرین بأساء أبناء الشیاطین واین مجازات ومکافات که مجمع علیه اولو العقل شده یا درین نشاه می باشد چنانکه معتقد اهل تناسخ است[93] یا در نشاۀ دیگر چنانکه معتقد اهل حق وملّت است وتقید بقید بدن عنصری جهت اخراج جسد مثالی است وقید مطلقا بجهت ادخال تناسخ بمعنی اعم بمذهب قائلین بفسخ ومسخ ورسخ وقید بجهت مجازات ومکافات اعمال بنابر اخراج[94] عود روح درین نشات بطریق اعجاز[95] چنانکه از انبیا صادر شده وقصّه عزیر پیغمبر و غیر آن یا بعنوان کرامات چنانچه از حضرت امیر المؤمنین صلوات الله علیه واقع شده[96] اینها بطریق اعجاز وکرامات است نه بطریق[97] مجازات ومکافات وهمچنین قصه رجعت که از حضرة صاحب الامر صلوات الله وتسلیمات علیه که[98] صادر خواهد شد یا بنابر انجاح آمال شیعیان بالجهت اثبات قاعدۀ امامت یا بنابر حکمت دیگر که سرّ آن بر ما منکشف نیست وهمچنین احیاء در قبر که بجهت سوال منکر ونکیر مي شد این قسم را تناسخ وبعث ونشور مصطلح نشده بلکه هر کدام را بحسب اختلاف حقیقه مسمی باسمی کردانیده اند پس بنابرین مقدمه عبارت شیخ الهی نسبت تناسخ نمودن وحمل بغیر مصطلح کردن وجهی ندارد چه تعلق روح بجسد مثالی چنانکه معتقد حکما است واز اهل ملت از بعضی نصاری نقل کرده اند ومنطوق احادیث منقول از حضرت ائمة معصومین صلوات الله علیهم اجمعین واردست که روح انسانی تا ازف قیامت متعلق ببدن مثالی

خوهد شد که در عالم مثال که باصطلاح حکمای اشراق هورقليا خوانند سعدا بنعيم واشقيا بعذاب اليم می باشند واز متقدمين متكلمين امام غزالى واز متاخرين غياث اهل التدقيق همين طريق رفته اند كه ارواح در عالم برزخ که از موت تا بحشر است بحسد مثالى خواهند بود ربطى بمقدمه تناسخ ندارد چه تناسخ چنانچه مذکور شد عبارت است از عود روح انسانی ببدن عنصری بجهت مجازاة ومكافاة اعمال
قال الفاضل التفتازانى اتفق المحققون من الفلاسفة والمليين على قضيت[99] المعاد واختلفوا في كيفيته فذهب[100] المسلمون إلى أنه جسماني فقط لأن الروح عندهم جسم لطيف[101] سار في البدن كماء الورد في الورود سريان النار في الفحم[102] وذهب الفلاسفة إلى أنه روحاني فقط لأن البدن ينعدم بصوره وأعراضه فلا يعاد والنفس جوهر مجرد باق لا بسبيل للفناء إليه[103] فيعود إلى عالم المجردات بقطع التعلقات وذهب كثير من علماء الإسلام كالإمام الغزالي والكعبي والحليمي والراغب والقاضي أبو زيد الدبوسي إلى القول بالمعاد الروحاني والجسماني جميعا ذهابا[104] إلى أن النفس جوهر مجرد بعود إلى البدن وهذا رأي كثير من الصوفية والشيعة[105] وبه يقولون[106] جمهور النصارى والتناسخية
قال الإمام الرازي إلا أن الفرق أن المسلمين يقولون بحدوث الأرواح وردّها إلى الأبدان لا في هذا العالم بل في الآخرة والتناسخية بقدمها وردّها إليها في هذا العالم وينكرون الآخرة والجنة والنار وإنما نبّهنا على هذا الفرق لأن غلب على الطباع العامة أن هذا المذهب يجب أن يكون كفرا وضلالا لكونه مما يذهب إليه التناسخية والنصارى ولا يقولون أن التناسخية إنما يكفرون لإنكارهم القيامة والجنة والنار والنصارى إنما يكفرون بقولهم التثليث و أما القول بالنفوس[107] المجردة فلا يدفع أصلا من أصول[108] الدين بل إنما يؤيّده ولقد بالغ الغزالي في تحقيق المعاد الروحاني وبيان أنواع الثواب والعقاب حتى سبق إلى كثير من الأوهام ودفع الشبهة عن بعض العوام أنه ينكر حشر الأجساد إقراء عليه وقد صرح به في مواضع من كتاب الإحياء وغيره[109] أنتهى عباره بالفاظ وصاحب صحائف سمرقندى ذكر كرده كه[110] واختلف اهل العالم في المعاد[111] فقال المحققون من الأولين والآخرين بجوازه وأنكره القدماء والفلاسفة والطبيعيين[112] وتوقف[113] جالينوس فإنه قال لم يظهر لي أن النفس غير المزاج فإذا كانت هو فعند الموت تصير معدومة ويمتنع المعاد لامتناع إعادة المعدوم وإن كانت جوهرا باقيا بعد فساد المزاج كان المعاد ممكنا ثم القائلون بالمعاد اختلفوا فمنهم من قال إن المعاد هو الجسماني فقط وهو قول أكثر المتكلمين لاعتقادهم أن النفس جسم ومنهم من ذهب إلى أنه روحاني فقط وهو قول الفلاسفة الإلهيين ومنهم من قال[114] إنه روحاني وجسماني جميعا[115] بين الشريعة والحكمة وهو قول كثير من المتكلمين[116] وأكثر النصارى ثم قال بعد ذلك وإنما قلنا إن الصادق أخبر بذلك[117] لاتفاق[118] الأنبياء على ذلك[119] غير موسى عليه السلام فإنه لم يذكر وما نزل عنه[120] في التورية[121] وأما الذين جاءوا بعده كحزقيل وشعيا عليهم السلام فقد وجد في كتبهم[122] ولذلك أقر اليهود[123] وأما الإنجيل فقد ذكر فيه أن الأخبار[124] يصيرون كالملائكة[125] ويكون لهم الحيوة الأبدية والسعادة السرمدية ويمكن حمل ذلك الكلام[126] على المعاد الروحاني وعلى[127] الجسماني وعليهما جميعا إليه[128] ذهب أكثر النصارى وأما[129] القرآن فقد جاء في[130] كثير من المواضع مثل قوله تعالى ﴿من يحي العظام وهي رميم قل يحييها الذي أنشأها أوّل مرّة﴾ و﴿أيحسب الإنسان أن لن[131] نجمع عظامه بلى قادرين على أن نسوّي بنانه﴾ ﴿أئذا كنا عظاما نخرة﴾ ﴿وقالوا لجلودهم لم شهدتم علينا﴾ ﴿أفلا يعلم إذا بعثر ما في القبور﴾ وأمثال ذلك كثيرة فإن قلت[132] دلالة

الألفاظ ليست قطعية فلا يمكن القطع بها لأن المعاد الروحاني مما لا يفهمه أكثر الناس فذكر[133] المعاد الجسماني تمثيلا للمعاد الروحاني قلت ثبت[134] بالتواتر تصريح الأنبياء عليهم السلام بظواهر[135] هذه الألفاظ فيحصل القطع وما ذكرتم في الوجه الثاني تصريح بكذب[136] الأنبياء أما الطبيعيون فلظنهم أن النفس جسم أو جسماني كما مر في أبحاث النفس واعتقاد[137] أن المعدوم لا يعاد أحالوا المعاد مطلقا والإلهيون وإن وافقوهم على امتناع المعاد الجسماني[138] لكن[139] لما اعتقدوا تجرد النفس وبقاءها بعد خراب[140] البدن وذهبوا إلى أن[141] المعاد روحاني ولعل مرادهم بالمعاد الروحاني قطع تعلق النفس عن البدن وإلا لا وجه لإطلاق لفظ المعاد على الباقي انتهى مقالته

وشارح طوالع در بحث معاد گفته كه القول بالمعاد الجسماني غير موقوف على إعدام الأجزاء بالكلية ولم يثبت بدليل قاطع عقلي أو سمعي[142] أن الله تعالى[143] يعدم الأجزاء ثم يعيدها والتمسك[144] بقوله تعالى ﴿كل شيء هالك إلا وجهه﴾ والهلاك بمعنى[145] الفناء ضعيف لأنا لا نسلم أن الهلاك هو الفناء بل الهلاك هو الخروج عن[146] حد الانتفاع وتفرق الأجزاء وخروجها عن حد الانتفاع يكون[147] هلاكا والحق أن الشيء في الآية بمعنى المشي[148]ء فمعنى الآية أن كل شيء هالك في حد ذاته غير هالك بالنظر إلى وجهه الكريم[149] وهو كذلك فإن كل شيء[150] بالنظر إلى ذاته ليس له وجود وبالنظر إلى ذاته[151] تعالى موجود فلا يحتاج[152] صرفها عن ظاهره[153] انتهى

واز اين كلام منقول ظاهر شد كه تناسخ عبارت است از عود روح انسانى ببدن عنصرى چنانكه مفاد لفظ مشعر بآنست وبقاى نفس بعد از خراب بدن وتعلق او بجسد مثالى را تناسخ نمي گويند اين كلام شيخ الهي كه فرموده دليلين الفاجر سربال القار ربطى به تناسخ ندارد همچنين سان[154] وتفسير قطب فلك تحقيق كه فرموده أي الجلود السود[155] التي[156] لانواع الحيوانان[157] چه امثال اين در آيات واحاديث نيز وارد شده درتفسير آية كريمة ﴿يوم ينفخ في الصور فتأتون أفواجا﴾

مفسرين ذكر كرده اند كه معناه أنهم تأتون في ذلك اليوم[158] فوجا فوجا حتى يتكامل اجتماعهم[159] وقيل جماعات مختلفة[160] وعن معاذ أن سأل رسول الله ﷺ فقال يا[161] معاذ سألت عن أمر عظيم من الأمور ثم أرسل عينيه وقال تحشر عشرة أصناف من أمتي بعضهم على صورة القردة وبعضهم على صورة الخنازير وبعضهم منكسون[162] أرجلهم فوق وجوههم يسجبون عليها[163] وبعضهم صما وبكما[164] وبعضهم يمضغون ألسنتهم فهي مدلّاة على صدورهم يسيل القيح في أفواههم يتقذر[165] أهل الجمع وبعضهم مقطعة أيديهم وأرجلهم وبعضهم[166] مصلبون على جذوع من نار وبعضهم أشد نتنا من الجيف وبعضهم ملبسون جبابا سابغة من قطران لاصقة[167] بجلودهم فأما الذين على صورة القردة فالقتات من الناس وأما الذين على صورة الخنازير فأهل السحت وأما المنكسون على وجوههم[168] فأكله الربوا[169] وأما العمي فالذين يجورون في الحكم وأما الصم البكم فهم[170] المعجبون بأعمالهم وأما الذين يمضغون ألسنتهم فالعلماء والقصاص الذين خالف أفعالهم[171] أعمالهم وأما الذين قطعت أيديهم وأرجلهم فهم الذين يؤذون الجيران وأما المصلبون على جذوع من نار[172] فهم[173] السعاة بالناس إلى السلطان وأما الذين[174] أشد نتنا من الجيف فالذين يتبعون الشهوات واللذات ومنعوا حق الله تعالى في[175] أموالهم وأما الذين يلبسون الجباب فأهل الفخر والكبر[176] والخيلاء

معلوم شد از اين كلام منقول كه مجرد تغير[177] صورت وهيئة موجب جواز اطلاق تناسخ نمى باشد وتناسخ بمعنى عود روح باشد ببدن عنصرى در اين نشاة بجهت مجازات

ومكافات اعمال واين معنى از كلام شيخ الهى و هم از كلام قطب المحققين معلوم
نموده
قال الشيخ الإلهي في كتاب المشارع والمطارحات في أبطال التناسخ بهذه العبارة
وما[178] يذكر في امتناع التناسخ[179] أن البدن بمزاجه[180] يستعد نفسا[181] من الواهب فإذا
انتقلت إليه علاقة المستنسخة فيحصل لحيوان واحد نفسان مستجددة ومستنسخة
متصادمة متدافعة وهو محال وأيضا فإن النقل إن كان عن النزول[182] عن الانسان فظاهر
أن أعداد الحيوان[183] تزيد على الإنسان والنبات على الحيوان بشيء لا يتقائس[184] فيفضل
ذوات النفوس على النفوس وهو محال وإن كان بالصعود[185] فالنفوس المنتقلة[186] تفضل
عن[187] الأبدان فتتمانع ومن الحيوانات الصغار أنواع تزيد[188] عدد نوع واحد على جميع
الحيوانات الكبار وكذا في النبات ولا[189] يصح ما ذكر وا وههنا تفصيل[190] يطلب[191] في[192]
بعض المواضع[193] لنا أنتهى عبارة بالفاظه

***

Notes

1 S. Ahmed, *What is Islam? The Importance of Being Islamic*, Princeton: Princeton University Press, 2016, p. 26.

2 L.W.C. van Lit, "The Commentary Tradition on Suhrawardī," in *Philosophy East & West* 68:2, 2018, pp. 539–563.

3 M. Dirayati, *Fankhā*, Tehran: Sāzmān-i asnād wa-kitābkhāna-i millī-i jumhūrī-i islāmī-i Īrān, 1390, vol. 19, p. 542. He ascribes two other works to Jīlānī, *al-Farā'id fī bayan kalimat al-tawḥīd* and *Anīs al-abrār fī mabāḥith al-janna wa-l-nār*. The latter I did indeed find in MS Majlis-i Shūrā-yi Millī 1593, ff. 120–261. The text discusses the afterlife drawing from Shīʿī tafsīr and ḥadīth sources which is in terms of subject relatively close to the current treatise. It does not use philosophy nor does it give any information on the author.

4 H. Corbin, "Prolégomènes," in *Opera Metaphysica et Mystica* [= Œuvres Philosophiques et Mystiques / Majmūʿa fī al-ḥikma al-ilāhiyya]. Suhrawardī, edited by H. Corbin. Orig. publ. 1945–1970. 4 vols. Tehran: Institut franco-iranien, 2009, vol. 1, p. lv; Corbin, H. *En islam iranien: Aspects Spirituels et Philosophiques*. 4 vols. Paris: Gallimard, 1971.

5 I am following Ziai's and Walbridge's translation, but based on Jīlānī's version of this sentence, which is slightly different from the edition of *Ḥikmat al-ishrāq*. Cf. Suhrawardī, *The Philosophy of Illumination* [= Ḥikmat Al-Ishrāq], transl. by J. Walbridge and H. Ziai, Provo: Brigham Young University Press, 1999, p. 158 (§ 268).

6 Suhrawardī, *al-Talwīḥāt*, in *Oeuvres Philosophiques*..., vol. 1, pp. 105–121.

7 J. Walbridge, "The Devotional and Occultist Works of Suhrawardi." *Ishrâq* 2 (2011): pp. 80–97.

8 Quṭb al-Dīn Shīrāzī, *Sharḥ Ḥikmat al-ishrāq* [= Commentary on Illuminating Wisdom]. Edited by A. Nourani and M. Mohaghegh. Tehran: Muʾassasah-i muṭālaʿāt al-islāmī, 2001, p. 524.

9 R. Freitag, *Seelenwanderung in Der Islamischen Häresie*. Berlin: Klaus Schwarz, 1985; Walker, P., "The Doctrine of Metempsychosis in Islam," in *Islamic Studies Presented to Charles J. Adams*, ed. by W.B. Hallaq and D.P. Little, Leiden, 1991, pp. 219–238; Keller, C.-A., "Le monde islamique et les doctrines de réincarnation," in *La réincarnation. Théories, raisonnements et appréciations. Un Symposium*, ed. C.-A. Keller, Bern: Peter Lang, 1986, pp. 181–203; E.R. Alexandrin, "Ràzì and His

Mediaeval Opponents: Discussions Concerning Tanàsukh and the Afterlife." *Cahiers de Studia Iranica* 26 (2002): 397–409; D. Gimaret, "Tanāsukh," *EĪ*, vol. 10, pp. 181b–183a.

10 P.B. Fenton, "New Light on Maimonidean Writings on Metempsychosis and the Influence of Avicenna," in *Avicenna and his Legacy*, ed. Y.T. Langermann, Turnhout: Brepols, 2010; pp. 341–68; W.S.W. Abdullah, "Ibn Sînâ and Abû al-Barakât al-Baghdâdî on the Origination of the Soul (hudûth al-nafs) and the Invalidation of its Transmigration (ibtâl al-tanâsukh)," *Islam & Science*, vol. 5, nr. 2 (2007): pp. 151–64.

11 V. Minorsky, "Ahl-i Ḥaḳḳ", *EĪ*, vol. 1, pp. 260a–263b; M. Khaksar, "Reincarnation as Perceived by the 'People of the Truth'", *Iran and the Caucasus*, vol. 13, no. 1 (2009), pp. 117–123.

12 All references to Corbin's editions in *Oeuvres Philosophiques…*: *al-Talwīḥāt*, vol. 1, p. 81, l. 11; *al-Mashāriʿ*, vol. 1, p. 499, l. 19; *Ḥikmat al-ishrāq*, vol. 2, p. 218, l. 7; *Partaw-nāmah*, vol. 3, p. 74, l. 9; *al-Alwāḥ*, vol. 4, p. 81, l. 13; *Kalimat al-taṣawwuf*, vol. 4, p. 120, l. 4; *al-Lamaḥāt*, vol. 4, p. 236, l. 3.

13 *al-Talwīḥāt*, vol. 1, p. 82.

14 *al-Talwīḥāt*, vol. 1, p. 86.

15 L.W.C. van Lit, *The World of Image in Islamic Philosophy: Ibn Sīnā, Suhrawardī, Shahrazūrī, and Beyond*, Edinburgh: Edinburgh University Press, 2017. See esp. pp. 33–36 where Fakhr al-Dīn Rāzī and Sayf al-Dīn Āmidī are discussed, who think that the version of Ibn Sīnā is still tantamount to metempsychosis.

16 *al-Talwīḥāt*, vol. 1, p. 90.

17 *al-Talwīḥāt*, vol. 1, p. 91.

18 *Ḥikmat al-ishrāq*, vol. 2, p. 230 / *The Philosophy of Illumination*, p. 149.

19 Perhaps to the exclusion of *Rūzī bā jamāʿat-i ṣūfīyān*, cf. Marcotte, "Suhrawardī's Realm of the Imaginal," p. 77; *Rūzī bā jamāʿat-i ṣūfīyān*, vol. 3, pp. 245, 247; translation in Suhrawardī, *The Philosophical Allegories and Mystical Treatises*, trans. W. Thackston. Costa Mesa, CA: Mazda Publishers, 1999, pp. 36, 37; Suhrawardī, *L'archange empourpré: Quinze traités et récits mystiques*, trans. H. Corbin. Paris: Fayard, 1976, pp. 371, 373.

20 S. Schmidtke, "The Doctrine of the Transmigration of Soul according to Shihāb Al-Dīn Al-Suhrawardī (Killed 587/1191) and His Followers." *Studia Iranica* 28 (1999): 237–54, p. 240.

21 Schmidtke, pp. 243–249.

22 Kāshānī, ʿAbd al-Razzāq. *Sharḥ Fuṣūṣ Al-Ḥikam*. Edited by M. Hadizadeh. Tehran: Anjuman-i asār va mufākhir-i farhangī, 2004, p. 141.

23 Mīr Dāmād. "Taʿlīqa ʿalā Ḥikmat al-ishrāq." In *Muṣannafāt-i Mīr Dāmād*, edited by A. Nourani, 523–27. Tehran: Anjuman-i āthār wa mufākhir-i farhangī, 2003.

24 Ibn Sīnā. *Traités Mystiques d'Abou Alî Al-Hosain B. Abdallâh B. Sînâ, Ou d'Avicenne*. Edited by A.F. Mehren. 2 vols. Leiden: Brill, 1889, p. 8.

25 Shīrāzī, Quṭb al-Dīn. *Durrat al-tāj li-ghurrat al-dubāj*. Edited by M. Mishkat. 5 vols. Tehran: Ḥikmat, 1385, vol. 1, pp. 175–176.

26 The statement is actually in the eighth section of the fifth chapter of the second part of *Ḥikmat al-ishrāq*.

27 Note that the last word, in the edition of Mīr Dāmād's text, is 'fire' (*al-nār*), whereas in the edition of Suhrawardī's text and in Jīlānī's essay it reads 'tar' (*al-qār*).

28 Literally: Has come to occupy a correct place and hit the mark, … *dar mawḍiʿ-i istiqāmat wa-maḥazz-i iṣābat wāqiʿ āmadah ast.*

29 I took the translation of passages from the Koran from A.J. Arberry.

30 H. Corbin, *La philosophie iranienne islamique aux XVII et XVIII siècles*. Paris: Buchet/Chastel, 1981, p. 356.

31 L.W.C. van Lit, *The World of Image in Islamic Philosophy*, pp. 152–160.

32 Mullā Ṣadrā, *al-Mabdaʾ wa-l-maʿād fī l-ḥikma l-mutaʿālīya*, ed. by M. Dhubayhi and J. Shah-Nazari. 2 vols. Tehran: Bunyād ḥikmat islāmī ṣadrā, 1381, vol. 2, pp. 552–554.

33 Ibid., pp. 656–657.

34 There is some disagreement about his death date. I rely on Ihsan Fazlioglu's entry on him in T. Hockey, et al. (eds.), *The Biographical Encyclopedia of Astronomers, Springer Reference*, New York: Springer, 2007, p. 1008.

35 For a translation see Bayḍāwī, ʿAbd Allāh, and Maḥmūd ibn ʿAbd al-Raḥmān Iṣfahānī, *Nature, Man and God in Medieval Islam*, transl. by J.W. Pollock and E.E. Calverley, 2 vols., Leiden: Brill, 2002, vol. 1, pp. 1042–1043.

36 I am following Ziai and Walbridge's translation, but based on Jīlānī's version of this sentence, which is slightly different from the edition of *Ḥikmat al-ishrāq*.

37 On Uzair, see H. Lazarus-Yaveh, "ʿUzayr," *EĪ*, vol. 10, p. 960.

38 See C.R. Lange, *Paradise and Hell in Islamic Traditions*. Cambridge: Cambridge University Press, 2015, pp. 125–126; G. Archer, *A Place Between Two Places: The Qurʾānic Barzakh*. Piscataway: Gorgias Press, 2017.

39 One may think here of reflections in popular scientific magazines on the regularly asked question whether we share any atoms with famous people from the past or whether we could breathe in the same oxygen as famous people such as Julius Caesar.

40 ط: وبعد .

41 ق: - .

42 س ح: مغلوب .

43 س ح: + لرضاء الله وأنه .

44 س ح: بأس، لكن في الشرح للعلامة الشيرازي يقال: "وفي نسخة 'بأساء'" .

45 ق: چين .

46 ط: ملام .

47 م أ: وإنما حظ الأخير أن يتعانى حفظ الشارد وجمع المفترق .

48 ق: + آن .

49 ط: علماء .

50 ط: + ثالث .

51 ط: + مولانا .

52 ق: - .

53 م د: النار .

54 ق: "در بيان اعضال" - .

55 م د: مبهجه .

56 م د: الرواقية .

57 م د: + كتاب .

58 ق: روح .

59 س ح: + أنه .

60 س ح: + لرضاء الله وأنه .

61 س ح: + على .

62 م د: النار .

63 م د: + حمل .

64 م د: + طريقه .

65 م د: فرموده اند .

66 ق: اقامت .

67 م د: ههنا يوجد الآية في التعليقة لمير داماد .

68 م د: + وضوء در .

69 م د: وجه نسبتی .
70 م د: + مسلك .
71 م د: + این .
72 م د: عقیده اصحاب .
73 م د: + واعتقاد صحت آن .
74 ق: و فتح .
75 ق: - .
76 ز: يسمى .
77 ز: فتهنأ .
78 ز: + وحدته والجلد .
79 ز: + به .
80 ز: الريح .
81 ز: القمض .
82 ز: لتجتمع .
83 ط: - .
84 ز: ونتن الريح على أن .
85 ز: كل ما .
86 ز: وعده .
87 ز: أو وعد، أو أوعد .
88 ز: ما .
89 ز: - .
90 ق: - .
91 ط: "در قرآن مجید" - .
92 ق: - .
93 ق: + یا در نشأة دیگر چنانکه معتقد اهل تناسخ است .
94 ق: - .
95 ق: - .
96 ق: - .
97 ط: بجهت .
98 ق: - .
99 ت: حقية .
100 ت: + جمهور .
101 ت: - .
102 ت: سريان النار في الفحم والماء في الورد .
103 ت: إليه للفناء .
104 ق: هاديا .
105 ت: + والكرامية .
106 ت: يقول .
107 ق: بنفوس .
108 ق: "من أصول" - .
109 ق: - .
110 ط: - .
111 ص: فيه .
112 ص: قدماء الفلاسفة الطبيعيين .
113 ص: + فيه .
114 ق: +إلى .
115 ص: جسماني وروحاني معا جمعا .

116 ص: المسلمين .
117 ص: - .
118 ص: + قول .
119 ق: بذلك .
120 ص: عليه .
121 ص: التوراة .
122 ص: فقد وجد في كتبهم كحزقيل وشعيا عليهما السلام .
123 ص: +به .
124 ص: الأخيار .
125 ص: ملائكة .
126 ص: - .
127 ق: - .
128 ق: "جميعا إليه" = معا .
129 ص: + في .
130 ق:- .
131 و في القرآن: ألّن .
132 ص: قيل .
133 ص: فذكروا .
134 ط: قد يثبت .
135 ص: + أمثال .
136 ص: بتكذيب .
137 ص: واعتقادهم .
138 ق: - .
139 ص: لكنهم .
140 ص: فناء .
141 ق: - .
142 إ: نقلي .
143 ط: "أن الله تعالى" - .
144 إ: + بنحو .
145 إ: - .
146 إ: من .
147 إ: فيكون .
148 إ: الممكن .
149 إ: - .
150 إ: + أي ممكن .
151 إ: الله .
152 إ: + إلى .
153 إ: ظاهرها .
154 ق: - .
155 ق: السواد .
156 ق: الذي .
157 ق: الحيوان .
158 ف م: ذلك المقام .
159 ف م: + قال عطاء .
160 ف م: روى صاحب الكشاف .
161 ق: "سأل رسول الله ﷺ فقال يا" - .
162 ط: + على .

163 ف م: + وبعضهم عمي.
164 ف م: صم وبكم.
165 ف م: يتقذرهم.
166 ط: -.
167 ف م: لازقة.
168 ق: +النار.
169 ف م: الربا.
170 ف م: -.
171 ف م: يخالف قولهم.
172 ف م: النار.
173 ف م: -.
174 ف م: + هم.
175 ف م: من.
176 ف م: الكبر والفخر.
177 ق: تعبير.
178 س م: مما.
179 ق: "بهذه العبارة وما يذكر في أمتناع التناسخ" -.
180 س م: لمزاجه.
181 ق: نفس، س م: لنفس.
182 س م: بالنزول.
183 س م: الحيوانات.
184 س م: يتقايس.
185 س م: + إلى الإنسان.
186 ق: -.
187 س م: على.
188 س م: يزيد.
189 س م: فلا.
190 ق: -.
191 س م: اطلب.
192 س م: من.
193 س م: مواضع.

Works cited

Abdullah, W.S.W., "Ibn Sînâ and Abû al-Barakât al-Baghdâdî on the Origination of the Soul (hudûth al-nafs) and the Invalidation of its Transmigration (ibtâl al-tanâsukh)," *Islam & Science*, vol. 5, nr. 2 (2007), pp. 151–64.

Ahmed, S., *What is Islam? The Importance of Being Islamic*, Princeton: Princeton University Press, 2016.

Alexandrin, E.R., "Ràzì and His Mediaeval Opponents: Discussions Concerning Tanàsukh and the Afterlife," in *Cahiers de Studia Iranica*, 26, 2002, pp. 397–409.

Archer, G., *A Place Between Two Places: The Qurʾānic Barzakh*, Piscataway: Gorgias Press, 2017.

Bayḍāwī, ʿAbd Allāh, and Maḥmūd ibn ʿAbd al-Raḥmān Iṣfahānī, *Nature, Man and God in Medieval Islam*, transl. by J.W. Pollock and E.E. Calverley, 2 vols., Leiden: Brill, 2002.

Corbin, H., *En islam iranien: Aspects Spirituels et Philosophiques*, 4 vols. Paris: Gallimard, 1971.

Corbin, H., *La philosophie iranienne islamique aux XVII et XVIII siècles*. Paris: Buchet/Chastel, 1981.

Corbin, H., *Opera Metaphysica et Mystica*, 1945–1970. 4 vols. Tehran: Institut franco-iranien, 2009.

Dirayati, M., *Fankhā*, Tehran: Sāzmān-i asnād wa-kitābkhāna-yi millī-yi jumhūrī-i islāmī-i Īrān, 1390, vol. 19

Fenton, P.B., "New Light on Maimonidean Writings on Metempsychosis and the Influence of Avicenna," in *Avicenna and his Legacy*, ed. Y.T. Langermann, Turnhout: Brepols, 2010, pp. 341–68.

Freitag, R., *Seelenwanderung in Der Islamischen Häresie*. Berlin: Klaus Schwarz, 1985.

Gimaret, D., *Encyclopaedia of Islam*, s.v. Tanāsukh.

Hockey, T., et al. (eds.), *The Biographical Encyclopedia of Astronomers, Springer Reference*, New York: Springer, 2007.

Ibn Sīnā, *Traités Mystiques d'Abou Alî Al-Hosain B. Abdallâh B. Sînâ, Ou d'Avicenne*, edited by A.F. Mehren. 2 vols. Leiden: Brill, 1889.

Kāshānī, ʿAbd al-Razzāq, *Sharḥ Fuṣūṣ Al-Ḥikam*, edited by M. Hadizadeh. Tehran: Anjuman-i athār va mufākhir-i farhangī, 2004.

Keller, C.-A., "Le monde islamique et les doctrines de réincarnation," in *La réincarnation. Théories, raisonnements et appréciations. Un Symposium*, ed. C.-A. Keller, Bern: Peter Lang, 1986, pp. 181–203.

Khaksar, M., "Reincarnation as Perceived by the 'People of the Truth,'" in *Iran and the Caucasus*, vol. 13, no. 1 (2009), pp. 117–123.

Lange, C.R., *Paradise and Hell in Islamic Traditions*. Cambridge: Cambridge University Press, 2015.

Lazarus-Yaveh, H., *Encyclopaedia of Islam*, s.v. ʿUzayr.

Lit, L.W.C. van, "The Commentary Tradition on Suhrawardī," *Philosophy East & West* 68:2, (2018), pp. 539–563.

Lit, L.W.C. van, *The World of Image in Islamic Philosophy: Ibn Sīnā, Suhrawardī, Shahrazūrī, and Beyond*, Edinburgh: Edinburgh University Press, 2017.

Minorsky, V., *Encyclopaedia of Islam*, s.v. Ahl-i Ḥaḳḳ.

Mīr Dāmād, "Taʿlīqa ʿalā Ḥikmat al-ishrāq," in *Muṣannafāt-i Mīr Dāmād*, edited by A. Nourani, Tehran: Anjuman-i āthār wa mufākhir-i farhangī, 2003, pp. 523–27.

Mullā Ṣadrā, *al-Mabdaʾ wa-l-maʿād fī l-ḥikma l-mutaʿālīya*, ed. by M. Dhubayhi and J. Shah-Nazari. 2 vols. Tehran: Bunyād ḥikmat islāmī ṣadrā, 1381/2002.

Quṭb al-Dīn Shīrāzī, *Sharḥ Ḥikmat al-ishrāq* (Commentary on Illuminating Wisdom), edited by A. Nourani and M. Mohaghegh. Tehran: Muʾassasah-i muṭālaʿāt al-islāmī, 2001.

Schmidtke, S., "The Doctrine of the Transmigration of Soul according to Shihāb Al-Dīn Al-Suhrawardī (Killed 587/1191) and His Followers." *Studia Iranica* 28 (1999): pp. 237–54.

Shīrāzī, Quṭb al-Dīn, *Durrat al-tāj li-ghurrat al-dubāj*, edited by M. Mishkat, 5 vols. Tehran: Ḥikmat, 1385/2006.

Suhrawardī, *L'archange empourpré: Quinze traités et récits mystiques*, trans. H. Corbin. Paris: Fayard, 1976.

Suhrawardī, *The Philosophical Allegories and Mystical Treatises*, trans. W. Thackston. Costa Mesa, CA: Mazda Publishers, 1999.

Suhrawardī, *The Philosophy of Illumination* (Ḥikmat al-Ishrāq), transl. by J. Walbridge and H. Ziai, Provo: Brigham Young University Press, 1999.

Walbridge, J., "The Devotional and Occultist Works of Suhrawardi." *Ishrâq* 2 (2011): 80–97.

Walker, P., "The Doctrine of Metempsychosis in Islam," in *Islamic Studies Presented to Charles J. Adams*, ed. by W.B. Hallaq and D.P. Little, Leiden, 1991, pp. 219–238.

Notes on Contributors

Martin van Bruinessen
is Professor Emeritus of Comparative Studies of Modern Muslim Societies at Utrecht University. He is an anthropologist with a strong interest in politics, history and philology, and much of his work straddles the boundaries between these disciplines. He has conducted extensive field research in Kurdistan (Turkey, Iran, Iraq, Syria) as well as Indonesia and Southeast Asia generally and has published numerous articles and books about both regions. After his formal retirement in 2011 he has held visiting professorships in London, Istanbul, Yogyakarta, and Singapore, which enabled him to continue field research and engage with colleagues in both regions. He is the editor-in-chief of the *Kurdish Studies Journal* (Brill). His most recent publications include «The Kurdish Medrese in Ottoman and Republican Times,» in *The Oxford Handbook of Religion in Turkey*, eds. Caroline Tee, Fabio Vicini and Philip C. Dorroll (Oxford University Press, 2024) and "The Abolition of the Caliphate, Secularization and Kurdish Nationalism," in *The Abolition of the Ottoman Caliphate, 1924: Debates and Implications*, eds. Elisa Giunchi and Nicola Melis (London: Routledge, 2024).

Arash Ghajarjazi
received his PhD from the Department of Philosophy and Religious Studies at Utrecht University. He works across the fields of media history, memory studies, and religious studies. Currently he is a Postdoc scholar for the ERC-Advanced Grant *Beyond Sharia: The Role of Sufism in Shaping Islam*, completing his monograph *Remembering Khayyam: Episodes of Unbelief in the Reception Histories of Persian Quatrains*. He has published *Irrationalities in Islam and Media in Nineteenth-Century Iran: Faces of Modernity.* Leiden: Leiden University Press, 2022.

Colin Imber
was Reader in Turkish at the University of Manchester until his retirement in 2005. Among other subjects, he has a particular interest in Islamic law and its application in the Ottoman Empire. He is the author of *The Ottoman Empire, 1300–1481* (Isis Press, Istanbul, 1989), *Ebu's-su'ud: the Islamic Legal Tradition* (Edinburgh University Press, 1997), *The Crusade of Varna* (Ashgate, 2006), *The Ottoman Empire, 1300–1650: The Structure of Power* (3rd edition, Red Globe Press, 2019) and editor of Norman Calder, *Islamic Jurisprudence in the Classical Era* (Cambridge University Press, 2010) and V.L. Ménage, *Ottoman Historical Documents* (Edinburgh University Press, 2021).

He has also published three volumes of articles: *Studies in Ottoman History and Law* (1996), *Warfare, Law and Pseudo-History* (2012) and *Mamluks, Muftis and Sipahis: an Ottoman Miscellany* (Isis Press, 1996, 2011, 2022).

Majdoddin Keyvani

(b. 1938) gained his B.A. in 1961, and his PhD from Wales University in 1978. Back in Tehran, he taught Linguistics, English language skills, and translation at several universities. He served as Principal of the University for Teachers' Education at Zahedan Branch (1974–1978). Since 1985 he has collaborated with the Centre for the Great Islamic Encyclopedia as translator, writer of entries and editor. He has also written articles for several other encyclopaedias such as *Encyclopedia of Persian Language and Literature* and a wide range of scholarly journals. He worked at the Encyclopedia of *Iranica* (2009–2010) and has served as the Editor-in-Chief of *Ayaneh-ye Miras* since 2013. His publications add up to over 390 Persian articles, reviews, obituaries and editorials, and 12 English articles. Further, he translated 22 works from English to Persian and A. Zarrinkub's *Pelle Pelle* from Persian into English (*Step* by *Step Up to Union with God:* ..., 2009, winner of Islamic Republic of Iran's World Award). Some of his translations from English are, *Principles of Language Study*, 1974; *Ruzbihan Baqli*: ..., 1998; *The Psychology of Reading*, 1999; Beyond *Faith and Infidelity:* ..., 1999; *Al-Hallaj*, 1999; *The Heritage of Sufism*, 3 volumes, 2005; *The Wine of Wisdom*: ..., 2006 (Winner of Islamic Republic of Iran's Yearbook Award, 2006).

Cornelis van Lit

received his PhD from the department of Philosophy and Religious Studies at Utrecht University. He is an expert on Islamic philosophy, formerly based at Utrecht University. His first book is entitled *The World of Image in Islamic Philosophy* (Edinburgh University Press, 2017), in which he studied Suhrawardi (d. 1191) and his commentators on their thinking on the imagination and the afterlife.

Zhinia Noorian

received her PhD from the department of Philosophy and Religious Studies at Utrecht University. Currently she is a Postdoc scholar for the ERC-Advanced Grant *Beyond Sharia: The Role of Sufism in Shaping Islam*, working on the project *Feminising Masculinity: Negotiating Gender Norms*. She has published *Parvin Etesami in the Literary and Religious Context of Twentieth-Century Iran: A Female Poet's Challenge to Patriarchy*, Leiden: Leiden University Press, 2023.

Lloyd Ridgeon
is Reader in Islamic Studies at Glasgow University. His education includes a B.A. in Modern Middle Eastern Studies from Durham University (UK), an M.A. in International Relations from the International University of Japan (IUJ), and a PhD from the University of Leeds (UK), where he was supervised by Professor Ian Netton. He has published widely on various aspects of mediaeval Persian Sufism, including monographs on ʿAzīz Nasafī (1998) and Awḥad al-Din Kirmānī (2018). He has also published on modern Sufism, focusing on the Anjuman-i Ukhuvvat and Zahīr al-Dawla of the Niʿmatullahī order. His work on modern Sufism also includes a study of the criticisms of Aḥmad Kasravī, titled *Sufi Castigator* (2006). He has edited three collections of essays: *Sufism: Sufis and Salafis in the Contemporary Age* (2015), *The Cambridge Companion to Sufism* (2015) and the *Routledge Handbook on Sufism* (2021). More recently he has paid attention to aspects of jurisprudence in Iran under the Islamic Republic, and has published a monograph on the topic of the *ḥijāb* and another monograph on *Ahmad Qābel and Contemporary Islamic Thought*, Cambridge: Cambridge University Press, 2023. He is also the chief editor of the peer reviewed *British Journal of Middle Eastern Studies*, which produces five issues per year. He served as editor of *IRAN*, the journal of BIPS from 2013– 2021.

Asghar Seyed-Gohrab
is Professor of Iranian and Persian Studies at Utrecht University in the Department of Philosophy and Religious Studies, and member of the Royal Netherlands Academy of Arts and Sciences (KNAW). He has published extensively on Persian literature, mysticism and religion. His publications range from Persian poetry to Sufism and the role of religious and mystical motifs and metaphors in the Iran-Iraq war (1980–1988) and how peaceful religious injunctions are used to justify violence. *Martyrdom, Mysticism and Dissent: The Poetry of the 1979 Iranian Revolution and the Iran-Iraq War (1980–1988)*, Berlin: De Gruyter, 2021. *Literature of the Early Twentieth Century: From the Constitutional Period to Reza Shah*, London and New York: I.B. Tauris, (2015, ed.). His most recent book is *Of Piety and Heresy: Abū Ḥāmid Muḥammad Ghazzālī's Persian Treatises on Antinomians*, Berlin: De Gruyter, 2024. Currently, he is the Principal Investigator (PI) of an ERC-Advanced Grant entitled *Beyond Sharia: The Role of Sufism in Shaping Islam* (www.beyondsharia.nl), examining Islamic non-conformist movements.

Amir Theilhaber
is a post doc researcher at the Department of History at Bielefeld University, where he works on his habilitation project "The Ethnological Collection of the Lippisches Landesmuseum in Peripheral Detmold. A Glocal History of Conglomeration, Fragmentation, Indifference and Contestation from 1835 to the Present." He

completed his BA in International Affairs at Vesalius College – Vrije Universiteit Brussel (2006), his MA in Islamic and Middle Eastern Studies at the Hebrew University Jerusalem (2009), and his PhD in History at the Technical University Berlin (2018). Theilhaber taught a course on the Aryan myth in global contexts at the Centre for Antisemitism Studies at the TU Berlin, was a Visiting Postdoctoral Fellow at the German Historical Institute in Washington DC (2019–20), and led an interdisciplinary provenance research project on the West African collections at the Lippisches Landesmuseum in Detmold (2021–24). He is the author of a book on the German Orientalist scholar and foreign minister Friedrich Rosen and the connections of Orientalist scholarship and international politics during the age of empire (De Gruyter, 2020).

Index

Iranian Studies Series

J.T.P. de Bruijn
Pearls of Meanings. Studies on Persian Art, Poetry, Ṣūfism and History of Iranian Studies in Europe
ISBN 978 90 8728 348 3

J.C. Bürgel & C. van Ruymbeke (eds.)
Nizāmī: A Key to the Treasure of the Hakim
ISBN 978 90 8728 097 0

J. Coumans
The Rubáiyát of Omar Khayyám. An Updated Bibliography
ISBN 978 90 8728 096 3

D. Farhosh-van Loon
Ayatollah Khomeini's Mystical Poetry and Its Reception in Iran and the Diaspora
ISBN 978 90 8728 401 5

B.M. Fomeshi
The Persian Whitman. Beyond a Literary Reception
ISBN 978 90 8728 335 3

N. Fozi
Reclaiming the Faravahar: Zoroastrian Survival in Contemporary Tehran
ISBN 978 90 8728 214 1

A. Ghajarjazi
Irrationalities in Islam and Media in Nineteenth-Century Iran. Faces of Modernity
ISBN 978 90 8728 398 8

R. Harris & M. Afsharian (eds.)
A Journal of Three Months' Walk in Persia in 1884 by Captain John Compton Pyne
ISBN 978 90 8728 262 2

A. Karimi-Hakkak
A Fire of Lilies. Perspectives on Literature and Politics in Modern Iran
ISBN 978 90 8728 329 2

M.M. Khorrami & A. Moosavi (eds.)
Losing Our Minds, Coming to Our Senses. Sensory Readings of Persian Literature and Culture
ISBN 978 90 8728 368 1

F. Lewis & S. Sharma (eds.)
The Necklace of the Pleiades. 24 Essays on Persian Literature, Culture and Religion
ISBN 978 90 8728 091 8

S. McGlinn (ed.)
Principles for Progress. Essays on Religion and Modernity by Abdu'l-Bahā
ISBN 978 90 8728 307 0

M.A. Nematollahi Mahani
The Holy Drama. Persian Passion Plays in Modern Iran
ISBN 978 90 8728 115 1

Z. Noorian
Parvin Etesami in the Literary and Religious Context of Twentieth-Century Iran. A Female Poet's Challenge to Patriarchy
ISBN 978 90 8728 412 1

C. Pérez González
Local Portraiture. Through the Lens of the 19th-Century Iranian Photographers
ISBN 978 90 8728 156 4

L. Rahimi Bahmany
Mirrors of Entrapment of Emancipation: Forugh Farrokhzad and Sylvia Plath
ISBN 978 90 8728 224 0

R. Rahmoni & G. van den Berg
The Epic of Barzu as Narrated by Jura Kamal
ISBN 978 90 8728 116 8

A. Sedighi
Agreement Restrictions in Persian
ISBN 978 90 8728 093 2

A. Sedighi
Persian in Use: An Elementary Textbook of Language and Culture
ISBN 978 90 8728 217 2

A.A. Seyed-Gohrab
Courtly Riddles. Enigmatic Embellishments in Early Persian Poetry
ISBN 978 90 8728 087 1

A.A. Seyed-Gohrab (ed.)
The Great Umar Khayyam: A Global Reception of the Rubáiyat
ISBN 978 90 8728 157 1

A.A. Seyed-Gohrab & S.R.M. McGlinn (eds.)
One Word – Yak Kaleme. 19th-Century Persian Treatise Introducing Western Codified Law
ISBN 978 90 8728 089 5

A.A. Seyed-Gohrab & S.R.M. McGlinn (eds.)
Safina Revealed. A Compendium of Persian Literature in 14th-Century Tabriz
ISBN 978 90 8728 088 8

A.A. Seyed-Gohrab, F. Doufikar-Aerts & S. McGlinn (eds.)
Embodiments of Evil: Gog and Magog. Interdisciplinary Studies of the 'Other' in Literature & Internet Texts
ISBN 978 90 8728 090 1

P. Shabani-Jadidi
Processing Compound Verbs in Persian: A Psycholinguistic Approach to Complex Predicates
ISBN 978 90 8728 208 0

B. Solati
The Reception of Ḥāfiẓ: The Sweet Poetic Language of Ḥāfiẓ in Nineteenth and Twentieth Century Persia
ISBN 978 90 8728 197 7

R. Tabandeh
The Rise of the Ni'matullāhī Order in 19th-Century Persia. Shi'ite Sufi Masters and Their Battle against Islamic Fundamentalism
ISBN 978 90 8728 367 4

S. Tabatabai
Father of Persian Verse. Rudaki and his Poetry
ISBN 978 90 8728 092 5

K. Talattof & A.A. Seyed-Gohrab (eds.)
Conflict and Development in Iranian Film
ISBN 978 90 8728 169 4

M. Van Zutphen (ed.)
A Story of Conquest and Adventure. The Large Farāmarznāme
ISBN 978 90 8728 272 1

R. Zipoli
Irreverent Persia. Invective, Satirical and Burlesque Poetry from the Origins to the Timurid Period (10th to 15th century)
ISBN 978 90 8728 227 1